DYNAMICS OF PAKISTAN'S FOREIGN POLICY

DYNAMICS OF PAKISTAN'S FOREIGN POLICY

S.S. BINDRA
Department of Political Science,
G.N.D. University, Amritsar

DEEP & DEEP PUBLICATIONS PVT. LTD.
F-159, Rajouri Garden, New Delhi-110027

DYNAMICS OF PAKISTAN'S FOREIGN POLICY

ISBN 978-81-8450-285-5

Typeset by S.S. COMPOSERS
3190, Mohindra Park, Shakur Basti, Delhi-110034.

Printed in India at MAYUR ENTERPRISES
WZ Plot No. 3, Gujjar Market, Tihar Village, New Delhi-110018.

Published by DEEP & DEEP PUBLICATIONS PVT. LTD.
F-159, Rajouri Garden, New Delhi-110027.
Phones: 25435369, 25440916
E-mail: ddpbooks@yahoo.co.in • ddpubs@gmail.com
Showroom:
2/13, Ansari Road, Daryaganj, New Delhi-110002 • Telefax: 23245122

Contents

Preface

Walter Carlonaes feels that it is hard to dispute the supposition that 'foreign policy' constitutes a form of behaviour emanating from or at least ascendable to human beings. In a few words, just as in other sphere of social sciences, we are here concerned primarily with aspects of human-beings or thought instrumentally.

In the recent years those who are associated with the foreign policy-making have acknowledged the complexity of the whole process. But to study the foreign policy process of a small developing state, one has to follow and analyse a different set of variables, because of vast differences in each country's political system, historical legacies, ideology, economy and culture, the most important variable which all the small developing states are sharing is poverty. They all lack power, possession of which is essential to have a say in international affairs. The four basic components of power are wealth (human and material), organization (formal and informal, status (ascribed and acquired) and will (conscious and sub-conscious).

A very acceptive approach is that the goals of a state's foreign policy should be limited to the pursuit of its self-interest, except for occasional mistakes. If this is so, all states single minded pursue this self-interest, then foreign policy problems are concerned with how to secure maximum advantage for oneself now or in the future. The capacity to attain the realization of interests in the future is national power. Keeping in mind this very assumption, if a problem arises in which a state's immediate self-interest is not apparent, then its interest becomes that of the maximization of power thus abetting the chances of its future realization of self-interested goals. Hans J. Morgenthau is considered to be the main champion of this approach by stressing the states pursue and (should pursue) their interest defined as power. This view has of course a respectable intellectual leverage, being available in general form in the writings of philosophers and amateur psychologists Nietzsche and Hobbes for example, who have postulated the general rule that all men pursue power. The drive for power that so many observers perceive in the world of international relations, need not be based on the presumption of a general institutional law of human behaviour, but instead be of a secondary nature deriving logically from the principles of a pursuit of self-interest. If the power is defined in the most general way to mean the ability to make others do what one wants, it would thus include not only force in a military sense, but also economic pressure, psychological influence and so on, then clearly power is indeed needed to pursue any ends that may be postulated and the pursuit of power becomes a necessary preliminary to the pursuit of any other goal or policy. It should be noted that one may prefer the most noble goals imaginable but the realistic attempt to attain them can only proceed by means and techniques of power.

Robert L. Wendzel wrote that as far as the foreign policy of a country is concerned, it comprises of:

(a) General assessment of state's economic, military and international positions.
(b) An appraisal of its capabilities in advising a self-reliance, caution, isolation, military potential, alignments, etc.
(c) Broad principles of conduct.
(d) National interests.
(e) The strategies, commitments undertaken to achieve a given object.

The guiding principles of Pakistan's foreign policy were pronounced by the founder of Pakistan Quaid-e-Azam Mohammed Ali Jinnah in 1948. "Our foreign policy is one of friendliness and good towards the nations of the world. We do not cherish aggressive designs against any country or nation. We believe in the principle of honesty and fair play in national and international dealings and are prepared to make our utmost contribution to the promotion of peace and prosperity among the nations of the world. Pakistan will never be found lacking in upholding the principles of the UN Charter." These principles were cosmetic only and the most important fact is foreign policy does not develop in vacuum.

The contours of foreign policy are shaped, particularly by the geo-political realities. The unique geo-strategic location of Pakistan has its own importance. It transcends South, Central Asia and West Asia and have the potential to become the inter-regional trading hub. Pakistan has positioned itself to offer trade and energy corridors to the Central Asian States. It places rather excessive demands in the domain of security since independence. Pakistan's security environment derives its origin from the circumstances in which Pakistan was created. The violence accompanying partition leading to the emergence of the two independent states of India and Pakistan generated hostility, which continued to affect relations between the two countries mainly because of the unresolved issue of Kashmir. Besides this, Pakistan instigation of terrorist activities in India, has also contributed for continuing tensions and conflict and shaped the unstable and tense security in the region. Pakistan's quest for security perspective is primarily shaped by the fundamental asymmetry that India, has especially in the area of defence capability. In order to fulfil this desire, Pakistan's foreign policy-makers succeeded in making all weather friendship particularly with China. Beijing and Islamabad have forged civilian and military contracts, traded nuclear secrets, exchanged intelligence and importantly, cooperated against common Indian and Soviet adversaries. More importantly, Islamabad considers Beijing to be the cornerstone of its foreign policy and has wielded significant political, economic and military influence in Islamabad. Leaders in both countries describe the relationship in lofty prose from "higher than the Himalayas" to "deeper than the Indian Ocean." For Pakistan, China has been everything but the US has been so, on the other hand, the China has leveraged Pakistan's volatile relationship with India to maintain strategic hedge against a close competitor in the region. To secure its strategic and economic needs, China has invested billion of dollars to build infrastructure in Pakistan. But the most important issue which the Chinese are nursing cautiously while China's border disputes with India is awaiting solution, the two neighbours have established strong economic relations by creating a mature framework. The variable of Chinese foreign policy is indicative of its broadening agenda in South and Central Asia. To form an axis was the major foreign policy decision of Pakistan.

The deteriorating situation in Pakistan is viewed with concern by both the US and the Chinese. They are for stability in Pakistan as it will bring enduring peace to South Asia.

Pakistan's search for security since its inception is endless. She sought security through outside alliances and worked painstakingly on building a relationship with the US. The Western-oriented anti-communist treaties and alliances Pakistan joined in mid-fifties became an important part of her foreign policy.

Foreign policy of a state is an extension of its domestic politics. Nowhere, it is true than in the field of economic development. The quest for economic progress has been the important plank of Pakistan's national as well as external policies. The economic dimension of relations between nations has over the years been accepted as the central role of diplomacy. It is being understood that the political and economic relations augment each other. In fact, one cannot function truly without the other. Over the years, Pakistan has focused her foreign policy objectives to reverse the net capital flow from the developing to the developed world, which forces the poor to sink deeper into the quagmire of poverty.

The US-Pakistan love-hate relationship has its own dimensions in the context of Pakistan's foreign policy's moves and initiatives. American policy towards Pakistan has been guided by political expediency. The US has given billion of $ to Pakistan to fight terrorists but without any significant results. The Americans have endorsed every Pakistani military dictator even though that started wars with India and moved the country towards dictatorship and into Jihadist embrace.

The US strongly believes that what happens in South-West Asia can profoundly affect its political, social and economic environment. The US stakes are high in Afghanistan because events in Pakistan directly affect Afghanistan. It is in US interest to see a stable and politically viable Pakistan. The US-Pakistan partnership is deeply in trouble since the Talibans were driven from Afghanistan in 2001. Pakistan's very integrity as a nation has been challenged directly. It is a well known fact that Pakistan has no effective control over the military and intelligence agencies. The majority of people of Paksitan are disillusioned with the Zardari government inability to address a wide array of domestic problems, including rising inflation and food shortages created by global developments beyond the government control. The country's economic crisis has deepened with widening trade and fiscal deficits and a slow down in investment. Promises to deal with the challenges of extremism and violence, especially those identified with spreading Talibanization have yielded little.

Pakistan's use of "militants" as a foreign policy tool has had a profoundly destabilizing impact on the region. Pakistan support of militant activity in Kashmir was directly responsible for one war with India in 1965 and contributed to the other wars, crisis situations and also in widening the gulf between the two neighbours..

In the initial stage of her existence a number of factors which emerged from the struggle for Pakistan determined its foreign policy to a considerable extent. Pakistan emerged on the world map with a build in alliance with Britain to protect her strategic interests in the region and to provide her a foothold. Another factor was the Muslim League leaders indebtedness to the British for their continuous support, guidance and inspiration during the struggle for freedom. Pakistan wanted to attain parity with India with the help of Britain and her allies.

"India factor" has always been a flash point for the foreign policy-makers of Pakistan, since its inception, terrorism and militancy have added another dimension in her foreign policy objectives. The US is actively involved in the counter-terrorist activities in the areas bordering Afghanistan which has proved a boom for Pakistan's economy. Billion of dollars have been pumped into Pakistan's kitty and still the process is going on. The situation is complicated and complex beyond control of both the US and Paksitan.

The Afghanistan (1979-89) crisis which emerged after the Soviet armed intervention not only increased the US involvement in the region but also further deteriorated Indo-Pak relations, created a civil war like situation in Kashmir valley, strengthened Pakistan's nuclear and missile programmes which resulted in the proliferation of nuclear weapons and also changed the whole context of the terrorist activities in the region. After the signing of the Geneva Accords in 1989, Pakistan redefined its foreign policy objectives, primarily in the case of Kashmir, where it launched a proxy war and started providing training to the misguided youths to get them involved in the terrorist activities in the Kashmir region.

Pakistan's foreign policy-makers are more successful in achieving their objectives as they adopted always "wait and watch" approach and react only when the time and situation demands. They got maximum benefits from the US in the form of economic and military assistance since joining of military pacts in the mid-fifties. The process is continuing as the US involvement in the region is deep-rooted.

It took more than 7 years (2002-10) to prepare manuscript of the book. During this period, the internal situations of Pakistan was in turmoil. Once again Pakistan returned to democratic rule, of course, very difficult to ascertain which type of political system will suit to Pakistan's political culture.

The study has covered nearly all the aspects of Pakistan's foreign policy but with some limitations, as, it was not possible to analyse all the moves of Pakistan's foreign policy-makers. The main emphasis is on the strong bonds between the geo-strategic location of Pakistan and defining, redefining of her foreign policy objectives.

My thanks are due for Prof. Stephen P. Cohen, Bruce Ridel, Pavneet Singh, of Brookings Institute, Washington, D.C. for providing me necessary input in the form of ideas for continuing research on Pakistan and other related issues of the region.

I have no words to thank Mr. G.S. Bhatia, my friend, of Deep & Deep Publications, who was always kind to me whenever I approached him for publication of my book.

Amritsar S.S. BINDRA

1

Analyzing Foreign Policy: Theoretical Perspective

The study of international politics and foreign policy has experienced over the years "the signs of sophistication which mark the end of adolescence." In the post-second world war era, the scholars engaged in the study of international relations became aware of important differences and limitations between their own interests and those of their pre-war predecessors. Mid-1940's was acknowledged as a period which constituted a major turning point in the study of international affairs. There seems to be a general agreement that during the post-world war period, interests have turned from solving problems and reforming institutions to understanding processes and identifying issues. There was a general feeling that international relations should be examined and guided systematically, whereas this was not a value to which pre-war scholars have been committed either fully or explicitly. The commitment of the scholars to analyse international relations systematically in fact raised a number of questions, particularly about its nomenclature, its entire scope or whether only certain types of relations were pertinent.[1]

Researchers, academicians, diplomats and authors felt

that, there were a variety of relations which got formed, across national boundaries and those economists who studied international trade and sociologists who laid emphasis on cultural interchange were as much students of international relations as were political scientists and historians who addressed themselves to the processes and consequences of diplomacy. But the trend to use loose and imprecise terms continued. The post-war attempts to systematize the field result in a broad understanding that international politics is only a sub-category of international relations, although the most "Important" one. Similarly, "the study of foreign policy has come to be recognized as an endeavour which is not concerned directly with international relations.[2]

But this assumption has always been a subject of discussion and the debate is still going on. Feliks Gross maintained that the international politics and foreign policy were identical and that it was only in the non-political sphere that separation of subject matter occurred.[3] Similarly, Russell[4] contended that "international politics" is really a study of the primary factors that enter into the politics of nations as reflected in current international developments. Sondermann has discussed, at least from various aspects, the linkage between international politics and foreign policy. He broadly concluded that:

> "There is a lack of clarity concerning the limits and contents of the study of international political relations and the linkage between this area of inquiry and related subjects, including foreign policy.
> They are "actor-oriented" and much more attention has been given to the study of foreign policies than to international politics properly.
> It seems highly desirable to indicate clearly the limits of the two fields, the differences in their respective focus, and the linkage between them."[5]

The two fields, for all practical as well as theoretical purposes, are closely knitted and that it is a matter of choice one wish to attach to one's efforts. It would seem only reasonable however, to say that in view of the preponderance of attention which has been centered on the study of foreign policy. This should be the name given to one's endeavours. The main reasons for rejecting the proposition that the two fields are identical that there do exist environmental factor, processes, compulsions and dynamics in the field of international politics which can neither logically nor conveniently be included in the study of foreign policy. The study of the foreign policies of the states is considered to be one of the most important aspects of the study of international political relations. But the latter is conveniently accepted as a broader field which also includes inquiry into other problems.[6]

Since foreign policy consist of selected national interests presumably formulated into a logically consistent whole that is then implemented. Any foreign policy is viewed analytically in three phases: conception, content and implementation. Conception generally is the strategic appraisal of what goals are to be achieved. Content is the result and reflection of that appraisal. Implementation looks to both the coordinating mechanisms within a state and the means by which it conveys its views and wishes to other states. Although inefficiencies and failures can be costly in any of these three phases, it is apparent that the most critical phase is conception.[7]

DIFFICULTIES IN FOREIGN POLICY-MAKING PROCESS

If nations vary in prudence with which they select their goals and in the scope of the interests that compose their policies, they are alike in confronting a number of difficulties in following a rational foreign policy. The first difficulty that a nation encounters is the achieving of a realistic view of the world with which its foreign policy is designed to deal. No nation even a superpower, has enough power to attempt to impose its will on uniformally hostile world. No nation even tries to do this. In practice, when the state is in the process of evolving a foreign policy, a calculation is generally made which power will be on its side, which power will be opposed and which power will be uncommitted. Consequently any foreign policy of a state examines a quick assessment of the positions and commitments likely to be made by other states. In this essentially strategic assessment, costly errors may be in ambush at every step along the logical path from the initial conception of objectives down to their detailed implementation.[8]

A reliable way to gauge the degree of prudence and appreciation of reality that characterizes any nation's approach to the formulation of foreign policy is to ask how addicted that nation is to reaching to a foreign policy problem with the initial question, "What should we do?" if it asks first, "What is it that we would like to see being done"? It has begun at the right end of the strategic analysis, particularly if it next asks, "Who might have to do it?" and "Who can realistically oppose it" and finally, "What is then left that only we can do"? Although all the three equations are important, the critical question is the second. This is where a realistic view of the world is absolutely desired.[9]

Another difficulty is a result of the fact that foreign policy objectives are generally expressed in abstract terms and that can; in fact whittle away the effectiveness of the policy. When foreign policy objectives are expressed in abstract terms, it becomes difficult to understand the essential idea of an objective. The trouble with abstract goals is that they must constantly be interpreted in terms of immediate, practical circumstances. Unless great care is taken, the abstract goal is lost in the shuffle of the practical situation. As a consequence, "policy may lose direction and, like the fictional knight, go galloping off in all directions."[10]

The third difficulty in following a rational foreign policy is that since events have a way of taking the bit in their teeth as it were and running away with the policy, whereas the policy is supposedly just the opposite? This process is cumulative. As George Kennan remarked: "Our action in the field of foreign policy is cumulative, it merges with a swelling stream of other human happenings and we cannot trace its effects with any exactness once it has entered the fluid substance of history."[11]

Harold Nicalson has also expressed somewhat the same views in one of his books. He gave trenchant expression to the way in which events may, with a will of their own, shape policy in unanticipated directions. "Nobody who has not watched "policy" expressing itself in day-to-day action can realize how seldom is the course of events determined by deliberately planned purpose or how often what in retrospect appears to have been a fully conscious intention was at the time governed and directed by that potent of all factors—"the chain of circumstances." Few indeed are the occasions on which any statesman sees his objective clearly before him and marches towards it with undeviating stride; numerous indeed are the occasions when a decision or an event, which at the same time wholly unimportant, leads almost fortuitously to another decisions which is no less incidental, until, little link by link, the chain of circumstances is forged."[12]

This kind of development may also mean that much more power is required for successful implementation of the policy anyone anticipated; and in the long-term, it may force the surrender of other foreign policy objectives for which power is no longer available, even such a decision would not have been made if it had been clear beforehand what was going to happen.[13]

The fourth difficulty concerning following a rational foreign policy is that foreign policy objectives or goals are sometimes mutually contradictory. A nation may unwittingly attempt to push to two goals that may be incompatible with each other. The contradiction may not turn to be serious, as long as goals are abstract, but when they are transformed into concrete embodiment and implementation, a conflict may occur which, if not, resolved, may cause a sort of schizophrenia in the national character. This kind of situation is much common with abstract than concrete goals, since, it is not difficult to find out the discrepancy in the latter case.[14]

These four difficulties in formulating a rational foreign policy can only be partially offset by a thorough attention of the conceptual phase of foreign policy. No matter, how much attention is given to conception, for example, there will be difficulty in checking as one thing will continue to lead to another once the policy is implemented, that decisions will necessarily often be taken under the mistaken belief that they lead to desired end, when in fact, this is not true. Even so, a mere "playing by ear" will not be sufficient. "If a nation is not clear about the direction in which it wishes to influence events often turbulent currents of international relations." But if a nation is clear about its goals, given the nature of the world it confronts, it can choose a policy content that is rationally relevant.[15]

Why do we study foreign policy? The first and most acceptable response to this question is to say that scholars and diplomats alike in the field of international relations are always interested in trying to understand what is going on at the international level. In spite of the fact that many important changes have occurred in international relations which, over the years, have broadened the range of actors, which are involved. It remains the case that, much if not most of what goes on, is in fact the product of various aspects of the foreign policy behaviour of one or more states. Since 1945, as the governmental activity has increased manifold in the welfare as well as warfare fields, resulted in increasing the powers and functions of the state. At one level at least, international behaviour consists of an interacting network of foreign policies.[16]

The importance for studying foreign policy becomes apparent if we examine proximity between the behaviour and critical issues involved in international relations that literally deal with the matters of life and death on a mega scale. An understanding of foreign policy in such a context is almost self-evidently, necessary to identify the patterns of behaviour perhaps fortuitously to avoid plunging into a major man-made disasters like a nuclear war.[17]

Other important reasons emanate from the relationship between foreign policy analysis and the broader study of international relations. First, foreign policy analysis, with its major focus with state and the ways in which the state relates to the international environment provides a very broad or micro perspective on international relations. This can be contrasted with a 'macro' perspective which attempts to explain international relations from the level of how states as actors rescue their own foreign policy objectives in the international system itself.[18]

Foreign policy's relevance in policy-making process provides another reason for its study. The field of international relations which has always close links with the governmental activity, the findings of the academics, when they make conceptual frameworks and broad formulations, potentially at least be directly concerned with policy-making apparatus of the government. In some countries, particularly in the US, where academics are inducted into government on the assumption that their ability to analyse foreign policy behaviour will help in improving the quality of foreign policy-making and implementation process. But the main fear in this context seems to be the standard of objectivity to the extent that analysts might be temped to offer explanation which the government would be pleased to hear. Nevertheless there is a link between the academic study of foreign policy and real world foreign policy-making.[19]

A major practical difficulty, however, a policy-maker often encounters is the fact that the feasible alternatives are limited by the past and one usually has only a narrow range of options from which to choose. The unpleasant truth seldom receives sufficient emphasis with the result that observers tend to exaggerate the number of realistic choices a policy-maker actually has. There are several facets to this concept. First, a nation's historical experience has a direct or indirect impact on the content of policy-maker's perception of various features of the international environment such as ethics, law and ideology. Second, one's perceptions of the past significantly influence the content of objectives and his choice of policy implementation instruments as well. Third, once a particular policy has existed for a while a degree of inertia seems to set in. Operations become routines and the underlying assumptions are not questioned. The fundamental American assumptions underlying the containment policy went for nearly two decades without being challenged. Fourth, once a policy is undertaken, those policy-makers responsible for its formulation and implementation have a vested interest in its success. Thus they would prefer to have the present policy succeed rather than consider other options and will make every effort to see that it does. Fifth, the execution of any policy invariably brings about commitment of some of the state's resources for its success. These may be economic, military and psychological, as well as political in the broadest sense and it is somewhat difficult to rearrange the allocation of resources. Sixth, once a policy is undertaken the state inevitably has invested some of its prestige. It is not only the individual policy-makers who may lose by failure, but also the nations itself. Finally, it is often assumed that there is some value in having a degree of certainty and stability in foreign policy; sudden changes would tend to produce just the reverse.[20]

These influences from the past often combine to produce what has been termed a policy of instrumentalism Roger Hilsman puts it this way: "Rather than tough grand decisions or grand alternatives, policy changes seem to come through a series of slight modifications of existing policy with the new policy emerging slowly and haltingly by small and usually tentative steps, a process of trial and error in which policy steps."[21]

Another problem develops if the policy-maker sees things only in terms of his own perspective; if he does not empathize and put himself in the other fellow's shoes. It is absolutely necessary when attempting to "understand" a problem that one tries and sees it from the point of view of each of the parties concerned. One must analyse the situation in one's own perception. This requires a concerted effort to "role play" to really "be" someone else for a while. It requires the development of what has been called "tough-minded empathy", one must see things from the other fellow's perspectives but also have the strength to independently evaluate the point of view.[22]

One of the most dangerous pitfalls a policy-maker must avoid is distortion due to preconception. To put it somewhat differently, he must be very careful to avoid prejudgments based on preconceived ideas about the source of information one would believe, its interpretation, about the intention and objectives of various parties, their capabilities, even about the identification of who is involved and what the issues may be. Changing one's image is difficult. It is difficult to admit one has been wrong and the problem is compounded by the fact that policy-makers often have an investment in its being right, once they are on the public record. In such a case contrary information may not be wanted because it is a threat. To President Eisenhower's credit, he began to accept the fact that (Vietnam Crisis) was primarily a domestic power struggle; he began to recognize that his preconceptions had prevented him from accurately assessing the situation.[23]

Another difficulty for policy-makers is that an event is seldom the result of a single cause and each policy affects more than one party (even if not so intended) one has to accept the fact that events are always inter-related and all decisions in whatever form are taken, have different effects. This really can be explained in two ways. First, it means that all decisions have both costs and benefits. Second, each decision has an impact on more than one party, and affects each party differently. As a policy-maker, one must analyse each situation analytically. He must also consider the potential effects of each choice. He must recognize that all of his alternatives have both advantages and disadvantages and chose the one with the best ratio. But he must do this within the confines of the second facet of differential effects, namely, the fact that every choice has several parties and the effect is different for each. Thus the alternative the policy-makers are seeking is the one that yields the best net cost benefit ratio when calculated in terms of the anticipated impact on all the parties' affected.[24]

The final difficulty is that often the policy-maker does not have enough time to analyse the problem thoroughly, things just happen too fast. Each of these difficulties can constitute an obstacle to effective policy and the policy-maker must try to avoid or overcome them in order to optimize his chances of success. Each broad consideration and each specific opinion must be carefully thought so that (1) its formulation is neither abstract nor over generalized, (2) it is compatible with the rest of one's policy, (3) the actions of implementation are consistent, (4) the policy is sufficiently flexible to allow for unanticipated contingencies yet it allows one to manage events as much as possible, (5) it recognizes the limitations of one's knowledge and influence, (6) it takes into account the realistic limitations on future choice given the dead hand of the past and yet is not limited to the *status quo,* (7) it avoids the distortions of action and information which preconceptions provide, (8) as much as possible it allows for sufficient time to analyse the significance of information and action, (9) it recognizes the inter-related nature of the causation of specific policies, (10) it allows for the different impact which decisions may have, and (11) it is based on a true, "understanding" of all parties in the situation.[25]

THE FORMULATION OF POLICY CONTENT

Looked at this way, the need is to prepare a conceptual strategy for foreign policy very clear. Its success or failure depends on how well it delineates the assumptions behind that policy and relates what is sought to what exists. If this task is done in a systematic manner, tactical failures in implementation may still frustrate the intent (the ways and means may fail) but the likelihood of success is still great. The assumptions of a nation-state about the international system is going to decisively influence in a big way the scope as well as the thrust of its behaviour. Nothing guarantee that a nation will match its role to its strength, that it will grasp the real interests, or that it will maximize its opportunities to save such real interests. Nations are destined to play a variety of roles and the opposition they encounter is generally determined and influenced by their own choice of actions. If they are in a position to play a vigorous and far-reacting roles, they may be facing numerous enemies and may be led in consequence to seek to balance such enemies with numerous allies. For all the nations there is a range of choice the minimum role may not help in eliminating the power problem, but the maximum role will multiply it.[26]

Each nation, assessing its power problem (its cluster of likely enemies) is concerned with its own total power both as a backing to its foreign policy as its measure of defensive or military capability. In assessing its power problem each state, if it is wise, follows a foreign policy strategy to maximize its total power resources while minimizing those available to its likely enemies. (Each nation out of prudence normally seeks to face in peace and war the least formidable group of likely enemies possibly). The size and power of this enemy group is most frequently countered by initiating and forming alliances but it is limited through policies that seek to give likely enemy states, a pause in focusing their power towards one's own state.[27]

Most studies of foreign policy are concerned with the purposes of state action, the form it takes, the processes which initiate it or the societical sources from which it derives. If we combine them or take singly, the conformation with substantive and methodology problems is quite obvious, not the least of which is the nature of the linkage between them. Take the case of goals of the foreign policy; they are a function of the processes by which they are formulated just as these in turn are influenced by the objectives which were sought in the past and aspired by society for the future. In the same way, the form and content of the state actions are determined partly by the resources available to system it and partly by the organizational and intellectual processes through which it was selected. Indeed, the inter-relationship of the different aspects of the foreign policy is so intricate that the societal factors which underlie state action are affected, through feedback, by the action itself and thus operate differently as sources of future action. In short, "like all behaviour, foreign policy action is sequential. It does not have a beginning, an existence, and an end. Rather, it is constantly unfolding and at any given moment is partly a function of what it was previously and what it may become in the future."[28]

Few aspects of the field are more resistant to classifying than the objectives that states pursue in their international relationships. Foreign policy goals are difficult to pronounce and the subject of extensive investigation. They are classified and conceptualized in a number of ways and means. Peace, security, power and prosperity have been identified as long range goals.[29]

Whenever two or more values clash, the relative importance of both must be carefully analysed, even if there is no agreement on the identity of their supreme value. This ranking of values is not easy because intensity fluctuates from case to case and is often determined by conditions. Values reach their full political significance only in action, when the situation actively applies them. In the most vague and most general form, this leads to what may be what be descended as a vision of the good life, an arrangement of the elements of reality—as perceived by the decision-maker—to approximate as closely as possible to value he holds. Needless to say when it comes to actual action, this vision can never be fully realised because the environment is always, at least to some degree, intractable. There is also same tension between the vision of a good life and life itself even when the vision is so moderate that it can be easily translated into concrete political programme. Some visions are quite utopian, completely unrealisable and most of them contain a sizable utopian element.[30]

While the vision of good life indicates only the general direction desirable for foreign policy, more specific principles of behaviour are deducted from it. To arrive at a political decision, a statesman must juxtapose his values and his environment and therefore we must investigate how he arrives at his knowledge about this environment.[31]

Each society especially when it deems itself a "nation" and has been organized into a state has to follow a social code that helps her to achieve a peculiar identity and which activates and energies all political action. If the prevailing concepts of "good" and "evil" could be rationalized within the boundaries of the society itself, they would have little or nothing to do with international affairs.

However, the situation has changed drastically, with the changes in international environment evident in every aspect, "national value structures have impingement upon the world outside their borders, social values have come to relate intimately with questions of foreign policy."[32]

The content of governmental action in the international arena is determined by the set of social values controlling the society at large. The rise of nationalism is responsible for making the foreign policy more "democratic" as governments became obliged to structure their international efforts so as to reflect the mass value judgments of the people they represented. The analytical apparatus of statecraft is no more than a standardized technique for translating the value preferences of a society into a workable frame for government action.[33]

Even from an analytical point of view, we must avoid becoming overly specific about the social values that underline the foreign policy. Values are seldom self-evident and the concepts of good and evil that a government chooses to pursue always stem from a mixture of sources within the society. We can identify at least five differing versions of "good" which are usually combined in a single foreign policy.

The good of the individual citizen primarily the wish to be secure in beliefs and prosperity as they become threatened by forces outside the society.

The good of the society at large: collective values normally including preservation of the social system, augmentation of its prestige, protection of its ideology and so on.

The good of the state (the juristic personality) as such the more common ingredients include self-preservation, security, well-being, and the strength of the political unit.

The good of "social interest group" in the state and society: these tend to be included to the maximum extent possible within the operative notion of the general interest and contribute largely to the shaping of public policy on a specific issue.

The good of the government itself and its personal values peculiar to membership in a public community that inescapably find expression in the activities of policy."[34]

One can say, the values maximised by the state in foreign policy are varied in origin and substance. It is the sacred duty of the diplomats and bureaucrats "charged with policy-making to shape the loud spectrum of needs and wants into some semblance of integrity and to apply the resulting value of synthesis to the phenomena of international politics." It is obvious for the statesman to compromise among competing values, accepting some of the cost of rejecting others, or he may prefer to build his approach to world affairs on a number of value choices.[35]

FOREIGN POLICY AND INTERNATIONAL POLITICS

The base of any foreign policy is a state's desire to maximize its value synthesis. Once a state starts implementing its foreign policy objectives, it has to move very cautiously on the international scene, however, it encounters other states, and each state is keen to protect its own value-based goals. Thus international politics is at bottom an exercise in the prosecution of value differences and grows less from the judgments we generally make about those conditions.[36]

Two basic approaches to foreign policy are very popular since the days of French Revolution. The ideological approach lays stress on the policies followed by a particular state *vis-à-vis* the rest of the world are merely expressions of prevailing political, social and religious beliefs. The advocates of this line of thinking are categorised as democratic, libertarian or socialist or peace-loving or aggressive. For example, in the beginning of the twentieth century, it was common among the scholars and diplomats to declare that the US or Britain or France had no foreign policy orientation and were not following liberal or conservative principles. This is one way to think about foreign policy, to the present day, it is the prevailing approach. This dominant approach views group relations primarily in psychological terms; as it gives preference to the motives or ideology of the leaders, or the governments "as the essential, if not the role determinant of policy." It further maintains that a democratic regime has a different policy outlook, an autocratic regime another, a communist regime a third, and a democratic socialist administration still another. And "foreign policy is considered a function of a political system in action or of the preference or convictions of political leaders who carry out its programmes."[37]

Because of reaction against the ideological approach to the study of foreign policy, the scholars started paying attention to the analytical approach. The ideological approach has been "shaken and discredited by contradictions, and it has faltered and failed in describing the continuities of objectives and purpose in the policies of states." It should perhaps have been obvious that conceptions in which foreign policy is nothing more than a by-product of domestic politics, could hardly do justice to the elements of continuity in national policy. Regardless of the intentions, social philosophy or religious outlook of the individuals, there are "broad strategic position and international role that must be safeguarded and its independence to be preserved." For Bolsheviks as well as Tsars, the approach and thinking of nation's statesmen, who stand guard over other country security and whose conception of that security has been formed and moulded by the same instructions and traditions, however, an intangible "national mind" which interprets the national interest, is itself a factor in the permanence of foreign policy." According to the advocates of analytical approach, foreign policy demands of policy-maker's choices and determination of basic order. For them, not only are the interests of a nation permanent in character and supreme but they also range themselves in a hierarchy of greater and lesser interests. In a classic statement as a guide in the formulation of Belgium's foreign policy but with relevance to general foreign policy-making process, Paul-Henry observed that, there must be a hierarchy in international obligations. The nations of a continent cannot reasonably be asked to consider with the same realism and sincerity of judgment affairs which directly concern them with events which are taking place thousands of kilometres away in regards where they have neither interests nor influence.[38]

Certain interests must be defended at all costs; others should be safeguarded under particular circumstances and certain others, although desirable, can never be defended. It is the task of foreign policy in the first instance to determine its own hierarchy of interests and next to examine the scale of interests revealed in the principles or practice of other foreign policies.[39]

Before 1950s, the traditional approach to analyse foreign policy was popular. But the trend changed afterwards, which determined the very idea of traditional assumptions by the application of a decision-making approach which has established its strong roots in the foreign policy analysis.

The international relations have over the years witnessed important changes, which has resulted in the widening of the range of actors, the scope of the issues and the complexity of the process involved, it remains a fact that what goes on in fact is the product of foreign policy behaviour of one or more states. Indeed governmental activity in the international sphere has been growing its importance to the extent that states, as agents of welfare as well as warfare, have increased their military as well as economic capabilities, particularly that post-second world war period of one level at least, international relations consists of an interacting network of foreign policies.

This can be illustrated by reflecting upon international developments in the late 1980s. The scholars and commentators agree that distinctive changes in east-west relations implemented in the Eastern European countries and the former Soviet Union, have had a potential impact on the international system as a whole.

The other important reasons emerged from the relationship between the foreign policy analysis and the broader study of international relations. First, foreign policy analysis with its focus on the state and the world which the state relates to the international environment produces is what might be called a micro-perspective which tends to explain international relations from the perspective of the state predisposes the analysis to highlight the differences between states in terms of their foreign policy behaviour.[40]

Still another factor for the study of foreign policy analysis is related with its relevance. As the branch of international relations which is most closely connected to government, the findings can be utilized by the foreign policy-makers from time to time.

Foreign policy has no links with the other areas of governmental activity. A foreign policy is directed at and must be implemented in the environment external to the state from the way of identifying a specially foreign area of the government activity, is to assume that this denotes not only the direction but also a particularly type of policy which is concerned with the vital security interests of the state.[41]

In the unethical universe of today, judgement and evaluation in terms of an ethnical consideration is hazardous and highly unpredictable. Hence a more instrumental approach to the evaluation of the foreign policy is suggested. It is based on the assumption that, at least for the time being, nation-states are here to stay and that their foreign policy must be evaluated in terms of successes and failures to implement the goals they pursue.

After the Second World War, many new states emerged on the world map and the UN with a clear aim to maintain international peace and security also come into being. These developments had further strengthened the fact of internationalism among states. Today, we see every government behave in a particular manner in relation to its relation to other government.

There is no consensus among the scholars as far as the relationship or distinction between international politics, international relations, world politics and foreign policy is concerned. How one defines these terms is largely influenced by what one wants to investigate is largely a function of his particular approach, model or theory.[42]

Most studies related with world politics or international politics in fact have been studies of foreign policy, "where policy is defined as the decisions that define goals, set precedents or lay down courses of action, and the actions taken to implement these decisions. These studies have concentrated on describing the interests, actions, and elements of power of the great powers."[43] Sondermann describes the distinction between the terms as more academic than real. "In simple and easy terms, it should be accepted as the difference between objectives and actions (decisions and politics) and the interaction between the two or the more states."[44]

Furthermore, in the international politics, the decisions, actions or reactions of the states can be challenged by anyone and "the states have no sure prospect that their decisions will prevail and must contend for their interests with other equally sovereign entities."[45] The matter related to foreign policy is too "central to the survival of the state, to be left to the same interplay of forces as domestic policies, too closely associated with the basic values of nationhood, to be an appropriate subject for partisan debate and factional advantage." This is the main reason that political theorists, constitution-makers, and politicians have been treating foreign policy as an independent and special field, which should be treated, by a government with utmost care and must be given top priority.[46] For Hobbes "the right of making war and peace with other nations and commonwealth that is to say, of course judging when it is for public good, and how great forces are to be assembled and aid for that end was one of the essential powers annexed to the sovereign."[47] For John Locke "the power of war and peace, leagues and alliances, and all the transactions constituted for the federative power which must necessarily be left to the prudence and wisdom of those who are responsible for running the affairs of the state.[48] Even in the modern world, foreign as a special area, having association with security and fundamental values of the state retains much of its force. But the preliminary difficulty related with the term foreign policy is that one has to see the specific area it covers in international politics. For some, the term means a fixed set of attitudes towards the international milieu, and plan of a country which may be implicit or explicit for the sole purpose of maintaining relationship with the outside world. A conscious feeling of what is or ought to be the country's place in the world, or some general guiding principles or attitudes, determining or influencing decisions on particular issues.[49]

For others, the term implies rather a field of related but distinct actions and issues in which policy formulation is not given preference, and is generally formulated in a disjoined fashion, particularly in response to crisis situations. Those who hold conviction in the former view of foreign policy as prominent area are concerned primarily with diplomacy and the threat of peace. Those who are showing interest in the latter view, feel that wars or threats of force are not always occurring in international relations, and political calculations should be given priority as they cover wide range of country foreign relation than national security and territorial integrity. They are not keen to include in their definition of foreign policy, commercial relations, the regulation of international commerce and travel, emigration and immigration, cultural policy, external investment and so on.[50]

To understand the term international relations, one may refer to all forms of interaction between the members of separate societies, whether government sponsored or otherwise. The analysis of foreign policy means the study of all aspects of international relations, including the study of trade unions, the international Red Cross, tourism, international trade, transportation, communication, and the development of international values and ethics.[51]

If we take into consideration the meaning given by scholars belonging to different schools of thought, then it would be a futile exercise to work in the direction of creating the consensus. The interpretation of a term given by a scholar and the relationship between them nearly two or three decades ago may not fit in the framework of present day international environment in which non-state actors are becoming more important and trying to establish their hegemony over the present day states.

By accepting and recognizing the waxing and waning that occurs very frequently in international environment, one is compelled to accord *defacto* recognition to the close interaction between foreign policy, international politics and international relations.

In the given situation, theorizing of foreign policy and international politics or relations become all the more important, if not acute. For building conceptual frameworks and models in these fields of research, one has to examine its various parts at the macro and micro-levels to single out the various variables which without losing their shape, are determining the foreign policy and also giving direction to the actors and non-state actors in international relations and politics.

Rosenau has rightly pointed out, "at the foreign policy level too, the forces of the past and then of the present can conflict, co-exist and synthesize. The choices and activities of foreign policy decision-makers can be guided by cultural norms and historical precedents or the choices and activities be guided by the changing demands that emanates from the international system or from the decision-makers of the society."[52]

FOREIGN POLICY-MAKING PROCESS

The main focus of foreign policy-making process has long been on the institutions of government that have been assigned the prime responsibility for its formulation and implementation. Because of the complexity of the institutional framework for making foreign policy and the frequency with which the institutions are altered, with formally or through usage, the national institutional outlook has also focused on inter-agency coordination as a technique for continuously unwieldy process of foreign policy formulation and agreement with the government.[53]

In the western democratic countries for the last seventy years, the making of foreign policy was visualized as an important function of the government because it was closely associated with the national interests, rather than special interests. Another important aspect of foreign policy-making process is that since it evokes a different political response, it is generally accepted that political institutions function differently when they confront different foreign policy issues. In addition of course, different institutions are also involved, in that some government agencies are concerned exclusively or substantially with foreign policy.[54]

Rosenau has suggested nine pre-conditions for creative theorising of foreign policy-making process. They are:

First, "to think historically, one has to avoid treating the task as that of formulating an appropriate definition of theory;

Second, one has to be clear when one aspires to empirical theory or value theory;

Third, one must be able to assume that human affairs are founded on the underlying order;

Fourth, one must be predisposed to ask about every event, every situation, or every observed phenomenon of what is it an instance;

Fifth, one must be ready to appreciate and accept the need to sacrifice for broad observations;

Sixth, one must be tolerant of ambiguity concerned about probabilities and distrustful of absolutes;

Seventh, one must be playful about international phenomenon;

Eighth, one must be genuinely puzzled by international phenomena; and

Ninth, one must be constantly ready to be proven wrong."[55]

To be very clear, foreign policy is considered to be a dependable variable but with a difference because foreign policy activities vary from one state to another and from one type of state to another. The general pubic is interested only with the policies that state declare, the decisions taken within the government circles, the actions actually taken by the government and the possible impact of the behaviour of governments and their official representatives. Foreign policy is considered to be the outcome of whatever foreign policy process exists within that state.[56]

One simple way to examine the various aspects of foreign policy is to break down into component parts—foreign and policy. Policy is accepted as a set of decisions or programmes that determine the behaviour of political elites and is a guide to an action or set of actions intended to realise the goals an organization has set for itself. Furthermore, choosing actions to achieve a goal is very important as far as the implementation of a policy is concerned. If we are to understand what foreign policy means, then one has to take the help of sovereignty and territory. Sovereignty applies to the territory that is in existence in the legal boundaries of a state. Foreign applies to anything that is just outside the legal boundaries where the state has no authority over the people and territory. "Foreign policy is thus a set of guidelines to choices being made about people, places and things beyond the boundaries of the state."[57]

From an analytical point of view, we should not be specific about the social values underlying foreign policy. The sources available in the society in fact guide a government to choose between the concepts of good and evil and on the contrary it is generally believed that values are seldom self-evident. Generally, five different versions of "good' are usually combined in a single foreign policy.[58]

The base of any foreign policy is a state's mission to maximize its value synthesis. Once it makes a place in the international scene and generally interacts with other states, each struggling for the accomplishment of its own value.[59]

Policy formulation is another aspect of foreign policy process. It is the first and important duty of the policy-makers to identify clearly who is involved in the particular situation they are examining. How many parties are there? What is their relationship? Who will be critical in determining the outcome? In a number of situations, the policy-makers are bound to face a number of problems. They should not ignore a number of factors like, first, the two primary parties, second, a primary party and a coalition of equals. Third, a primary party and a coalition headed by a dominant party, two or more coalitions of equals, fifth, every primary party, and last two or more coalitions with each headed by a dominant party. The policy-maker must attempt to determine which configuration characterises the situation on question and what in terms of the appropriate target for his policy.[60]

For example, who really is involved with various Middle East conflicts? Do the disputes revolve around an Arab coalition of equals and Israel?

Is it Israel against an Arab coalition? What role does the Russia play? Do the Russians and Americans hold the trump cards? Are there really several primary parties but no cohesive alliance? Do the Palestinian Arabs really have the key? If so, which Palestinian Arabs? Are the critical parties, the Arab oil states or the oil companies? Are inter-Arab disputes ultimately more important than Arab Israel Conflicts? The discussion on this issue could go on and on, because to determine who is involved, is very critical and difficult too. It is largely accepted that the policy-makers must deal with each crises on merit he is planning to formulate effective policy.[61]

I. National Interest and Foreign Policy

National interest is accepted as the key, "concept in foreign policy." It amounts to be the sum-total of all the national values, pertaining to the nation and to the state but national in both meanings of the word. This concept is rather vague and ambiguous. One common sense definition describes it as the general and continuing ends for which the nation acts. A major ambiguity arises when it is used in non-specific terms, without any sufficient clarification and by a degree of continuity and by its connection, with political action. National interest can describe the aspiration of the state; it can be used also operationally, in application at the actual policies and programmes pursued, it can be used polemically in political arrangement to explain, rationalise or criticise. The recurrent controversies "on foreign policy often stem these ambiguities and not only from the different ideas about the substance of the national interest."[62]

In the theory of international relations, we find different views on the nature of national interest. At the one end is the realist who feels that national interest and the national power cannot be reported and measured in terms of material growth, primarily military strength. On the other end are the extreme idealists or utopians who would identify rational interest with some universal moral aspirations of the entire mankind, such as the external peace or human brotherhood and be willing to sacrifice the material power of the nation for the moral upliftment of the mankind. Between these extremes are a whole range of qualified, or moderate, realists and idealists, who would be willing to combine the material interests and power of the state with some broader and more general and universal objectives, indifferent degrees, dependency on their realist or idealists bias and arrive at a synthetic conception of national interest.[63]

There may be difference of opinion on the meaning of national interest. But the concepts of the national power are central on core values of the society which includes the welfare of the nation, the security of political beliefs, national way of life, territorial integrity and policies and programmes that seek to create and preserve a favourable international environment. Past experiences and judgements and attitudes also condition the judgements of the circumstances on which political leaders base their policy decisions. Some states attempt to protect their policy decisions and they attempt to protect what they conceive to be their national interests by providing a given *status quo* by expanding their territory or area of influence, by attempting to reduce foreign threat or danger and others by striving to dominate the weak states. These policies sometimes involve making alliances. Still other states seek to reconcile their interests with the international environment by adopting policies of isolation, non-alignment or neutralism. The fact that states have similar objectives tell us little about the methods they may follow to achieve them.[64]

National interest and foreign policy-makings process have traditionally been acknowledged by the diplomats and academicians as strongly interlinked. The importance of national interest has been universally recognized. As Morganthau has rightly pointed out that "it is the assumption of universality of the national interest, in time and space which enables us to understand the foreign policy." Regardless of all the differences in personality, social environment, convictions and preferences, their actions can take place within a narrow range when they were faced with the task of protecting and promoting the rational core of the national interest.

The reason for neglect of national interest as a key concept in the study of international relations is three-fold.

Many scholars believe that the nation-states should not be the primary focus of the study of international relations and hence the interests of states should be subordinated to the study of international organization and international integration.

Scholars who earlier rejected the realist school of international politics because of its efforts to give precedence to the national interest military power, found no other suitable basis for discussing the goals of states.

Some have decided that the term national interest is methodologically so vague and closely defined by diplomats and military planners that it is impossible to formulate generally acceptable guidelines.[65]

All statesmen are governed by their respective national interests but this does not mean that they can never agree on anything. On the contrary, they often do, but only on the basis of their conceptions of their national interests. If a statesman agrees to concessions, he does so only when he is convinced that this brings some advantage to his state, directly or indirectly. Furthermore, cooperation is conditional upon the existence of a suitable framework, of reasonably suitable stable international order within which the actions of other states are predictable and therefore rational foreign policy is possible. From here stems the interest of all states in this international order, again according to their individual national advantage, if they find this order congenial, they support it and, if necessary, defend it, if uncongenial, they endeavour to alter it accordingly.[66]

Throughout the history of political thought, man has been seeking a supreme value which could be used as general yardstick. Unfortunately, the very fact that so many conflict theories have arisen, casts some doubt on the general validity of any of them. The popular yardstick of 'national interest' is too vague and that of 'power' is insufficient. Power has, in fact, been the necessary condition of self-preservation and a state which ignores this condition persistently cannot escape the danger of disappearing. This does not mean that the yardstick is or cannot be persistently applied to all values in all situations; indeed, it is sometimes ignored and even deliberately acted against.[67]

Simply offering a definition of national interest, does not, however, provide the scholars or policy-makers with any guidelines to help identify such an interest. We are to locate some of the basic interests of nation-states and these nations' needs that form the understanding of their foreign policy. They may be described as under:

1. *Defence Interests*: The protection of the nation-state and its citizen against the threat of physical violence directed from another state or organization, extremely inspired threat to its system of government.
2. *Economic Interests*: The enhancement of the nation-state's economic well-being in relation with other states.
3. *World Order Interests*: The maintenance of an international political and economic system in which the nation-state system may feel secure and its citizens and commerce may operate peacefully outside the borders.
4. *Ideological Interests*: The protection and furtherance of a set of values that the citizens of a nation-state share and believe, are to be universally accepted.

Several assumptions have been made about basic national interests. First, the order is in which they appear does not suggest any priority of one over another, although it may be argued that unless a nation-state can defend its territory and citizens—even through a strong defence or in alliance with a major power or both—none of the other three interests are likely to match much. Second, it is obvious that these four basic interests are not mutually exclusive and that policy-makers must accept trade offers among them. For example, the economic interests of certain countries within the state may sometimes be sacrificed in order to enhance a world interest involving another country whose friendship and cooperation are needed it to enhance the stability in an important part of the world. Third, a nation's ideology is an important part of its national interest although it may be adhered to as strongly as the other, it is nevertheless important in determining how a person acts to international issues.[68]

In sum, the four basic national interests outlined above are dynamic factors conditioning the behaviour of nation-states and changes in priority among them are usually measured in years and decades rather than in months. In democracies of the western type, these changes emphasis on the basic interests are decided after much debate in their legislatures and they are usually sustained when the new governments come to power.[69]

It is the national interest which reflects the foreign policy objectives of a country. The development of national interest (which may remain an abstract concept) is considered to be as the first step in formulating a foreign policy. Before the concept may actually serve as a guide to action, the statesman must grapple with a classic problem: reconciliation of ends and means. The ends of state action in international politics—the national interest and such national goals as may be derived from it—are postulated a priority—before policy can be made, the statesman somehow conceal the facts of his problem, including whatever means he has at his disposal, with the conceptual system formed by his set of ends. In specific political situations, one of the most difficult problems faced by policy-makers is determination of the most appropriate relationship between abstract ends and concrete means. Any confusion of the ends means relationship, any loss of appreciation of the value roots of policy, or any reluctance to remain firmly committed to long range concepts of interests, cannot help but deprive a foreign policy of vigour, effectiveness and flexibility. A government that succumbs to these dangers quickly find themselves thrust on the strategic defensive and to a major extent, placed at the mercy of others who know more precisely what they are trying to accomplish. There is no substitute for a clearly rationalized and thoroughly understood purpose in foreign policy, especially in the contemporary period, which is an end of the great change in the international milieu.[70]

We can, however, be quite explicit about its functions. As the overriding purpose governing the state's relations with outside world, it serves two purposes; it gives policy a general orientation towards the external environment and more importantly, it serves as the controlling criteria of choice in immediate situation. The dominant view of national interest, in other words, dictates the nature of a state's long-term efforts in foreign policy and governs what it does in a short-term context. National interest thus flows from the application of a highly generalized value synthesis to the overall situation in which a state is placed, in world politics. It is, within the terms of its social origin, relatively slow to change and change is evolutionary rather than revolutionary. National interest provides the necessary measures of consistency to national policy of a state, consciously adhering to its national interest in a rapidly changing situation, is more likely to maintain its balance and continue to progress towards to goals, than it would if it changed its interest in adapting to new situation.[71]

2. The Aims of Foreign Policy

What then is foreign policy about? What efforts are made by various governments to achieve it? We must beware of thinking that, because states are often referred to as 'actors' in the international system, their foreign policy begins with themselves between the outside and the inside. The primary task of the policy-maker is to articulate the country's external interests and order in some scheme of relative importance. The articulation and ordering of interests must be continuously changing through time.[72]

No state can accomplish everything it wishes in its foreign policy. The ends of policy are unlimited, but the means are sharply limited both in logic and fact. Even powerful states have an operative system of priorities that govern their policy choices and that they allocate funds in their respective budgets respectively. It is not an easy task to rank the priorities that govern their policy choices and they allocate funds in their respective budgets. It is very difficult to rank the priorities of interests, goals and objectives particularly in determining that relative claims that each has on the state's resources. A state that attempts to conduct its foreign policy without priorities or with its priority system vague or unimpressive rapidly discovered priorities imposed upon it by force or circumstances. It is also significant to judge the importance of different problems; otherwise all issues would tend to become equally significant. In foreign policy matters top priority thus tend to be assigned on the basis of recent occurrences and immediate needs. The choice priorities become a significant plank of foreign policy process.

However, as far as the foreign policy is concerned, every country tries effectively, first, with the preservation of its independence and security, and second, with the pursuit and protection of the economic interest groups. Deeply involved with these interests in the case of the major powers, at least are a concern with opposing any penetration and manipulation by foreign countries and different belief system and an unblushing effort to accomplish some active penetration and manipulation of their own. Finally, closely related to the national security, economic and clandestine warfare interests of each major power are its policies of economic aid to foreign nations, its efforts to spread its own national and ideological propaganda in foreign countries and its support of cultural and scientific exchange missions favourable to that end.[73]

When one speaks of 'objective' he is talking about 'ends of the policy.' However, it should not be assumed that it is possible to neatly distinguish between 'means and ends' and that the 'ends' are definite and final. Few objectives are ends in themselves. Instead they are usually means to the achievements of further ends (which in turn often means to further ends and so forth). What the situation involves is a means and chains of varying degrees of complexity.[74]

The states are multipurpose organizations pursuing many practical, very often selfish objectives. Joseph Frankel feels that 'if we consider the making of foreign policy, the choice of its objectives, as a rational activity, we can usually analyse it as to exploration of the environment, in order to find out the restraints upon our actions as well as the opportunities to secure ourselves and estimate the likely cost to be incurred'[75]. Furthermore, the policy objectives are naturally to be pursued in the real world or in the real politics of interaction of states which in fact is 'operational environment.' But it is very difficult to clearly define the term 'operational environment' and information about the term can never be complete and is also of some variance with it.[76] At the same time, one should not take it for granted that the 'operational environment' is always harmonious and the realization of its real nature would weed out conflict totally contrary to the assumptions, the 'operational environment', harbours many potential conflicts and fuller understanding of their nature as well as of the restrains operating may increase rather than decrease conflict.[77]

As far as the types of aims and objectives are concerned, they vary from nation to nation and region to region. The nation by nation description of policies would be largely a recapitulation. There are three broad categories of objectives, i.e. fundamental, middle range and special immediate objectives. All states try to achieve fundamental objectives and the most important in this is pure survival. A state would not mind in adopting every means available to crush those forces which would dare to challenge its sovereignty because only sovereign independent nation commands respect. Another one is territorial integrity that is often considered a matter of survival.[78]

The preservation of a state's belief system from external proposed change has often been considered a very important fundamental objective. The states are emotionally attached with their own principles, beliefs, values, customs and traditions by which they live to the utmost that they would always be ready to protect and maintain them. A state would also be willing to protect the existing political and economic system from the extremely imposed change.[79]

The achievement of a satisfactory prestige level in an international arena is one of the most serious problems of foreign policy process. How much prestige and status is required in a given contact? One serious problem that often complicates for prestige concerns about the criteria of high status, a state may wish prestige in terms of certain aspects of its own ego image, but may receive generous deterrence in other terms that do not meet its requirements. A reputation for high level of artistic achievement, for example is of little significance to a state that wishes for a rank as a major military power. The difficulties implicit in any attempt to 'win' prestige; however, have not served to deter states from the attempt.[80]

Another common objective of state is well-being. After the higher priority objective of self-preservation and security permitted to the maximum by the state's situation. It also tries to improve the actual conditions of the existence of its citizen both conceptually and practically, the welfare of all rather than that of an individual. The unit of calculations is 'the economy' and the measures of prosperity tend today to be those familiar 'macro-economic' concepts 'gross national product' and the 'rate of economic growth' of course there may be no real clash between collective well-being and the economic welfare of the individuals and even when such a conflict develop it is only on an explicitly 'gun or butter'. In case of unavoidable divergence of interest, however, the normal pattern of political value choices dictates the intrinsic superiority of collective well-being of any individual or group interests.[81]

The fundamental objectives are considered to be conservative in nature. In most cases, they are integrated and often they interact with another for limited resources. The policy-maker is usually confronted with an uncertain choice among related alternatives none of which is totally acceptable or unacceptable. For a better understanding of a country's foreign policy, it would be worthwhile to analyse it separately, one must remember that in reality things are much more complicated.

Holsti has divided middle range objectives into three categories and has also examined middle range objectives analytically. Military capability, industrial development, scientific and technological skills, etc. have become one of the great national goals and are sought with almost as much commitment of resources as the securing of some core values and interests. Self-extensions of territory is a popular foreign policy objective. Some states are always interested even though they do not need the territory is its neighbour. Territorial expansion becomes an end in itself whether it fulfils any strategic, economic or social needs or not.[82]

The policy-maker must be clear-headed in achieving the middle range objectives. Whatever is in their mind must be coherent and consistent as far as possible because strength and effort would be dissipated of the work of the right hand than of the left. Inconsistency is very dangerous in the sense that it feeds ammunition for propaganda to the opponents.[83]

There are specific immediate objectives which the policy-makers would like to achieve whenever the need arose. They are spontaneous and quick action is always required to achieve them. The situation and the circumstances prevailing both are important in this context and particularly the correct assessment of these variables mainly depends upon the ability and intellect of the policy-makers.[84]

Suppose a state has realized that there exists a threat to its survival because of its failure in sufficiently achieving the middle range objectives, having also links with the economic growth and to strengthen it one is in need of petroleum but has very little in his possession. In this particular situation, the specific immediate objective would be to obtain petroleum in the most feasible manner. After careful analysis of the situation, the policy-makers would try to explore whether they should initiate a long-term trade policy, aiming to purchase the product or to approach to some international agency for immediate help or to adopt coercive methods to achieve that particular cause.[85]

It will be interesting to examine what are the

universally accepted sources of the foreign policy objectives and from where do they originate? Some objectives seem to spring from several sources while others are just allowed to develop and all attempts at the classification level distort their reality to some extent. It is pertinent and important for all the policy-makers to know where objectives came from, if he is really keen to know everything and would like to influence the future goals formation and attempt to task no matter, how different, it is?

The identification of resources may be helpful in understanding the aims and objectives of the foreign policy-makers. Roger Hilsman has rightly pointed out that, 'Very often policy is the sum of congeneries of separate or only vaguely related actions. On other occasions, it is an uneasy, even internally inconsistent, compromise among competitive goals or mixture of alternative means for achieving a single goal rather than through grand decisions or ground alternatives, policy changes seem to come through a series of slight modifications of exiting policies emerging slowly by small and usually tentative steps.'[86]

The most significant element that may influence the calculations of decision-makers is ideology. It is difficult for an actor on the political scene to conceal the true nature of political actions behind the mask of political ideology.[87]

The ideolization of world politics is not a new trend. Their roots are lying in the contemporary era and have always been fertile source of international conflict and 'generally creates obstacles, in the peaceful resolutions of all conflicts'. They are considered to be irrational and are full of emotional contents. But they can be easily used to obscure the real facts of situation or the real motives of ambitious leaders they frustrate efforts to find areas of agreement; they are hard to deal with international problems without sacrificing national honour or prestige; they turn international conferences into propaganda venues instead of creating opportunities for the accommodation of diplomacy.[88]

The term ideology 'is related with the modern moving ideas, including many of the isms'—Nationalism, anti-Imperialism, Totalitarianism, Communism, Fascism, Nazism, Marxism, Socialism, Liberalism, and Collectivism and so on.

As far as its significance in world politics is concerned, in a number of cases the ideologies are supposed to be linked with the national power of a country. 'Without power of some kind, an ideology, even one which aspires to universalism ... is a passive harmless pattern of related ideas...?"[89]

Interestingly, the policy-makers of a state are least bothered about its terminology and definition. They are interested in its operational aspects. To what extent do these ideas and views in life and the world influence the actual formulation and implementation of policy? Are they more important than other considerations such as law, ethics and capability or less so? These and similar questions may be critical as the policy-makers try to understand and anticipate the actions of the opposite numbers. Unfortunately there seldom is satisfactory answer.[90]

An ideological approach to world political problems displays certain marked characteristics:

1. Ideology leads inescapably to the formulation of a problem in moral terms. An international dispute thus becomes a clash between good and evil with the stakes never less than absolute vindication or total defeat.
2. Ideological controversy which is inevitable in any contact between states embodying total belief system is not susceptible to compromise and accommodation. No ideology permits bargaining with evil.
3. Ideologically-oriented policies can never 'succeed' in the sense that strategic calculations can be crowned with success. States cannot kill ideas, wiping out a population in no way destroys their unpopular beliefs.[91]

The role of ideology in international politics or the degree to which it affects the formulation of a state's foreign policy or the resulting implications for international politics, have become an increasingly important question. This issue has been magnified by the challenges of present day ideological formulation of world politics. One important question arises whether government adhere strictly to a foreign policy formulated according to dogmatic tenets or whether follows the traditional method of realistic appraisal of concrete situation within the context of its individual national interests and the relevant information available concerning the situation.[92]

Another question involves concerning the overlap of theory and reality. Are not both ideology and realistic appraisal present, although in varying degrees, in the formulation of foreign policy by almost all states? Every state is equipped with a priority system for the determination of foreign policy goals and tactics. There are certain levels of action in which either ideology or realism is predominant or between two, some sort of balance is achieved. There is, however, nc fixed relationship that can be postulated; rather ideology and realistic appraisal meet in each distant situation of foreign policy, with different degree of emphasis. In this parameter, ideology plays the smallest role in the most restricted choice situation, but becomes increasingly effective when there is greater freedom of choice of alternative action possibilities. In attempting to discover which tendency—ideology or realistic appraisal operates more strongly, it must be remembered that a state can remain consistent with its ideology tenets although its ideology may of course, become the source for postulation of national interest and long range goals. If these aspirations are deeply rooted in the social dynamic of the people and if the government is to adapt tactics, a successful foreign policy is possible. But ideology intrudes into situational analysis and the range of state action is to cast in terms of imperatives of belief, state of craft in the classic sense is left helpless.

All of us have ideologies of some sort so that we do not have to deal with each issue on a purely provisional and isolated basis. In politics one can understand this when one uses broad terms as liberal, radical, reactionary, hawk, pacifist and others of course, some people's ideologies are much more tightly organized and coherent not to say rigid than others. Here we use the term ideology in the same way as Holsti uses belief system. 'A set of system through which information concerning the physical and social environment is received. It orients the individual to his environment defining it for him its salient characteristics... In addition to organizing perceptions into a meaningful guide for behaviour, the belief system has the function of the establishment of goals and the ordering of preferences.'[93]

3. How is the Foreign Policy Made and Implemented?

There is no general agreement about the most suitable framework for the analysis and comparison of foreign policies although a fair degree of agreement exists about what are likely to be the most significant factors. A strong agreement can be made in favour of an explicit scheme, without claiming special theoretical virtues for it. The significant factors are arranged in five groups:

1. Capabilities and salient characteristics, especially those based on geography and historical traditions.
2. Major features of the decision-making machinery.
3. Major issues of foreign policy and the means to meet commitments.
4. Attitude to the most important states and blocs.
5. Attitude to international order.[94]

As the foreign policy is an area of governmental activity which is concerned with the state and other actors, particularly other state in the international system and developing an understanding of foreign policy behaviour is an important activity. Trying to analyse that behaviour, though, presents a number of intellectual challenges which range from defining basic terms to more fundamental methodological problems. Attempts to resolve these problems led analysts to adopt some simplifying of conventional assumptions about that behaviour. These assumptions collectively have produced what might be called a traditional approach to analysis which has been very influential. From 1950s, these traditional assumptions have been undermined by the application of a decision-making approach which makes different assumptions about foreign policy behaviour. While this approach in turn has generated a number of problems, it has established what few foreign policy analysts would now dispute, namely that an understanding of the way in which policy is made is central to an understanding of the substance of foreign policy. Certainly, the focus on the decision or policy-making process has laid the analytical ground work for an understanding based on the foreign policy system.[95]

One particular approach to the study of foreign policy has been so pervasive over the years that it can be referred to as a traditional approach. One of the attractions of this approach is that it is based upon conventional and straight-forward assumptions about foreign policy. One has to scarcely need to think very hard about any particular example of foreign policy in action to realize that we tend to assume that states have coherent foreign policies which are exemplified by particular actions; that governments have goals or objectives towards which their policies are directed and the governments calculate not only particular courses of action but also the consequences of that action. Foreign policy is the product of national behaviour.[96]

Joseph Nye has summarized these conventional assumptions which underpin traditional analysis rather more formally under the label of 'state centric realism.' The state rather than any other international actor is regarded as the foreign policy-making unit. More importantly, the state, or the government acting on behalf of the state, is treated as a monolithic actor; in other words, it is government activity whose behaviour is broadly analogous to that of purposeful individual. These two assumptions, Nye suggests are usually harnessed to realist analysis which explains state behaviour in terms of an inter-state struggle for power. This serves to reinforce the treatment of the state as a 'billiard ball' interacting with other essentially similar entities. As realist characterizes the international environment as hostile and dangerous, it follows that state behaviour is analysed from the perspective of that environment, forces external rather than internal to the state are regarded as the major determinant of foreign policy. The ability of the states to survive and prosper in such an environment thus provides a focal point for analysis. Survival is seen to hinge around the skilful of means to ends, power to purposes.[97]

The state is considered to be the supreme unit of social organization to encourage social communication or interactions of any kind across state boundaries just for its own sake. But such communication or interaction is required only when there is a genuine need for the achievement of some policy objectives which cannot be achieved by any other mean or by state activity within its boundaries. Interestingly, the intensity of state interaction varies from period to period and within each period, from state to state. The past shows a 'propensity to self-sufficiency, to the restriction of international intercourse.'[98]

The entire foreign policy organization of a state exists for the purpose of making and executing decisions to protect the state's interests. Basic ingredients of the decision-making process are common in all the nations of the world irrespective of their status. As 'foreign policy is not made by electronic computers, it is formulated by men who lack mathematical decisions, but also do possess judgements.' It is a well known notion that decision-making processes are common in all the nations of the world irrespective of their status and decision-making must be based on the understanding of what the decision itself is about. No policy can be chosen without an appreciation of the problem to which the decision is to offset. To begin with, if two officials in any government judgements are to be understood, the same set of facts in an identical problem terms, each would bring his own personality, professional and organizational bias, and each may have its own source of information. 'An important element in any problem analysis is the early selection of an objective to the attainment of which the nation's efforts will be committed.' Since all operational decisions are made in terms postulated goals, the identification and evaluation of strategic objectives constitute a major step in the process of problem identification.[99]

Decision-making theory is basically a conceptual framework. It furnishes a comprehensive and useful checklist of the factors which ought to take into account in any attempt to analyse policy-making, either as a generalized process or as process in a specific case. The theory serves to identify a large number of relevant variables, and it suggests interesting possible inter-relationship among these variables nor does it necessarily contain hypothesis that would lead to predictive capability concerning the kind of substantive policy which a decision-maker might choose in a given situation.[100]

When one goes through the works of Stanley Hoffman, Henry Kissinger and Morgenthau, and one reads about decision-making approach and its various aspects,[101] scholars such as Graham Allison, Alexander George, Holsti, Robert North, Rosenau, Burton Spain and Richard Snyder have sought to dissect the 'belief systems' of individual decision-makers and to assess the impact of idiosyncratic role of bureaucratic, national and systematic variables of various types.[102]

Snyder, Bruch and Spain in their work sought to focus on specific decision-makers who speak and act in the name of the state. According to them, the so-called real and objective world does not matter? What matters were the perceptions of decision-makers; these perceptions shape the policy-makers views of reality and also motivate their subsequent decisions. They compared the team of high level officials advising the chief executive to a massive filter that processes countless variables, including the decision-maker's beliefs and roles, bureaucratic demands, political and social interests and the constraints on their policies that arise in the rest of the world.[103]

Rosenau's contribution to decision-making approach is also significant. His concept of issue area has helped to internationalize the notion that there is no such thing as a single, static decision-making team for all foreign policy, rather, such teams varies in composition with the issue area in question. Further, Rosenau worked with linkage theory dramatized the interdependence of domestic and international politics. Indeed foreign and domestic policies are intimately linked; they can be separated only for the purpose of analysis and at the expense of some distorting of reality.[104]

Joseph Frankel performs a useful service when he points out that some foreign policy decisions may be highly irrational while other approach much closer to rationality. Especially during periods of crisis, such issues, as the Irish question, or Alsace-Lorraine or Arab-Israel conflict, or the anti-imperial movement in Indonesia and Kenya, do not lend themselves entirely too national analysis. But in some cases, and over the long haul, governments with limited resources are constrained by the imperatives of economy and diplomatic prudence to strike a national balance between the principle of minimum cost and maximum comprehensiveness in which the important political values are ignored. Frankel concludes that foreign policy bureaucracies generally strive towards the application of reason for the sake of avoiding errors. This final comment on the question, "every specific decision usually leads to action which requires explanation to the general public in the traditional terms of rationality." This often leads to rationalization; a spurious explanation on national grounds of decisions taken for other reasons; but at the same time it constitutes a powerful argument for the decision-makers to take into account this rational, consideration before their final decision. Rationalization is generally considered debasement of reason but actually it is also a powerful rational influence.[105]

Charles Lindblem feels that faced with a given problem, the rational decision-making first clarifies his or her values, goals, and objectives and then orders there is some way (usually in a transitive, most of least desired ranking). Then decision-makers list all the important possible ways to achieve goals and investigate all the important consequences of each alternative identified. Then the decision-makers comprise the consequences of various alternatives. Finally the decision-makers chooses the decision or policy alternative with the consequences that most closely match the goals. Another version of ideal decision-maker is provided by Irving Janis and Ralph Mann. They list seven criteria for achieving what they call 'vigilant information processing.' They are the following:

1. Thoroughly canvass a wide range of alternative course of action.
2. Survey the full range of objectives to be fulfilled and the values implicated by choice.
3. Carefully weighs whatever he or she knows about the costs and risks of negative consequences that each alternative could produce.

4. Intensively searches for new information relevant to further evaluation of the alternatives.
5. Correctly assimilates and takes into account any new information or expert judgements to which he is exposed even when information or judgements do not support the course of action he initiatively prefers.
6. Re-examines the positive and negative consequences of all known alternatives, including those originally regarded as unacceptable before making a final choice.
7. Making detailed provisions for implementing or executing the chosen course of action! With special attention to contingency plans that might be required if any of various risks materializes.[106]

The key concepts and assumptions generated by this approach have been more important than any other.

For the development of foreign policy analysis, there are three central concepts, decisions, decision-maker and the decision-making process. The major assumptions which underpin the use of these concepts are visible. Foreign policy is, in essence, a series of decisions made by a group of people who can be labelled decision-makers. Foreign policy decisions do not simply emerge in response to external stimuli rather they are processed through identifiable machinery within the state. Broadly, adopting this approach gears foreign policy analysis to the task of explaining the behaviour of an individual or, more typically, a group of people operating within a structured environment who decide (or choose) to pursue one course of action rather than another.[107]

In some respects decision-making analysis has reinforced traditional assumptions. Decision-making analysis have also tends to reinforce 'rational actor' assumptions by assuming a rational decision-making process. Faced by the question, why does a typical decision-maker choose to pursue one course of action rather than another, analysts have tends to assume that the process begins with a clear objective or set of objectives. The foreign policy decision-maker, like any rational behaviour considers possible courses of action and evaluates the likely consequences of each in terms costs and benefits. The decision-maker then selects the course of action most likely to achieve the desired goal.[108]

There are, of course, good reasons for assuming rational behaviour. In the first place, we are predisposed to view man as a rational human-being. There is a powerful tradition, certainly in the western philosophical thought, of assuming rational purposeful behaviour. Another practical reason for assuming rationality is that this assumption has made foreign policy-making process an easy to understand and analyse its every aspect. As Sidney Verba puts it 'If the decision-makers behaved rationally, the observer knowing the rules of rationality, can rehearse the decision-making process in his own mind, and if he knows the decision-maker's goals, can both predict the decision and understand why the particular decision was made.[109]

Another reason for assuming rationality relates to the importance of foreign policy behaviour. It is very confronting to assume that foreign policy decision-makers act rationally, especially when 'life or death' decisions are being taken. Indeed some scholars have argued that decision-makers are most likely to behave rationally in crisis situation, when there is considerable pressure on them to weigh very carefully the consequence of their actions. Even if, as other analysts have, argued a rationalistic conception is an imperfect guide to actual foreign policy-making, it remains an important ideal type both for scholars and practitioners providing an important reference point for evaluating the decision-making performance.[110]

The decision-making approach may have reinforced certain aspects of foreign policy analysis but it has also offered some important challenges to traditional assumptions. In general terms it offers a behavioural rather than a realist approach to the study. The object of that study is no longer the state which is both abstract and ascribed with human qualities by traditional analysts. Decision-makers focus on the behaviour of those, who make decision on behalf of the state? For them the state becomes, by definitions, its decision-makers. The fact that decision-makers, unlike detractions, can be observed (and questioned if they are alive) opens up the possibility that the relevant behaviour can be accurately observed and rigorously analysed. The most subversive aspect of decision-making as applied to the study of foreign policy has been the focus on the decision-making process. Indeed, it can be argued that the most important contribution of the approach has been to instil a general awareness that foreign policy is, to a greater or lesser extent, a product of the way it is made. Anyone who wants to understand foreign policy (the decision or policy process) must comprehend the substance of that policy.[111]

Rosenau had observed in the early 1970s that "for many years, the policy-making process was simply assumed as a necessary prerequisite to the initiation of state action. Today it is common place to presume that what a state does, it is in no small way a function of how it decides what to do—in other words, foreign policy action is product of decisions and the way decisions are made may constantly affect their content."[112]

There are a number of difficulties one may face if we are to study any foreign policy. Decision-making will never be straight, forward. Even the term 'decision-making' is misleading since it implies that foreign policy can be broken down into a series of observable decisions: 'conscious choices as in case game of political chess.'

Any study of a state's foreign policy over a given period quickly reveals that rather than a series of quick decisions, there is a continuing and confusing flow. Of action made up of a mixture of political decisions, non-political decisions, and bureaucratic procedures continuations of previous policy and sheer accident. For both practitioners and observers, the reality of policy-making is extremely messy.[113]

The system approach can serve as a framework for analysis, an organizing device which is sufficiently broad and flexible to encompass the major processes and interactions involved in producing foreign policies. The system approach cannot itself explain foreign policy but it does help the analyst to construct explanations by setting out range of variables involved and the possible inter-relationships between them.[114]

A foreign policy system like other system does not

operate in a vacuum. The behaviour to use systems language the: 'outputs generated by the system are conditioned by influences which operate outside the boundaries of the system but which can and do serve as significant input' into the foreign policy system. From a system perspective they are seen to motivate, modify, constrain or some other way affect the workings and operations of the foreign policy system. One simple way of thinking about these environmental factors is to see them as a collection of demands and constraints which have an impact on foreign policy. Some of these factors can be located conveniently in the domestic environment of the state and some in the international environment that is common to all states. However, economic processes cross the boundaries of the states and its international environment too.[115]

This does not mean that concept of decision-making is meaningless. Rather one should realize that the idea of decision-making does not refer only to the making of conscious choices, but also to a range of personal, organizational, institutional and environmental factors which also help account for the flow of events. Not all that goes on in the realm of decision-making is actually a decision—in the sense of being a single human choice—and one must find some way in which to characterize the range and depth of the political activity which produces foreign policy actions.[116]

To do this, students of foreign policy have employed the main principles of system analysis to examine the activities involved in the decisions-making process. This involves viewing foreign policy as if it was a system. In reality, one knows that human behaviour and organizations do not actually exist as a system: only organizations and machines are tangible systems in operation. In other words, one can begin to describe the complex business of foreign policy by using the metaphor of a system.[117]

All of this has created something of a revolution in political science, for systems analysis became almost overnight with all the zeal of a revolution, a new approach which has failed to revolutionize the study of international politics. It has nevertheless left us with a well developed awareness of how to use at least the metaphor of a system as way of organizing thoughts and achieving greater understanding of the phenomenon that make up foreign policy analysis. The system is not trying to explain everything that happens in foreign policy process and so the idea of a general foreign policy system won't be very helpful. The use of the systems approach is an aid to understand the foreign policy process. If the search for understanding must, ultimately be initiated, then the proper use of the system approach allows us to differentiate and explore a number of possible lines of explanation, which collectively can enable us better to understand the nature of foreign policy.[118]

There are broadly three types of explanations which can be derived from the system approach. The first type operates at the level of the international system and regards the foreign policy system as a sub-system of the international system. Theories which operate at this level see foreign policy as the response of that sub-system to the structure of the international system. These are general system theories rather than perspectives derived from the foreign policy system, but they do offer descriptions, explanations and prediction about foreign policy behaviour. A second type of explanation to foreign policy is through a group of theories which can be described as 'input-output'. Their prime behaviour is to relate the inputs to that system from both the domestic and external environment of the state.[119]

The larger question however is how the system as a whole and the policy process works? Each perspective offers different sorts of in-sights into the operation of the system, whether by focusing on organizational behaviour and bureaucratic policies, cognitive processes or problems of implementation. By focusing attention on particular aspect of the policy process, each perspective can consider a relatively small number of variables and can thus deal effectively with manageable researchable questions.

4. Policy Implementation Process

The policy implementation instruments which have been duly recognized in international affairs and diplomatic channels include, the trade policy and the foreign aid. These are the part and parcel of the economic capability of a state.

As the economic strength is required to build the capability, the policy-maker should not ignore the potential influence of the economic tools and consider their options carefully. In international politics and environment, it is not possible to draw a line as far as economic options are concerned, since almost every aspect of economic activity could conceivably be used as a weapon. For political ends, the policy-makers are facing a large number of difficulties as far as making of choice is concerned. Their choice has become limited because of two simple reasons:

1. If the economic capability of a nation is too weak and this option is either closed or it simply does not exist.
2. Sometimes, the domestic environment prevailing in a country prevent him in using these, he thinks that would be helpful in achieving a particular objective. In simple words, the policy-maker's options are determined by the milieu in his own state.[120]

Just as modern nations are politically and technologically interdependent so do they rely upon each other sources and commodities that enable them to develop and sustain viable economics? For almost any national endeavour, whether it is to establish or increase standards of living or to produce capabilities and resources that can be used for domestic or foreign policy purposes, reliance on others has become one of the paramount conditions of modern international relations. Needs that cannot be fulfilled within the national frontiers help create dependencies on other states. Degree of need is one variable element in the successful exercise of influence in international politics. Because economic resources are often scare—but necessary to fulfil national values and aspirations—need in the modern world frequently of an economic nature and possession of these resources could be transformed easily into political influence? It is the need for key raw materials by industrial powers that helps explain how 'weak' countries, as measured by military or economic capabilities, are able to influence the actions of the 'strong'. Economic resources are among the major capabilities that can be mobilized for political purposes.[121]

Economic needs and capabilities are not of course, distributed equally in the international system. Degrees of dependence upon trade as a component of overall economic activity vary considerably among states. Trade instruments of foreign policy are normally used for three purposes:

1. To achieve any foreign policy objective by exploiting need and dependence and offering economic rewards or threatening or imposing economic punishments.
2. To increase a state's capabilities or deprive a potential enemy of capabilities.
3. To create an economic satellite that guarantees markets and resources of supply or help maintain political obedience in satellites or 'spheres of influence' by creating a relationship of economic dependence. Power and influence do not only flow from the major powers or those who possess military might is illustrated in the oil embargo imposed by the Arab countries against Western Europe, Japan and the US in 1973.[122]

Trade occurs among nations precisely because there are differences in costs of production between them,[123] some commodities or goods cannot be produced in particular countries at all; they can be produced in other countries at a comparatively low cost. Consequently, the first group of states must trade rather than produce; and second group finds it advantageous to marketing rather than producing; and the third group sees that it can obtain goods which it cannot produce or which it can produce only at high cost, by selling its cheaply produced goods to the states where production of those goods is more costly or perhaps impossible. Since the natural endowment of countries is different, the classifications of states into these three groups differ in respect of specific products.[124]

Perhaps the most obvious difference among states is the

factor of production in natural resources and geographic position. Some states are favoured with minerals, fertile soil, natural flora and fauna, climatic advantages and general topographic amenability, or with some of these assets, or other assets are poor in some or even virtually all of these. In some countries labour is abundant; in others it's scare and relatively expensive. For historic or natural reasons or a combination of them, some states have a high proposition of skilled labour; in others the proposition is low. Advanced countries, with ample capital, are able to develop and maintain industrial produces unknown to the under-developed states. One producing state may be located near populous areas and potential markets, whereas some states, favourably situated in other respects, may be unable to bear the added burden of transportation. Collectively these factors are of tremendous importance because fundamentally international trade occurs because of international differences in costs. From this, it seems to follow that from a purely economic point of view a country will profit most when it specializes in the area, of its greatest comparative advantage. When a particular country enjoys no such advantage, theoretically its greatest economic gain will come from specialization in those products in which it is burdened with the latest comparative disadvantages.[125]

Foreign aid is another important variable which has a deep impact on the economic growth of a country. The international transfer of economic resources is the main plank of foreign aid. The flow of public assistance consists of grants and loans, including technical assistance from a donor government or international organization to other governments or enterprises in recipient countries. The forms and purposes of financial and technical assistance are extremely varied. The pure economic function of this type of aid is quite significant. They are the historical evaluation of aid programme, the appraisal of the relative merits and demerits of different types of aid, the criteria for the effective use of aid and the burden of aid.[126]

There are number of ways in which foreign aid to a state can be rendered, but need not involve the explicit transfer of resources. Sometimes preferential treatment is given to less developed countries in the form of tariff reductions and special import quotas. In this way, these measures are helpful in increasing the relative earning power of the exports of the less developed countries.[127] J.E. Spero feels that, 'aid in many cases reinforced the political links of dependence. It provided access to the North for economic, i.e. decision-making in the South. The granting of aid and the conditions placed on that aid provided important tools for influencing policies in recipient countries'[128].

Another important aspect of foreign aid in the context of foreign policy is the preservation of external sovereignty in the context of heavy dependence on foreign aid; also needs the diversification of the source of foreign aid. It is a basic principle of the science of international relations that the aid giving state act largely in their own interests and giving of aid for other reasons constitute the exception rather than the rule.[129] It is unquestionably true that foreign aid has had a desirable though small redistributing effect on world health. It is less clear that foreign aid leads to direct political influence upon the recipient country. This is particularly true where the aid given by one country is the sole source of another foreign assistance, it still does not uniformly follow that the recipient country will follow the lead of the donor country in foreign affairs.[130]

Foreign aid for the economic development is a widely accepted phenomenon. The under-development is at least primarily because of the result of loss of capital and technological know-how. Similarly, a nation may suffer from human deficiencies, which preclude economic development. This gap can be filled with foreign aid.[131]

Political stability is accepted as one of the pre-requisite for satisfactory economic growth and development. It may be any form of system, democratic or rightist, authoritarian without a modicum of stability, it is somewhat difficult to carry out its investment programmes effectively, train its labour force effectively or consistently expand its GNP services and per capita income, while planning disjuncture may on occasions act as a positive stimulus to development, political violence and chronic mass unrest, are generally viewed as constraints to rapid economic progress, sufficient disruption inevitably occurs in the economic and planning sectors without borrowing additional problems from the political arena. Foreign economic aid contributes to the overall development process, it is argued by providing the recipient government with greater decision-making flexibility through funds which can be used to reduce the strains caused by inflation, foreign exchange deficit or investment shortfalls at specific project areas. Foreign military assistance may similarly be employed to boost regime structures. Thus foreign aid reinforces orderly political relationship and thereby enhances economic growth and development.[132]

The economic development as part of the foreign policy aid programme is considered to be linked directly with the foreign policy-making process. The policy-makers are usually alert about the needs of his country's economy and adopt all possible means to strengthen it. But the national interest is never ignored because of its significance in a country's political process. The under-developed countries make the choice of aid giving country after carefully analyzing the international environment prevailing. Gone are the days when the superpowers were virtually running the foreign affairs departments of the under-developed countries.

There are in existence some intangible implementation instruments. They are widely applied and are not new to the students of foreign policy analysis. The objectives of these means, actions that are preferably designed to 'communicate with the influence of the masses in another country or involve various communications designed to signal one's own policy-making counterparts' often a negotiating situation develops and one seeks either to solve a problem via an agreement or just to certain benefits from the negotiating process itself.[133]

Foreign policy-making process is deeply rooted in the perceptions of various determinants which directly or indirectly are responsible for making the foreign policy of a country workable. The non-permanent variables are more important as compared to the permanent ones in the sense that the former are to be understood in a better way if one has to really see how they are having their impact on the foreign policy-making process. In this regard the developed and least developed countries, diplomats are to be more cautious and must learn how to tackle successfully the growing demands of the developing nations.

The contributions of various scholars in understanding the various aspects of foreign policy at least definitely help in analyzing crisis situations which comes in the orbit of foreign policy-makers. One aspect of foreign policy which is not debatable is that it requires a lot of patience, understanding and skills to analyse or take a decisive policy on any foreign policy issue.

Notes and References

1. James N. Rosenau, (ed.), International Politics and Foreign Policy: A Study in Research and Theory (New York, 1961), p. 5.
2. *Ibid.*, pp. 5-6.
3. Feliks Gross, Foreign Policy Analysis (New York 1954), pp. 4, 24, 49 as cited in Fred A. Sondermann, "The Linkage Between Foreign Policy and International Politics" in *Ibid.*, p. 9.
4. Russell H. Fifield, "The Introductory Course in International Relations", *The American Political Science Review*, Vol. XLII, 1948, p. 1190, as cited in *Ibid.*
5. Fred A. Sondermann, "The Linkage Between Foreign Policy and International Relations", in James N. Rosenau, n. 1, p. 12.
6. *Ibid.*, p. 12.
7. Frederick H. Hartmann, The Relations of Nations (New York, 1973), p. 67.
8. *Ibid*, p. 68.
9. *Ibid.*
10. *Ibid*, p. 70.
11. George Kennan, American Diplomacy, 1900-1950 (Chicago, 1951), p. 50 as cited in *Ibid.*, p. 71.
12. Harold Nicholson, The Congress of Vienna (New York, 1946), pp. 19-20 as cited in *Ibid.*, p. 71.
13. *Ibid.*
14. *Ibid.*, pp. 71-72.
15. *Ibid.*, p. 73.
16. Brain White, "Analyzing Foreign Policy: Problems and Approaches," in Michael Clarke and Brain White (eds.) Understanding Foreign Policy: The Foreign Policy System Approach (Vermont, 1989), p. 2.
17. *Ibid.*, p. 3.
18. *Ibid.*, Also see J.D. Singer, "The Levels of Analysis Problem in International Relations," in K. Knorr and S. Verba, (eds.) The International System: Theortical Essays (Princeton, 1961), pp. 77-92.

This classic essay sets the issue within the general context of International Relations.

19. *Ibid.*
20. Robert L. Wendzel, International Relations (London, 1977) pp. 217-218. For a discussion of bureaucratic politics in connection with the third and fourth points see, Louis E. Koeing, The Chief Executive (New York, 1968), Richard Neustdt, Presidential Power: The Politics of Leadership (New York, 1960), Joseph De Rivera, The Psychological Dimension in Foreign Policy (Ohio, 1968), I.M. Destler, Presidents, Bureaucrats and Foreign Policy. The Politics of Organizational Reforms (New Jersey, 1974), Theodore Sorensen, Kennedy (New York, 1965), Hadley Cantril, The Human Dimension: Experiences in Policy Research (Bruns Wick, 1967).
21. Roger Hilsman, The Politics of Policy-making in Defence and Foreign Affairs (New York, 1971), p. 5 as cited in *Ibid.*, pp. 218-19.
22. Ralaph K. White, Nobody Wanted War: Misperception in Vietnam and other Wars (New York, 1968), pp. 32-33.
23. Robert L. Oendzel, n. 20, pp. 224-27.
24. *Ibid*, pp. 227-33.
25. *Ibid*, pp. 233-37.
26. Frederick H. Hartman, n. 7, p. 82.
27. *Ibid.*
28. James, N. Rosenau, n. 1, p. 141.
29. *Ibid.*
30. Joseph Frankel, International Politics, Conflict and Harmony (London, 1973), p. 114.
31. *Ibid.*, pp. 88-89.
32. Charles O. Larche, Jr., Abdul A. Said, Concepts of International Politics (New Delhi, 1972), p. 23.
33. *Ibid.*
34. *Ibid.*, pp. 23-24.
35. *Ibid.*, p. 24.
36. *Ibid.*, p. 25.
37. Kenneth W. Thomson and Roy C. Macridis, "The Comparative Study of Foreign Policy", in Roy C. Macridis (ed.) "Foreign Policy in *World Politics*" (Englewood Cliffs, 1972), pp. 1-2.
38. *Ibid.*, pp. 1-3.
39. *Ibid.*, p. 3.
40. S.S. Bindra, US Foreign Policy Process (New Delhi, 2005), pp. 20-22.
41. *Ibid.*, p. 21.
42. K.J. Holsti, International Politics: A Framework for Analysis (New Delhi, 1928), pp. 20-21.
43. *Ibid.*, p. 21.
44. *Ibid.*
45. William Wallace, Foreign Policy and Political Process (London, 1971), p. 28.

46. *Ibid.*, p. 9.
47. Thomas Hobbes, Levithan (Oxford, 1960) Chapter 18, p. 117, as cited in *Ibid.*
48. John Locke, The Second Treatise of Government (Oxford, 1948), Chapter 12, pp. 72-73, as acted in *Ibid.*
49. Dorthy Pickles, "French Foreign Policy," in F.S. Northedge, The Foreign Policies of Powers (London 1968) p. 127. Also see Arnold Wolfers, Discord and Collaboration: Essays on International Politics (Batimore, 1962), Roy E. Jones, Analyzing Foreign Policy: An Introduction to Some Conceptual Problems (London, 1970).
50. William Wallace, n. 45, p. 11, Also see, F.H. Hinsley, "On the Present State and the Future Development of the International System, "*World Politics*", Vol. XX, 1967-68. Rogers D. Masters, "World Politics as a Primitive Political System", *World Politics*, Vol. XVI. 1963, pp. 163-64.
51. K.J. Holsti, n. 42, p. 21. For an understanding and more information see, Richard Brody, "Three Conceptual Schemes for the Study of International Relations" in Richard Synder, *et. al.* (ed.) Foreign Policy Decision-making: An Approach to the Study of International Politics (New York, 1962), Mortan A. Kaplan, "Is International Relations a Discipline," *Journal of Politics*, Vol. XXIII, No. 161, 1973, pp. 462-67, Charles P. Kindleberger, "Scientific International Politics", *World Politics*, Vol. X, 1956, pp. 63-88, Charles A. Mcclelland, "The Function of Theory in International Relations", *Journal of Conflict Resolution*, Vol. IV, 1960, pp. 303-36.
52. James N. Rosenau, The Scientific Study of Foreign Policy (New Delhi, 1981), pp. 318-19.
53. Bernard C. Cohen, "Foreign Policy", in David L. Sills (ed.) *International Encyclopaedia of Social Sciences*, Vol. V, (New York, 1968), p. 530.
54. *Ibid.*
55. James N. Rosenau, n. 52, pp. 20-31.
56. Bruce Russtt and Harvey Starr, The *World Politics*: The Menu for Choice (Bombay, 1986), p. 191.
57. *Ibid.*, Also see, C. Lindblom, The Policy-making Process (London, 1963), D. Vital, The Making of British Foreign Policy (London, 1968).
58. Charles O Lerche, *et. al.*, n. 32, p. 24.
59. *Ibid.*
60. Robert Wendzel, 20, pp. 39-40.
61. *Ibid.*, p. 43.
62. Joseph Frankel, n. 30, p. 85.
63. J. Bandhyopadhyaya, The Making of India's Foreign Policy (New Delhi, 1976), 112.
64. Norman J. Padelford *et. al.* The Dynamics of International Politics (New York, 1976), p. 112.
65. Donald E. Neuchterlein, National Interest and Presidential Leadership (Boulder, 1978), p. XIII.

66. Jpseph Frankel, n. 30, pp. 86-88.
67. *Ibid.*
68. Donald E. Neuchterlein , n. 65, p. 5.
69. *Ibid*, pp. 7-8
70. Charles O Lerche *et al.*, n. 32, pp. 25-27.
71. *Ibid.*
72. F.S. Northedge, n. 49, p. 15.
73. Karl W. Deutch, The Analysis of International Relations (New Delhi, 1989), p. 97.
74. Keith R. Legg and Joseph F. Morrison Political and the International System: An Introduction (New York, 1971), pp. 140-42.
75. Joseph Frankel, n. 30, p. 114.
76. *Ibid.*
77. *Ibid.*
78. Robert L. Wendzel, n. 20, pp. 44-45. Also see for more details, Howard H. Lenter, Foreign Policy Analysis: A Comparative and Conceptual Approach (Ohio, 1974), John P. Lowell, Foreign Policy in Perspective Strategy, (New York, 1972).
79. *Ibid.*, pp. 45-46.
80. Charles O. Lerche, n. 32, p. 29. Also see Robert C. Good, "National Interest and Moral Theory: The Debate Among Contemporary Political Realist, in Rogers Hilsman and Robert C. Good (ed.) Foreign Policy in the Sixties: The Issues and the Instruments (Baltimore, 1962).
81. *Ibid.*, p.
82. K.J. Holsti, n. 42.
83. Fredrick H. Hartman, The Relationship of Nations (New York, 1967), p. 73.
84. *Ibid.*, Also see, Charles B. Marshall, The Limits of Foreign Policy (New York, 1949), Kurt, L., "How Foreign Policy in Made? (New York, 1984), Bernard, C. Cohen, The Political Process and Foreign Policy (Princeton, 1957), Walter Lippmann, Public Opinion (New York, 1982), Louis, L. Halle, Civilization and Foreign Policy (New York, 1952).
85. Robert L. Wendzel, n. 20, pp. 47-48. An Excellent example of this kind of analytical approach may be found in, William D. Coplin *et al.*, American Foreign Policy: An Introduction to Analysis and Evaluation (Duxbury, 1974), pp. 86-86. Donald James, International Politics Today, (New York, 1971), pp. 90-94.
86. Roger Hilsman, To Move a Nation: The Politics of Foreign Policy in the Administration of John F. Kennedy (New York, 1967), p. 5.
87. Norman D. Palmer and Howard D. Parkins, International Relations: The World Community is Transition (Calcutta, 1970), p. 72.
88. *Ibid.*, p. 75.
89. *Ibid.*
90. Robert L. Wendzel, n. 20, p. 21.

91. Charles O. Lerche, n. 32. pp. 209-10.
92. *Ibid.*
93. *Ibid.*, p. 211.
94. Joseph Frankel, n. 30, p. 31.
95. Brain White, n. 16, p. 1.
96. *Ibid.*, pp. 10-11.
97. Also see, G.T. Allison, Essence of Decision (Boston, 1977), J.S. Nye *et al.*, New Dimensions of World Politics (London, 1975), pp. 30-40.
98. Joseph Frankel, n. 30, p. 11.
99. Charles O. Lerche, n. 32, p. 46-52.
100. James N. Rosenau, "The Premises and Promises of Decision-making Analysis, "In James C. Charles Worth (ed.) Contemporary Political Analysis (New York, 1967), pp. 208-09.
101. See, Stanley Hoffman, Primary or World Orders American Foreign Policy Since the Cold War, (New York, 1978), Henry A. Kissinger, American Foreign Policy, (New York, 1977) and White House Years (Boston, 1970), Hans J. Morganthau, A New Foreign Policy for the United States (New York, 1969).
102. See for more details, Richard C. Synder, *et al.*, Foreign Policy Decision-making: An Approach to the Study of International Politics (New York, 1962), Robert C. North, "Perception and Action in the 1914 Crisis", in John C. Farrel and J. Smith (ed.) Image and Reality in World Politics (New York, 1967), David Bray Brooke and Charles Lindblom, A Strategy of Decision: Policy Evaluation in a Social Process (New York, 1963), Glenn D. Paige, The Korean Decision (New York, 1968), John W. Spanier, Foreign Policy is Made (New York, 1974), Theodre C. Sorensen, Decision-making in the White House (New York, 1963), Harold Laswell, The Decision Process: Seven Categories of Functional Analysis (College Park, 1956).
103. *Ibid.*
104. James N Rosenau, n. 100.
105. Joseph Frankel, The Making of Foreign Policy: An Analysis of Decision-making (New York, 1963), p. 174.
106. Charles E. Lindblem, The Policy-making Process (Englewood Cliffs, 1968), Irving Janis and Kalph Mann, Decision-making (New York, 1977).
107. Brain White, n. 16, p. 10.
108. *Ibid.*, For a more developed attempt to evaluate the impact of decision-making approach on the study of foreign policy, see, B.P. White, "Decision-making Analysts" in T. Taylor, (London, 1978), pp. 141-164.
109. S. Verba, Assumptions of Rationally and Non-rationally in Models of International System", James N. Rosenau, International Politics and Foreign Policy (New York, 1969), p. 225.
110. Brain White, n. 16, pp. 13-15.
111. *Ibid.*
112. Michael Clarke, "The Foreign Policy System: A Framework for Analysis", in Michael Clarke and Brian White, n. 16, p. 27.

113. *Ibid.*, pp. 27-55.
114. *Ibid.*
115. *Ibid.*
116. *Ibid.*, p. 28.
117. *Ibid.*, p. 31.
118. *Ibid.*, pp. 54-55. Also see, CF Hermann, Crisis in Foreign Policy (New York, 1969), pp. 29-30, R.W. Cox and H.K. Jacobson, The Anatomy of Influence: Decision-making in International Organization (New Havens, 1974).
119. See, Morton Kaplan, System and Process in International Politics (New York, 1964), R. Rosecrance, Action and Reaction in World Politics (Boston, 1963) and International Relations: Peace or War. (New York, 1973).
120. Robert L. Wendzel, n. 20, pp. 137-38.
121. K.J. Holsti, n. 42, pp. 242-43.
122. *Ibid.*, pp. 247-50.
123. Walter Krause, International Economist (Boston, 1965), p. 6.
124. Normal D. Palmer and Howard C. Parkins, n. 87, p. 137.
125. *Ibid.*, pp. 138-39.
126. Gerald M. Meier, "Foreign Aid's Economic Aspects", in David L. Sills (ed.) *International Encyclopaedia of Social Sciences*, Vol. V. (New York, 1960, pp. 521-22. Also See, Robert L. Asher, Grants Aids and Local Currencies: Their Role in Foreign Aid (Washington, 1961), Alarm D. Neale, The Flow of Resources: Rich to Poor Countries. (Cambridge, 1961), John A Pinws, International Coal Sharing (Baltimore, 1965).
127. Jagdish Bhagwat and Richard S. Eckaus, Foreign Aid, (Baltimore, 1970), p. 7.
128. John Edolman Spero, The Politics of International Economic Aid (London, 1981), p. 160. See for more details, Goran Ohlim, Foreign Aid Policies Reconsidered (Paris, 1966), Robert S. Walters, American and Soviet Aid: A Comparative Analysis (Pitsburg, 1970).
129. Edward S. Mason, Foreign Aid and Foreign Policy (New York, 1966), p. 47.
130. Richard Rosecronce, International Relations, Peace or War (New York, 1972), p. 258.
131. Robert K. Carr, *et. al.*, American Democracy in Theory and Practice (New York, 1986), p. 482.
132. Eric D. Newsom, "Uniting the Tools of Force and Diplomacy to Enhance Security", Electronic Journals Public Affair Office, US Embassy, New Delhi, May 2000, p. 9.
133. Robert L. Wendzel, n. 20, p. 175.

2

Pakistan's Quest for Security

Pakistan emerged on the world map as sovereign independent nation in August 1947 and since then, it has always been in the grip of insecurity. Foreign policy is often considered as the first line of defence of any country. This fact has also close relationship with Pakistan, which has been beset by a difficult security position from the very beginning. Indeed "the country can be said to have had a baptism of fire. It has more or less thrown into the vortex of international cross currents before it could even stand on its feet."[1] The foreign policy-making process of Pakistan is determined by national interests. The foreign policy aims and objectives, enlightened or conceived by her leaders from time to time, keeping in mind the needs and requirements of their country, like the geo-political situation and needs, to build strong economic and military capabilities. But Pakistan's foreign policy-makers knew well that they have to give proper attention to the ideology which formed the basis of Pakistan and the commitments made during the struggle for Pakistan, the sort of equation established by the Muslim League leaders with the neo-colonial power before and after formation of Pakistan and the mode of achieving independence. Besides this the foreign policy of Pakistan was tailed to the domestic and international environments prevailing.[2] The most important factor which has its own relevance in the context of the Pakistan's foreign and security policies is the definite role of the armed forces in the internal and external affairs. The army has always or otherwise upper hand and any ruler, may be democratically elected cannot dare, to ignore the army top brass. It has always been a well established fact of Pakistan political process.

INDIA FACTOR: A DETERMINANT

"India factor" is considered to be the strongest one as far as the determinants of its foreign policy are concerned. Pakistan's attitude towards India has been determined by her own reading; perception of Indian intentions, motivations and aspirations both in national and international spheres—Pakistan has never been convinced that she can ever trust India, a bigger and more powerful neighbour. Pakistan has failed to establish her complete national identity and even after more than sixty-two years of her existence is still trying its best to establish her national identity. It has, therefore, been Pakistan's constant endeavour to prove that the idea that inspired the Muslim League to seek Pakistan was quite sound and still relevant in the contemporary world. That is regarded as "a major factor in Pakistan's efforts to disown the common heritage and the geopolitical independence of the India-Pakistan sub-continent."[3]

A.K. Fazlul Haq, known as Sher-e-Bangla, the mover of the Lahore Resolution of 1940 had challenged the existence of Pakistan when he said that he considered those to be the enemies of India who had divided it. He declared: "we are fellow workers in the common cause. If we have the common cause in view it is idle to say that I am Bengali, someone is a Bihari, and someone is something else.... India exists as a whole.... I shall dedicate my service to the cause of the motherland and work with those who will try to win for India—Hindustan and Pakistan—a place among the countries of the world."[4] He declared that in removing the parries which existed between the Bengalis, he "would not take note of the fact that there was a political division of the province into East and West Bengal."[5] Others both in East Pakistan and

West Pakistan had similar nostalgic memories, but dared not think loudly for the fear of dire consequences. It is clear even to a novice that India and Pakistan leaders wanted a dignified position—as actors rather than objects—in a world still organized on the traditional basis of the European to move sovereign states system. They wanted further to maintain the essence of their ancient cultures and traditions, adapting them as necessary to modernize their societies so that they could deal with western nations on an equal basis. This was proving to be far more difficult than was imagined at the time of independence, but they were intensifying their efforts rather than retreating into ineffectual demography. "Although Indian and Pakistani leaders realized that their long-term task were domestic rather than international, they did not have the luxury of a lengthy quite period to devote largely to addressing their internal problems. Ancient religious and cultural antipathies between Hindus and Muslims had taken on a political collaboration during the struggle for independence and led to bitter hostility between the two new states. Their hostility, together Soviet-American antagonism and the rise of communist China, drew South Asia into the cold war in ways that were more tragic (arms race) and beneficial (foreign aid for development)."[6]

Since the British left the Indian sub-continent, "by virtue of its location, population, combination of actual weakness and potential strength and efforts at nation building, the South Asian sub-continent is an important example of that shifting struggle. For instance, it illustrates equally well the complexity of problems in the post-war politics of Asia. But is South Asia infact, a forum of world politics in the same sense? That is to say, the West Asia has been at the centre of the contest between Western nations and the communist world. To be sure, India, Pakistan, the US, the Soviet Union, communist China and their various national interests came into striking juxtaposition in South Asia." International political relations in South Asia are so closely intertwined that a change in one nation's policy almost invariably leads to a shift—sometimes subtle, sometimes dramatic in the policies of the other nations. Not only foreign policies but also ideologies, economic conditions and policies and strategies have their own role to play in South Asia.[7]

It is neither necessary, nor possible to answer with precision the question whether the India sub-continent is a critical focus of world politics as other areas of great power confrontation. The great powers demonstrate their foreign policy interests in the sub-continent and regard it as an area for accommodation and adjustments. That has been the case historically and it continues even today.

There was a growing belief that the struggle between the west and the communists would be decided in the Third World. South Asia with half the population of the non-communist Africa and Asia combined and locked between a turbulent Middle East and an unstable South East Asia was regarded as an area of vital importance. No doubt, the picture is now somewhat different if not entirely changed, particularly after the disintegration of the Soviet Union, number of independent countries emerged in the Central Asian region which has been the source of attraction for the foreign policy-makers of the US because of their strategic location and not so cordial relations with the former Soviet Union.[8]

Indeed if India and Pakistan were unable to withstand the communists and to make the transition from traditional to modern societies, what hope was there fora nation to be well prepared for the struggle? That was probably a right thinking of scholars and diplomats at that time.[9]

Underlying the view of India and Pakistan importance was the widespread eviction that the underdeveloped areas, thought of almost as a unit had to demonstrate to their peoples within a reasonably short time that they would succeed in the tasks of modernization as non-communist societies. From 1947 to 1967 India enjoyed a degree of domestic political stability that was virtually unique in the underdeveloped world.[10] Pakistan was less fortunate in early years to have stable governments, generally during military rules. There was a brief spell of civilian rule in Pakistan in parts, but that too could not provide any democratic setup. Again it was under army rule, and a civilian Prime Minister with all its strings in the hands of the President.

The problem of national security was considered to be major one for the newly independent states of South Asia.

The rapid political changes which were visible in this region had posed for the new states of South Asia the problem of national security, was practically insoluble in terms of traditional theory and practice which linked national security primarily to military strength and strategy. The naval and air powers of all the states of this region were negligible and grossly insufficient for guarding the sea and also the vast skies of this area. Their armies were not only inadequate for guarding the long frontiers; they were also divided and locked up within the area due to the lack of organization integration at the sub-system level. Nor was it possible in the changed political environment in the area and in the world as a whole for new states to exercise harmony over the neighbouring areas, should they desire to do so.[11]

Faced with an enormous security problems, and without any development of industrial land and military base, the South Asian states chose to adopt a relatively dynamic and manipulative foreign policy for safeguarding their national security. India started off with her policy of non-aligned, an active role in the UN and expressed its faith in disarmament and world peace and the ideal of Asian solidarity all of which were intended to safeguard her national security. Pakistan on the other hand started thinking on different lines. It began with an elementary hatred and fear of India and the goal of pan Islamic solidarity, then passed through a period of complete dependence on the west for its military and economic needs, if not politically and then gradually leaned heavily towards China and at the same time working for cordial relationship with the former USSR, but did not abandon the advantages of her alliance with the West. These twists and turns in the foreign policies of India and Pakistan, have infact, been much more complex. Although they have been grouping in haphazard and inarticulate manner.[12]

The use of foreign policy by the South Asian states for the purpose of safeguarding their national security, as well as for playing a decisive role on the international political scene has of course been "facilitated by the new objective conditions in which they function, including the growth of international law and organization and the neutralization of the big powers through the cold war and the balance of nuclear deterrence." Moreover while depending primarily on foreign policy for safeguarding their national security and playing an important role in world affairs, the South Asian states at the same time steadily increased their military and industrial strength, which had shown that they did not believe that in the long-run national security, could be safeguarded without adequate industrial and military power.[13]

The Islamic Republic of Pakistan "was created to be the state organization of Muslim nation of the Indian sub-continent. It does not posses a history of national unity; it has no common language, nor uniform culture. The force behind its establishment was based very largely on a feeling of insecurity."[14] Insecurity from whom? Probably all the moves of Pakistan's foreign policy revolve around the Indian foreign policy. The feelings of mistrust and fear from India are the prominent variables of Pakistan's foreign policy process. Mutual fear and mistrust have conditioned the whole international outlook of the two nations. "From the day Pakistan emerged on the world map as sovereign independent nation, the main plank of Pakistan's foreign policy has been to obtain a shield against a possible attack from India."[15] The Government of Pakistan and its political elites feel that India from the very beginning did not like the emergence of Pakistan and the main aim of Indian foreign policy has always been to destroy and weaken Pakistan.[16]

A Pakistani scholar was of the view that "Indian" efforts immediately after independence to undo Pakistan, particularly its attempt to seize Kashmir, were the main causes for its bitterness and sense of insecurity which gripped the Pakistani policy-makers from the outset. This perception was to have a profound influence on the formulation of their defence and foreign policies. In the years that followed, the Pakistani foreign policy-makers were more or less convinced that India which is several times bigger than Pakistan in size and resources was always in search of an opportunity to remove it from the world map. "In their perception, India's hostile designs not only consisted of the conventional methods of warfare (to begin within Kashmir) but also included diverse political and other pressures, including a psychological war of relations, propaganda questioning the very *raison de etre* of Pakistan's creation."[17]

To overcome these challenges to the security of Pakistan the first task of the "Pakistan diplomacy was therefore, to somehow prepare the blueprint of foreign policy which could find an equalizer against India. This has ever since remained the most important pre-occupation of Pakistan's foreign and defence policies." But in the later years, there were many ups and downs in Pakistan foreign policy. In search of security, Pakistan joined Commonwealth and hoped that the British would help her in solving the problems with India, particularly which the partition of India had produced. But it was disappointed when found out soon enough evidence that the Commonwealth under the British patronage was not willing to discussion any bilateral dispute between member states.[18]

Soon after independence, Pakistan also explored Pan-Islamism to see if it could bring the weight age of the numerous Islamic states behind it with respect to India. however, it could not succeeded in its mission and its call "for an Islamic bloc even aroused uneasiness in countries like Egypt which were seemingly warned that Pakistan would become a rival for leadership in the Islamic World" Egypt's opposition to the formulation of an Islamic bloc was reiterated by President Nasser who on a visit to Pakistan said, "I do not wish to use Islam in international politics."[19]

Thus the Pakistani foreign policy-makers found themselves in a dilemma. Tensions with India showed no signs of abatement. The Pakistani efforts to mobilize the UN support as well as the Commonwealth against India's intransigence in Kashmir were making no headway. The Islamic countries were quite weak and in any event were not at all in a position responding positively for the formulation of an Islamic bloc. The Soviet Union did not show much interest in Pakistan in the formative years and had convinced the ruling elites of Pakistan that they should not hope for any economic aid from the Soviet bloc. Pakistan was in desperate need to somehow find an equalizer against a belligerent India.[20]

NEHRU AND INDIAN FOREIGN POLICY

On the other hand, the Indian foreign policy-makers were quite confident. Nehru was holding the charge of Ministry for External Affair too, in the hope of giving a desired shape, to the country's foreign policy, keeping in mind its needs and of course the national interest. While delivering a speech at the Indian Council of World Affairs, New Delhi on 2 March 1949, Nehru spoke at length on the evoluation of Indian foreign policy in general and India's relationship with its immediate neighbours in particular. If there erupted a war or conflict any where in the world, it would have a tremendous impact on the foreign policy process of India in a big way. India's foreign policy was to be shaped keeping into consideration all the possible areas of conflict, trade, economic interest, etc. Nevertheless the nearby countries always had a special interest in one another and India must inevitably think in terms of her relation with the countries bordering her by land and sea.[21]

In regard to Pakistan, "the position has been a peculiar owing to the way Pakistan was formed and India was divided. And there have been not only all the upsets that you all know but something much deeper and that is a complete emotional upset of all the people in India and Pakistan because of this... There is also no doubt at all in any mind that it is inevitable for India and Pakistan to have very close relations with each other—sometimes or others in the future."[22] He strongly believed that we could be either hostile to each other or very friendly with each other, whatever period of hostility might intervene in between, because the interests of both the countries were so interlinked.[23]

The political environment prevailing in both the countries at the time of partition of British India, and afterwards, for nearly a decade, played a significant role in shaping Nehru's Pakistan policy on the one hand and Pakistan's India policy on the other. The attitude of the political elites of the Indian National Congress and the Muslim League towards each other created fear, suspicions and feelings of insecurity between them.[24]

The partition of British India on the basis of "Two

Nations Theory" created "two new states with religious boundaries that made geographical non-sense." The intention behind the partition was intended to avert the threat of civil war between Hindus and Muslims. But the forces behind it "failed to anticipate the sectarian massacres and forced migration to which they were condemning Hindu and Muslim minorities left behind in the divided territories.[25]

The Muslims ruled India for 800 years and the British for nearly 200 years. The Hindus were convinced that the domination of minority over the majority would not prevail and it would soon end as the Hindus were without power for more than 1000 years. In the case of Muslims, it was argued that having ruled for more than 800 years over India, they should be equally associated with the governance of the country.[26] These two opposite and altogether different psyches shaped the freedom struggle. Some wise men, including political elites with nationalist outlook from both the communities tried their best to end the Hindu-Muslim disunity by unfolding a secular and united India inspired by modern concept of economic growth, democracy and creation of an egalitarian society based on social justice, emancipation of women from their age old bondage, and building up India with modern scientific culture and had helped the west to grow fast after agricultural and industrial revolutions.[27] K.L. Gauba, an eminent political figure of pre-partition felt that "the empire of Pakistan is founded no less on fear—feared Hindu domination, fear of Hindu exploitation, fear of Hindu absorption. It is an empire founded on an inferiority complex."[28]

Although Nehru succeeded in preventing India's developing into a theorocratic state like Pakistan, he could not check the rise of Hindu revivalism and fundamentalism, and further strengthening its roots in the Indian politics and society altogether and later years under his successors, it was to play an increasingly ominous role. Hindu revivalism fed in particular, on the guilt by association which tarred the large majority of Muslims who stayed on in India after partition. M.J. Akbar, explains the peculiar dilemma which the existence of Pakistan created for the Indian Muslims. "The guilt of that still remains, the price that has to be paid still remains. The real tragedy is that the price of partition is not being paid by the people who got Pakistan but by Muslims in India....? The memory of a nation divided is a powerful one. It seeks into decisions, subconsciously or unconsciously some rules. It creates an aura of suspicion, around the Indian Muslims, it adds to the argument that the Muslims cannot be trusted.[29]

MUSLIM LEAGUE AND PAKISTAN'S FOREIGN POLICY

There is very little evidence of any active participation by any Muslim League leader in the process of foreign policy formulations in the early years. It would have not been irrelevant to mention here that a political party of Muslim League stature had never showed an evidence of an international outlook before 1947.[30] Its concern for international affairs in pre-1947 days was evidenced only in cases where the interests of some Muslim countries were involved. The horizon of League never extended beyond the Muslim countries of West Asia and Africa.[31] After independence, the Muslim League engaged itself in the national affairs of the country. Especially after the death of Jinnah and the assassination of Liaquat Ali Khan, its time and energy were devoted more to the pursuit of the personal power at home than to the process of foreign policy-making. Only when the Muslim League went out of office in 1956, its leaders began to show interest in the country's foreign policy toward the Suez Crisis in 1956.[32]

The Muslim league also did not anywhere define what the Islamic State would be like. Probably to avoid sectarian conflicts, it continued to be a vague concept. Jinnah was not in a position to formulate his views on Islam, minorities and economic matters before tabling the resolution on Pakistan. He deliberately did not prepare the nation for an agreed ideology of the proposed state of Pakistan. Thus, Pakistan having not spelt out clearly what it meant, made the Muslim League an umbrella organization to all types of people having different ideas, concepts and policies contrary to this Congress formulated its views on secularism, social justice, land reforms, economic growth or the eradications of poverty.

Pakistan nurtured feudalism and continues to live with feudal structures with orthodox Islam as its base."[33]

Though the leaders of the Congress who stood for a united India spoke lightly of Hindu-Muslim differences and ascribed these solely to the British policy of divide and rule, Jinnah believed Pakistan had "started the moment first non-Muslim was converted to Islam..... (because) as soon as Hindus embraced Islam he was out cast not only religiously but also socially, culturally and economically... Throughout the ages Hindus and Muslims... had not merged their entities—that was the basis for Pakistan."[34]

Indeed it is difficult to think of any two religions more anti-theatrical to each other than Hindustism and Islam. Islam is the youngest of the universal religions. Its basic doctrine is brief and explicit: belief in one powerful God, in Mohammed his messenger and in the *Quran* as the message. Hinduism on the other hand, is an ancient religion and has no central dogma or agreed scripture. "Hinduism as a faith, is vague amorphous, many sided, all the things to all men. It is hardly possible to define it, or indeed to say definitely whether it is a religion or not, in the usual sense of the word."[35]

The Pakistanis, having got their wish had a sense of fulfilment and were mentally better conditioned to let bygones be bygones. Practical good sense also demanded that Pakistan should also try to turn down the heat. She was the weaker of the two parties and dependent on Indian mercy for her share of the joint assets. Jinnah, on entering the Governor General house in Karachi as the Governor General of independent Pakistan, said, "Never expected to see Pakistan in my life time. We have to be very grateful to God for what we have achieved."[36]

As Governor General while addressing the Constituent Assembly on 11 August, Jinnah made it clear that it was impossible to avoid the problem of minorities, being in one domain or the other. The partition was inevitable and if you will work in cooperation of, burying hatchet, you are bound to succeed. If you change your past and work together in a spirit that everyone of you matter, to what community to one belongs, no matter, what relations he had with you in the past "no matter what is his colour, caste or creed, is first, second and last a citizen of this state. With equal rights, privileges and obligations, there will be no need to the progress you will make."[37] No where in this speech he mentioned that the Pakistan would be an Islamic state and where Islam would be given preference over other religions. He was confident that in due course of time all this angulations of the majority community, the Hindus, or the Muslim community—having Pathans, Punjabis, Shias, and Sunnis and so on will come to an end. Among the Hindus, you have Brahmins Vaishnavites, Khatris and Bengalis so on—will vanish. This division in both the communities was responsible for causing the delay in the transfer of power. He further emphasized that we must learn a lesson from this "you are free to go to your mosques or any other place of worship in the state of Pakistan. You may belong to any religion or caste or creed that has nothing to do with the business of the state. In the new state of Pakistan, there would not be any distinction between one community and another, no discrimination between one caste and creed or another would be allowed to exist. In the course of time; Hindus would cease to be Hindus and Muslims would cease to be Muslims not in the religious sense because that is the personal faith of each individual but with political sense as citizen of the state."[38] It was he who forcefully launched a tirade against the Hindus and the Indian National Congress and compelled the British to implement the "Two Nations Theory."[39]

But there was something else in his mind about the nature of the state to be established in Pakistan, if the views expressed in his writings and interviews in the beginning of 1948, were any indication. By that time, the communal tension between the two communities had substantially eased and governments of both the countries succeeded in curtailing communal violence and the activities of the undesirable elements. In a recorded speech which was for the people of the US and Australia, while discussing the constitution of Pakistan, he refused to accept categorically that what would be the shape of the constitution of Pakistan but at the same time, he further stated that: "it will be of a democratic type, embodying the essential principles of Islam.

Today, they are as applicable in actual life as they were 1300 years ago. Islam and his ideals have taught us democracy. It has taught equality of mankind, justice and fair play to everybody.... In any case, Pakistan in not going to be theocratic state to be ruled by the priests with a divine mission."[40]

Jinnah had infact never imagined that there would be a large scale cross migration and communal tension would take a worst turn. He was confident that non-Muslims in Pakistan would accept the citizenship in their respective countries of their own choice.[41]

Immediately after the death of Jinnah, the controversy regarding the interpretation of Islam developed into a storm "though its first rumbling could be heard even during his life time." The *Ulema* did not like the democratic and liberal institutions of the west as they were repugnant to the teachings of the *Quran* and *Sunna* and if western type of state—would be incorporated in the future, constitution of Pakistan, it would naturally amount to be betrayal of the ideals for which the state of Pakistan had been founded after a prolonged struggle. Their interpretation of Islam was different. They regarded it not in terms of precedents, i.e. the practices and institutions that were in existence in the country. They were for strong executive and did not favour parliamentary system of government and institution. They felt that the Islamic law Shariat was comprehensive and therefore was capable of meeting the need of the hour. They insisted that not only on the framing of laws but appointing the experts of Islamic law to integrate.[42]

The fundamentalists after partition could not do much but were extremely important themselves so far were compelling the moderates to make their views more explicit. As was expected the modernists views on the nature of the state be established in Pakistan were legalistic nationalistic and democratic and were mainly based on Iqbal ideology of limitations of Ijtihad and the renew ability of Ijma. They forcefully advocated that "Ijma be instutionalized in the legislative assembly."[43] The modernists also felt that the Islamic legal heritage should not be ignored. On the contrary, the Islamic Parliament would be competent to interpret the sources[44] or legislations which were antagonistic to the concerns and traditions and to what the prophet Mohammed had said.

Until 1947, the ideologists of the movement for Pakistan confined themselves to popularizing the slogan of an independent state of Indian Muslims. Exactly what implied was not stressed at that time. But with the achievement of political independence, the problem of its practical implementation loomed large. A sharp controversy flared up around the question of what kind of state it was to be. As it proved the very idea of Islamic state was far from being acceptable to all members of Pakistan society.[45] The forces that opposed it were not so numerous as they were diversified in social character. The adaptation of Islam as the official ideology of the new state conflicted with the interests of the religious minorities, who saw in it a threat to civil and economic rights.[46]

It was also opposed by some Muslims, mostly those with European educational background, who wanted their state systems and social institutions to be modelled on West. Then, of course, there were the more progressive elements of Pakistan society who were committed to secular democratic forms of government.[47]

Serious differences even cropped up among the supporters of the Islamic state themselves, while recognizing Islam as an official ideology, most theorists argue that there was no distinctly Muslim type of state. They pointed out that the prophet did not prescribe the manner in which his successor was to be chosen, or leave any instruction as to the running of the government. The prophet, merely bequeathed his followers some principles to guide them in policies and gave them the liberty to select the form in which those principles should be applied in their own times.[48]

One can be easily misled if we casually examine the public pronouncements, made by the religious and political elites in Pakistan in the beginning. When the Constituent Assembly was in session of course so far as Maudoodi, *Ulema* and other fundamentalist leaders were concerned, it was the unprecedented social and economic upheaval, to mobilize the people on the issue of Kashmir, divergent social interests, to encourage private and provincial efforts for the rehabilitation of refugees. to promote a tolerant attitude towards the Hindu minority in accordance with the Islamic traditions were some of the factors which had created such an environment that the need for the Islamic character of constitution was felt by the leadership of Pakistan.[49] Maulana Shabir Ahmed Usmani, President of the Jammial-at-*ulema*-i-islam, Sharif of NWFP, Maulana Akram Khan, President of the provincial Muslims League (a figure of some importance in religious circles of East Pakistan). Maulana Abdullah-al-Baquil, all these gentlemen were active in and outside the Constituent Assembly and were strongly advocating that Islamic state must be created in Pakistan. Usmani expressed his doubts in an address to a conference of his party unit in East Pakistan. He said that *Ulema* had played an important role in the achievement of Pakistan and Pakistan was founded in order to become an Islamic state. He mentioned the various countries where the constitutions were based on Islamic principles. They were Afghanistan, Iraq, Iran and Saudi Arabia. He demanded that the Constituent Assembly "should set-up a committee consisting of eminent *Ulema* and thinkers... to prepare a draft and present it to the Assembly."[50]

POLITICAL SET-UP OF PAKISTAN

One can easily conclude from the Constituent Assembly proceedings and the various resolutions tabled in it that there were serious differences among its members regarding the future political set-up of Pakistan. Jinnah's untimely death and Liaquat Ali Khan's assassination created a vacuum in the political process of Pakistan. Quaid-e-Azam, the Father of Pakistan, was a realist who never permitted his vision to be obscured by emotionalism. He was an ardent Muslim and a true leader who always spoke in simple and straight-forward manner. He was a cautious man and weighed pros and cons of a policy. before recommending it to anyone. Some of his significant qualities were his independence of thought, courage, integrity, ability and perseverance. His strict sense of discipline enabled him to reconcile to the loss of political allies rather than tolerate indiscipline. His character was above-board, his integrity was unimpeachable and his abilities were unbeatable. He clearly pointed out in his correspondence to Nationalist Muslims where they had erred and how they were playing into the hands of those who were attempting to trap Muslims into accepting solutions which would have led to the establishment of the entire Muslim nations in a recalled united India ruled by the ruthless brute force of a Hindu majority.[51]

Jinnah's contribution to the institutional framework of Pakistan was appreciated by all. First, he had a legalistic approach to politics. Thus while, acknowledging the unjust and perverse nature of the Radcliff Award, he reminded Pakistan that "we had argued to allude by it and it is binding upon us." Second, he demonstrated a spirit of self-introspections, leading to a flexible approach to men and matters. About his struggle for separate home land for Indian Muslims, he acknowledged: "may be that view is correct, may be it is not, that remains to be seen." Third, in his views state identities and loyalties, state enjoyed a superior status to all other social identities. He advised those Muslims who stayed back in India "to give unflinching loyalty to the state in which they happened to be. "Finally the state was conceived by Jinnah as an institution capable of making and maintaining rational laws." Thus the state was a tremendously resourceful machinery to work for the welfare of the society." He judged the strength or weakness of the state in terms of legal, financial and administrative resources on the one hand and the challenging task on the other.[52]

Jinnah's "leadership projected a sense of national destiny and a legalistic-constitutional approach to exercise a legitimate authority. While he generally did not create new institutions, he gave a new ethos to the existing institutions of the state, thereby lending them a spirit of legalism; he affected a new relationship between the state and society in Pakistan within an overall framework of protection of individual rights. The tremendous lightening potential of Jinnah's charisma was exercised in favour of the core institution of the state.[53]

He tried to build Pakistan's political framework on

sound footings. He was clear in his ideas and outlook. It will be wise to framework his views on Pakistan's foreign policy. Pakistan's foreign policy under Jinnah represented a confluence of three variables: the Quaid's world views of cosmology, the security compulsions of the new state of Pakistan and the then international environment where the whole world was divided into two power blocs, led by the US and the USSR respectively. To these overarching influences one must add the historical fact that the Muslim League which spearheaded the struggle for the creation of Pakistan under the leadership of Jinnah was "devoid of a coherent international outlook. Unlike the Congress, the Muslim League had few emotional or intellectual commitments" apart from the "historical sympathy and interest of the Muslim of India for other Muslim counters of West and North Africa.[54] This general lack of a foreign policy orientation of the Muslim League enabled Jinnah, despite his falling health to define the strategic parameters of Pakistan's foreign policy according to his predictions. Pakistan did not have a full time foreign minister until December 1947" and all papers were sent to Jinnah for information or taking any decision.[55]

The basic tenets of the foreign policy of Pakistan were outlined by Jinnah at a press conference in Delhi on 14 July 1947. He remarked that the new state of Pakistan "will be most friendly to all the nations. We stand for the peace of the world." We will make our contribution whatever we can. These ideas were further elaborated on 15 August 1947, when as Governor General of Pakistan he said, "our objective should be peace within and peace without. We want to live peacefully and maintain cordial relations with our neighbours and with world at large. We stand by the UN Charter and will gladly make our contribution to the peace and prosperity of the world."[56]

Regarding non-alignment, Jinnah in his broadcast talk to the people of the US in February 1948 said, "Our foreign policy is one of friendliness and goodwill towards all the nations of the world. We do not cherish aggressive designs against any country or nation. We believe in the principle of honesty and fair play in national and international dealings and are prepared to make our contribution to the promotion of peace and prosperity among the nations of the world. Pakistan will never be found lacking in extending its material and moral support to oppressed and suppressed peoples of the world and in upholding the principles of the UN Charter."[57]

Jinnah world view may be called rationalistic, such a characterization warranted by the fact that "Jinnah's appeal to religion was always ambiguous, certainly it was not characteristic of his political style before 1937 and evidence suggests that his use of the communal factor was a political tactic, not an ideological commitment. For example, on the emotionally charged issue of Khilafat in Turkey in 1920, Jinnah as a true constitutionalist rejected "the false and dangerous religious frenzy" of the "zealots, both Hindus and Muslims" since it threatened the stability of the existing political structures and orderly progress along moderate and nationalist lines. Jinnah vehemently opposed the partition of Palestine and the establishment of Israel in 1948. In a cable to President Truman urging him to "uphold the rights of the Arabs" and thus "avoid the greatest consequences and repercussions.[58]

Similarly, Pakistan provided all possible "diplomatic and material assistance to the liberation movements in Indonesia, Malaysia, Libya, Tunisia, Morocco, Nigeria and Algeria." Jinnah gave open and unflinching support to North African Arabs in their struggle to throw off the French yoke. He "considered the Dutch attack on Indonesia as an attack on Pakistan itself and refused transit facilities to Dutch ships and planes, carrying war material to Indonesia.[59]

Soon after partition, Pakistan was faced with a hostile security environment. The most serious threat to Pakistan security emanated from India which never reconciled itself to the idea of the partition of the British India. The Indian leaders harboured grave reservation about the partition. J.L. Nehru, for example, said, "The proposal to allow certain parts to secede if they so will be painful for any one of us to contemplate. Expressing the similar view, the resolution of the All India Congress Committee (AICC) on the partition plan, adopted on 15 June 1947 stated that: "geography and mountains and the seas fashioned India as she is and no human agency can change the shape or come in the way of final destiny. Economic circumstances and the insistent demands of international affairs make the unity of India more necessary. The picture of India we have learnt to cherish will remain in our minds and hearts. The AICC earnestly trusts that when the present passions subsided, India's problem will be viewed in their proper perspective and the false doctrine of two nations in India will be discredited and discarded by all."[60]

In October 1947, Field Marshal Claude Auchinleck reported to the British Prime Minister Attlee that: "the present Indian cabinet are implacably determined to do all in their power to prevent the establishment of the Dominion of Pakistan on a firm basis."[61]

POLITICAL INSTABILITY IN PAKISTAN

Political incertainty is a part of political culture of Pakistan. Since its inception, we find continuity and change in the political process of Pakistan. The political chaos and confusion prevailing in Pakistan in its formative years had an impact on the making of its foreign policy, opportunism and unprincipled lust for power in the people who came at the helm of affairs in Pakistan after the assassination of Prime Minister, Liaquat Ali Khan, also added an irrational touch to the formulation of foreign policy. Apparently, there were two facets of the problem. One, the element which gained control over the levers of powers after Liaquat, were not of representative character and the politicians who rather became professional, in their lust for power, pawned themselves much as one changes one's shoes.[62]

Ironically, there was nothing surprising in that, and both the factors were embedded in the struggle for Pakistan. It is well-known that the movement of Pakistan was controlled and effectively run by the Muslims of Bengal and those of the Hindu majority provinces who cared always of Hindu domination. The Muslim League's standing in the areas in the former West Pakistan, was nebulous. In Punjab, the Muslim League was eclipsed by the unionists, a combination of Muslims, Hindus and Sikhs who were running the government: in North West Frontier Province (NWFP), the Congress was in power, and in Sind, at best, the League hold was precarious.[63]

After the creation of Pakistan, the migrant element from India, took the command of the country as the Governor General and Prime Minister. But, after the death of Jinnah and Liaquat Ali Khan, there was no political leader of their stature in Pakistan and the civil service which mostly belonged to the wealthy and landowning classes, quietly grabbed all the powers and distributed patronage among politicians. The Bengali elements right from the beginning went into political wildness while the residue refugee's elements had no roots either in East or West Pakistan. The West Pakistan Muslim League politicians were proverbially opportunist. The Muslim Leaguers as a lot in the pre-partition period got their inspiration from the British bureaucracy and they had little complications in transferring their loyalties to the Pakistani civil services.[64]

There is no evidence to suggest that Jinnah and Liaquat aimed at reforming the bureaucratic order inherited from the British Raj. However, Jinnah was emphatic in suggesting that the bureaucracy must change its attitude. He propounded an attitudinal change among civil servants that would reflect the spirit of an independent people in conformity with democratic ideals. He was aware of the lingering effects of colonial rule on the mental make up of the bureaucracy. He advised the bureaucracy to descend from the position of the "ruling class" to that of the "servants of the people". Jinnah noted, "I know we are saddled with old legacy, old mentality, old psychology and it haunts our footsteps, but it is up to you how to act as true servants of the people even at the risk of any minister or ministry trying to interfere with you in the discharge of your duties as civil servants." In return of this political neutral and independent role of the bureaucracy, Jinnah promised security, safeguards and protections of the interest of the civil servants. He was of the opinion that civil servants be loyal to the government in power, implement and execute its policies and be judicious and independent in advising the government.[65]

Instead of aloofness and arrogance, he suggested that the bureaucracy should show warmth, affection and compassion for the people in their dealings as well as for comprehending their problems. To inculcate this attitude change among the civil servants, in his speeches, he advised the officers to concentrate on the following points:

Remain a non-political and serve the people,
Perform as servants of society and not act as rulers,
Show tolerance and respect towards the demands of the people,
Subject, patronage and promote merit, and
Do not yield to pressure.

He also emphasized the need for developing respect and understanding between the politicians and bureaucracy. He suggested that the political parties and political leaders must respect the sanctity of civil service. He cautioned the civil servants not to support any political party. Simultaneously, he warned the political leaders to stay away from influencing the services and not to interfere with their working or use them for their ends.[66]

He was conscious of the fact that in a newly emerging country where democracy was not fully planted, the political government would get enormous pressure from the political parties and leadership. Therefore, time and again, he advised the civil servants to show determination in resisting pressures from the party in power and stay independent and neutral in performing their duties. He also recognized the integrationist role of the bureaucracy in a country where regional voices persisted. Therefore, the bureaucracy was perceived as the symbol of federation unity, despite constraints. It continues to stand out as a unifying force in institutional forms.[67]

The bureaucracy wielded considerable impact on foreign policy of Pakistan. The Civil Service of Pakistan (CSP), the direct descendent of the Indian Civil Service, protected its power and status without taking into consideration its impact on the social and political system of Pakistan. According to Hasan Sahib, "The impact on socio-economic, planning and administration has been disastrous, making the country pay clearly in terms of widening management gap, acute misadministration and a colossal waste of human and psychical resources. In the political field, it has nourished and supported autocratic military or dictatorial regimes and prevented the march of democracy and promoted the continuation of British imperial rule.[68]

The high or elite bureaucracy in Pakistan was exceptionally powerful and enjoying exceptional privileges. They did not like the behaviour and manner of functioning of politicians and the way they worked and consolidate their position had produced abrasive reactions that characterized Pakistan Government. The administrative set-up of Pakistan has always been dominated by intraservice rivalries which resulted in the isolation of the dominant bureaucrats from the larger administrative system.[69]

The political instability in Pakistan, probably, was responsible for increasing the role of bureaucracy in the first decade of its existence. The lack of strong party system encouraged the civil servants to manipulate the situation. A leading Pakistani scholar wrote: "in Pakistan, the army and the bureaucracy had played a dominant and decisive role, the "seize of power in 1958 by General Ayub Khan in the name of the army was just a dramatic movement in that continuing domination. The army came to the limelight during crisis, but the bureaucracy actively dominated the political scene then and in normal times. In the first decade after independence, the façade of parliamentary government obscured the role of bureaucracy and did its bidding. However, when radical political parties posed a challenge to its authority, the bureaucracy put an end to the constitutional apparatus of government and assumed power directly."[70]

But "paternalism" of Pakistan's elite bureaucracy should be examined, observed and analyzed against the political and social culture of Pakistan. All the more important is the ways and means suggested to tone up the Pakistan's administration and political authority must be seen in this larger context."[71]

The political environment prevailing in the first decade was complex and confusing particularly after the permanent departure of Jinnah and Liaquat. The "Muslim League was unable to present to the public either a convincing programme or an inspiring leader. It had therefore to turn for support to local politicians and local issues" for survival.[72]

POLITICAL MILIEU 1947-1957

The electorates of Pakistan were predominately rural. They were poor, illiterate and demanding too. They were only in a position to understand either a very general idea "such as Pakistan and the triumph of Islam, or a very particular idea, such as the curtailment of the power of this landlord or that policeman", *Jagirdars* and *Zamidars, Pirs* and *Mirs, Makhdooms, Khans* and *Nawabs* were having vast political influence. They were very active in political arenas. The political map of Pakistan, was dotted with the signs of entrenched area of personal political power.[73]

L.F. Rushbrook Williams, a noted analyst of Pakistan affairs was of the view that, "during the period which immediately followed Quaid-e-Azam's death, there developed a fierce competition for influence, wealth, power and prestige between the various interests and personalities which made up political life. The arena in which the competition manifested itself was the organization for framing the constitution which was to give final expression to Pakistan polity."[74]

What would be the nature of political system to be established in Pakistan? It was not possible to install a federal structure in Pakistan because the ruling elites were not for it. Their style of functioning and policies pursued by them to protect their vested interests had created an ambiguous political environment in the country. The Muslim League failed to create Islamic State according to the *Quran* and the *Sunna*. Nobody was aware in Pakistan what the Islamic State actually meant. The orthodox lobby dominated by the *Mullah* and the *Ulemas* had desired the installation of unitary form of government but the logic of situation prevailing in Pakistan with the presence of a number of distinct nationalities *Bangalis, Punjabis, Pathans, Baluchis* and *Sindhis* with strong cultural identities, demanded that a federal structure would be most suitable for Pakistan.[75]

How was power to be divided between the centre and the provinces and between East and West Pakistan?[76] It was really a million dollars question. As Pakistan was divided into West and East Pakistan and the two different social set-ups were working in both the wings. The people of Eastern wing were dissatisfied with the policies pursued by the western wing political and bureaucratic elites towards them. They were totally alienated from the people of the Western wing. If the members of the Constituent Assembly had taken into consideration the problems and needs of the Eastern wing, and granted it some sort of political autonomy, perhaps, the disintegration could not have taken place in the year 1971.

How far the shape of a modern state could be squared with the principles of Islam?[77] That was another serious matter which was before the Constituent Assembly of Pakistan. As the basis of the partition was on the basis of "Two Nations Theory", it was not an easy task, to frame the constitution of Pakistan based on Islamic principles the *Quran* and the *Sunna*. The chances of the survival of such types of states based on religious guidelines, and ruled by the fundamentalists are very bleak as they won't be able to maintain social, economic, cultural, educational and technological relations with other people of the world because of the fundamental differences in their approach and values.[78]

How the different competing interests—landlords, religious leaders, businessmen, and industrialists—could receive recognition to their claim to power and influence?[79] These groups were represented very well in the Constituent Assembly of Pakistan. They clashed with each other when the various issues in which they had direct or indirect interest, were debated in the Assembly. In fact, it was not at all possible to accept the views and demands of every group.

The first step in the direction of framing the constitution for Pakistan was the adoption of the Resolution in March 1949 on the "Aims and Objectives of the Constitution, popularly known as the Objective Resolution by the Constituent Assembly." This Resolution was tabled by Late Prime Minister Liaquat Ali Khan. It strongly recommended that the future Constitution of Pakistan should be according to the principles and values of Islam. It was clearly mentioned in the Preamble of the Resolution that the sovereignty of the God would be supreme and declared that state authority must be subservient to God. But it recognized the supreme authority of the peoples as they were empowered to choose by adopting the process of elections, their representatives who in turn would run the affairs of the state. The principles of democracy, freedom, equality, tolerance and social justice would be fully incorporated in the new constitution. The Muslims of the Islamic state would mould their lives individually and collectively according to the requirements of the *Quran* and the *Sunna*. It also recognized the existence of minorities in Pakistan. They would be free to profess the religion of their choice. There should not be any restriction if the minorities wanted to develop their own culture. The political set-up of Pakistan would be based on federal principles in which the units would enjoy authority but the central authority would impose certain limitations and restrictions on their powers.

It would be the duty of the state to provide adequate protection to the backward classes, and also the minorities. Their legitimate interests would be given due recognition.[80]

The Resolution was aimed to satisfy both the *Ulema* as well as the modernists as was clearly evident from its contents. The fundamentalists were satisfied as they would read in it the contours of a democratic secular state.[81]

An eminent scholar Sisir Gupta felt that "the making of a constitution has been an unusually perplexing task in Pakistan. The peculiarities of the country's geography, the history of its people and the conditions in which the state took its birth, have combined to make Pakistan a unique country with a unique constitution, that would reconcile the conflicting interests and trends within the country to the satisfaction of all concerned."[82] The people of Pakistan were not happy with the working of the Constituent Assembly. It was formed in a non-democratic way and had also lost its credentials. The opposition was not performing its duty in the manner which was required. The government did not think much of the constituent immunity of the Assembly members. The seats that, for various reasons fell vacant were filled by co-optation. Sessions were as a rule very short lasting only for one to eight days (only the last two sessions, lasted for 28 days). The decisions on the constitutional matters were virtually taken behind closed doors, at the sittings of the Muslim League Co-option fact... The decisions were submitted to the Constituent Assembly and adopted without any voting and considerations.[83]

The Assembly was dissolved in 1954, by the then Governor General of Pakistan, Gulam Mohammad, on the ground that it had lost the confidence of the people. He was probably correct in his estimate, since it had for a long time represented nothing but the interests of those who happened to compose it.[84]

In February 1956, the first Constitution of Pakistan was accepted. Though parliamentary form of Government was established under the 1956 Constitution, but it failed to provide a desirable political system to Pakistan. The party system was not in good shape. The Muslim League was the only party which was established at the grass root level. But it was also faction ridden. In East Bengal Awami League was having strong political base. There was a political chaos prevailing.[85]

The parties in Pakistan became the vehicle for politician's political careers. Generally new parties were formed when a career seemed to be making no progress in an old party. Some parties were formed entirely from among members' legislatures and constituted in fact a temporary grouping within an assembly for the purpose of making or breaking a ministry. These factors hampered the growth of a workable system of responsible government.[86]

Besides political reasons, there was some economic aspect of the political crisis in Pakistan which ultimately led to the emergence of army on the political scene of Pakistan, led by General Ayub Khan. The economy was in bad shape in 1957-58. The agricultural output in Pakistan decreased to 4.2 percent and the yield in the rice was about 6 percent in 1958. The growing food imports had an adverse impact on the economic position of the country. During the first nine months of 1958, Pakistan balance trade showed a deficit of Rs. 470.7 million. From December 1957 to September 1958, the currency reserve fell by Rs. 1.021 million to Rs. 765 million. The Pakistan economy was further strained by the worsening conditions of foreign trade, the fact that the US curtailed its purchase of Pakistan commodities, the fall of the prices on the world market for such import items of Pakistan such as jute (price of which dropped by $5-10 per ton) and cotton and the reduced export of wood, hides, etc. The settlement and employment of millions of refugees from India was also an important problem which was awaiting solution. To settle the refugees from India required large funds. There was a sharp increase in the prices of principal consumer goods, mainly due to the abolition of price control in February 1958 which "served the interests of the top strata of the country propertied classes." Despite the seriousness of the situation only Rs. 290 million—out of a total of Rs. 2600 million—was allocated to health services under the Sixth Year Plan of Development (1951-57) and a mere 6.2 percent of the total expenditure of First Five Year Plan (1955-60) was earmarked for educational purposes and even these modest targets were not achieved.[87]

The political instability in Pakistan in the first decade of Pakistan gave a somewhat different shape to Pakistan domestic and foreign policy. At the domestic front, people were fed up with the frequent change in leadership[88] and the absence of any strong leader of international repute. There was no end between the fight of Eastern and Western wings. Leaders from both the wings were busy in levelling charges and counter-charges against each other. Robert Laporte summed up the internal situation of that time as such. He said, "most of the period (from 1947-56) was spent in trying to reach on some constitutional consensus. During this period, the only institutional developments which occurred, took place within the civilian and military bureaucracies, cabinets and Prime Ministers came and went, but the civil servants and military leadership re-found position of importance and power in the new state."[89]

President Ayub in his autobiography made it clear that the "unprincipled" behaviour of Pakistani landlords, lawyers and civil servants turned politicians led directly to the 1958 Coup. Laporte feels that: military bureaucrats in league with

Iskandar Mirza chose to move and perform the coup in the name of parliamentary corruption and immorality is untenable. At any rate, the instability of this period and the inability of the civilian politicians in and out of parliament to appease the military civilian bureaucratic coalition did contribute to the abandonment of the parliamentary democratic façade."[90]

It was during that period that Pakistan leadership decided to align with the US and formally joined the US sponsored military alliance that was considered to be a main foreign policy decision. There was a political uncertainty. The only supreme body existed during most of the period was the Constituent Assembly. But the Assembly was faction ridden and failed to do anything worthwhile. It took more than eight years to produce a constitution which was to be abrogated by President Ayub.

The bureaucracy was in total control of the power in Pakistan. All the major foreign policy decisions were taken by the bureaucrats with politicians having little role to play. They in league with their military counterparts were in total control of the foreign and defence affairs of Pakistan. Probably, the political instability and fast deteriorating economic conditions had driven Pakistan towards the US and her allies.

PAKISTAN'S SECURITY NEEDS AND JOINING OF MILITARY PACTS

Pakistan's policy-makers in defence of their country's military alignment with the west repeatedly referred to certain unique defence problems of Pakistan *vis-à-vis* India and *vis-à-vis* major powers like Soviet Union—the latter of historic origin because of the strategic areas of West Pakistan and the Soviet's interests in obtaining access to warm water ports and above all the West Asian oil resources. Infact Pakistan's defence requirements were far out of proportions to its actual defence capacity it built on its own resources. Thus, Pakistan argued that she had to align herself militarily with the US because of the certain threatening Indian postures. Pakistanis thinking was that because of the military weakness of Pakistanis, compounded by the physical separation of the two parts of the country, Pakistan had to seek military aid. Some would say that even West Pakistan with all its martial traditions did not have enough territory to defend itself in depth against a massive onslaught by a superior power... Thus Pakistan maintained that, it had to obtain military hardware in sufficient quantity to deter a country like India from launching a military attack.[91]

From the beginning, it was apparent to Pakistan that even though it might feel compelled to join western military alliances, it would have to pay heavily in terms of various deprivations that it would suffer.[92]

The Indian leadership strongly felt that Pakistan had committed a grave "political sin" by accepting the US military aid from 1956 onwards. It resulted in the weaking of the "area of peace" as it brought cold war to the Indian sub-continent and opened the gates once again for the return of the empire.[93] Pakistan's pronouncement that to secure herself, she had joined the defence pacts, seemed to be a fraud. SEATO only provided Pakistan with obsolete arms and humiliating aid, nothing but suspicion and hostility from the countries which had before respected Pakistan's actions and reactions in various international forums. It was instrumental in compelling the USSR to "whole heartedly" support India's stand on Kashmir and it frequently started using veto in India's favour in order to check the cheap moves of the US and Britain."[94]

What are the main bases of regional pacts? This question needs to be examined at same length because of its sensitive nature. The states joining such pacts and arrangements must obviously have a common interest in the region but it is not necessarily to be situated in that region. The geographer's definition of region has no association with regional arrangements which are founded in the modern world because the revaluations in the modern communication system have further brought the world more closer. That is why, oceans and mountains are no longer considered as serious barriers between territories. No doubt physical continuity and common, social, cultural and economic backgrounds do help in forming regional arrangements but are not indispensable for them. As all the members of SEATO are neither situated in geographically limited areas nor they are bound by ties of common culture and traditions. The basis of these arrangements these days is the common desire of the participating countries to preserve their respective countries from aggression. The common ideology is the pivotal factor which usually influences the states to enter into regional pacts. Another important factor which induces states to make regional arrangements is the common urge for security. The growing realization that mutual aid and technical assistance can help in subverting the well-being of the people also instigates the states to enter into regional pacts.[95]

The Government of Pakistan had signed the pacts, of course, keeping in mind their security and defence needs. Pakistan was the only country from Asia to join the SEATO and CENTO. It was associated with the US through not one but four mutual security arrangements and sometimes regarded as "America's most allied ally in Asia."[96]

President Ayub Khan in his autobiography had examined various factors which were behind Pakistan's move.

First, the main aim was to oblige the US which was giving large scale economic aid to help in building Pakistan economy. He further clarified that "membership of this organization would in any way strengthen the position of the Eastern part of Pakistan, then he was obviously overlooking the fact that the real danger to Pakistan was from India which surrounded it on all sides."[97] In fact that was the thinking of some western scholars too that the motives behind Pakistan's interests in SEATO was the possibility of being able to get military aid to strengthen Eastern Pakistan to meet a potential enemy.[98] President Ayub was convinced that the East Pakistan was facing danger from India. It was the India factor which once again played an important role and affected considerably the minds of Pakistan foreign policy-makers.

Second, it entered into military pacts to seek safeguards, not against communism but also against India or any other country that might have aggressive intentions against her. The Indiān attitude towards Kashmir and various other unresolved problems probably "indicated that the Hindu majority in India would like to see the two countries reunited. The fear of India had created suspicion and hatred in the minds of the Pakistan people. The danger of going red or being conquered by a communist power was unthinkable as compared with the immediate and continuing danger of forcible merger with India.[99]

The Pakistan government and commonmen were under the impression that after joining SEATO and other pacts, the US would help Pakistan in strengthening her economic condition, unqualified moral and political support in finding an amicable solution of the Kashmir and other disputes. But the hopes of Pakistan were soon belied when the US did not show any signs that it would be going to take the Kashmir issue more seriously. On the other hand, there were enough indications that the US administration desired to be friendlier with the Nehru Government. In December 1955 when top leaders of the USSR, Khrushchev and Bulganian during their Indian visit, categorically declared on the Indian soil that Kashmir was an integral part of India, and while in Pakistan, the Soviet leaders came out with the statement by declaring their support for the need of creation of Pakhtoonistan, a state to be carved out of Pakistani territory. It was expected that the US administration would repudiate the statement of the Soviet leaders. But the mysterious silence of Washington sent shock waves in Pakistan and her people were greatly disappointed.[100]

In Pakistan, there has hardly been a meaningful debate on the multi-dimensional problems of national security. And many leaders have, by and large able to give recognition to the official "line that the nation would eat grass, rather than weaken its military capability. Needless to say, the insecurity syndrome has been accentuated by the formidable military build up of the belligerent "big brother" across the border."[101]

Ironically, whenever, there is a proposal or any suggestion to cut the defence expenditure by mutual consent between the two neighbours, New Delhi has always put forward the arguement that India cannot be equated with Pakistan, since it has to reckon with other sources of threat to its national security. "To argue for a unilateral down-sizing of the armed forces, or opting out of the arms race in the region, without a corresponding Indian gesture, is therefore no less than asking for a moon."[102]

There is no hope that both the countries would divert their funds from guns to development and letting the common people at some stage have a more tangible reward for the toil and sweat, than illusions of national honour and glory. Now that militaryism has acquired a degree of legitimacy more than ever before and people in both countries have been overwhelmed by a chauvinistic tide, holding a brief for a non-military approach to national security is indeed a tall order. Nevertheless, the fact remains that equating security with military capability is an oversimplified, short-sighted view of the problem.[103]

The security of the country does not hinge on the prowess of its fighting force, but there must be a popular resistance to any manifestation of foreign domination. The people must have a sense of belonging to their country, the motivation to defend national interest, "and the will to act in unison in the face of an external threat, in order to rally round force in defence of national interest."[104]

Third, the Middle East rich in natural resources particularly oil, could be a source of conflict between the Soviet Union and the Western world. It was a common feeling at that time once such a situation would develop it would seriously affect the security of Pakistan. The leadership of Pakistan wanted to be associated with the any proposed arrangement in the future for the security and defence of West Asia. It also hopes to "get certain measure of protection against Indian designs in the Middle East." Furthermore, Pakistan wanted to secure its own position and to contribute to general consolidation and stability of the entire region, particularly of the Muslim world. Some Arab countries were of the opinion that Pakistan would guard the interests of the western powers and the US in this area.[105]

Fourth, the economy of Pakistan was not growing rapidly and extra efforts were required to put it back on rails. There was a necessity of developing the country to provide the people, with better living conditions and with the help of this process the bonds of friendship and unity would be strengthened between the peoples of the two wings. Pakistan was to look for external assistance to build up the social overhead and provide the initial capital investment. Without maintaining good and friendly relations with the US and other western nations, it was not possible to build the basic infrastructure.[106]

In return to economic assistance Pakistan, offered to the US her goodwill and growing opportunities for collaborations in the field of trade and industry.[107]

Fifth, during 1950-53, the economic and political conditions of Pakistan were not favourable. The internal weakness "drove the rulers of Pakistan to make an alliance with the US." She strongly felt that informalities with the Commonwealth did not give them the strength which would compensate for their internal political instability and economic weakness.[108]

Sixth, Pakistan was feeling insecure because of certain threatening Indian postures which emerged out of the Indo-Pak conflict, particularly the Kashmir problem. It was not possible that even with all its martial traditions and military capability, Pakistan was not in a position to defend itself against a massive "onslaught by a superior power." And Pakistan "had to obtain military hardwares in sufficient quantity and of such a nature as to deter a country like India from launching a military attack."[109] As declared by Feroz Khan Noon, the then Minister for External Affairs of Pakistan "we want them (Member of the Baghdad Pact) for our defence.... Our first duty is to strengthen our defence particularly against India no matter what others might say."[110]

Last but not the least, Pakistan is a Middle Eastern as well as South Asian country, by joining hands with the US and other Western countries, it wanted to deter India from attacking over East Pakistan which was sharing land and sea borders with India.[111]

The US interest in creation and sponsoring of the military alliances were well known. It wanted "to establish a counterpoise to communism that had impelled that Christian world to help the Muslim world for the first time in history." Because of the strategic and economic importance of the Muslim world, the US and its allies thought it to befriend the

Muslims. The Muslim world also needed material assistance and technical collaboration for the speedily development because it was having plenty of material and human resources and there was no reason why they should not avail that opportunity? There was some logic in the argument that if a larger number of countries from the Muslim world had joined Baghdad Pact because it had provided excellent opportunities and a unique platform for the Muslim countries to get to know one another and to coordinate their policies and plans. At that very juncture, the Muslim World had no forum where they could discuss the common issues and problems they were facing and explore other areas of cooperation.[112]

The US had its own thinking when it invited Pakistan to join military pacts. It wanted, certainly to achieve number of its foreign policy objectives:

First, she had in mind to establish military basis on the Pakistani territory and wanted to utilize that facility for keeping a watch on the Soviet Union, People's Republic of China, India, Afghanistan and Nepal.

Second, the US also did not want at that time that India should be allowed to establish its hegemony in the South Asian Affairs because the US administration did not like Nehru's foreign policy moves, particularly his policy of non-alignment.[113]

Third, the US defence analysts knew very well that how strategically Pakistani territory was important for them. It was keen to strengthen its position in South-East and West Asia. Pakistan could be utilized to an advantage in any event of war and more so, to contain the march of communism in Asia.[114]

Pakistan got substantially in economic and military spheres from the US and its allies after joining the military alliances. But it adversely affected Pakistan in many ways. From the outset Pakistan was aware that she had to pay heavily in terms of various deprivations when the negotiations for the signing of the pacts were in progress. Nehru made it clear that "whole context of the Kashmir issue will change if military aid comes to Pakistan." This fact proved correct and the climate of the Indian sub-continent was changed altogether and bilateral negotiations to solve the Indo-Pakistan problems were unthinkable. Afterwards, the tension between the two countries increased and created mistrust in the minds of Indian leadership and the peoples, regarding the intentions of the Pakistani Government. The relations of the two countries had reached the lowest ebb. The military alliances "became a constant factor in the reaction and counter-reaction which characterized subsequent relations between the two suspicious neighbours."[115]

Pakistan also lost the opportunity for maintaining cordial and close relationship with the Soviet Union. Because of the lack of any contact between the leadership of the two countries, a number of misunderstandings cropped up and Soviet leadership started leaning towards India. This more than nullified whatever economic and military advantages Pakistan gained from the pacts.[116]

The affairs of the Indian sub-continent were also further complicated, with the US as the third party. A beginning was made of the US active role in the affairs of the sub-continent. The US moves were considered anti-Indian and the Government of India thence forward become more cautious and lost faith in the moves initiated by the US administrations to improve relations with India.[117]

The intentions of both the US and Pakistan were almost different as far as the military pacts were concerned. Primarily the spirit behind the creation of defence pacts was to contain the Soviet influence in the world. The SEATO documents categorically stated that the US would be exclusively available against the communist aggression.

As far as the Kashmir issue was concerned, it was further complicated because of the alliances. The Pakistani leadership was warned well in advance by the Prime Minister Nehru about the impact of joining the alliance on the Kashmir, but Pakistani leadership did not pay any attention and wanted to keep the issue alive in order to strengthen its political position. It knew that without neutralizing the Soviet support to India in and outside the UN on the Kashmir issue, it was not possible to solve it.

The economic aid factor was also not taken into consideration by the Pakistan leadership accordingly. The economic aid given by the US was used to build up the defence capability of 'Pakistan. Probably', it was purely a political move in the hope of winning the people of Pakistan who were fed up with the political chaos prevailing in Pakistan. The Pakistani, leadership, bureaucracy and military bureaucracy, tried their best to exploit the feelings of the Pakistani people. The joining of military pacts was widely welcomed by the people and it was propagated that it would help in solving the Kashmir issue. The people were made to attach themselves emotionally with the Kashmir issue.

PAKISTAN AND THE US, THE USSR AND CHINA

To strengthen its security, Pakistan from the very beginning started playing safe on the foreign policy front. It adopted a very cautious approach as far as the foreign policy-making process was concerned. But from 1947 to 1954 it believed strongly in the "wait and watch foreign policy." On the other hand, its neighbour India, did not waste time and categorically announced that it would like to follow the non-alignment foreign policy. In the first six years of its existence, Pakistan remained busy in finding the solution of the various issues that the partition of British India produced. There was uncertainty on the home front in Pakistan and its leadership wanted quick solution to its problems with India.

Pakistan made the beginning of her foreign policy by showing her sympathies with the US and the Western powers. In April 1950, the then Deputy Foreign Minister of Pakistan declared that "we do not regard ourselves as member of either or any bloc" and intend to establish good relations with both the superpowers.[118] When the General Assembly was discussing the Korean Crisis, Pakistan voted in favour of the "Uniting for Peace Resolution." It also appreciated the Japanese Peace Treaty.

Pakistan immediately after independence established economic and cultural relations with the Soviet Union, despite delay in formally establishing diplomatic relations, "for which the mental reservations of the league leaders towards the Soviet Union were responsible." The cultural, medical and trade delegations were exchanged.[119]

As it turned out under Stalin, the Soviet policy towards both India and Pakistan showed certain ideological reservations. The Soviet Union saw the hand of imperialism behind the developments in the sub-continent and treated India and Pakistan as bourgeois pro-west states. Moscow thus showed little interest in getting close to either India or Pakistan. However, the developments took place in 1949, which brought new thinking in Moscow as well as in Karachi. The US extended an invitation to Indian Prime Minister Nehru to visit the US and this was readily accepted. Also India decided to stay on in the Commonwealth even after becoming a republic. Both of these moves drew criticism from the Soviets who then looked more supportively towards Pakistan.[120]

But Pakistan's "bid to assume the leadership of the Pan-Islamic forces provide stumbling bloc for the improvement of relations with the Soviet Union. Moscow condemned the convening of the first Islamic Economic Conference in Karachi. The growing pro-west orientation also made the Russian suspicious and there were adverse comments in the Soviet press. Pakistan's attitude in the Korean War also prevented the development of friendly ties with the USSR. In London, Liaquat Ali Khan publicly announced Pakistan full support to the UN and denounced North Korea action as a clear case of aggression. A Soviet weekly on international affairs described this as Liaquat Ali Khan's "servile zeal." Between 1950 and 1952, the Soviet press on several occasions voiced suspicion that Pakistan was moving close to the American camp to win the US support on Kashmir—9 August 1950, carried a report about an assurance, the American Ambassador had given to Pakistan's of support on Kashmir in return for Pakistan participation in the Korean War.[121]

Dyakov in his work published in 1952 was expressing the general Soviet attitude when he wrote that Pakistan was used chiefly by Anglo-American imperialism for strengthening its influence in the Near and Middle East and that in the UN, the Government of Pakistan "supports American policy much more openly than the Indian government." Dyakov made scathing criticism of Pan-Islamic and observed that "in foreign policy the task of Pan-Islamism is to mask the Pakistan" government's reactionary policy of scrapping together an anti-Soviet bloc among the Near and Middle East. By Pan-Islamic slogan and by raising the common interests of all Muslims in the world, the Muslim League is trying to conceal the dependence of Pakistan's present policy on British and American diktats and to veil Pakistan's role as the bridgehead of the Anglo-American bloc...."[122]

The Soviet Union had shown her keenness to strengthen its relations with Pakistan. On 2 June 1949, the Soviet Union formally invited Liaquat Ali Khan and his wife to visit Moscow, which was promptly accepted by Liaquat Ali Khan. Pakistan's Ambassador to the US, M.A.H. Isphani wrote to Liaquat on 7 September 1949: "Your acceptance of the invitation to visit Moscow was a master piece in strategy." Isphani letter reflected the mood of the group headed by the Prime Minister, who wished to use the Russian gesture to enhance Pakistan's importance—one of the basic foreign policy objectives has been to attain parity with India in politics and diplomacy not in military might. Indeed, the public in Pakistan welcomed the Soviet invitation as a way to balance the set back of Nehru's invitation from President Truman. Some however were not so enthusiastic about Liaquat's visit to Moscow. The then Pakistan's Minister for External Affairs, Zafrullah Khan was leading the group and he sought influential foreign support. The British government was contacted, and it responded with subtle pressure on Pakistan. The tussle between the two groups frustrated Liaquat Ali Khan visit to Moscow. In the manner, a great opportunity to cultivate Pakistan and the Soviet Union was lost. Then the Soviet attitude towards Pakistan, never friendly, began to turn harsh, and it was not until the mid-sixties that the two nations exchanged visits by Heads of States. When Ayub Khan landed at Moscow in April 1965, Soviet Premier Kasygin said: "At least the Head of Pakistan government could land in Moscow."[123]

Later, a myth developed in some Pakistani circles, particularly those with left orientations that Moscow had turned against Pakistan in the year that followed because of the Liaquat Ali Khan's failure to visit the Soviet Union whereas he did go to the US. Incidentally Moscow itself further argued that the alleged rebuff to the Soviet Union inevitably led to profound adverse consequences, as subsequently seen. A careful appraisal, however, shows that there was no noteworthy strains in Pakistan's bilateral relations with the USSR in between 1949-53. Most importantly the Soviet Union did not veto any Security Council resolution on Kashmir. Moreover, Pakistan and the Soviet Union exchanged Ambassadors. Infact, the relations with the Soviet Union turned sour only around 1954 when Pakistan decided to join the military alliances sponsored by the US. That was the Moscow's displeasure with Pakistan and not the inability of Liaquat Ali Khan to visit the Soviet Union for which, he could not be any case, held personally responsible, invitations are often extended but not always often availed. Failure to visit a country in response to its invitations has hardly ever become the cause of long-term estrangement. So Pakistan was in a dilemma. The Islamic countries were acutely weak and in any event, were not responding to Pakistan's suggestion for an Islamic bloc. The Soviet Union was not forthcoming and was not really in a position to extend large scale assistance to anyone.[124]

Pakistan turning towards the West was not an unnatural alliance. In ideological terms Pakistan, fell closer to the West rather than to communism. Moreover, the Russian had been on an expansionist course southwards since the previous two centuries and had annexed vast Muslim territories in Central Asia with which the Pakistani people had age old links. This had aroused a negative perception in Pakistan about Russian intentions.[125]

Because of the intensity of the global struggle between the western and the communist nations, the US tried to rally the non-communist nations of the world to prevent further communist expansion. Seeking to disrupt the western efforts, the Soviet Union tried to demonstrate to the new nations of Asia and the Middle East that they had aligned themselves with the west.[126]

When the US became involved in the affairs of the South Asia after the Korean War, its interests were generally considered to be the following:

- that the sub-continent be militarily secure from external attack;
- that India and Pakistan assume some of the responsibility for the defence of Asia;
- that the two countries cooperate politically with the US and the western powers;
- that the quarrels between India and Pakistan and between them and their neighbours, be settled or kept at least under control;
- that both countries make sufficient political, economic and social progress to enable their non-communist governments to continue in power; and
- that they be willing to provide the US with transit rights, communication facilities and perhaps even military bases if necessary. In sum, the US wanted the two countries to be secure, to co-operate with the west to hold the communists at an arm's length and to enjoy political stability and economic progress. The interests of other western countries were regarded as much the same, although it was generally recognized that the US and the UK would be most directly involved.[127]

American attitude varied over whether defence of the sub-continent or development of the two nations should receive top priority. The two views were more complex than a simple preference for placing either military or economic considerations first. Indeed, development and security are not really alternatives, because neither can exist without the other, both are sought. Economic aid is one instrument to faster development and security, military aid can be another to get security and hence development. Moreover, attitudes tended to shift back and forth overtime. After the Korean War (while the French were fighting in Indo-China) military considerations were stressed. By the late 1950s, there was a shift in emphasis towards economic development, but with the 1962 Sino-India War, the relative emphasis on military considerations came to the fore again for a time.[128]

Among the factors of global setting those particularly conditioning Pakistan's foreign policy were the interests, objectives and perceptions of the three big powers, the US, the USSR and China and their power conflict. Among those the following factors were notable:

- The US-USSR global, or the East-West conflict which was the principal, conditioning factor in international politics since 1945;
- Sino-Soviet conflict which developed in the early 1960s;
- The Sino-Soviet entente which developed in 1970s and which was expected to take the form of Beijing-Washington-Tokyo Axis with Islamabad likely to join; and
- The Chinese objectives of assuming a dominant unchallengeable position in Asia (including South and South-East Asia) and also taking the unquestionable leadership of the Afro-Asian World.[129]

Infact, with the beginning of the cold war the US administration suddenly realized the importance of Pakistan. Since 1947 "containment deliberately designed to the expansion of communism" was the principal object of the American foreign policy.[130] As a result, for a decade and a half after the Second World War, the US identified security with alliances. Henry Kissinger felt that "for the first time, foreign policy has become global. In the past, the various continents conducted their foreign policy in isolation. Throughout much of history, the foreign policy of Europe was scarcely affected by events in Asia. Commenting on the formulation of foreign policy, he further said:

- the number of participants in the international order has increased and their nature has altered;
- their technical ability to effect each other has vastly grown; and
- the scope of their purpose has expanded.[131]

But the Government of Pakistan was quick to recognize the People's Republic of China and accepted the communist regime as a *dejure* government of China. It was hopeful that their friendly relations and mutual understandings would be strengthened in future[132] as its foreign policy-makers knew that, if they succeeded in getting the whole of Kashmir, the communist China would be their next-door neighbour,[133] Pakistan gesture was welcomed by China and she was equally keen to be friendlier to Pakistan. Being the largest populated Muslim country, Pakistan could be helpful in establishing Chinese influence in the Middle-East region. The oil of that area was a major source of attraction for the Chinese too.[134] But during the Korean Crisis, Pakistan sided with the US and that strained its relations with the communist regime.[135]

But interestingly, when Pakistan joined the military alliances in 1954, there was no strong reaction in the Chinese capital. It seemed, the Chinese accepted it mildly because it was a general feeling in China that Pakistan membership of SEATO would not in any way create any misunderstanding between the two.[136] One plank "of this new US-oriented foreign policy of Mohammed Ali took the shape of some kind of a verbal crusade against the aims and objectives of international communism as well as against the Soviet Union." Significally towards China, the then Pakistan Prime Minister Mohammad Ali showed, "more circumspection and caution." He deliberately did not mention the name of China when Ali criticized those countries that were professing communism. The Government of Pakistan gave a signal to the US administration that she was not interested in Chinese but Pakistan also "took such a posture as to show that she was determined to lend all her support to the US for containing the Chinese communism in Asia.[137] But Mohammed Ali always very cautiously skipped the Chinese reference whenever he spoke about the spread or dangers of communism.

At the Bandung Conference too, there was an understanding between the Chinese Prime Minister and the Pakistani Prime Minister Mohammed Ali Bogra. During the Prime Ministership of Bogra, the Chinese relations with

Pakistan improved considerably. At the Bandung, Bogra was successful in convincing his Chinese counterpart that Pakistan joining of military pacts was not against China in any way but it was mainly to maintain parity with India in the area of defence, and to get economic aid for the economic growth of the country.[138]

The Chinese from 1949 to 1964 took deep interest in the South Asian affairs that it was a formative phase of Chinese diplomacy in the region. Kashmir was the main issue which had over-shadowed others. When the Soviets declared their open support for India by declaring unequivocally that the accession of Kashmir to India was final and complete thereby rejecting Pakistan's case on Kashmir. This possibly was the Soviet retaliatory measure against Pakistan's close military and political entente with the Western bloc. But this vital pronouncement on Kashmir by the Soviet leaders greatly disturbed the power balance in the Indian sub-continent, a great power sided with a contending party in what was a localized bilateral dispute. Apparently, it had extremely good relations with India. The Soviet Union had already committed itself to India's stand regarding the conflict in which Anglo-American machinations "were alleged to have been in operation. Beijing, therefore, could have declared its support to Kashmir, making a complete polarization between the communist and non-communist bloc on this issue." But China had kept its cards secret which it did not then open fully. The strategic importance of Kashmir, China could not afford to overlook. According to an expert opinion, it is convenient and true to control Asia in a Kashmir's focus. It is a point in which China, the former USSR, India, Pakistan and indeed Afghanistan meet. There are few points more strategically situated in any part of the world. For sheer proximity of Kashmir to the Pamir regions of the Central Asia, the place has a special appeal to China, apart from his nearness to Delhi.[139]

A western observer of Pakistani affairs Rushbrook Williams claimed that in early 1955, after Bandung, Pakistan received the hints of a likely rapture between India and China. He revealed that following the Bandung Conference "Karachi received—as I have been assured on an unimpeachable authority, a private message from Beijing. The Chinese people's Government assured the Government of Pakistan that there was no conceivable clash of interests between the two countries which could imperil their friendly relations, but that this position did not apply to Indo-Chinese relations in which a definite conflict of interests could be expected in the future."[140]

Inspite of the fact that the US was pleading Pakistan's case on Kashmir in and outside the UN sometimes mildly and vigorously too, the Chinese were keenly watching and analyzing every event in the region with restrain and caution. The Sino-India relations were going from bad to worse. Norman D. Palmer, a renowned political analyst had divided Sino-India relations into three main chronological periods.

From 1949-54, a period of limited relations, with numerous gestures of friendship from India's side and considerable observation on Chinese sides.

From 1954-59, the Hindi-Chini Bhai Bhai period when on the surface Sino-Indian relations were remarkably good and whereas beneath the surface there were numerous points of friction. The open warfare in October 1962 and strained and limited relations ever since with China assuming a distinctly hostile pose.[141]

The Soviet Union continued efforts to improve relations with Pakistan even after later joining hands with the US. The proclamation of Pakistan as a Republic was described in an article in *Izvestia* of 23 March 1956 as an important event in the life of the country, signifying the advancement on the path of national development. In the same year, the USSR announced a gift of 16,500 tons of rice to help Pakistan to tide over a food crisis and several cultural delegations were also sent to Pakistan. But the military coup, led by General Ayub Khan in 1958 was not liked by the Soviet Union. The coup brought Ayub Khan to power who was considered to be the architect in forging military alliances with the west. The report of the Central Committee of the Communist Party of the Soviet Union (CPSU) to the 21st party Congress held that the military coup in Pakistan was indication of the fact that "an attack is developing against the democratic gains of people who have won national independence."[142]

From early 1956, a campaign was launched against the US administration for its alleged indifference to the Pakistani cause in Kashmir. As feeling emerged among the people of Pakistan that China was more dependable than the US as it did not say anything against Pakistan and the Kashmir issue in spite of the fact that Pakistan was a member of the military pacts. Hamidual Haq Chaudhery, the then Minister for External Affairs of Pakistan while participating in a discussion in the National Assembly of Pakistan appreciated the feeling of the members who were critical of the US attitude of the Kashmir. He assured the House that Pakistan would try to further strengthen its relations with the Chinese.[143]

In October 1956, H.S. Suhrawardy assumed the office of the Prime Minister of Pakistan and visited China for twelve days. He wanted to convince the Chinese that alignment with the western countries did not mean a total ban of friendly relations with the communist countries. During his visit, he not only praised the economic growth achieved by the Chinese but also appreciated their domestic and external policies. He did not miss the opportunity by specially appreciating the development projects launched by the Chinese.[144] The Chinese considered Pakistan more important than India because of Pakistan's indifferent relations with the Soviet Union.

To reciprocate, the Chinese Premier also visited Pakistan in December 1956. The Government of Pakistan was expecting that Chinese would declare their support for Pakistan on the Kashmir issue, but were disappointed when the Chinese advised the Pakistani leadership that the problems be solved by sitting across the table bilaterally as China was not in favour of any third party intervention in the dispute.[145] The Pakistan leadership got some relief because the Chinese Premier at least had recognized the Kashmir as a disputed territory and the accession of Kashmir with India as not final.

But Suhrawardy was not sincere in her efforts to improve relations with the Chinese. The main inhibiting factor was his excessive reliance on the military pacts which he sought to use as shield against Indian possible aggression.

Not for a moment it occurred to the Pakistani leaders that China at that time—was desirous in its own interest of forging close friendship with Pakistan." Even within the framework of military pacts, Pakistan with diplomatic ingenuity, could have established a more smooth and workable relations with Beijing. That was done later but could have been in reality easier if Suhrawardy had shown genuine interest in this matter.[146]

The Chinese were not much enthusiastic when Ayub Khan came into power, because they did not expect much from the military ruler who was pro-US in his outlook and behaviour.[147]

In the late fifties the US-Pak relations were at its Zenith. Sino-Soviet differences were an open secret and the Sino-Indian relations were fast deteriorating. The US got the opportunity "that of realizing its long cherished ambition to spread its influence over India."[148] The document entitled United States Foreign Policy complied by the Senate Foreign Relations Committee in August 1959 set out the following objectives:

- Use of bilateral aid to stimulate cooperation among the developing countries of Asia.
- Re-examination of the role of local military forces and the US bases in Asia in relations to US strategic political and economic objectives.
- Inclusion of the countries leaning towards communism. India and Pakistan were specially mentioned in this connection.[149]

When the Sino-Indian differences were on the point of no return, Senator Kennedy desired that the US must tilt towards India. He said whatever battle might be in this headline, no struggle in the world deserves more time and attention from this administration on the next—than that now which groups the attentions of all as in the battle between India and China.... And that is the struggle between India and China for the economic and political leadership in the east, for the rest of all Asia, for the opportunity to demonstrate whose way of life is the better.... It should be obvious that the outcome of this competition will vitally affect the future of all Asia—the comprehensive strength of Red and free nations—and inevitably the strength and standing of our country... It is not enough that we participate on a clash basis, for temporary relief. We must be willing to join with other western nations in a serious long range programme of long-term loans, backed up by technical and agricultural assistance—designed to enable India to win that race with Red China. We want India to be a free and thriving leader of a free and thriving Asia. But if our interest appears to be a purely selfish, anti-community and part of the cold war—if it appears to be the Indian people that our motives are purely political—then we shall play into the hands of communist and neutralist propagandist, cruelly distort America's image abroad and undo much of the psychological effort that we expect from our generosity."[150]

When Senator Kennedy became the President of the US, he showed his keenness to contain communism in Asia, with the help of economically strengthened, free and neutral nations, supported by the US. The value of military bases had been reduced by the spectacular advances made in missile technology. These developments and other factors were probably responsible for the change in the strategy of the US. It started laying more emphasis on economic aid than military bases and alliances. The ability to fire a missile from the US territory in case of a threatened attack or if a vital interest of the US was facing a danger had resulted in reducing dependence on allies on account of the military bases in their territories intended to compromise the US freedom of actions in the service of its interests in international relation.[151]

Ayub Khan's foreign policy moves were not welcomed in Pakistan as he was known to be more close to the US. It was argued by his critics that for the development of Pakistan, cooperation of other countries was required and China was considered to be the most suitable. The China-Pakistan lobby was led by Altaf Hussain, editor of Pakistan's leading English newspaper, *the Dawn* and M.A.H. Isphani.[152]

Pakistan needed an opportunity to open her heart for the Chinese. The much needed desire of those who were keen to form Pakistan-China axis the opportunity was provided by the Sino-Indian war of 1962. The Chinese were condemned by the US and its allies. The Washington Post wrote that "India is in greater peril than it had been at any time since its independence.... If India requests military assistance from the US....... Help to the limit of prudence, should be given..... The defence of India should have very high priority indeed."[153]

The Kennedy Administration has supported India at the risk of alienating Pakistan. In fact, "this was the opportunity for which the US had been yearning from the time of partition—its cherished dream was coming for reality."[154] The Indian Government also approached to the US for military assistance because of the indifferent attitude adopted by the Soviet Union. The US readily agreed to provide them military aid which the Nehru Government accepted.[155]

President Kennedy sent Harriman to India to study the ground realities and make suitable recommendations. He told the Kennedy Administration that there was a need to provide military aid in order to strengthen the military capability of India. He also reviewed India's relations with the Soviet Union which in his opinion in no way would affect the process of the normalization of Indo-US relations because Nehru made it clear to Harriman that the Soviet Union had no objection if India was to collect arms from the US and other western countries.[156]

It was supposed to be an unconditional offer of the US. But in real sense, it was not. Nehru and Kennedy had reached on an understanding that after the war India and Pakistan would discuss the Kashmir issue and would try to amicably solve it. Pakistan was upset and there were anti-US feelings in the minds of its leadership. Pakistan openly supported the Chinese and declared India an aggressor. Kennedy Administration tried to clear the doubts and assured Pakistan that Kashmir issue once again would be more alive, which was lying on the agenda of the UN Security Council.

In spite of the US assurances, the Pak-US relations had reached at the lowest ebb after the Sino-India war of 1962. It was believed in Pakistan that the western countries including the US had overreacted to the crisis. The US had been provided with an opportunity "of making a vowed fight against communism."[157] Furthermore, the western military aid had changed the balance of power in the Indian sub-continent in India's favour. Pakistan which was always suspicious of Indian intentions failed to view the situation created with equinimity."[158]

There was a feeling among the people of Pakistan that at the time of any future India-Pak war, the US would be on Pakistan's side. But it was always the thinking of the US that the pacts signed with Pakistan were "intended to provide defence only against communist aggression." The US Ambassador to India Chester Bowl had confirmed the worst fear of Pakistan. He made it clear that at the time of the Indo-Pak war, the US would act through the UN.[159]

Z.A. Bhutto, then Pakistan Minister for External Affairs, made a lengthy statement in the Pakistan National Assembly on the country's foreign policy. He described the Sino-Indian crisis "perhaps the gravest one the people of Pakistan are faced with" and as a result of the US military aid to India, Pakistan's foreign policy is in the process of being reshaped. There is an agonizing re-appraisal and rethinking as a result of circumstances that have been brought into operation in the political life of this country."[160]

He accepted that in the past on a number of occasions, Pakistani foreign policy planners thought it necessary to reformulate the foreign policy but the circumstances prevailing at that time had no comparison with the atmosphere created after the decision of the US to supply arms to India. He said that "a new important element introduced by new circumstances and events compel us to reconsider Pakistan's basic position.... What has made the situation all the more alarming and all the more disturbing is the fact that India is in a position to onslaught its military strength in a formidable and powerful manner. This is being achieved by India through the assistance of western powers."[161]

He informed the house that Pakistan had conveyed both to the US and the UK its genuine fears and apprehensions. But they are least bothered about the security and integrity of Pakistan and "feel that their global policy and their global interests require the containment of international communism, and they feel that there is a real threat to India from communist China." The Government of Pakistan was not satisfied with the explanations of the western powers and Bhutto described these assurances as false and impractical and in pragmatic terms they were meaningless.[162]

He demanded more arms from the US "to maintain a balance between India and Pakistan. Without the balance, the peace in the sub-continent will be difficult if not almost impossible to maintain." He blamed the western powers for deteriorating the relations and it was their duty to "arrest this deterioration" by devising ways and means.[163]

He declared that if there would be war between India and Pakistan, "the international situation is such today that Pakistan would not be alone in that conflict... an attack from India on Pakistan is no longer confined to the security and territorial integrity of Pakistan." It "involves the territorial integrity and security of the largest state in Asia and therefore, this element and this new factor brought in the situation is a very important element and a very important factor."[164]

Almost all the members who participated in the debate on Pakistan's foreign policy was furious. They demanded that Pakistan should quit the SEATO and CENTO Khattak was of the opinion that these two pacts made our security even more insecure.... We must never lose sight of the fact that the US primarily wanted India as its ally, but Nehru rejected alignment with any bloc. In the face of Indian refusal, the US drafted us into alliances, but rude shock awaited us the day India agreed to come into the American camp."[165]

The participants had shown their happiness, that the Sino-Pakistan friendship was growing and both the countries had also solved their bilateral problems. They were confident that in the hour of crisis, China would have been on their side. But some members were not sure whether China would really help Pakistan in case of war with India.[166]

Z.A. Bhutto indicated that there would be some basic changes in the basic foreign policy assumptions. Indirectly he issued a warning to the US and her western allies that the people and leadership of Pakistan did not like the way, India was treated during the Sino-Indian war of 1962.

SINO-PAK AXIS: NEED OF THE HOUR

The evaluation of the special relationship between China and Pakistan is best analysed in a conceptual framework where ideological considerations are replaced by a security interests and real politic as prime determinants of the relationship between the two states. From a purely geographical perspective, Pakistan's neither a close neighbour of China nor it does share an extensive frontier with it. Inaccessible terrains provide a common frontier in the icy Himalayan Mountains. This frontier was deliberately created by Pakistan in 1963 by ceding parts of Kashmir, claimed by India, to China other durable links like the 766 kilometers long Karakoram highway, the only others land route between the two countries, the Khunjerali pass was created in 1978 as part of a conscious two-way effort by both the countries. Different motives and mechanisms were responsible for the continuance of close Sino-Pakistan cooperation between the 1950s to the present day. This multi-dimensional cooperation has had several results:

- It has kept alive Pakistani pretensions to a status of equality with India and helped it pose a strategic challenge to the much larger country.
- It has enabled China, as also the US, the former Soviet Union and to a much lesser extent the European powers to play a larger than life role in South Asian affairs as aid givers, advisors, military suppliers would be mediators
- Strategic cooperation with Pakistan has enabled China to develop relations with the Muslim World and make friendship with the US.[167]

During the 1960s, the closeness of the relationship between China and Pakistan was evident from expression of political support each gave to the other at times of tension with India. During the 1962 war, Mohammad Ali, Minister for External Affairs of Pakistan said that "we feel that this conflict stems from India's unrealistic and fallacious foreign policy."[168] This same period saw China also witnessed providing sympathy and support to Pakistan. Negotiations for a Sino-Pakistan boundary settlement started a week before the outbreak of the Sino-Indian conflict. Within a few months, Pakistan and China reached on a complete agreement, in principle, on the location and alignment of their borders. During the negotiations, China endorsed Pakistan's call for a plebiscite in Kashmir and agreed to occupy a part of Azad Kashmir which Pakistan was willing to handover in spite of India's protests and claims to these territories. The Indian Government in a protest note to China on 2 March 1963 blamed the latter for intending to destroy the accord and amity which had been developing between India and Pakistan as a result of the joint talks between the two countries on Kashmir and other related issues.[169] It was generally believed that by signing the Border Agreement with Chuna. Pakistan had further complicated the Kashmir issue.[170] It was also a move from the Chinese to improve their image on the world political scene by "presenting herself as a reasonable and friendly power."[171] The Pakistan government settled the border problems with China because of the belligerent attitude of the latter. The Chinese had very good roads on their sides of the border and they could easily capture any Pakistani territory they desired.[172]

The agreement gave a further boost to Sino-Pakistan ties. By the end of 1963, India became the common enemy of both China and Pakistan. But the tension with India was not the only factor which determined Pakistan's China policy. There were other reasons too, such as Pakistan's desire for enhanced security, diversification of commercial connection, an assessment that the Chinese threat to the Indian sub-continent was remote, Pakistan would march towards political stability and growing demands from the leaders of various political parties and peoples that Pakistan must adopt an independent foreign policy, the general thaw in the cold war and the emergence of feelings in Pakistan political circles that the US herself might at a proper time eventually might establish diplomatic relations with China as she had done in the case of Soviet Union.[173]

In 1964, China tested its first nuclear device. The possession of large quantities of sophisticated weapons received from the US (as a part of the SEATO and CENTO treaties) and the support of nuclear China emboldened Pakistan to launch offensive against India in the Rann of Kutch in May 1965. China backed Pakistan through its state owned media. This they had committed themselves to do. In December 1963, the Chinese Vice-Minister for Foreign Trade, Nan Han Chen, said during a visit to Pakistan, "if ever there is a war between India and Pakistan, China will surely support Pakistan, not India.[174]

In May 1964, after the demise of J.L. Nehru, political environment in the Indian sub-continent changed considerably. The Soviet Union also showed keen interest in normalizing relations with Pakistan because of its growing differences with the Chinese. She was worried about the formation of the Sino-Pakistan Axis and wanted to wean Pakistan away from China. It knew very well that the alienation of Pakistan from the US was growing and it was a proper environment for the Russians to act.

There were a number of reasons because of which USSR-Pak relationship could not develop. First, the attitude of the Soviet Union towards the Kashmir issue was totally unfavourable for Pakistan. Second, the Soviets were the major source of military aid to India. They also helped in building economic and industrial capacities of India which directly or indirectly augmented India's war potential against Pakistan. The Soviet Union for reasons best known to her leadership helped India. The reasons were:

- ideological differences with China;
- to boost up opposition to Chinese strength and its influence in the region; and
- to check India's leanings towards the US.[175]

The interaction and personal contacts between the leadership of Pakistan and the Soviet Union at various levels during 1964-65, removed a number of misunderstandings and paved the way for the visit of President Ayub Khan to Soviet Union in April 1965. It was the first direct personal contact in

18 years between the top leader of Pakistan and the Soviet Union.[176]

The shift in Pakistan foreign policy was beneficial for the Soviet Union also. It was believed that "the Soviet Union did not want a hostile Pakistan backed by the US to be replaced by a hostile supported by China... This Soviet aim could be achieved only by softening of its attitude towards Pakistan by the assumption of a rather neutral role in Indo-Pakistan disputes. It could also be accelerating the pace of Soviet economic assistance to Pakistan.[177]

Another way was to adopt a neutral attitude towards Indo-Pakistan bilateral problems. The attitude of the US and its allies was at time based on the same pattern. During the Rann of Kutch dispute and Indo-Pak War of 1965, not only the US and Britain, the USSR also adopted an indifferent role. During the Rann of Kutch dispute, they significantly and characteristically sought as usual to equate Pakistan with India. The Soviet Union appealed to both the countries to resolve their differences through peaceful moves.[178] The Soviets were not keen to annoy Pakistan by openly supporting the Indian view point. It was in fact a green signal to Pakistan that in the wake of her attack on India, the USSR would adopt a neutral posture.[179]

During Indian Prime Minister Lal Bahadur Shastri's visit to the USSR in May 1965, on the heels of the President Ayub visit to Moscow, there was evident change in the Soviet Union policy towards India, particularly the Kashmir issue. In the Indo-Soviet Joint statement, there was no mention of the Kashmir issue and the dispute on the Rann of Kutch. Commenting on the Soviet attitude the Economist of London wrote, "In short the Russians made it plain that they had no intention of getting involved in India's problems with its neighbours... Lal Bahadur's and Kosygin's public exchanges were remarkably cardial. Russian reservations were clear enough between the lines. Kosygin was clearly thinking of Pakistan when he said that peace loving countries and people need not take any development in Russian-Indian ties directed against them... The impression left was that the Russian would aim to keep both Pakistan and India looking equally to Moscow as friends."[180]

SOVIET POLICY OF APPEASEMENT TOWARDS PAKISTAN

Earlier when President Ayub visited Moscow along with his Minister for External affairs Z.A. Bhutto, the former with his "honest, patient and straight-forward efforts" created an atmosphere of goodwill at Moscow. But Bhutto had created embarrassing situation for Ayub by adopting a tough attitude towards India which infact irritated the Soviet leaders—particularly Brezhnev, who appeared to be more pro-Indian than Kosygin. Ayub had on several occasions tried to stop Bhutto to keep quiet by speaking in Urdu, to avoid further embarrassment. There were several formal meetings between the Soviet and Pakistani leaders in which they agreed on a number of important issues – "the two sides considered their bilateral relations, touching particularly upon such matters as the Soviet stand on Kashmir, Soviet arms aid to India, Pakistan's membership of Western pacts, American bases in Pakistan and Pakistan's request for Soviet arms."[181]

Ayub tried to convince the Soviet leaders of the threat to Pakistan's security and territorial integrity as a result of India's huge military build up to which USSR was the biggest contributor. The Soviets replied that they had sold some "small quantity of arms" only since 1964 after "the Chinese had inflicted a humiliating defeat on India" only after rightist elements in India had started a campaign to make India ally with the US and Britain and join the West military pacts. According to the Soviet leaders, "if the Soviet Union had refused to supply arms to India, it would have crippled liberal elements in India who wanted India to remain non-aligned." Defending the military aid to India, Kosygin pointed out that "the Soviet Union provides arms to those countries that were fighting colonialism and imperialism... India is in the struggle." Ayub was skeptical "which imperialism is India suffering from?" he asked. Brezhnev went further and dismissed Pakistan's fears of Indian military build up, "India is a neutralist country and does not participate in the war", Ayub replied, "Pakistan is one-fifth of India in terms of resources, military strength, etc. and if India were to fear Pakistan, it would be like the Soviet Union fearing Poland." Imperialism's legacy, not USSR arms to India, seemed to be what the Soviet leaders thought was the source of Indo-Pakistani tensions.[182]

Contering Pakistan's objections to Indian arms supplier, the Soviet leaders questioned Pakistani membership in CENTO and SEATO. Pakistan was forced to join pacts "owing to constant Indian threats," Ayub said, adding that Pakistan had begun a process of disengagement from them. Besides Ayub claimed Pakistan's membership in SEATO had prevented American reliance upon the treaty organization in the Vietnam War. As for CENTO, according to Ayub "there is no life in it." Ayub claimed that by initiating the Regional Council for Development (RCD) with Iran and Turkey, Pakistan had virtually put CENTO "in cold storage."[183]

At one stage, the Soviet leadership even said that they won't insist upon Pakistan's withdrawal from the defence pacts as a pre-condition for the betterment of their relations but they put forward some suggestions:

- Prohibition of foreign military bases on its territory.
- Prohibition of foreign nuclear weapons on its territory.

Limitation or termination of military cooperation with military blocs. Initially, the Pakistani leaders were somewhat convinced that if they would implement the suggestions given by the Soviet Union, they were going to see a change in the Soviet's stand on Kashmir, on military assistance to India or on military supplies to Pakistan. But subsequently, it was made known to them that Soviet Union was not willing to make any departure from its policy regardless of Pakistani action.[184]

The 1960s were, therefore the decade of what was termed "bilateralism" in Pakistan's foreign policy when it sought to establish, with some success equally good relations with the two power blocs—the US, the USSR and of course, China too—"even though three were deeply antagonistic to each other. This balancing act was a high point in Pakistani diplomacy. Indeed during the decade of the 1960s, Pakistan appeared to be more genuinely non-aligned, than India." It was an achievement of Pakistan foreign policy that, despite its very strong relationship with India, the Soviets did not stand with India during Rann of Kutch dispute and the Indo-Pak war of 1965. The Soviets tried their best to pacify the two neighbours and avoid the war, but their efforts failed. But they were successful on the other front, after the war, they persuaded both India and Pakistan to sit together across the table and solve their problems that emerged out of the 1965 war. The Tashkent Declaration of January 1966, "brokered by the Soviet Union, marked a high point of Moscow's diplomacy in the sub-continent."[185]

On the other hand, the Soviets did not accept fully or in public, Pakistan "analysis of the situation in the sub-continent as a result of the Ayub's visit to Moscow. They did not subsequently change policy, Ayub effectively presented his own viewpoint, however, the Soviet leaders gained first hand information of Pakistan's difficulties and it seemed they got some realization that the military build up of India by them "was not altogether unjustified." The Soviets also felt that "Pakistan also truly wanted to follow an independent foreign policy and to reduce its commitments to the western allies. Thus Soviet-Pakistani relations were no longer bogged down in suspicion and distrust and Ayub's visit could be labeled an event of momentous importance in the changing pattern of the policies of South Asia. Pakistan, an ally of the US and later a close friend of China, had begun a new era of understanding if not friendship with the USSR.[186]

The Soviet activities in Pakistan increased after the Tashkent Declaration. There was a change visible between the two countries, when in the first week of May 1966, Pakistan learned about the Soviet Union decision to supply arms to India. The media in Pakistan reacted sharply. *The Morning News* wrote, "The continued outpouring of Russian military aid to India, in the circumstances of that country's obduracy against the paths of people and of its currents preventive bellicosity is tantamount to stroking the fire."[187] *Pakistan Times* was of the view that: "The induction of new arms in the region would only make the position of smaller powers like Pakistan, more vulnerable. The most ironic part of the situation is that, having played a leading role as a peacemaker between India and Pakistan at Tashkent, Russia should now pursue a policy which is tantamount to stroking the fire."[188]

The Soviet Union never liked the idea of promoting the arms race between India and Pakistan as it would have been harmful to the economic development of the two countries. But, when Pakistan was getting continuous supply of arms from the US and it posed a threat to India's security, it supplied with a reasonable quantity of arms to help meet normal defence requirements which acquired a new urgency in the light of China's hostility."[189]

In 1968, Moscow also agreed to supply S-47 fighter bombers to India. It was protested by Pakistan. When Kosygin visited Pakistan, he was greeted with the slogans "Give us tanks, not tractors" and "Down with India" and so on. President Ayub without mincing words raised the issue of Kashmir with the Soviet Prime Minister and further said, "that when people begin to fear for their security and survival, other issues get relegated to the background. The only effective way to meet the situation is to remove the cause of that fear. This involves an examination of fundamentals. The fear cannot be overcome by mere assurances. So long as fear remains, tension persists."[190]

The Soviet Premier was in a tight spot. He restated the basic objectives of the Soviet foreign policy very clearly by declaring, "the Soviet Union has good normal relations practically with all these (Middle-East and South Asian) countries including the close neighbours of Pakistan... We are strangers to designs of using the relations with one country to the detriment of its relations with others... To sow the seeds of discord between the states and peoples which have freed themselves, to seek to confront each other is a favourable policy of colonizer. They seek to pursue it now after they have been thrown away... The creation of an atmosphere of mutual trust between countries of South Asia, settlement of disputes by means of negotiations and taking into account the mutual interests would cut the ground under the feet of imperialists and would prevent them from pumping their insidious policy."[191]

Following a trip to the USSR by a Pakistan military delegation led by Yahya Khan, the Commander-in-Chief of Pakistani Army, the USSR agreed to supply arms to Pakistan. The Indian and the US Governments reacted sharply when the Soviet decision was made public on 17 July 1968. Indian Prime Minister, Indira Gandhi addressed a letter to the Soviet Premier to underline the strain which the supply of lethal weapons would put in Indo-Soviets relations.[192] There were protest demonstrations and rallies in India in front of the Soviet Embassy. The issue was, widely debated in the Indian Parliament. It was an anxiety among the members about the change of the Soviet attitude towards the Kashmir issue. Indira Gandhi tried to convince the members of both the Houses that there was no change visible in the Soviet Union as far as Kashmir was concerned.[193]

On the other hand, the US Congress was bent upon in cutting foreign aid funds and strongly opposed any extensive military assistance to foreign governments. There was little the US could do to counter the Soviet Union. The US officials were particularly concerned with the inroads that the Soviet Union had made into Pakistan.[194]

The changes were also evident to the Pakistan attitude towards the US. It was a general feeling among the people of Pakistan that the joining hands with the US by signing the military pacts, Pakistan had gained nothing worthwhile. The solution of the Kashmir issue was nowhere insight. On 20 May 1968, the then Minister for External Affairs of Pakistan, Arshad Hussain, told the National Assembly during Question Hour that the Pakistan Government had served on the US authorities a notice for the termination of the lease of American Communication Unit at Badar Ber near Peshawar. Answering questions, he said that Pakistan's participation in SEATO and CENTO was under constant review of the foreign policy and defence analysts. Over the years, the situation in the region had witnessed great change and the Government of Pakistan from time to time examines the impact of these alliances following the beginning of the narrowing of the gap between the two superpowers. The cooperation between the US and the USSR as well as between the regional members of the CENTO was on the increase. As politics was considered to be a process of constant adjustment to changing circumstances, that was why the government of Pakistan was compelled to take this decision.[195]

President Yahya was restless when he could not get any response from the US regarding the arms supply. He issued a warning to the US administration that if the US took a longtime to decide on the question of arms to Pakistan, he would not mind in opening the other options for acquiring arms for the Pakistan military.[196]

On 7 October 1970, the Nixon Administration ultimately announced that limited amount of lethal weapons would be provided to Pakistan, particularly like B-57 bombers and interceptors but not tanks.[197] The White House spokesman made it clear that the US decision would not affect in anyway the relative military strength of India and Pakistan.[198] Naturally, the US decision was resisted by the Government of India.[199] The *New York Times* in an editorial wrote that the US Government was already involved deeply in South-East Asia and this decision would incredibly add fuel to another potentially explosive situation in South Asia by supplying arms to Pakistan. It advised the US Government that instead of arming either side for another round of conflict, it should use all the diplomatic energies to try to resolve the decisive issue that threaten to engulf the sub-continent once more in fratricidal war.[200] *The Statesman* felt that the US administrations has concern not to lose all leverage to Pakistan's first ever General Elections, need not be doubted.[201]

The environment prevailing in the Indian sub-continent in the late sixties affected the foreign policy moves of Pakistan. The Bangladesh crisis followed by the war between India and Pakistan had changed the foreign policy priorities of the US, the USSR and China. The war resulted in the dismemberment of Pakistan and added new dimensions to Pakistan's foreign policy. The break up of Pakistan had increased disparity and imbalance between India and Pakistan.

The normalization of the Sino-US relations was another historical event of the early seventies. Pakistan played a major role in arranging the secret visit of the US Secretary of

State Henry Kissinger to Beijing which paved the ways for the establishing of the formal recognition of the People's Republic of China by the Nixon Administration and a permanent seat in the UN Security Council.

The decisive "pre-eminence" that India seemed to gain in the sub-continent in the wake of the Indo-Pak war of 1971 had considerably been "undermined by the perceptible change in the sub-continent strategic equation due to the increased collusion between the US and China in favour of Pakistan." The China factor which was nowhere in the 1950s posed a severe security threat to India and any talk of India's military edge over Pakistan without taking into account "China factor" infact would be ignoring the realities. Since then the Chinese had been arming Pakistan and infact mainly responsible for the nuclear proliferation in South Asia. It helped Pakistan considerably in the development of missile technology and strengthening of nuclear capability. To examine the Reagan Administration decision to rearm Pakistan, one has to take into account the increased strategic role of China in the affairs of the Indian Sub-continent. In this regard one of the important studies made by Francis Fukayama of the Rand Corporation need to be examined. His study conceded that "Pakistan major pre-occupation was and would remain India" and that despite Soviet presence in Afghanistan, the bulk of Pakistani forces were deployed against India. Pakistan's thrust, a perception which Fukayama accepted was that "India acting as a Soviet proxy, might attack Pakistan in the east" in the event of Soviet pressure on Pakistan from the west, or India and Soviet Union would mount a coordinated attack from both east and west."[202]

It was on this assumption that Fukayama had recommended, the rearming of Pakistan, not only to "improve the defence against Afghanistan, but against India as well and upgrading of the 1959 Executive Agreement between the US and Pakistan into a full-fledge treaty "to enable Pakistan to face both the Soviet Union and India." He added that by meeting the demands of Pakistan, the US would strengthen its relations with China, additionally India would feel threatened enough by a rearmed Pakistan to agree to cooperate with US. In any case, he said "the US can afford to ignore India."[203]

There was a general assumption that Pakistan would be "groomed" into the role of "America's regional Cuba" by the US after the Russian army entered into Afghanistan. The US was thinking the reinforcement of the Rapid Deployment Force with other military measures, prompting of more military aid into some of the pro-west Gulf States and proving arms assistance to Afghan rebels. The Indian Ocean strategy of the US centered on Diego Garcia was largely a result of the energy crisis. Both the superpowers had since, then been intensely competing between themselves to increase their naval presence in the Indian Ocean. It was a moot question who would come first. But one could hardly ignore the sudden rise in their oceanic strength after 1973. This competition was further intensified due to the politico military developments in the Gulf regions, the most important, being the Russian intervention in Afghanistan.[204]

The countries around Afghanistan had to be militarily strengthened with American assistance. Pakistan was offered $400 million which of course it did not accept describing the amount as "peanuts" only: President Zia-ul-Haq was not opposed to American aid. He was keen to bargain because he correctly understood the American need of Pakistan in its Gulf strategy. President Reagan roped Pakistan waging American, "Jehad" against the Soviet Union in West Asia and Gulf region. The US sought to make Pakistan a "frontline state" against Russian threat in the area it was to supply arms and weapons to Afghan gorillas through Pakistan. The Zia regime argued that Russian presence in Afghanistan had posed danger to its security and the US military assistance would help it in containing this threat. Pakistan earlier asked for the replacement of the 1959 Executive Agreement by a defence treaty between Washington and Islamabad. But of late it seemed to having second thoughts on it. A full-scale defence treaty would militate against the membership of the NAM. Further, it also realized that its open collaboration might invite Russian anger and retaliation which it wanted to avoid at any cost.[205]

REAGAN ADMINISTRATION: SOME NEW INITIATIVES

During Reagan Administration, the US-Pak relations had reverted back to the relationship of the fifties. Reagan argument was arming of Pakistan would prevent the Soviet Union "from moving in this direction and thus prevent it from fulfiling its expansionist ambitions." He went to the extent of exempting Pakistan from the Symington Amendment, "on the basis that a strong and independent Pakistan was in the mutual interest of both countries."[206]

Again, beneath that move laid the foreign policy objectives of the US too. It was "motivated by its own strategic compulsions and global perceptions of international policies." The US desired to establish its own hegemony in South-West Asia through Pakistan. The State Department was of the view that Pakistan could play an important role in the training and maintenance of the well-stocked but under-developed armies of the oil rich states.[207]

No doubt, Pakistan gained substantially in terms of aid, but had to pay heavily, as its relations with the Muslim countries, particularly Egypt, Saudi Arabia and Afghanistan became tense. It also antagonized the Soviet Union, for it again made Pakistan an American stooge. Therefore, after 1962, Pakistan adopted the small power strategy of balancing the interests of the super powers by moving towards a policy of partial alignment. By 1978, it had freed itself from the compulsions of the US alliances and was able to follow independent foreign policy. It also succeeded in forcing the US to reconcile to itself, that Pakistan was on its way to detonate a nuclear device in the future, rather the US found Pakistan a hard bargainer because the help that it was getting from Saudi Arabia and its wish to improve relations with the Soviet Union.[208]

Pakistan also took some risks, primarily by confronting the Soviet Union. Moscow repeatedly warned Pakistan that it was playing with the fire and threatened with dire consequences. There were many strategists who advised caution and retreat. However, Zia saw the communist take over in Kabul and later entry of the Red Army into Afghanistan as a mortal threat to Pakistan itself and decided as he put it to fight the battle for Pakistan inside Afghanistan. He held the view that for more than a century, Russia had been following a policy of relentless expansion in Central Asia as a result of which one Muslim state after another had been conquered and annexed. Imperial Russian successor, the Soviet Union, had shown itself to be even more expansionist. From the historical perspective, the Soviet entry in Afghanistan could not be considered an isolated event. Afghanistan was to be the gateway to Pakistan and to the warm waters and central zone of the oil rich Gulf States which were perceived to be the real Soviet agenda.[209]

President Zia had clearly also had personal motives in following a policy of activism in Afghanistan and that was to "enrich himself more deeply in power in Pakistan by securing responsibility and international aid for the military regime which had become relatively sequesrated, in particular after the execution of former Prime Minister Z.A. Bhutto."[210]

President Zia stood firm in the view that it made more sense to try to hold back the Soviets in Afghanistan since Pakistan turn would come next, whether or not it acquiesced in the Soviet presence in Afghanistan. Moreover, he calculated that Afghans had a proud history of resisting foreign occupiers and the country terrain was well-suited for guerilla resistance. Zia and his military associates General Rehman Khan, the Head of ISI who was to play a key role in the military planning were also encouraged by the example of Vietnam where guerilla has blocked every efforts of the US and France. Both were compelled to leave the territory of Vietnam.[211]

Pakistan got more than $5.1 billion of military aid from the US till 1990. In addition, the US provided her $35 billion of aid which was to be transferred to the Afghan rebels. But the US aid to Pakistan created an imbalance in South Asia. India also started strengthening her military capability. An armed race started between the two neighbours. Pakistan continued its efforts to acquire nuclear capability. A large chunk of aid was used to acquire nuclear equipments, technology and enriched uranium. Pakistan since its inception is trying to seek parity with India. There were calculated efforts by Pakistan to negate India's conventional superiority.[212]

In the meanwhile Pakistan continued to build it nuclear capability with the economic aid provided by the US. We can say, "The US subsidies the nuclear weapons programme of Pakistan by proxy. Pakistan also got high technology weapons system, from the US on lease and through sales too. In 1986, it was an open secret that Pakistan had crossed the nuclear threshold. The offer made by the US of AWACS which, the defence analyst believed would alter the air power balance in the region.[213] The Afghanistan crisis proved to be very beneficial for the Pakistan rulers. They got everything they desired from the US, in spite of the fact that its scientists and defence experts were busy in providing the Pakistani Army much sought-after, the nuclear weapons.

In mid-1987, it was reported that Pakistan in a clandestine deal, had imported the US made sophisticated instruments and advanced computer equipment that could be used in making nuclear bombs. Top American and Hong Kong businessmen were indicated for illegally exporting to Pakistan such equipments. Leonard Specter, a leading US expert on nuclear proliferation said that, "the next time India and Pakistan go to war, each side must assume the other had a bomb."[214]

Technically, many US officials however argued that Islamabad does not have nuclear weapons, by claiming it was "one screw driver turn away." That claim had been made to justify, the US aid to Pakistan.[215] After the death of President Zia in a plane crash, Pakistan continued its weapons-oriented programme. The nuclear programme was neither stopped nor slowed down and was continued with great vigour.[216] Jagjit Singh, former Director of Indian Institute for Defence Studies and Analyst said that "there is a national consensus in Pakistan on the nuclear programme which is not likely to change with the death of General Zia." He believed that for Islamabad, the nuclear programme was not a military strategic issue but a political magnet attracting diverse political ideologies into its realm.[217]

After the Geneva Accords of 1989, the Russians left Afghanistan and the US became more serious about the nuclear porgramme of Pakistan. Under the Pressler Amendments, all types of military and economic aid was cutoff to Pakistan. But it could not deter Pakistan from achieving the desired nuclear capability, and detonation of nuclear devices in May 1998.[218]

Another important phase of Pakistan foreign policy was considered to be of (1988-99), characterized by successive party-based civilian governments in a post-Zia scenario. Two issue areas from the previous years revealing around the Kashmir dispute and war in Afghanistan continued to determine the direction of foreign policy. There was a consensus among people on the official policy on Kashmir especially in North Pakistan. A policy of support for the struggle of Kashmir from independence from India throughout the 1990s has enjoyed considerable backing from the public.[219]

On a parallel line, the developments in Afghanistan were also of major concern for the foreign policy planners of Pakistan. Pakistan Afghan policy remained a favourite, because it first led to the withdrawal of the Soviet troops from Afghanistan and secondly, before the US action in Afghanistan, it was "perceived as helping a pro-Pakistan militia—The Taliban to establish stability in that country."[220]

China factor has always been very significant if we analyze the various foreign policy moves of Pakistan since the beginning of seventies. China has a communist socio-economic and political structure in which People's Liberation Army plays an important role in the formulation of foreign relations and defence co-operation with other countries. A major "arena of cooperation which became the basis of a close relationship between China and Pakistan has been the defence sector, in addition to the economic and political collaborations. "Mutually beneficial relation between the armed forces of the two countries have served as an interrupted and sustainable factor of continuity in the overall bilateral relationship."[221]

There had been some ups and downs due to the circumstantial and personal indications of the elected ruling elites when Z.A. Bhutto, was the Prime Minister, the relationship between the two were moving at a very high pace and it was considered to be a remarkable development. Bhutto due to his own charismatic personality and partly due to the socialistic orientation in his policies, had been able to tremendously strengthen Pak-China Axis.[222]

But since 1988, experts on Pak-China relations suggest that although the relations are over developing, they are however lacking the extent of depth the two countries used to have. They attribute this deficiency to the level of maturity of the young Pakistani leadership General (Retd.) Mirza Aslam Beg, "since the early sixties a very meaningful relationship had developed between the leadership of the two countries, but this is now lacking depth because the younger leadership had not been able to maintain the level of contact needed, and our relations have remained static.[223]

The end of the 1970s witnessed developments of immense importance in the region which had their influence throughout the course of next few decades. First, the success of the Islamic Revolution in Iraq and its hostility towards the US in February 1979. Second, the invasions of Afghanistan by the Soviet troops on 27 December 1979 and their subsequent withdrawal from their country.[224]

But the Soviet invasion changed the political scenario of the region. Pakistan was faced by two hostile fronts and its security was gravely threatened. The early 1980s witnessed the extensive engagement of two superpowers in Afghanistan. China condemned the Soviet military intervention in Afghanistan as a "hegemonic action" that violated the sovereignty and independence of Afghanistan and posed a grave threat to peace and security in Asia and the whole world. A formal protest was lodged with the Soviet Ambassador in Beijing and a demand that the Soviet Union should immediately stop its aggression and intervention in Afghanistan and that as Afghanistan was China's neighbour, the Soviet armed invasion of that country posed a threat to China's security. China seriously felt that the Soviet move threatened the security and internal stability of their long-term ally Pakistan.[225]

Support to Pakistan was the major feature of China's Afghan policy. Pakistan and China coordinated their strategies to deal with the situation arising out of the Soviet military intervention of Afghanistan. China provided covertly through Pakistan, military supplies of US $200 million annually to the Afghan rebels. China also agreed to provide the US with listening posts to monitor Soviet Central Asia through secret station established in the western Chinese province of Xinjiang. During this decade, the US Central Intelligence Agency (CIA) Pakistan's Inter-Services Intelligence (ISI) and the Chinese Intelligence Services(CIS) developed a close cooperation and collaborative relationship based on the convergent perception of Soviet Union and exchange of information.[226]

THE SINO-PAK ENTENTE

Large scale and sustained assistance to Pakistan's military development has been one of the most important dimensions of the Sino-Pak entente. It was unaffected by the Sino-Indian rapprochement. Between 1956, when the PRC began giving aid to non-communist countries and the mid-1980s, Pakistan was the top ranking recipient of Chinese assistance, outranking the next highest recipient (Sri-Lanka) by 500 percent. During that period, China extended between $400 million and $1 billion aid to Pakistan. Much of this aid was military. China has been along with the US, Pakistan's major suppliers; China has far more understanding of Pakistan's perspectives. Twice when the US suspended arms aid to Pakistan in 1965 and in 1990—China stepped in to meet Pakistan's needs. After the US cut-off aid in 1965, China was for a period the only nation willing to extend significant military assistance to Pakistan. Again, after the US suspension of military aid in 1990, Chinese equipment substituted for American. China also provided major shipments of military hardware to Pakistan in the run-up to both the 1965 and 1971 wars. Following Pakistan's defeat in the 1971 war, for example, China deferred for 200 million and wrote off another $110 million of earlier loans. Chinese shipments of tanks, Jet fighters, trucks and small arms helped Pakistan rebuild its shattered armed forces after the 1971 defeat.[227]

Chinese supported Pakistan's military modernization efforts in the mid-1980s. In terms of air force capabilities, between 1986 and 1988, China delivered 90 F-5A fighters and 60 F-7 fighters to Pakistan. In 1987 Pakistan ordered another

150 F-7 fighters from China to be fitted with the US General Electric-made F-404 engines and the US designed avionics and fire control systems. This hybrid modernalized version of the MIG-21 which Pakistan began to deploy in 1989, is a highly modernized version of the MIG 21, with high engineer performance lethally and weapons carrying ability. It is also one-fifth of the cost of a US made F-16 aircraft. The F-7 fighters were to replace the F-6 as Pakistan's main ground support air-crafts. China also helped Pakistan to modernize its tank force. In the early 80s, it also set-up the Heavy Rebuilding Factory outside Rawalpindi to overhaul those F-59s and manufacture many parts, including the engine for that tank.[228]

Pakistan came to be cultivated by China mainly because of two reasons in the conduct of global policies:

- Pakistan was looked upon as a link to the Middle East, and
- In the regional initiatives, Chinese strategy was to forge closer links with South Asian countries to create a sub-regional balance to counter the Indian pre-eminence in South Asia. The Chinese were able to project two contradictory stands in pursuit of their long-term and short-term policies. It was able to convince its special friends, that despite its potential resources, China would never behave like a superpower and within the regional context, it was able to project an image of a weighty neighbour, particularly in South Asia and Pakistan had sought countervailing authority that China had willingly provided.[229]

The Chinese turned out to be most willing proponents of military collaborations and technology transfers. They had three reasons for doing so—

- Military collaboration would allow developments of greater links with Pakistan;
- The arms supply to Pakistan could be a show case

for potential exports to other third world countries; and

- It would help them to subsidies their own RED programme.[230]

The South Asian region was also affected by the post-cold war developments. Amongst these were India's improved relations with US and China. Pakistan viewed the developing Sino-Pakistan ties as a threat to its deep-rooted friendship with China. China had reinsured repeatedly, that developing ties with India would not beat the cost of its friendship with Pakistan. Pakistan also attached some positive angle to this developing relationship. Pakistan's then Seceretary General of the Ministry of Foreign Affairs, Akram Zaki said, "we think that China would exercise a restraining influence on India's ambitions in the region. We welcome the development."[231]

PRC was keen to persuade India to delink Sino-Indian and Sino-Pakistan relations. In areas where the two sides India and China disagreed, they should discuss those disagreements, but not let those disputes block progress in other areas. Where agreement was possible, the two sides should move ahead. Improvements in Sino-Indian relations should not be held hostage to intractable issues like the border dispute or Sino-Pakistan relations China's policy of delinking emerged clearly during PRC Foreign Minister Huang Hua's visit to India in June 1981, then A.B. Vajpayee, India's Minister for External Affairs had established the precedent of formally presenting India's objections about the Sino-Indian military link during his visit to Beijing in February 1979. While insisting on unconventional China-Pakistan and China-India ties, Beijing offered New Delhi a different sort of peace offer. China would no longer take sides in intra-South Asian disputes by supporting other South Asian countries that came into conflict with India. The origin of this policy seemed primarily linked to Beijing desire to counter-Soviet activities in South Asia. Beijing concluded that conflict among South Asian nations created opportunities Moscow might exploit. But China's leaders must have understood the utility of this approach in lessening Indian opposition to continuing and expanding Chinese ties with India's South Asian neighbours. This new orientation did not take place overnight. On several occasions during the 1980s China continued to take sides in intra-South Asian disputes, i.e. during the Sri-Lankan Indian confrontation of 1986-87 and in the Kashmir dispute up to 1990. But it did signal an important new direction in China's South Asian policy a direction very different from the 1960s and early 1970s. India would utilize the Chinese concessions to the fullest insisting that China redeem its promise by adopting a more truly neutral stance and such issues as Kashmir. China's links with the South Asian countries remained unaffected. The principle of delinkage was established in the Sino-Indian Joint communiqué issued at the Conclusion of Premier Li Peng's visit to India. After summarizing the measures taken to advance better relations, the communiqué said: the two sides stated that the improvement and development of Sino-Indian relations affect their existing friendly relations and cooperation with other countries. It clearly meant that China's links with Pakistan need not be curtailed for the sake of better ties with India. Regarding Sino-Pakistan ties, Li Peng told reporters that, while Sino-Indian ties were improving, China is willing to maintain and develop friendly relations with India, Pakistan and all other countries in South Asia on the basis of the Five Principles of Peaceful Co-existence. In other words, Sino-Pakistan and Sino-Indian relations would develop independently of each other Implicit in Li Peng comments was the conclusion that Indian attempts to limit the Sino-Pakistan ties by linking them to the Sino-Indian ties would violate the Five Principles of Peaceful Co-existence to which India had agreed.[232]

Interestingly Indian rapprochement with China proceeded parallel to and unaffected by, robust Chinese assistance to Pakistan's nuclear weapons, missile and other programmes. To gain an understanding of the global context which still sustains the Sino-Pakistan politico military relationship, one must explain why the US which is the only super power left, does not feel threatened by the close coordination between these two allies considering the successive US administration turned a blind eye to repeated transgression by China of the Missile Technology Central Regime and even of the Non-proliferation Treaty. It is clear that the US felt itself unable to enforce its non-proliferation agenda on Pakistan and China. What is significant is that after the withdrawal of the Soviet Union from Afghanistan and dissolution of the wars and pacts, the sole super power was unable to prevent China from continuing to help Pakistan to develop nuclear weapons and the means to deliver them. The US knew well what was going on, for, according to a CIA report, "During the last half of 1996 China was the most significant supplier of Weapons of Mass Destruction (WMD), goods and technology to foreign countries. The Chinese provided a tremendous variety of assistance to both Iran's and Pakistan's ballistic missiles programmes. China was also the primary source of nuclear-related equipment and technology to Pakistan.[233]

Far from punishing China, for such blatant violations of the treaty obligations, the US has been an active salesman of military equipments to China since 1978. Under the Clinton Administration, the US took further steps to enhance military cooperation between China and Pakistan making renewed engagement with these two countries, an important part of its strategy in South Asia. The visits of the Chinese Defence Minister to Washington in December 1996, the Chinese Premier visit in September 1997 and the visit of the US Security of Defence, William Cohn to Beijing in December 1998, solidified this cooperation despite concerns that China had been helping Pakistan's nuclear weapon's programme. President Clinton went further and gave a certification to the US Congress in January 1998 that "China is not assisting and will not assist any non-nuclear weapon state either directly or indirectly in acquiring nuclear explosive devices or the material or components for such devices."[234]

Sino-Pakistani collaboration has altered the balance of power in the region and the clandestine nature of Sino-Pakistani transactions has promoted a culture of disbelief and mistrust countries in the region will now be suspicious of signing any arms control or disarmament agreement with China who although an adherent to MTCR shows nothing but disdain for the treaty. It would be difficult to sell to India public opinions any security arrangement that does not include foolproof verification provisions.[235]

China for all practical purposes has intervened directly in South Asian affairs by supplying missiles or missiles technology to Pakistan so altering the power balance. The international community believes that China's prime motive in transferring missile technology to Pakistan is profit. The profit is channalized into the Chinese arms industruy.[236]

Western scholars have, by and large, ignored the longer strategic interests of the Chinese. The transfer of missile technology is most likely part of a larger game plan. It is possible that China has been demanding certain strategic concessions from Pakistan for the transfer of forbidden items and Pakistan is used as a base by Pakistan.[237]

China's missile trade with Pakistan has caused more international concern than its missile trade with virtually any other country and China's most serious confrontation with the US over ballistic missile proliferation have involved alleged transfers of M-II ballistic missile-related technology to Pakistan when on 6 April 1998, Pakistan successfully tested a new medium range surface to surface Gauri missile with a range of 1500 Kilometers, Washington reacted sharply and started examining any role China may have had in the development of the Gauri Missile, in violation of China's commitment to allude by the MTCR guidelines. But the Chinese denied the allegations and also any involvement. According to the Chinese Foreign Ministry spokesman Zhu Bangzao, as for whether China helped Pakistan, I can say that there is no connection whatsoever, he further stated that "As for the United States investigating this issue, I believe that is unreasonable and groundless."[238]

The 1990s witnessed a strategic shift, and in its efforts to build ties with the US, Beijing had come under tremendous pressure not to supply sensitive military technologies to countries like Pakistan and Iran. As China has emerged now more strongly on the economic and military areas, these pressures are bound to increase. There was likelihood that Sino-Pakistan defence cooperation would be limited because of the number of reasons. First, both sides are not necessarily in congruence in terms of their anti-Indian sentiments, Beijing ties with India have become warmer. Pakistan is always worried about whenever any step is initiated in this direction. But just like Moscow, Beijing may one day become sensitive to India's protests against its weapons supplies to Pakistan.

Second, China is going through a rapid modernization process in which factors like ideology and good relations that once determined friendship are gradually being discarded in favour of pure commercial interests. The fate of various defence deals would increasingly be determined by China's national interests as well as hard gains in terms of foreign exchange.

Third, China might not continue to appreciate the liberties being taken by the Pakistan, like its support to still various terrorists organizations and also its harbouring with Islamic fundamental organizations in Pakistan occupied Kashmir (POK) who sometimes create problems in China's Xinjiang Province.

Then there is always a constant pressure from the US on China not to supply certain sensitive technicalities to Pakistan. Beijing may also get irked by the fact that Pakistan itself continues to enjoy close ties with the US and keeps projecting Washington as its alternative supplier of advance defence technologies.

China has lately been working hard to improve the technological edge of its weapons systems. However, as it succeeds in developing more advanced weapons, China just like other major powers, may not like to export its state of the art equipment to any other country especially if this happens to be the neighbourhood. This may also be the consequence of conditions imposed by countries supplying such frontier technologies to the Chinese.[239]

As the situation in Afghanistan and Iraq is still complicated and the US is holding all the strings, it is overlooking the Chinese stakes in the Pak-China defence collaboration and it has not done any thing substantial to dissuade China. No doubt, China is still a partner of the US in the struggle against terrorism. Therefore, the chances are that Pakistan will continue to get required supplies for its nuclear and missile manufacturing facilities without any hindrance.[240]

Modification of its position on Kashmir was another element of China's effort to balance rapprochement with India and continue entente with Pakistan. Apparently in response to the insistent Pakistan demands for support on the Kashmir issue and to avoid misunderstandings with over the issue, NPC Chairman Wan Li travelled to Islamabad in early May 1990 for discussion. The differences between the two are clear when their speeches are juxtaposed. At a banquet welcoming Wan, Speaker of the Pakistan National Assembly Mehraj Khalid praised the Pakistan-China bond for upholding the UN Charter and referred to Pakistan's support of the struggle of the Kashmiri people for self-determination: Wan merely termed the Sino-Indian relations a model of friendly cooperation between countries of different social systems. He made no mention of the UN resolutions. Instead he said China "appreciated" Pakistan's willingness to solve the problem through negotiations. Prime Minister Benazir Bhutto also travelled to Beijing to personally lobby for Chinese support for referral of the Kashmir issue to the UN. But Beijing refused. China would not become involved in the Kashmir issue, "The existing issues between India and Pakistan—including the Kashmir issue must in the end be resolved properly through patience and bilateral dialogue", a Chinese Foreign Ministry spokesman said.[241]

Beijing was not in favour of the Islamabad efforts to internationalize the Kashmir issue. By early 1990 Pakistan was considering mobilizing international support for the convening of a special session of the UN General Assembly on the Kashmir issue. But the Chinese advised the Pakistan Government against efforts to bring the Kashmir issue before or convening a special session of the UN. There was simply too little interest on this issue, they said India was more than satisfied with the Chinese position on Kashmir. High level Indian diplomats and political leaders were happy with the Chinese adopting a balanced approach on Kashmir. China had abandoned its old passion of support for Pakistan on this issue. Nor had it made any moves to involve the UN. China's primary objective was to avoid a conflict between India and Pakistan and to this end, it had encouraged de-escalation and all trends in this direction.[242]

Six more years of Sino-Indian rapprochement produced very encouraging and acceptable results, producing further pro-incremental pro-Indian shifts in Beijing Kashmir policy. Several days before President Jiang Zemin's December 1966 visit to India and Pakistan China's Ambassador to India told the media, "we do not stand for internationalization of the Kashmir issue" thereby directly and publicity rejecting Pakistan's approach to the problem. Addressing Pakistan Senate, Jiang urged the resolution of Pakistani-Indian disputes via, "consultations and negotiations." Throughout his forty-five minute of his speech Jiang did not mention Kashmir, a fact that Indian observers saw is highly significant.[243]

Measured against earlier periods, China deterrent support for Pakistan has declined under the Sino-Indian normalization process which is still on. While this should be considered a significant development, one should not assume that, Pakistan leaders were particularly unhappy with China's stance during the 1990s crisis when the armies of both the countries were facing each other while they would undoubtfully have stronger nuances in China's choice of words. They nonetheless felt that China's pro-peace stand benefited Pakistan. The people of Pakistan and elite groups were not unhappy with the Chinese stance. They saw China as a reliable friend unlike the US, could be counted on the emergencies Subtleties of languages were less important to them than underlying perceptions and purposes and these, they understood Beijing need to mince words for the sake of pleasing India but were confident that "when push come to shove, China would be there." Pakistan journalists' sometimes exerted Chinese leadership to speak bluntly and when they declined to do so, the journalists misinterpreted China's intentions, according to Chinese diplomatic sources. On these occasions Chinese diplomats sought these reports out and explained to them that in view of the long friendship between China and Pakistan, a friendship tested by adversity, China would not abandon Pakistan in the event of a crisis. Mostly journalists understood and appreciated their comments.[244]

For Beijing sustaining a strong Pakistan independent of Indian domination and linked militarily to China is a fundamental element of maintaining a position *vis-a-vis* India. If India was unable to uncouple China and Pakistan, subordinate Pakistan or destroy its military potential. India would be able to concentrate its forces against China. While there was no indication of a major war between India and China in the immediate future in certain circumstances, Indian leaders might decide on war with China. The main precondition for such a war would be to improve India's relations with Pakistan so that India could avoid a two front war. In other words, a prudent Chinese policy would sustain Pakistan war against India.[245]

Whatever validity of these observations, it is clear that Indian security planners believe that, in the event of an all out Sino-Indian war or a major Indo-Pakistani war, Pakistan or China would enter the conflict against India. Thus India must keep guard in the west while dealing with any northern challenge, Indian contingency planning for a major war with Pakistan typically assumes Chinese intervention, the scenarios are many. One variant vetted in the early 1990s envisioned a decisive ten day war with Pakistan in retaliation for the "low-intensity proxy war", India believes Pakistan has been waging against India since 1980s. In response to increasing support for terrorists in Punjab, Kashmir and other areas of India, India decides to administer a decisive blow to "break Pakistan's will to support terrorism and insurgency." Indian forces are hypothetically ordered to destroy, Pakistan's "war-making potential which underpins her confidence in persisting with her destabilizing efforts" against India: "you will generate and maintain high levels of psychological shock (sic) to bring the lesson home to the government of Pakistan and its people that such actions of theirs has invited this retaliation. Under these circumstances, "it would be sensible to assume that China will also get into the act. Short of such extreme outcomes, one is left to ponder the balance of gain in the China-Pakistan-India accommodation. India has secured an important shift in China's policy on Kashmir and in Beijing approach to other intra-South Asian disputes. Beijing also now uses its influence with Islamabad to discourage resort to force to solve or internationalize the Kashmir problem. China would not necessarily like to see a final, definitive resolution of the Kashmir question since that could recast the India-Pakistan relations and reduction in China's leverage. But neither does it wish to see a major Indo-Pakistan conflict that would force it to side between the two contradictory stands of its policy. This too would be a major gain for India.

Yet India has also been compelled to acquiesce to a steady increase in Pakistan's military capabilities, with China playing a crucial role in the process. It is probably fair to assume that, without China's large-scale, sustained and comprehensive assistance, Pakistan military capabilities would be far less patent and far less threatening to India than they are today. The mutual trust, familiarity and parallel interests that constitute that core remain unchanged by Sino-Indian rapprochement. This constitutes a major constraint on India's freedom to act.[246]

When India carried out its tests on 11 May 1998, China's condemnations were of a low key. However, by May 13 when the text of the letters of Prime Minister A.B. Vajpayee to President Clinton and other leaders was released, Beijing attitude underwent a sea-change and its criticism of India's additional tests became much stronger. The second series of Indian tests led China to make four important points. One, that India's action reflected an outrageous contempt for the common will of the international community "in favour of the CTBT." Two, India was using the China threat as an excuse for the development of its own nuclear weapons. Three, India was seeking "hegemony" in South Asia. Four, "the international community should adopt a common position by strongly demanding that India immediately stop its nuclear development programme."[247]

Pakistan's then Foreign Secretary, Shamshad Ahmed, visited Beijing immediately after the tests and on his return, indicated that "China has not pressed Pakistan not to go nuclear and left to Pakistan to decide what was in its national interests."[248]

The Chinese Premier, Jiang Zemin, firmly blamed New Delhi for the tension in South Asia, in his first direct reaction to the nuclear tests by India and Pakistan on 3 June 1988. He accused India of targeting both China and Pakistan and pointed out that "the nuclear cooperation between China and Pakistan was strictly peaceful, in the area of technology of nuclear reactors and all installations concerned are under the control of the International Atomic Energy Agency (IAEA)." On the same day, the official "China Daily" criticize India for its long admiration to became a world power and wanted that the long running India-Pakistan dispute is like a sleeping volcano beneath the nuclear threat."[249]

The post-nuclear situation in South Asia figured prominently in talks with President Clinton during his visit to China from 25 June to 3 July 1998. The joint statement condemned the nuclear tests by India and Pakistan, called on them to sign the CTBT and NPT and urged a peaceful settlement of political problems including that over Kashmir, through dialogue.[250] China and the US agreed to work together to contain the dangers likely to arise from the nuclearization of South Asia.[251]

While joining the US in reiterating the position taken by the P-5 countries, China maintained its view that the primary responsibility for trigging the nuclear stand off in South Asia was that of India. Within the P-5, opposition in conceding the status of a nuclear power to India, and to becoming a permanent member of the Security Council on the basis of its overt nuclear capability was strongest from China. At the same time, the bilateral relations between China and India remained cordial, assisting Pakistan with economic problems arising from the sanctions in the wake of the tests, notably though balance of payments support.[252]

By conducting nuclear tests Pakistan had established certain parity. However, the ground realities do not tally with this superficial equation. It is necessary for the international community to ascertain the real capabilities and politico-strategic equations behind Pakistan's nuclear capabilities. In this regard. It is necessary to properly take stock of not only the Sino-Pakistan nuclear cooperation but also to verify the clandestine assistance it received from various other NPT signatories in the eighties and early nineties. Secondly, the aid provided by China, especially since 1992 when it formally became a part of the NPT, must be accounted for. India must launch a diplomatic and media oftensive to project that its nuclear capability and status are certainly not only superior but substantially different from Pakistan. Whereas when India launched its nuclear research, even before independence, it was with a view not only to gain strategic depth but also a sustainable scientific role to develop its nuclear capability and rose the living standard of the Indian people.[253]

The Sino-Pak relations are on sound footings and the process of CBMS between China and India, Pakistan and India is going on. But the most important development of the last decade is, there is overall change in the perception of the Chinese leaders, they have reshaped their foreign policy objectives. Keeping in mind of course, the international environment and fast changing strategic equations in the world, the Chinese leadership has become more cautious and successfully achieved its foreign policy objectives. CRS Report of the US Congress, entitled "China in World Affairs—US Policy" prepared by Robert G. Sutter had acknowledged way back in 1995 that backed by impressive economic growth and steadily increasing military power, China's international influence has grown substantially. Few years back, China's leaders appeared as an isolated and troubled regime following the suppression of pro-democracy demonstrations at Tiananman Square in 1989.[254] In many important aspects, Chinese leaders since the late 1970s have generally followed pragmatic policies that have integrated China's economy more closely with the rest of the world. The result has been a foreign policy seeking greater economic advantage in order to improve the material standard of living of the Chinese people and to increase support for continued Chinese communist rule seeking economic advantage. It has prompted Chinese leaders to be more flexible than in the past on differences with neighbours and to curb action disruptive to the prevailing *status quo* in Asian and world affairs.[255]

Although optimists judge that China's growing economic and military power will be moderated by an ever-widening web of international interdependence, skeptics suspect that greater power would allow China to be more assertive in backing nationalistic territorial or other demands of course; actual Chinese policy could turn out to be moderate on some issues, trade disputes and more assertive on other territorial disputes. Political and economic developments inside China in the years to come would partly determine whether Beijing follows an accommodating or assertive foreign policy.[256]

Chinese foreign policy supported China's new quest to achieve economic modernization as effectively as possible. It did so by helping to promote economic contacts with various countries that could benefit China's moderate and helping to maintain a stable and secure environment by Asian and World Affairs that was conducive to Chinese modernization efforts. In this context, the Chinese leaders put aside post-ideological, political and other constraints to beneficial economic and technical interchange with a wide range of developing and developed countries. They halted or cut back support to Maoist insurgents or political groups that would impede smooth economic exchanges abroad,, cut back sharply on Chinese foreign assistance to the Third World and showed an increased willingness to pedal post-Maoist pretensions to change the world. Chinese leaders focused their foreign policy concerns on establishing a "peaceful environment" around China's periphery in Asia.[257]

Chinese leaders put aside past by autarchy and self-reliance and allowed the Chinese economy to become increasingly broad competitive. Beijing made efforts to meet the requirements of the US and others regarding market access, intellectual property rights and other economic issues and strove to become member of WTO. Chinese leaders duly accepted commitments and responsibilities stemming from participation with such international economic organization as the World Bank, the Asian Development Bank and the Asian Pacific Economic Cooperation (APEC).[258]

For many previous decades until the mid-1990s, China regularly criticized the structure of the international system and complained that other powers colluded against its interests. Beijing now increasingly appears to be embracing the current constellation of international constitutions, rules and norms as a means through which to promote and pursue its national interests. China is now working within the system opposed to criticizing and challenging its evidence of the changes in the Chinese diplomacy abroad. China has expanded the breadth and depth of its bilateral relations, joined various regional and international agreements and increased the quality of its participation in multinational organization Beijing embrace of multi-lateral institutions represents one of the most dramatic shifts in its foreign relations in the early 1990s. China was varying of such forums as venues that would criticize and can strain China. Beijing now views participation as a means to shape international rules, improve relations with neighbouring countries (especially in South Asian and South East Asian) and limits what it perceived as under global influence.[259]

While all these trends are important, China still faces serious obstacles to becoming a high profile much less a dominant player in the international community. Even as the country diplomacy become more active, Chinese leaders need to grapple with several political, social and economic challenges. Chinese new diplomacy presents Asian and American leaders with both opportunities and challenges, along-term task for the entire international communities consistent with regional stability and security.[260]

Notes and References

1. Shahid M. Amir, Pakistan's Foreign Policy: A Reappraisal (New York, 2000), p. 2.
2. Sangat Singh, Pakistan's Foreign Policy: An Appraisal (Bombay, 1970), p. 1.
3. *Ibid.*, 37-38. Arif Hussain a noted Pakistani scholar felt that Pakistan "has been conscious of the fact that geographically she has never an entity. A conquered Egypt would still remain Egypt but Pakistan would be forgotten if it were, say, annexed to another state, it would lack the national unity to preserve its identity." See Arif Hussain, Pakistan, Its Ideology and Foreign Policy, (London, 1966).
4. *The Hindu*, 5 May 1964.
5. *Ibid.*, 6 May.
6. William J. Barnds, India, Pakistan and the Great Powers (London, 1972), p. X.
7. *Ibid.*, pp. 1-2
8. *Ibid.*, pp. 2-8
9. *Ibid.*
10. *Ibid.*
11. J. Bandyopadhyaya, "Making of Foreign Policy: A Tentative Sub-

System Model for South Asia" in S.P. Verma and K.P. Misra, Foreign Policies in South Asia (ed.) (Bombay, nd), p. 29.

12. *Ibid.*, pp. 29-30.
13. *Ibid.*, pp. 29-32.
14. Keith B. Callard, Pakistan: A Political Study (London, 1967), p. 11.
15. G.W. Chaudhury, Pakistan's Relations with India (Meerut, 1971), p. 185.
16. M.A. Khan, Friends Not Masters (London, 1967), p. 114. Also see, S.M. Burke, Pakistan's Foreign Policy: An Historical Analysis (London, 1973), and Main Springs of Pakistan's Foreign Policies (Minneapolis, 1974), pp. 50-53.
17. Shahid A. Amin, n. 1, p. 39.
18. *Ibid.*, p. 40.
19. *Ibid.*, pp. 40-41.
20. *Ibid.*
21. Jawahar Lal Nehru, India's Foreign Policy (New Delhi, 1971), p. 42.
22. *Ibid.*, p. 2.
23. Sukhwant S. Bindra, "Nehru's Pakistan Policy", in Sunnera Kapoor (ed.) Thought and Vision of Jawaharlal Nehru (New Delhi, 2005), pp. 139-140.
24. Frank Moreas, Witness to an Era: India 20th to the Present Day (Delhi, 1973), pp. 220-21.
25. Mark Tully and Zaheer Masani, From Raj to Rajiv: 40 years of Indian Independence (New Delhi, 1988), pp. 13-14.
26. S.K. Datta and Rajiv Sharma, Pakistan From Jinnah to Jehad (New Delhi, 2002), p. 2.
27. *Ibid.*
28. K.L. Gauba, The Consequences of Pakistan (Lahore, 1946), pp. IX and X.
29. Mark Tully and Zaheer Masani, n. 24, pp. 23-24. M.J. Akbar is a leading Muslim Journalist in India.
30. Khalid Bin Sayeed, Pakistan: The Formative Phase (London, 1968), pp. 176-210.
31. Sisir Gupta, "Islam as a Factor in Pakistan's Foreign Policy" in Donald E. Smith (ed.), South Asian Policies and Religion. (Princeton, 1966), pp. 428-31.
32. *The Dawn*. 17 November 1956.
33. S.K. Datta and Rajiv Sharma, n. 26, pp. 26-27.
34. Jamil-ud-Din Ahmed (ed.), Recent Speeches and Writings of Mr. Jinnah, Vol. 1, (Lahore, 1960), pp. 19 and 22.
35. J.L. Nehru, Discovery of India (London, 1960), p. 63.
36. Hector Bolitho, Jinnah (London, 1954), p. 195.
37. Quaid-e-Azam Mohammed Ali Jinnah's Speeches as Governor General of Pakistan, 1947-48 (Karachi, n.d.), p. 8.
38. *Ibid.*

39. S.S. Bindra, Politics of Islamisation with Special Reference to Pakistan (New Delhi, 1990), p. 77.
40. Quaid-e-Azam Mohammad Ali Jinnah's Speeches, n. 37, 97.
41. Mohammed Munir, From Jinnah to Zia (New Delhi, 1981).
42. K.P. Misra, *et. al.* Pakistan: Search for Constitutional Consensus (New Delhi, 1967), pp. 11-12.
43. Leonard Binder, "Pakistan and the Modern Islamic Nationalist Theory", *The Middle East Journal*, Vol. XXVI, No. 21, Winter 1958; p. 53.
44. *Ibid.*
45. S.A.A. Maudoodi, Towards Understanding Islam (Lahore, 1948), pp. 16-19.
46. M.J. Stepanavants, Pakistan: Philospphy and Sociology (Moscow, 1971), p. 81.
47. *Ibid.*
48. *Ibid.*, pp. 81-82
49. Leonard Binder, Religion and Politics in Pakistan (Barkley, 1961), p. 117.
50. *Ibid.*, pp. 139-41.
51. S. Razi Wasti, "Quadi-e-Azam: Founder of the State", *Pakistan Journal of History and Culture*, Vol. XII, No. 122, Jan. to Dec. 1991, pp. 75-76.
52. Mohammed Wasim, "Quaid-e-Azam and State Building in Pakistan" in *Ibid.*, pp. 127-28.
53. *Ibid.*, pp. 128-30.
54. Syed Rifaat Hussain, "Quaid-e-Azam and Pakistan's Foreign Policy, *Pakistan Journal of History and Culture*, Vol. XII, No. 2, Jan. Dec. 1991, p. 138.
55. Saeeduddin Ahmed Dar, "Foreign Policy of Pakistan: 1947-48" in Ahmed Hussain Dani (ed.), World Scholars on Quaid-e-Azam Mohammed Ali Jinnah (Islamabad, 1979), p. 369 as cited in *Ibid.*
56. Quaid-e-Azam Mohammed Ali Jinnah, n. 37, pp. 55-56.
57. *Ibid.*, pp. 157-58.
58. "Quaid-e-Azam and the Muslim World", in Ahman Hassan Dani, n. 55, p. 362.
59. *Ibid.*
60. Latif Ahmed Sherwani (ed.), Resolution to Pakistan (1940-47), (Karachi, 1969), pp. 247-48.
61. As cited in Saeeduddin Ahmed Dar, "Foreign Policy of Pakistan 1947-19", in Ahmad Hassan Dani, n. 55, p. 363.
62. Sangat Singh, n. 2, p. 30.
63. *Ibid.*, pp. 30-31.
64. *Ibid.*, p. 31.
65. Saeed Shafquat, Quaid-e-Azam and Bureaucracy in Pakistan, *Journal of History and Culture*, Vol. XII, No. 2, Jan.-Dec. 1991, p. 133.
66. *Ibid.*, pp. 134-35.

67. *Ibid.*, 99. 135-37.
68. Hasan Sahab, Brahmans and Bureaucrats: A Critique of an Administrative System of Pakistan (Lahore, 1973), pp. 4-5.
69. Shahid Javed Burki, "Twenty Years of Civil Service in Pakistan", Asian.
70. Hamza Alvi, "Army and Bureaucracy in Pakistan, *International Socialist Journal*, Vol. III, No. 14, March-April 1966, pp. 88-89.
71. Lawrence Ziring, The Ayub Khan Era: Politics in Pakistan, 1958-69 (New York, 1971), p. 141.
72. Keith B. Collard, Pakistan: A Political Study (London, 1957), p. 49.
73. *Ibid.*, pp. 49-50.
74. L.F. Rushbrook Williams, The State of Pakistan (London, 1966), p. 139.
75. Satish Kumar, "Problems of Federal Society in Pakistan, "In Pandav Nayak (ed.), Pakistan, Society and Politics, (New Delhi, 1984), pp. 22-23.
76. L.F. Rushbrook Williams, n. 74, p. 132.
77. *Ibid.*
78. S.S. Bindra, Determinants of Pakistan's Foreign Policy (New Delhi, 1988), pp. 152-53.
79. L.F. Runbrook Williams, n. 74, pp. 139-40.
80. S.S. Bindra, n. 78, p. 155.
81. Kalim Bahadur, "Problems in the Evolution of a Constitutional Framework of Pakistan" in Pandav Nayak, n. 75, pp. 34-35.
82. Sisir Gupta, "Constitution Making in Pakistan", *Foreign Affairs Reports*, Vol. II No. 6, pp. 68-69.
83. Keith Callard, n. 73, pp. 89-90. Also see M. Ahmed, Government and Politics in Pakistan (Karachi, 1959).
84. L.F. Rushbrook Williams, n. 74, p. 143.
85. Sisir Gupta, "Political Trends in Pakistan," *Foreign Affairs Reports*, Vol. V, No. 12, December 1956, p. 135.
86. Keith B. Callard, Political Forces in Pakistan 1947-57 (New York, 1959), pp. 24-25.
87. Y.V. Ganpovsky and L.R. Garden Palonskaya, A History of Pakistan (Moscow, 1964), pp. 293-97.
88. From 1947 until the coup in Pakistan in October 1958. There had been a total of seven Prime Ministers, from September 1956 until October 1958, four individuals occupied this position one of these I.H. Chundigar, held office for only two months.
89. Robert Laporte Jr. Power and Privielge (Barkely, 1975), p. 41.
90. *Ibid.*, pp. 43-44.
91. Khalid B. Sayeed, "Preliminary Analysis of Pakistan's Foreign Policy," in S.P. Varma and K.P. Misra, Foreign Policies in South Asia (New Delhi, n.d.), p. 73.
92. *Ibid.*

93. Michael Breacher, "Elite, Images and Foreign Policy Choices," *Pacific Affairs*, Vol. II, Nos. 1-2, Spring and Summer 1967, p. 78.
94. M.A.H. Isphani, "The Ire of Pakistan", *Asian Review*, Vol. I, No. 1, November 1967, p. 16.
95. Mohammad, Ahsan Chaudhri, "The Principle of Regional Pacts," *Pakistan Horizon*, Vol. VIII, No. 3, September 1955, pp. 428-30. Also See, Werner Levi, The Fundamentals of World Organisation (Minnesota, 1951).
96. Mohammad Ayub Khan, n. 16, p. 130.
97. *Ibid.*, p. 157.
98. Lord Birdwood, "Pakistan in Global Strategy," *Pakistan Horizon*, Vol. IX, No. 2, June 1955, p. 350.
99. Mohammed Ahsan Chaudhri, "Pakistan and the United States," *Pakistan Horizon*, Vol. IX, No. 4, December 1956, p. 200.
100. *Ibid.*, p. 201.
101. Khalid Mahmood, "Governance and National Security of Pakistan A Case Study" in Dipankar Banerjee, Security Studies in South Asia (New Delhi, 2000), p. 131.
102. *Ibid.*, p. 132.
103. *Ibid.*
104. *Ibid.*
105. M.A Khan, n. 16, p. 155.
106. *Ibid.*, p. 118.
107. *Ibid.*, p. 119.
108. K.B. Sayeed, n. 91, p. 73.
109. *Ibid.*
110. Quoted in K.B. Sayeed, "South-East Asia in Pakistan's Foreign Policy," *Pacific Affairs*, Vol. XXIV, No. 2, Summer 1961, p. 212.
111. K.P. Karunakaran, India In World Affairs, Feb. 1950 to December 1953 (Calcutta, 1958), p. 150. Also see, V.B. Kulkarni, Pakistan: A Historical Survey of Indo-Pak Relations (Bombay, 1958).
112. M.A. Khan, n. 16, pp. 154-55.
113. H.R. Gupta, The Kutch Affairs (Delhi, 1969),p. 26 Also see Wayne Wilocox, "American Policy Towards South Asia," *Asia Affairs*, Vol. IV, Part 2, June 1973, p. 129.
114. Rafiushan Qureshi, The Nation of Pakistan (London, 1969), p. 96.
115. Russel Brines, Indo-Pakistan's Relations (London, 1968), p. 104.
116. M.A. Khan, n. 16, p. 158.
117. Tanvir Sultan, Indo-US Relations (New Delhi, 1982), pp. 75-76.
118. *New York Times*, 15 April 1950.
119. Devendra Kaushik, Soviet Relations with India and Pakistan (Delhi, 1974), pp. 33-35.
120. Shahid. M. Armin, n. 1, p. 41.
121. Devendra Kaushik, n. 119, pp. 33-34.
122. Cited in *Central Asian Review*, Vol. V, No. 2, 1957, pp. 166-69. See *Ibid.*, pp. 34-35.

123. G.W. Chaudhury, India, Pakistan, Bangladesh and the Major Powers (New York, 1975), pp. 12-15.
124. Shahid M. Amin., n. 1, pp. 40-43.
125. *Ibid.*
126. Russel Brines, n. 115, p. 4.
127. *Ibid.*, pp. 4-5.
128. *Ibid.*, p. 6.
129. D.C. Jha, "The Basic Foundations and Determinants of Pakistan's Foreign Policy" in Surendra Chopra, Perspectives on Pakistan's Foreign Policy (Amritsar, 1983), p. 32.
130. William J. Carieton, The Revolution in American Foreign Policy (New York, 1967), p. 163 as cited in *Ibid.*
131. Henry A. Kissinger, American Foreign Policy: Three Essays (New York, 1969), pp. 54-70.
132. For details, see the press statement issued by the Government of Pakistan on 4 January 1950. *The Dawn*, 5 January 1950.
133. A.P. Jain, In Kashmir What Really happened, (Bombay, 1972).
134. B.N. Goswami, Pakistan and China: A Study of Their Relations (Bombay, 1971), p. 9.
135. S.S. Bindra, "Foundation of the Sino-Pakistan Axis: A Brief Survey of Sino-Pak relations from 1953-65", *Kurukshetra University Research Journal*, Vol. IX 1975, p. 178.
136. Russel Brines, n. 115, p. 183.
137. B.N. Gosami, n. 134, p. 29.
138. *Ibid.*
139. *Ibid.*, p. 47.
140. L.F. Rushbrook Williams, n. 74, p. 120.
141. Norman D. Palmer, "China's Relations with India and Pakistan," *Current History*, Vol. IX, No. 361, Winter 1965, p. 140.
142. *The Pravada*, 28 January 1959 as cited in Devendra Kaushik, n. 119, p. 78.
143. *Pakistan National Assembly Debates*, Vol. I, No. 2, 26, Mann, 1956, pp. 65-68.
144. For details of the visit see, *The Dawn* and *Pakistan Times*, 19 October to November 1956.
145. *The Dawn*, 23 and 24 November 1956.
146. B.N. Goswami, n. 134, p. 59.
147. Balwant Bhaneja, The Politics of Triangle (Delhi, 1973), p. 51.
148. Z.A. Bhutto, The Myth of Independence (London, 1969), p. 48.
149. *Ibid.*, p. 49.
150. Cited in *Ibid.*, pp. 53-54.
151. *Ibid.*, p. 55.
152. B.N. Goswami, n. 134, pp. 73-76.
153. *Washington Post* (ed.), "India in Peral," 22 October 1962. Also see *New York Times* (ed.), "China Threat Grown," 23 October, 1962,

Christian Science Monitor (ed.), "Agony of Truth", 2 November 1962, Washington Evening Star (ed.), "India's Back to Wall," 26 October 1962.

154. Z.A. Bhutto, n. 148, p. 62.
155. For More details see, *Department of State Bulletin*, Vol. XL VII, No. 1223, 3 December 1962, pp. 837-38.
156. *New York Times*, 4 December 1962.
157. Staff Studies, "Pakistan and the Sino-India Dispute-II *Pakistan Horizon*, Vol. XVI, No. 1, 1963, p. 65.
158. *Ibid.*, pp. 66-67.
159. Staff Studies, "Pakistan and the West—Quarterly Survey", *Pakistan Horizon*, Vol. XVI, No. 3, Third Quarter, 1963, pp. 260-61.
160. *National Assembly Debates of Pakistan*, Vol. II, No. 26, 17 July 1963, p. 1662.
161. *Ibid.*
162. *Ibid.*, p. 1664.
163. *Ibid.*, p. 1665.
164. *Ibid.*, p. 1666.
165. *Ibid.*, p. 1667.
166. *Ibid.*, p. 1666.
167. Shri Prakash, "Sino-Pakistan Relations: Peace Initiatives", Vol. V, No. 324, May-December 1999, p. 125.
168. *Ibid.*, pp. 126-27.
169. See for more details, Sino-Pakistan Border Agreement: Some Facts (Delhi, Government of India, n.d.).
170. *Canbera Times*, 6 March 1963, *Globe and Mail*, 6 March 1963, *New York Post*, 6 March 1963.
171. Khalid Bind Sayeed, "Pakistan's Foreign Policy: An Analysis of Pakistan's Fears and Interests", *Asian Survey*, Vol. IV, No. 3, March 1964, p. 749.
172. *Ibid.*
173. Anwar Syed, "The Parties of Sino-Pakistan Agreements, *Orbis*, Vol. II, No. 3, 1967, p. 799.
174. Shri Parkash, n. 167, p. 127.
175. M.A.H. Isphani, "The Foreign Policy of Pakistan 1947-64," *Pakistan Horizon*, Vol. XVII, No. 3, Third quarter, 1964, p. 249.
176. Devendra Kaushik, n. 119, p. 83.
177. Mohammed Ayub, "Pakistan's Soviet Policy: A Balance Sheet in M.S. Rajan (ed.) *Studies in Politics* (New Delhi, 1971), p. 235.
178. Current Digest of The Soviet Press, Vol. XXII, No. 34, 15 September 1965, pp. 15-16.
179. S.S. Bindra, "Soviet Union as Peace-maker in the Indian Sub-Continent," *International Behavioural Scientist*, Vol. VII, No. 4, December 1974, p. 74.
180. *The Economist*, Vol. LLXV, 22-28 May 1965, p. 897.
181. G.W. Chaudhury, n. 123, pp. 42-43.

182. *Ibid.*, p. 43.
183. *Ibid.*
184. *Ibid.*, pp. 43-44.
185. Shahid, M. Amin, n. 1, pp. 50-51.
186. G.W. Chaudhary, n. 123, p. 44.
187. *Morning News* (ed.), "Stoking in the Fire", 23 May 1966.
188. *Pakistan Times* (ed.), "Soviet Arms to India", 23 May 1966.
189. Devendra Kaushik, "Soviet Union Pakistan's Policy" in Surendra Chopra, Perspectives on Pakistan's Foreign Policy (Amritsar, 1983), p. 258.
190. *The Dawn*, 18 April 1968.
191. *Ibid.*
192. *Times of India*, 11 July 1968. Also see, Amrita Bazaar Patiala, (ed.) "Arms Aid," 18 July 1968, *Indian Express*, (ed.) Arms Aid for Pakistan, 12 July 1968.
193. *Rajya Sabha Debates*, Vol. LXV, Nos. 2 and 3, 23-34, February 1969, Cols. 310-412 and 524-96.
194. *Hindustan Times*, 11 July 1968.
195. *Pakistan National Assembly Debates*, Vol. I, No. 11, 20 May 1968, pp. 808-809.
196. *The Patriot*, I April 1970.
197. *Times of India*, 8 October 1970.
198. *Ibid.*, 9 October 1970.
199. *Lok Sabha Debates*, Vol. XLV, No. 1, 9 November 1970, Col. 808-809.
200. *New York Times*, (ed.) "Arms for Pakistan, "11 October 1970.
201. *The Statesman*, (ed.) "Arms for Pakistan" 10 October 1970. Also see, *Indian Express*, (ed.), "Arms for Islamabad," 22 October 1970, Krishan Bhatia, "US Arms to Pakistan," *Hindustan Times*, 14 October 1970, *The Mainstream* (ed.), "Wrong Focus", 14 November 1970, *The Statesman* (ed.), More About Arms," 13 November 1970, Giri Lala Jain, "US Arms for Pakistan: Factors Behind the Decision", *Times of India*, 20 October 1970, "US Arms Supply to Pakistan", *"Indian and Foreign Review,"* Vol. VIII, No. 2, Novermber 1970.
202. J.K. Baral and V. Eshwar Anand, "United States Arms Supply to Pakistan: A Study of America's South Asian Diplomacy," Surendra Chopra, n. 189, p. 227.
203. *Ibid.*
204. *Ibid.*, pp. 228-29
205. *Ibid.*, pp. 229-30.
206. Leela Yadav, "Pakistan's Foreign Policy: An Analysis of Pakistan's Relations with the United States of America," in Surendra Chopra, n. 189, pp. 218-20.
207. *Ibid.*, p. 221
208. *Ibid.*, p. 223.
209. Shahid M. Amin, n. 1, pp. 87-88.
210. *Ibid.*

211. *Ibid.*, pp. 88-89.
212. Aditya Chibber, National Security Doctrine: An Indian Imperative (New Delhi, 1990), pp. 85-87.
213. *Ibid.*
214. S.S. Bindra, Determinents of Pakistan's Foreign Policy (New Delhi, 1988), p. 288.
215. *The Tribune*, 3 July 1988.
216. *Ibid.*
217. *Ibid.*, 8 September 1988.
218. *Ibid.*, 20 August 1988.
219. Mohammed Wasim, "Dialectic Between Domestic Politics Foreign Policy," in Christoph Jaffrelot, Pakistan Nationalism Without Nehru? (New Delhi, 2002), p. 278.
220. *Ibid.*, pp. 278-79.
221. Fazal-ur-Rahman, "Pakistan's Relations with China", *Peace Initiatives*, Vol. V. No. 3 and 4, May-December 1989, p. 173.
222. *Ibid.*
223. *Ibid.*
224. *Ibid.*, pp. 179-80.
225. *Ibid.*
226. *Ibid.*
227. John W. Garver, Protracted Contest: Sino-Indian Rivalry in the Twentieth Century (New Delhi, 2001), pp. 234-235.
228. *Ibid.*, p. 235.
229. T.K. Hussain, "China and South Asia," in P.L. Bhola, (ed.), A Perceptual Framework of Sino Indian Relations (Jaipur, n.d.), p. 176.
230. Abha Dixit, "Enduring Sino-Pak Relations," Strategic Analysis, Vol. XII, No. IX, December 1989, pp. 986-87.
231. Fazal-ur-Rahman, n. 221, p. 182
232. John W. Garver, n. 227, pp. 219-23.
233. Shri Parkash, n. 167, p, 129.
234. Cited in Chintamani Mahapatra, "The US, China and the Gauri Missile," Strategic Analysis, Vol. XXII, No. 3, June 1998, p. 364.
235. Rajiv Nayan, "Sino-Pakistan Missile Cooperation", *Peace Initiatives*, Vol. V, No. 394, May-December 1998.
236. *Ibid.*, p. 81.
237. *Ibid.*
238. See "American Views on China's Missile Exports and Assistance to Pakistan", *Peace Initiatives*, Vol. V, No. 394, May-December 1999, pp. 84-85.
239. M.V. Rajpal, "China's Nuclear Arsenal and Missile Defence", *Strategic Analysis*, Vol. XXVI, No. 1, Jan.-March 2002, p. 78.
240. John W. Garver, n. 227, pp. 228-29.
241. *Ibid.*, p. 231.
242. *Ibid.*

243. *Ibid.*
244. *Ibid.*, p. 241.
245. *Ibid.*, p. 242
246. *Ibid.*
247. Maqbool Ahmed Bhatty, "China's Emerging Role in The World," *Peace Initiatives*, Vol. 324, May-Dec. 1999, p. 164.
248. *The Dawn*, 21 May 1998.
249. *The Tribune*, 4 June 1998.
250. *The Dawn*, 13 July 1998
251. Maqbool Ahmad Bhatty, n. 247, p. 164.
252. *Ibid.*, pp. 164-65.
253. M.K. Rappai, "Nuclear Factor in India-China Relations", *Asian Strategic Review*, 1998-99 (New Delhi, November 1999), p. 326.
254. Congressional Research Service, 92-265, 31 January 1995, See www.far.org/ma/crs/92-265.htm
255. *Ibid.*
256. *Ibid.*
257. *Ibid.*
258. *Ibid.*
259. Evens Mederas and M. Taylor Fravel, "The Changing Face of Chinese Diplomacy, See www.rand.org/community/112503
260. *Ibid.*

3

Indo-Pak Relations: Areas of Conflict and Co-operation

Pakistan's foreign policy must be understood and analyzed by keeping into consideration various internal as well as external factors. These factors are never stable and keep on changing with the change of political environment in the world as well as in Pakistan. She has been always considered a country with western orientations. An Indian scholar strongly believes that orientation towards the west was writ large in the very concept of Pakistan. Pakistan emerged "with a built-in alliance with Britain."[1]

On the eve of Indian independence, the British were keen to have strong foot-hold in the new nation, i.e. Pakistan and were therefore bent upon creating opportunities to have influence there. Some British political elites wanted to put Sikhs against the Muslims in the hope of getting some advantage out of their mutual conflict. But, this proposition under which the Sikhs were to be given autonomous status in their majority dominated area was purely a British idea without the blessings of Mohammad Ali Jinnah or of Master Tara Singh, the Sikh leader. These two leaders counted most, but they did not see eye to eye on the problem. The Sikhs along with Hindus from Pakistan, rather preferred to settle down in India.[2]

Another area where the British intervened with their own selfish motives was the Kashmir issue which got complicated after Pakistan sponsored tribals invasion of the state, which ultimately decided to be a part of India after formally signing the Instrument of Accession. The British were well versed with the constitutional position in Kashmir and the situation that emerged after the decision of Maharaja Hari Singh of Kashmir, to join hands with India, but instead they chose to apply cold war standards to Kashmir, ignored Pakistan's aggression and wanted the leadership of both the countries to have a compromise solution. By adopting this line of action, the British in and outside the UN Security Council, manipulated everything in such a way that the Britain at once got an upper hand over in establishing guidelines for Pakistan's foreign policy. The British or for that matter the western powers during the heydays of the cold war, were never interested in the settlement of the Kashmir problem, since that would deprive them of the lever with which to drive Pakistan on the desired path. The British wanted to hold all the strings of Pakistan with a view to serving their colonial and strategic interests in the region. These were: one the vast political influence and commercial interests in West Asia; particularly access to oil in the Persian Gulf too, the physical control over large stretches on the South Arabian Coast line and the Persian Gulf, with the strategic Port of Aden and other minor ports. Three, the trade routes to Sinking through Pakistan occupied Kashmir and four, the need to prevent Russia from gaining, through political influence or otherwise, the access to hot waters in the region. Pakistan was thought to be pivot of the British designs.[3]

On the eve of independence, it was assumed that India would not be a member of Commonwealth while it was taken for granted that Pakistan would be an active member. However, the British diplomats succeeded in convincing Nehru to remain in Commonwealth. Both the new dominions did not quit Commonwealth and it was described as a notable achievement of the British diplomacy in the region.[4]

Nehru, who was the Chief Spokesman of the Congress party on external affairs, declared that India would never agree to have any constitutional link with the British after independence. To Nehru, the idea behind Dominion status of a mother country closely connected with her daughter nations, all of them having a common cultural background seemed totally inapplicable to India. Earlier on many occasions the Congress had committed itself to severing the Commonwealth link. On 2 January, 1930 the Congress Working Committee decided that 26 January was to be observed as Purna Swaraj Day (Complete Independence Day). A declaration drafted at that meeting was read to the people all over India on 26 January 1930 as part of the celebrations and recitations was repeated annually till independence became a fact. The declaration stated: 'The British Government in India has not only deprived the Indian people of their freedom but has based itself in the exploitation of the masses and has ruined India economically, politically, culturally and spiritually. We believe therefore that India must sever the British connections and attain Purna Swaraj.[5]

The Muslim League on the other hand had no anti-British traditions. As a matter of fact, when the Second World War was in progress and the allied powers were facing difficult situation, the Congress party first declined to cooperate in the war efforts and, subsequently launched the famous 'Quit India Movement', the more estranged Congress became from the British Government, the more were the latter forced to rely on the Muslims. For their part, the Muslims fully realized they had little chance of winning Pakistan against the opposition of the much more powerful Congress party unless they were backed by the British. The Muslim League rejected 'Quit India' Resolution and allowed the Muslims to cooperate in the war efforts.[6]

Naturally, however, this special relationship between the British Government and the Indian Muslims, could endure only as long as, it was suitable for both of them. It was clearly beneficial for the British to back Muslim minority while she intended to rule over India and had to keep the Hindu majority in check. But once she had decided to handover power the balance of her national interest immediately shifted in the direction of favouring the Hindus, for it seemed clear that whether India remained united or was split in into two, the Hindus of India under the banner of the Congress party would be a far more important factor in international life than the Muslims. The Labour party at that time happened to be in office in the UK greatly facilitated the process of rapprochement between Britain and the Congress leadership. Labour traditionally had been sympathetic to Congress causes and many members of the top echelons in both parties had long been on terms of personal friendship with one another. Attlee, Cripps, Pethick-Lawrence and others in Labour ranks admired the Congress leaders as progressive intellectuals fighting for the freedom of their country. Jinnah and the League on the other hand were pictured by them as reactionaries and treated with scant respect. This was visibly brought out in a BBC-TV 'conversation' between Attlee and Francis Williams in 1959:

Attlee: Never liked Jinnah I knew him as long as 1927 I never liked him.

William: Why?

Attlee: I don't think he was very genuine, you know I thought...a great deal of his ambition was for Master Jinnah rather than anything else.[7]

Personal friendship between Labour and Congress leaders notwithstanding, the task before the British statesmen was a formidable one, because the lost ground had to be recovered. Britain had to soothe the feeling of hostility between herself and the Congress party, which had launched the Quit India Movement. The relations between the two had become worse and by demonstrating positive actions to the satisfaction of the Congress leaders that the game of favouring Muslims finally ended. Mountbatten's much greater concern for Indian than for Pakistan susceptibilities in the matter of Commonwealth membership was not the only question regarding which Pakistan felt that the representatives of Britain had favoured India against Pakistan. They thought that the Redcliff Award was grossly unfair to them and that the date of transfer of power had been advanced, from June 1948, to August, 1947, under the pressure of the Congress party.[8]

Pakistan's main problems were related to India. Her appraisal of the British or any other country's attitude towards herself after independence depended their attitude on those issues. Z.A. Bhutto, a former Prime Minister of Pakistan, was of the view that since independence, Pakistan's foreign relations have evolved in stages, partly influenced by changing conditions and partly by sentiments and subjective judgements which invariably influence the thought of new nations. To arrive at a true and unbiased appreciation of Pakistan's role in the sub-continent, in Asia and the world, it is necessary to examine relations with states not on a temporary basis, but on that of a deeper consideration of world events and the objective facts that influence relations of nation-states, large and small. Political theorists, particularly in Pakistan, were inclined to make policy assessments out of immediate developments and jump to hasty and arbitrary conclusions. Difficulties arose from our habit of reaching rigid conclusions and persisting in them. It is necessary to make a departure from old habits of thought for the sake of a cleaner appreciation of facts. Indeed, the true implications of any happenings can only be judged if every major development is viewed in its proper place in the vast puzzle of international power politics.[9]

The traditional method of conducting foreign affairs in the nineteenth and the first half of the twentieth centuries was meant of forming regional alliances in order to maintain a balance of power among the various groupings of the Great Powers with the help of the smaller powers. It was possible to maintain peace with this very delicate balance and peace was disturbed only when the balance, at any given time, tilted in favour of one group or the other. In those days, the smaller nations could influence the policy and the alignment of great powers by indulging in various political permutations and combinations.[10]

All the same everything changed after the end of the Second World War, with the emergence of global powers which, in addition, to having all the attributes of Great Powers in the classical sense were at the same time much more powerful and played a larger role in determining the destinies of people all over the world. The emergence of these powers had changed the whole concept of conducting affairs of a state. The task of smaller nations in which all the developing countries fall in determining their relationship with global powers and in furthering their national interest had become more complex and difficult. The small nations which do not understand and analyse the various diplomatic moves in a proper perspective are doomed to frustration, sense of helplessness, isolation, and perhaps eventual extinctions. As a developing nation, Pakistan must have understood how to conduct its affairs in this new situation.[11]

A developing nation, Pakistan has always conducted its foreign policy moves in a very successful manner and achieved the desired results. Kalim Siddiqui, a noted journalist, was of the opinion that Pakistan's external behaviour had to be considered in the light of several factors. He referred to the images of various nations created by the propaganda of their opponents. Thus, the US, Wealthy powerful interventionist, the USSR; strong, idealist, revolutionary powerful, the UK; imperialist, cunning, would sell a refrigerator to an Eskimo, etc.[12]

All the more important is that Pakistan's domestic and regional realities have shaped its foreign policy within certain parameters. Domestically, Pakistan continues to grapple with inadequate nation-building as its ethno-linguistic, regional and secret Asian cleavages persist as the most important feature of Pakistan political life. Given the depth of these divisions, the limited experiment with democracy during the late 1980s was perhaps doomed with the absence of a sense of nationhood in Pakistan today. Regionally, Pakistan is constrained by its long and acrimonious relations with its more powerful neighbour India. The flare up of hostilities between the two countries in the spring of 1999 in Kashmir and their mutual nuclear tests of May and June 1998 highlight the fact that Pakistan must devote its attention in preparing for and yet avoiding all out war with India.

India's dominant position in South Asia hinders Pakistan from having significant influence in the region. Iran blocks Pakistan from expanding its influence towards the Arabian Peninsula although the large number of Pakistani guest workers on the other side of the Persian Gulf do provide Pakistan with some basis for close ties with those countries. Still the world's sixth largest country can only look north towards Central Asia, if it wishes to engage in any serious power projection or expansionist foreign policy desires. Thus for a combination of reasons, Afghanistan has become a key to Pakistan's foreign policy, providing it both an entry point to Central Asia, a battle ground on which it can confront Iran in proxy and the potential for strategic depth in relation to India. At the same time, India's shadow looms so large over Pakistan that it is easy (and not entirely misleading) for Pakistan's officials to present their activities in Afghanistan as merely a shadow to the outside world.[13]

Every move of Pakistan in the arena of international politics revolves around India. It always feels scared about India and since its inception in one way or the other has been trying to be at par with India. It is really difficult to analyse every aspect of Indo-Pak relations as one has to take into consideration so many dimensions. Pakistan's relations with other nations of the world, whether big or small, are always conditioned by one sole factor, how; it's going to affect its relations with India. From the very beginning, in fact, when the idea of Pakistan, as a separate state was voiced by first Mohammed Iqbal (the poet philosopher) at the first session of the All India Muslim League in 1930 at Allahabad, its political elites have been trying to attain parity. The Muslim League demand for parity between itself and the Congress party and between the Muslim and Hindu nations made since 1940s has also considerably conditioned Pakistan's foreign policy behaviour. The Pakistan fight for the said parity was illustrated in the letter written by Jinnah to Lord Linlithgo on 1 July 1940, the Resolution of the Muslim Executive Council in July 1945 and the memorandum presented by the League to the Cabinet Mission on 11 July 1946. Even after Pakistan's creation, its leaders have feverishly tried to attain the same and in the words of Keith Callard 'the primary aim of Pakistan is equality of status, to be even with India'[14]. He adds that 'Pakistan reacting hysterically to any suggestion that India outranks her in prestige or status. But the fact has been that Pakistan that emerged as a result of partition of the sub-continent was very weak and small *vis-a-vis* India.' It was in Jinnah's words 'a maimed, mutilated and moth-eaten Pakistan'.[15] This created an obsession in Pakistan and moved it to go all out in search, on the one hand, of a 'plus factor' and on the other hand, to do whatever is negatively possible to reduce the imbalance between Pakistan and India. Bhutto emphatically said that 'Pakistan will always need a plus factor for coping with India.'[16]

So far both nations have fought four major wars, detonated nuclear devices, initiated and implemented a number of Confidence Building Measures (CBMs), signed a number of declarations and agreements, starting with notably, Indus Water Treaty of 1960, 'Tashkent Declaration and Simla Agreement, etc. But their relations are far from friendly. The most important and unsolved issue is the Kashmir, which has become alarming because of its international implications as it 'contains the seeds of nuclear holocaust... the region is the site and source of some of the world's major terrorist groups. Besides Al Qaida, these include a number of groups based in, or tolerated by Pakistan and India itself has tolerated or encouraged various terrorist groups, operating in nearby states and its own terrorist problems are existent quite apart from Kashmir.'[17]

The origin of the Indo-Pakistan conflict has been traced to a number of causes—the failure of the British to smoothly transfer power and 'manage a peaceful and politically acceptable partition, the deeply rooted political rivalries among the sub-continent's major religious communities, Hindu, Sikhs and Muslims, the struggle for control over Kashmir and Kashmir's importance to the national identities and the greed or personal short-sightedness of leaders on both sides of the borders—in particular Nehru's fascination for Kashmir and his Brahmanical arrogance (the Pakistani interpretation) or Mohammed Ali Jinnah's vanity, short-sightedness and religious zeal (the Indian interpretation).'[18]

Religious intolerance continues to be one of the main characteristics of Pakistan which is symbolized by the official name given to the country as 'Islamic Republic of Pakistan'. The armed forces have played a definite role in Pakistan and it is considered to be highly politicized. These two factors also contributed in widening the gulf between India and Pakistan.

Many observers have characterized Pakistan as a failed state or even a 'rogue' state, particularly, for its support to the Taliban regime in Afghanistan prior to the September 11 terrorist attacks 'Armed with nuclear weapons and sympathetic to separatist and radical Islamist groups operating against arc-rival India, Pakistan is also portrayed as helpless and on the verge of imminent catastrophe even as it commands a powerful military capability.'[19]

Up to the mid-sixties, both the countries remained busy in solving the problems and issues that emerged as a result of the partition. The evacuee property problem, the minority issue, the problem of the sharing of river water, the division of military stores and the integration of princely states, etc. were solved by adopting peaceful as well as other methods. One aspect of the Indo-Pak relations has struck deep roots, i.e. peaceful methods are the only way out to sort out the differences by creating a stable environment in the sub-continent.

In the past, Indian efforts to improve people to people relations were suspected. Similar was the position of India's efforts to promote friendly relations and achieve a detente with Pakistan, of the type Canada has with the US. Interestingly once Pakistan's Minister for External Affairs said that "even if India were to treat us with yielding love, tomorrow we should only regard it as a trap." The same thing was repeated by, late Z.A. Bhutto when he said, "We are fully aware of the treacherous nature of India and we do not want to endanger the existence of Pakistan in the name of cooperation."[20]

Pakistani leadership in the past, particularly up to the mid-nineties was adamant to take any concrete step to normalize relations with India. They felt that once Pakistan agreed to normalize relations with India, the very *raison d'etre* for the partition of India would cease to exist and it would be a matter of time before Pakistan is sucked into India's geographical orbit. For these reasons up to the end of seventies, Pakistan did not encourage cultural exchanges, open borders, or general relaxation of visas with India as it would not be possible to mislead the people, the spontaneous outburst of fraternal feelings during religious pilgrims to

India and Pakistan pointed to the deeper yearnings of the people in the two countries for coming closer. That caused concern among Pakistani leaders who felt the need of a sustained campaign against the nature of Hinduism and highlight the basic conflict between Hinduism and Islam. In the process, history was destroyed and the picture of continuous conflict between the two religious groups, which culminated in the creation of Pakistan, was depicted. The main theme of Pakistani propaganda was two-fold, "misrepresentation of India, both in internal and external matters. Externally India was represented to be expansionist, a successor to the British imperialism, desiring Vishal Bharat, (Greater India), from the Oxus, or better still, from the Suez to the Mekong. Pertinently this sort of analysis emanated from the top."[21]

In an article in the journal of Foreign Affairs, President Ayub stated that "the Indian leaders have often stated that their true border extends from the Hindu Kush mountains to the Mekong river, this is to say, whether the influence of Hinduism had existed in the past. This early friendly overtures to China were based on the hope that there would be an understanding between them and China over the respective spheres of influence in Asia, and they would recognize and endorse India's claim."[22]

The story of Indo-Pak relations is history of two neighbours having different religious ideologies, socio-economic systems, international perceptions, national interests and foreign policy objectives.

However, Hindu-Muslim rivalry is considered to be the basic cause which, over the years, kept the two countries apart. Since the eighth century B.C when the Arabs made in-roads in to India and established a foot-hold in Sind, the rivalries between the two religious communities has been going on. It has been further strengthened by the power hungry politicians and fanatic Hindu-Muslim leaders. During the freedom struggle, the Muslim League was considered to be the sole organization of Muslims. It tried its best, in order to implement the 'Two Nations Theory', to widen the gulf between the Hindus and the Muslims. Mohammed Ali Jinnah had always branded the Congress party as a purely Hindu body. Before 1937, the differences were based on prejudices and social attitudes between the two communities, but thereafter, they were institutionalized and the Congress-Muslim rivalry became more bitter.[23]

The partition of India on the basis of religion further embittered the conflict. It was commonly reminded that Muslim owed the creation of Pakistan to the Congress in the sense that had the leaders of the Congress party treated the Muslims at par with the Hindus, there would have been no Muslim separatism and therefore no Pakistan. The Congress party never made any serious attempt to understand the problems of the Muslims.[24] It had no definite policy on this matter and always tried to meet the crisis as it arose. Coupland, Lord Eustace Percy, Sir Stanley Reed, Sir Ivor Jennings, Sir Francis Tucker, Ian Stephens, Rush Brook Williams, Penderal Moon and other competent judges of Indian affairs were unanimous that the arrogance of the Congress had sparked the partition of India. It led Jinnah resigning from the Congress party, he also strongly believed that Hindus and Muslims differed in ideas and outlooks, conducted modus of behaviour and he demanded the division of the country on these points.[25] The creation of Pakistan gave the Hindu-Muslim divide a permanent constitutional form.[26]

The unstable political conditions in Pakistan created a tense atmosphere between the two. The Muslim league, the party of big landlords and bourgeoisie, the intelligentsia, the peasantry and even the working class, started running the affairs of Pakistan after its emergence as an independent nation. No single party or public organization could, in the post-partition period, compete with the power and influence of the Muslim League up to 1954. It dominated the political life of Pakistan and controlled the Government at the centre as well as in the provinces. Liaquat Ali Khan, the first Prime Minister of Pakistan (August 1947-October 1951) expressed the true sense or affairs when he said, "I have always considered me as the Prime Minister of the League. I never regard myself as the Prime Minister chosen by the members of the Constituent Assembly."[27]

From August 1947 to October 1958, the political

environment in Pakistan was not conducive to the smooth running of any type of political system. The main consideration during this period was the making of a new political system. It was dominated by the strategic elite comprising the political leadership from across the border as well as Punjabi-based army and bureaucracy. Both the charismatic leadership of Quaid-e-Azam and 'Two Nations Theory' emerged as strong legitimizing forces and their multifarious interpretations manifested in increasing divisions in the body politic along ethnic, regional and class lines. Indian hostility provided an overall perceptive for operationalizing these resources of legitimacy. Similarly, the institution of the army took measures to assert it and rapidly came to occupied a pivotal position in the new political centre.[28]

Hindu-Muslim rivalry which has its roots in the past probably is one of the root causes of the tension between the two which will always remain. It's just not possible to eradicate this notion but somewhat congenial atmosphere can be created. Z.A. Bhutto felt that eminent historians who have exercised a powerful influence over the Indian mind, having elaborated the concept of Mother India as not only the Motherland of the Hindus, but also the Holy Land of the Hindus from the Himalayan to Cape Comorian. This veneration for Bharat Mata, which is Arya Varb (Aryan Homeland), is the central theme of Hinduism, the strongest mythology, philosophy, cosmogony and religion that the world has ever seen. The Aryans from whom the Brahmans claim their descend, lived for many centuries in Punjab before they advanced eastwards across northern India, conquering the indigenous Dasyus, the earliest Hindu Holy Scriptures, Rig Vedas and the Upnishds, were composed by the Rishis.

In the Hindu, national consciousness, as inspired by many great Hindu writers of the last century, the sub-continent is conceived as a unity—one and indivisible from the Khyber Hills to the far South, with the North-West, which is now Pakistan, its heart and soul. Geographical India was never completely united under one rule, except British and nominally for a few years under the Mughal Emperor Aurangzeb. Before that, the first Indian Empire, that of the

Maurya's, had extended over the whole of northern India, reaching into Afghanistan and some parts of the Southern Peninsula and Indian influence spread eastwards across the ocean to Cambodia and Java. Brahmanical religious and cultural influence was more extensive than the frontiers of any single Indian Empire in the past. The Hindu religion expressly extols the concept of Chatra Pati or the Lord Paramount, a ruler who conquers and dominates his neighbours and extends his sway from ocean to ocean. This kind of consciousness of past greatness, regenerated by many Indian writers to inspire Hindu cultural and political revival, has been the mainspring of twentieth century Indian nationalism. Discovery of India by Nehru explains how the most westernized of Hindu minds fell captive to this spell of the "essential Hinduness of India."

The advent of Islam in force in the eleventh century brought not only a loss of political power, but also outrage to the dominant religion. An Indian scholar analyzing the reasons for the Hindu-Muslims rivalry wrote, "The Muslim conquest of India could not be made innocuous for the Hindus through the caste system. The conquest was an extension into a new country of a well established and mature society, with a fully developed way of life and a living culture. The final conquest of India was the adventure of a Muslim King whose main territories lay outside India but even when the subordination of the new Muslim empire to an external Muslim Kingdom was ended, as it very soon was, Muslim rule in the country remained the rule of colonial people who never forgot their affiliation with the wider Islamic world."

As if that was not enough, the Hindus on their side had an almost equal contribution to make. By the time the new invasions began, they had completely lost whatever assimilating power and adaptability they had unhardened into a closed society with a conviction of its own superiority which mounted to megalomania. There could thus be no question of absorbing even a neutral foreigner.[29]

Bhutto further said, "Fed on centuries of hatred, their sense of injury received at Muslim hands reinforced by religious dogmas, all Hindu movements have conceived the assimilation of the Muslim minority as part of their objective differing only in their methods. The Hindu Mahasabha and the RSSS (Rashtriya Swaym Sevak Sangh) were committed to violence and the forcible conversion of Muslims into the lowest strata of Indian society. Gandhi's method was more subtle. He frequently spoke of Muslims as blood brothers and held out innumerable assurances that their rights would be safeguarded under a Congress governed India, but whenever called upon to define their rights and share of political power in an independent India, he invariably evaded a clear answer. Nehru with his background of association with Muslim culture not to speak of his Cambridge education and revival of Marxist philosophy dismissed the fact of a separate Muslim culture in the sub-continent. He asked, "What is the Muslim culture? Is it Persian Aryan culture or the Arab Semantic One? The only difference between a Hindu and the Muslim that he could discern was that the Hindu wore the Dhoti and the Muslim a Pajama and a Turkish Fez."

Bhutto was of the view that the Indian leaders agreed to Pakistan only when it became clear to them that partition was inevitable and that they had to concede to this division as a price for the transfer of power from British to Indian hands. In the light of these historical and psychological factors which govern the Indian attitude towards Pakistan, it was believed that Indian leaders had tolerated Pakistan because there was no option before them and they were not in a capacity to destroy it. Bhutto strongly felt that, "if they could forge this power as they are endeavouring to do by the augmentation of their military forces, they would end partition and reabsorb Pakistan into the India of their dreams. They have pronounced Pakistan as their chief enemy. The whole aim of Indian diplomacy under Nehru and his succession has been to isolate our country so that, when India has built up sufficient strength, she could overwhelm and absorb us as quickly as possible."

The founder of Pakistan, Mohammed Ali Jinnah, who was known as "the Ambassador of Hindu-Muslim unity" and the Indian National Congress regarded him as an apostle of their movement at the height of his career, he did his utmost with all his fervour and enthusiasm of his earlier days, to promote the cause of Indian independence, so that Hindus and Muslims could live side by side within a single polity and find their emancipation under one roof. The fact that he failed was in itself significant. Failure as such would have depressed a lesser man. Jinnah, whose single-mindedness and stamina had become a legend, could hardly be deterred by failure alone. Experience had shown him that the Indian leaders sought the cooperation of Muslims not as equals but only as a means to eliminate their identity. For some years, he remained abroad, aloof from the tortures of Indian politics. Only when approached by such Muslim leaders as Maulana Mohammed Ali did he return to fulfil his historic mission? For the Muslim league, he formulated a policy of total confrontation, steadfastly refusing to succumb to the lures and promises of cooperation with which Congress sought to distract or entice him. He was relentless in the pursuit of his objectives and would not be defeated from his course by either the sweet words of Sarojini Naidu, or the hypnotic dialectics of M.K. Gandhi.

In abandoning his advocacy of Hindu-Muslim unity, the founder of Pakistan left a lesson which has, with the passage of time, became clearer in its relevance. The fact that the Hindus and the Muslims of the sub-continent constituted two separate nationalities formed the foundation of the edifice of Pakistan. When this was first propounded as the Muslim's political objective, the leaders of the Muslim League were ridiculed not only by the Indian National Congress and the British, but also by many eminent Muslims. It seemed to them preposterous that, after nearly two hundred years of united existence under one yoke as the most precious gem in the crown of British Empire, the country should be rent as under. Subsequent events became part of history. Pakistan was achieved as a result of an overwhelming popular decision, in which the Muslims of the sub-continent including those who knew that they would not form a part of Pakistan cast their votes for its creation.

Bhutto was also vocal in accusing India for exploiting every conceivable situation in Pakistan's internal affairs continued to be exploited by her with the aim of aggravating Pakistan's difficulties and weakening its national integrity too.

It was no coincidence that the genesis of every Indo-Pak conflict was because of the Indian hostility. The origin of the Jammu and Kashmir dispute, the events leading to passing of the UN Resolutions of 1948 and 1949, the numerous mediation attempts by the UN, bilateral negotiations, India's repeated attempts to frustrate any settlement and finally her remuneration of solemn international commitments, a tale of consistent ill-will.

Her policy of evictions left no doubt that India's principal objective was the obliteration of Pakistan. The meanest intellect in the sub-continent must be aware of the vicious circle of communal disturbances, exodus and repercussions in the reverse direction. It was axiomatic in the circumstances that oppression of minorities in one country has inevitable ramification in the other. Moreover, it was highly probable that, if as a result such oppressions, any significant migration ensures, it would provoke the minority community and create a law and order crisis of grave magnitude.

From time immemorial, the exponents of Greater Bharat have maintained that its political, cultural and economic hegemony should extend from the Hindu Kush to Mekong. Throughout Indian history, political philosophers have propounded this theme at such length and such frequency that it has become part of the tradition which modern India has inherited. The fact that it was nearly a thousand years since India was in a position to take and step towards that glorious objective has not diminished either the intensity or the extent of that unavering ambition. As a first step towards this realization, Pakistan must be neutralized but ultimately the semi-religious concept of Akhand Bharat demands the end of Pakistan itself.

Z.A. Bhutto, who later ruled over Pakistan for nearly six years, was considered to be having strong anti-Indian attitude. The seeds of antagonism has been sown so deep in the minds of the leadership of Pakistan that even the younger generation not untouched. It is a hard fact that the communal malady which originated before partition did not subside with the creation of India and Pakistan. It got transformed into an Indo-Pakistan rivalry and conflict and also provided a ground for great power intrusion and intervention in the sub-continent because the Hindu-Muslim communalism had led step by step an unfolding hostility that imprisoned the leadership and people of India and Pakistan. It increased their burdens and limited their freedom.

The Hindu-Muslim rivalry factor's contribution in widening the gulf between the two neighbours will never ever diminish. It has in fact become an attitude and psychological factor. Still there are some sections of political, social and religious elites in both the countries and even in common strata of society, who are always in search of an opportunity to use the card of Hindu-Muslim rivalry. In fact, the wounds of partition are still alive, particularly the stories of carnage and large-scale violence, which erupted after the Hindu, Muslim and Sikh, had selected their places for living.

The war of succession continued at a mad pace for several months after independence with its horrible loss of life and property and the migration of millions of dazed and disputed men, women and children on both sides, it left lasting scars on the minds of all Pakistanis and Indians. Since half a million persons were mercilessly slaughtered and no less than fourteen million crossed the international border, smaller Pakistan, having received 1.7 million more refugees than India, had a much greater problem of rehabilitation. She was at the same time, faced with an over-whelming task of setting up of new administration from scratch, amidst conditions of bitter confusion. The early years after independence when the wounds of partition were raw, were especially difficult. Even Gandhi, normally the apostle of non-violence could not escape the evil spell of those furious days and added to the prevailing tension by some of his prayer meeting pronouncements.[30] On 26 September for instance he threatened that, 'if Pakistan persistently refuses to see it prosper or continues to be minimized, the Indian Government would have to go to war against it. Governor General Jinnah complained, it is very unfortunate that vigorous propaganda has been going on that Pakistan is merely a temporary madness (and) that Pakistan will have to come into the union as a repentant erring son... It is now clear beyond doubt that it was well planned, well organized, well directed and the object of it all was to paralyze the new born Dominion of Pakistan."[31]

Several arguments have been advanced purporting to explain the 'cause' of the creation of Pakistan. One was the pull exerted by the distinctive Muslim social order which could not flourish in the non-Muslim Hindu environment of India. A similar idea was that Pakistan was pushed into existence precisely by that non-Muslim environment. Another argument was that the essentially secular, economic interests of the Muslim bourgeoisies led them to seek institutional protection. The British themselves have been blamed credited for the partition of India and the establishment of Pakistan by their policy of divide and rule. The British pitted the communal sections of India against one another in order to neutralize their political effects. While it was in the interest of British to prevent all India political movements, it would not have served their purpose to provoke inter-community conflict and resulting disorder. In their attempts to impose rational western modes of governance on their subjects, they stimulated self-awareness. Moreover, as they moved towards self-government and established electorates based on religion, they contributed to Muslim political consciousness was another hypothesis concerning the competition for power among various groups and aspiring leaders. As is the case almost everywhere, there is insufficient room at the top for all people who think they should be there. One solution to this is to carve out one's political system, an approach that appeals especially to groups that are likely to be confined to permanent minority status.[32]

The explanation for the creation of Pakistan no doubt lies in some combinations of these arguments. But one thing is clear; all of them have an ingredient in common and that is Islam. The political and social essence of Pakistan is Islam. Attempts to separate Pakistan, its conception and history from Islam either in theory or in the real world of politics, calls into question the country's very identity. In a real sense, Pakistan is trying to establish a political system based on Islamic teachings.

As far as its attitude towards India is concerned Hindu-Muslim rivalry has played a very important role in determining Pakistan's foreign policy every aspect of it in the initial years, but now its impact has decreased considerably, because of the emergence of various trends and change visible in the national and international environments.

KASHMIR ISSUE: SOME DIMENSIONS

Kashmir has been well recognized as a product of partition which has all the years determined the relationship of India and Pakistan. Every move of both the countries on the world political scene is by one way or the other related with it. It has kept India and Pakistan divided and has also largely influenced the international outlook of the two countries. Many a times, it has caused embarrassing situation for the friends and allies of the two countries. Because of this dispute the two countries are spending huge sums of money on arms and this phenomena has greatly affected the economic development of the two countries.[33]

Its importance lays in the fact that it has helped the elites of Pakistan to rationalize their hostility towards India and strengthen their hate India campaign. It is helpful from containing discontent within and to divert unprofitable channels in order to keep their hold over the masses.[34] For the Government of Pakistan, the Kashmir is not merely a struggle for territory but something more, i.e. struggle for her ideology.[35] If in India, the Kashmir issue is connected with prestige or principle; in Pakistan, it looks like a matter of life and death. Any hostile power installed in Kashmir can dominate Pakistan military and at the hour of crisis can threaten at close range the vital road and rail communications from Lahore to Peshawar. She can control the waters of Chenab and Jhelum on which the economy of Pakistan is based. In short for strategic, economic and ethnological factors, the Government of Pakistan is pleading her case and will not allow any hostile and potentially hostile power to hold the administration of Kashmir.[36] Mohammed Ayub Khan in his autobiography has also emphasized that 'security of Pakistan is closely linked with the solution of Kashmir'[37].

The State of Jammu and Kashmir with its present boundaries was founded by Maharaja Gulab Singh. Initially, he had secured in 1820, the principality of Jammu from Maharaja Ranjit Singh of Punjab in recognition of his loyal services and was authorized to rule over the territory as a (King). By the time of Maharaja Ranjit Singh's death in 1839, he had consolidated his power in the area by subjugating and confiscating the Jagirs of many feudal chiefs.

After the Anglo-Sikh War, the East India Company concluded a treaty with Raja Gulab Singh on 16 March 1846. The treaty is popularly known as the Treaty of Amritsar. Under it, Kashmir was sold to Gulab Singh for cash payment of Rs. 75 lakhs. It recognized Gulab Singh as the Maharaja of Jammu & Kashmir.

The State of Jammu and Kashmir lies between 32.170 and 36.580 north latitude and 73.260 and 80.300 east longitude. The total area of the state was 2,22,236 sq. km. Out of this area, Pakistan had occupied 78,114 sq. km. and has illegally ceded 5180 sq. km. to China. Thus leaving 1,61,387 sq. km. with the people of Jammu and Kashmir who had earlier acceded to India.

The present State of Jammu and Kashmir consists of three divisions, i.e. (i) Kashmir, consisting of 15,948 sq. km., (ii) Jammu, having 26,293 sq. km., and (iii) Ladakh Division covering an area of 59,146 sq. km. the State has common borders with India, Pakistan and China. The climate of the State ranges from arctic cold of Ladakh to the tropical heat of Jammu plain. The valley of Kashmir, which is the only plain in the State is extremely cold in winter and has a moderate climate in summer. Kashmiri and Dogri are the languages spoken in the State. Ladakhis speak a language which is akin to Tibetan language. Urdu in Persian script, is the official language of the State.[38]

Pakistan has links with the State, through the Jhelum valley road connecting Srinagar with Rawalpindi. Between Srinagar and Jammu town runs a road through the Bannihal pass and from Jammu two roads spread out, one in the direction of Sialkot and another in the direction of Pathankot in India.[39]

The geographical situation of the State was such that it would be bounded on all sides by the new Dominion of

Pakistan. Its only access to the outside world by road lay through the Jhelum valley road which ran through Pakistan via Rawalpindi. The only rail line connecting the State with the outside world lay through Sialkot in Pakistan. Its postal and telegraphic services operated through areas that were close to Pakistan.

The State was dependent for all its important supplies like salt, sugar and petrol and other necessities of life on their safe and continued transit through areas that would form part of Pakistan. The tourist transit traffic which was a major source of income and revenue came via Rawalpindi. The only route available for the export of its valuable fruit was the Jhelum valley route. Its timber could be drafted down only in the Jhelum River which ran into Pakistan.

THE INSTRUMENT OF ACCESSION: SOME FACTS

The Maharaja of Kashmir, who could not decide to accede to India or to Pakistan, was trapped by the tribal raiders in their net. These raiders were openly supported by Pakistan and they were in fact, Pakistani soldiers. When the raiders were about to capture the Srinagar Airport, the Maharaja of Kashmir agreed to Kashmir accession to India and signed the Instrument of Accession on 26 October 1947. After the lapse of the British Paramouncy in August 1947, it had become optional for the princely states to accede to India or Pakistan or remain independent. By 15 August 1947, almost all the princely states, with three exceptions had acceded to India or Pakistan, on the same basis as the principle underlying the partition of British India, namely, non-Muslim majority areas joined India and Muslim majority states joined Pakistan. The three which stood out were Junagadh, Hyderabad and Kashmir.

Thus, (a) 597 states out of 600 acceded to India or Pakistan, in accordance with the religion accepted by the majority of the population in each case, and (b) in all three cases in which the rulers had indicated that their wish to go against the principle of partition, India compelled them to abandon the idea on the ground that their action would violate the principle on which the division of the sub-continent had been affected. Furthermore, the Muslim League had desired to include the whole of the predominently Muslim provinces of Bengal and Punjab in Pakistan but at the Congress insistence, they were divided so that the Hindu parts could join India. The trouble over Kashmir arose, according to a Pakistan scholar, when India laid claim to every single Hindu majority area on the ground that participation of the sub-continent was effected on communal lines, at the same time, she denied Muslim Kashmir to Pakistan.[40]

The Indian spokesman while pleading the Indian case for Kashmir singled out two basic facts and desired that the rest of the world must concede that the Pakistan has been the 'aggressor' in Kashmir. The first is that, the tribal invasion of Kashmir which was launched on 22 October 1947 and the second is the open intervention of the Pakistani armed forces inside Kashmir in the first week of May 1948. The Indian Government completely ignored the developments and provocation that led to the creation of chaos in the valley. The fact of the matter is that United Nations (UN) did not pronounce Pakistan as an aggressor and these occurrences notwithstanding, India agreed in the UN Security Council that the people of Kashmir should be allowed to decide their own future by a plebiscite, thus making the holding of a plebiscite the central issue in the dispute.[41]

A direct approach by India for getting Kashmir was clearly impossible because at that very time, she was pressuring Junagadh and Hyderabad to accede with her, on the ground that they had Hindu majority by which criterion Muslim obviously was to join Pakistan. India therefore did not demand Kashmir accession openly but employed political pressure behind the scene to create situation in which the appearance would be that the majority of the people of Kashmir wished to join India at their own will.[42]

Acharya Kirplani, President of the Indian National Congress, Maharaja of Patiala, Kapurthala and Faridkot and the rulers of the Punjab Hill States, visited the valley and were on a noble mission of persuading the Maharaja of Kashmir to join India. The members of the Muslim Conference had also been pressing the Maharaja to join

Pakistan and on 19 July 1947, passed a Resolution to this effect. Trouble started towards the end of July when the Maharaja ordered his Muslim subjects to surrender their arms to the police. The Muslim got annoyed and responded by organizing themselves as guerrillas in the hills of Poonch, an area dominated by ex-servicemen who had fought in the Second World War in the ranks of the British Army, while the tough warriors of Poonch held their own against the Maharaja forces, the Muslims in Jammu province, where Hindus formed a considerable portion of the population and where Sikhs and other militants from India had infiltrated.[43]

Korbel, who had analysed the Kashmir issue very closely, was of the opinion that 'if the struggle for Kashmir was a struggle for territory', if it was a struggle for national resources or for manpower or for strategic position, or for any of the other prizes for which nations traditionally contest, it might well have been solved some years ago, it might no longer constitute for the entire sub-continent, the meaning that today it remains.

Primarily what makes the problem of Kashmir, the high insoluble debate that is, what makes the leaders of both 'contending parties to dispute in such bitterness and compromise with such grudging reticence, what makes the whole history of its attempted settlement such a record of frustration, annoyance and exasperation is something more than these traditional causes for international disputes. The real cause of all the bitterness and bloodshed, the recalcitrance and the suspicion that have characterized the Kashmir dispute in the uncompromising struggle for two ways of life, two concepts of political organizations, two scales of values, two spiritual attitudes, find these selves locked in deadly conflict, a conflict in which Kashmir has become both symbol and background.

Simply, these two irrevocably opposed positions may be characterized this: To India the sub-continent is inescapably one nation. To Pakistan, it is just inescapability. The examination of the intensity of these two beliefs, their nature, their origins and the events that were and remain the expression of their conflict is essential to the full understanding of this conflict's present day symbol Kashmir.[44]

Korbel analysis is still very much relevant even today. There is no change .in the attitude of the leadership of both the countries on the various aspects of the Kashmir issue. Only the circumstances and the environments are different. There is no visible change in the perception and outlook of both the countries.

After the Kashmir, formal accession with India, the real problem emerged with Pakistan Government when it declared that accession was a fraud perpetrated on the people of Kashmir by its cowardly ruler with the aggressive help of the Government of India. The Indian Government gave an assurance to the people of Kashmir about the holding of plebiscite by saying that 'as soon as law and order have been restored in Kashmir and its soil cleared of the invaders a plebiscite would be held.'[45]

In the original text of the Instrument of Accession, there was no mention of holding of plebiscite in the valley after the normalization of situation. It clearly said that:

1. I hereby declare that I accede to the dominion of India with the intent that the Governor General of India, the Dominion Legislature, the Federal Court and any other Dominion authority established for the purpose of the Dominion shall, by virtue of this my Instrument of Accession but subject always to the terms thereof and for the purposes only of the Dominion, exercise in relation to the State of Jammu and Kashmir (hereinafter referred to as 'this State') such functions as may be vested within by the Government of India Act, 1935, as in force in the Dominion of India, on the 15th Day of the August 1947 (which Act as to so in force in hereafter referred to as 'the Act'.
2. I hereby assume the obligation of ensuring that due effect is given to the provisions of the Act within this State so far as they are applicable therein by virtue of this my Instrument of Accession.
3. I accept the matters specified in the scheduled hereto as the matters with respect to which the dominion legislature may make laws for the State.

4. I hereby declare that I accede to the Dominion of India on the assurance that if an agreement is made between the Governor General and the Ruler of the State whereby any functions in relation to the administration in this State of any law of the Dominion Legislature shall be exercised by the Ruler of this State, then any such agreement shall be deemed to form part of this Instrument and shall be construed to have effect accordingly.
5. The terms of my Instrument of Accession shall not be varied by any amendment of the Act or the Indian Independence Act, 1947, unless such amendment is accepted by me by Instrument Supplementary to this Instrument
6. Nothing in this Instrument shall empower the Dominion Legislature to make any law for this State authorizing the compulsory acquisition of land for any purpose, but I hereby undertake that should the Dominion for the purpose of a Dominion law which applies in the State deem it necessary to acquire any land, I will at their request acquire the land at their expense, or if the land belongs to me transfer it to them on such terms as may be agreed or, in default of agreement, determined by an arbitrator to be appointed by the Chief Justice of India.
7. Nothing in this Instrument shall be deemed to commit in any way to acceptance of any future constitution of India or fetter my discretion to enter into arrangement to the government of India under any such future constitution.
8. Nothing in this Instrument affects the continuance of my sovereignty in and over this State, or, save as provided by or under this Instrument, the exercise of any powers, authority and rights now enjoyed by me as Ruler of this State or the validity of any law at present in force in the State.
9. I hereby declare that I execute this Instrument on behalf of this State and that any reference in this

> Instrument to me or to the Ruler of the State is to be construed as including a reference to my heirs and successors.[46]

The Instrument of Accession was accepted formally by the Governor General of India Lord Mountbatten on 27 October 1947. In his reply, he said that, 'in the special circumstances maintained by your highness, my Government has decided to accept that accession of Kashmir State to the Dominion of India. In consistence with their policy that in the case of any state where the issue of accession has been the subject of dispute, the question of accession should be decided in accordance with the wishes of the people of the state, it is my Government's wish that as soon as law and order have been restored in Kashmir and her soil cleared of all invaders, the question of the state's accession should be settled by a reference to the people.'[47]

Now question arises when there was no mention of holding of plebiscite in the valley in the original text of the Instrument of Accession which was responsible for adding the plebiscite offer? So far, it is not clear why this clause was added. Furthermore, this clause was against the original text of the Instrument wherein under the clause 5, it was stated clearly that no changes can be made in the text and nature of the Instrument without the permission of the Maharaja. We can say by offering the holding of plebiscite, Nehru Government violated in clear terms the spirit of the Instrument of Accession.

When Pakistan came to know about this plebiscite offer, it termed the Instrument of Accession as provisional, based on fraud and violence. The Government of Pakistan communiqué to the Indian Government on 30 October 1947, not only traced under which circumstances the accession was finalized, but also blamed the Nehru Government responsible for the whole situation. The communiqué said that, 'the Government of Pakistan cannot accept the version of the circumstances in which Kashmir acceded to the Indian Dominion...calling attention to the repeated attempts of Pakistan to improve its relations with Kashmir...the threat to call outside help amounted almost to an ultimatum and showed that the real aim of the Kashmir Government's policy was to seek an opportunity to join the Indian Dominion by a *coup d'etat*. It further pointed out that 'in the opinion of the Government of Pakistan, the course of these negotiations clearly shows that Kashmir Government had never any intention of maintaining 'friendly relations with Pakistan and that at any rate as early as 15 October, they had made up their mind to call in outside assistance, presumably after ascertaining the attitude of the Government of India by secret negotiations which have been going on for weeks.' The Government of Pakistan denied consistently the raiding into Kashmir valley by people from Pakistan, 'The Pathan raid was provoked by the use of Kashmir troops to attack and kill Muslims in Kashmir and Jammu and for this the policy of the Government of Kashmir was solely responsible. The Kashmir Government must have been fully aware of the inevitability of the Pathan reaction. Their deliberate refusal to consider several suggestions that the Government of Pakistan made for a meeting of the representatives of both to handle the situation jointly by friendly cooperation and it at the same time hatched a conspiracy with the Indian Government to enable them to use this raid as the occasion for putting into effect the pre-planned scheme for the accession of Kashmir and for the occupation of Kashmir by Indian troops with the object of holding down the people of Kashmir who have driven to rebellion by this well-calculated and carefully planned aggression... The reference to plebiscite in Kashmir is merely put forward to mislead, as it ostensibly seems effective, but as a practical proposition, it remains on paper. If the Indian Government are allowed to act freely and unfettered, as they please by virtue of having already occupied Kashmir and landed their troops there, then their eldorado of plebiscite will prove a mirage'[48].

Lord Mountbatten held a meeting with Jinnah at Lahore in November 1947 to solve the various issues related with the Kashmir issue, but failed. Again on 8 December, a meeting of the Joint Defence Council (JDC) was held at Lahore in which Nehru and Mountbatten participated. But it did not produce any fruitful results. Even, Lord Mountbatten was convinced that negotiated settlement of the Kashmir issue was practically impossible.[49]

The main argument of Pakistan was that if self-determination was the governing principle for the partition of India, then the people of Kashmir should be allowed to exercise this right and refers to the Mountbatten's note on 'reference to the people' while, the accession of Kashmir. India contended that this assurance of 'reference to the people' was a unilateral offer to the people of Kashmir and had nothing to do with Pakistan. Besides, elections have been held frequently in Kashmir and people have participated and made their choice. In the words of a Pakistan scholar, 'if Pakistan accepts the tribal areas as having confined their loyalty to Pakistan, why the elections in Kashmir cannot be taken as a confirmation? If the reason is that no party with a programme other than continued accession to India came up, similar objection can be made against the tribal confirmation of loyalty.[50]

The issue became more complicated after the decision of the Nehru Government to refer the issue to the UN Security Council. Even before the formal accession of Kashmir to India, Nehru anticipated that Pakistan would attempt to seize Kashmir by force and was convinced that Maharaja Forces would not be in a position to stop invaders unless a popular resistance was organized. In a letter to Patel, then Home Minister of India, on 27 September 1947 he gave the following perceptive assessment of the situation prevailing in the valley. It is obvious to me from the reports I have received that the situation there (Kashmir) is dangerous and deteriorating one. The Muslim League workers are making preparations to enter Kashmir in considerable numbers. The approach of winter is going to cut-off Kashmir from the rest of the world. The only normal route then is via Jhelum valley. The Jammu route can hardly be used during winter and air-traffic is also suspended.

I understand that the Pakistan strategy is to infiltrate into Kashmir now and to take some big action as soon as Kashmir is more or less isolated because of the coming winter.

Whether this strategy succeeds or not, it depends upon the forces opposed to it I rather doubt if the Maharaja and the state forces can meet the situation by themselves without some popular help... obviously the only major group that can side with them is the National Conference under Sheikh Abdulah's leadership.

Indeed, it seems to me that there is no other course open to the Maharaja but thus: to release Sheikh Abdullah and the National Conference leaders, to make a friendly approach to them, seek their cooperation and make them feel that this is really meant and then to declare for accession to the Indian Union. Once the State accedes to India, it will become very difficult for Pakistan to invade it officially or unofficially without coming into conflict with Indian Union. If however there is delay to the accession, then Pakistan will go ahead without much fear of consequences, especially when the winter isolated Kashmir.[51]

Pakistan in order to put pressure on Maharaja stepped up the level of infiltration, causing a material change in the ground situation, Punjabis and other Pakistani nationals were sent to carry out irregular warfare against the Maharaja's forces. Though Pakistan Government always refuted the charges and disclaimed responsibility, the raiders received weapons transport and overall direction from Pakistani authorities. As a result of the stepped up invasion, the Maharaja's forces suffered significant reverses and on 15 October 1947 the Dewan of Kashmir sent a telegram to Attlee, appealing to him to advise Pakistani Government to deal fairly with Kashmir. Pakistan was thus able to mount clandestine military pressure against the Maharaja along a strip of border territory in Jammu province. This was an area where pockets of pro-Pakistani sentiments existed on account of cross border ethnic affinities. Pakistan was able to exploit the fact that large number of Poonch soldiers served in its army as a result of the decision to allot to her the Muslim units of the army of undivided India.[52]

The tactics followed in the border area of Jammu could not be replicated in other areas of the State where there was a little local support for Pakistan. Thus it was envisaged that the conquest of the valley of Kashmir would be affected through a massive tribal invasion along the main highway linking Rawalpindi to Srinagar via the towns of Dormel and Muzzafarabad. In the absence of any significant political support in the Kashmir valley, the 'raid' could not take the form of an outright invasion by the tribal irregulars. On 22 October 1947, Pakistan launched the invasion of valley. The India Government anticipated that Pakistan would try to seize Kashmir by force of arms. It therefore took a prompt decision to assist the State with military supplies. Patel wrote to the Defence Minister Baldev Singh on 7 October: 'I hope arrangements are being made to send immediately supplies of arms and ammunition to Kashmir. If necessary, we must arrange to send them by air. I think the question of military assistance in time of emergency must claim the attention of our Defence Council as soon as possible. There is no time to lose.'[53]

The decision that arms should be supplied to Kashmir on top priority was simply derailed by the Commander-in-Chief, General Lockhart, acting in collusion with Field Marshall Auchinleck; Lockhart took the position that no arms were available in Delhi. Army Headquarters asked about the availability of arms. The latter raised the question: could arms be supplied to states which had not yet acceded to either Dominion? In this connection, reference was made to a decision taken by the (JDC) that no arms should be available to Hyderabad without the Council approval. Though the decision was specific to Hyderabad, it furnished a pretext for stalling action on the Government's decision. Auchinleck and Lockhart knew that Pakistan would protest vigorously if military supplies were sent to the Maharaja and they were reluctant to get drawn to an inter-dominian controversy. Despite increasing urgent appeals from the Kashmir State authorities, no arms were made available by the Indian Army till 22 October when Pakistan launched the invasion in the Jhelum valley by tribal lashkers.[54]

However, tribal invasions precipitated matters and it was then conveniently asserted that Abdullah and his National Conference represented the majority in Kashmir and their opinion for India was a sufficient declaration of the popular will. Meanwhile efforts by the leadership to settle the issue continued. On 2 November 1947, the day after the Mountbatten-Jinnah meeting, Nehru made a public offer to hold a referendum under UN auspices. He announced in a radio broadcast: 'We on our part have no intention of using our troops in Kashmir when the danger of invasion has passed. We have declared that the fate of the people is ultimately to be decided by the people. We are prepared when peace and law and order have been established to have a referendum held under auspices like the UN.' Nehru move was welcomed by the British Government. Prime Minister Attle rushed to congratulate Nehru on his initiative. He called, 'I may say so it seems to me that you have made a noteable step towards the restoration of mutual confidence (with Pakistan) by the announcement made in your broadcast yesterday. The Pakistan reaction took Attlee by surprise. Liaquat Ali Khan rejected the Indian offer in the most violent terms in a cable to Attlee: 'It is full of most dangerous potentialities. What the Indian Government calls restoration of law and order is no more than an attempt to oppress, kill, terrorize and drive out the Muslim population of Jammu and Kashmir. The composition of the population is entirely changed, Nehru has even avoided the use of the word plebiscite and has spoken of referendum which might mean anything. After the Indian Government has established complete mastery over the territories of Jammu and Kashmir and the holding of a plebiscite or referendum will be purely a farce.'[55]

Liaquat spelled out the Pakistani proposals on the lines that Jinnah had indicated earlier to Mountbatten. These, he said, comprised the following:

1. To put an immediate stop to fighting, the two Governments should be authorized to issue a pro-proclamation forthwith giving 48 hours notice to the two opposing forces to stop fighting. Governor General of Pakistan has no control over the forces of the provisional Government of Kashmir or engaged in fighting, but he will warn them in the clearest terms that if they do not obey (call) to ceasefire immediately, the forces of the two Dominions will declare war on them.
2. Both forces of the Indian Dominion and the tribesmen to withdraw simultaneously and with

utmost expedition from Jammu and Kashmir state territory.

3. The two Governor Generals are to be given powers to restore peace, undertaking the administration of Jammu and Kashmir state and arrange for plebiscite without delay and under their joint control and supervision.[56]

Attlee commended these proposals as a promising starting point for discussion but rejected Liaquat's allegations against Nehru and sought to minimize the differences in the two approaches, 'I cannot believe that Nehru pledges have the sinister implications which you suggest', he informed Liaquat Ali Khan 'it seems to me therefore that both you and the Prime Minister of India have put forward proposals, which also differ in form, are broadly based on the same principles.'[57]

In reality the divergence between the two positions was formidable. Pakistan attempts to seize Kashmir by clandestine employment of irregulars had misfired, precipitating the state's accession to India. Pakistan tried to reverse the events by diplomatic means. Her proposals totally disregarded the fact of accession; they sought also to set aside the authority of both the Maharaja and the most popular political party by transferring control jointly to Jinnah and Mountbatten, India's stand was based on the fact that the state had legally acceded to India, with the support of largest and most popular political organization. She was prepared to accept referendum under UN auspices but only after the raiders had been expelled and order had been restored. The idea that Pakistan irregulars should be replaced by regular Pakistani army troops was legally and politically unacceptable to her. This was the chance that Mountbatten sought to avail to bridge through negotiations on margins of the (JDC) session in November and December 1947.[58]

Nehru was quite disturbed when he had learnt that his intentions were under scanner in Pakistan. He was sensitive to the need for allaying Pakistani misapprehension concerning India's intentions and preventing the outbreak of a war between the two new states; he shared his thinking in one of the periodic circular letters he wrote to the Chief Ministers of the Indian states.

He wrote, 'Recent events' in Kashmir and partly our action in Babriwad and Mangal has been a severe blow to the Pakistani Government. They have a terrible sense of frustration. Already, they were being overwhelmed by their problems. The vast number of Muslim refugees who have gone to Pakistan are a terrible burden on them and they cannot look after them. Because of all this, they are suffering from the delusion that the Government of India are conspiring to destroy Pakistan. That of course, is completely false. There is no conspiracy and there is no desire to destroy their state in anyway. Any such attempt would lead to grave injury to us. War is a dangerous thing and must be avoided. Only those who do not understand it or its consequence talk lightly of war. From the military point of view, there is little doubt that if there was war between India and Pakistan, Pakistan as a state would perish. But undoubtedly India would suffer very great injury and all our schemes of progress would have to be pushed aside for many years. Therefore, we must do our utmost to avoid war and that is our definite policy. Both statesmanship and expediency as well as humanity, requires this.[59]

The atmosphere of goodwill created in the sub-continent came under stress on the eve of the (JDC) meeting when in telegrams to Nehru and Attlee, Liaquat Ali Khan dismissed Sheikh Abdullah as a 'quisling' and once more accused the Indian Government of attempting to eliminate the entire Muslim population of Jammu and Kashmir. Smarting from these vicious attacks, Nehru had virtually decided to call-off the talks but was discarded from doing so by Mountbatten.

On 27 November 1947, the (JDC) meeting was held in New Delhi in a 'frosty atmosphere'. Nehru broached the question of Kashmir and it was left to Mountbatten to introduce the subject by recounting his efforts towards paving the way for a plebiscite following the state's accession to India. Nehru and Liaquat followed by giving an account of developments from their respective viewpoints. Mountbatten then proceeded to place before the JDC, the proposals based on the discussions. He made it clear that there was full agreement on the following points:

1. That a plebiscite should be held under an independent body like the UN,
2. That as soon as the situation had cleaned up, Indian troops would be withdrawn, except from small garrisons at vital strategic points to prevent further raids,
3. The full freedom of speech would be permitted,
4. That the refugees would be allowed to return to the state. Before these, the Pakistani Government had desired that Sheikh Abdullah should form a coalition with the opposition parties,
5. UN representatives should be sent for as early as possible to speed up the plebiscite process and to act as preliminary observes, and
6. Alternatively, an entirely new administration should be set-up in Kashmir which the people of Kashmir would accept as important.[60]

There were certain difficulties, like mainly on the question of residual Indian military force in the state and could the Pakistan Government appeal to the raiders, local rebels and the people in Pakistan who were assisting them only after they were in a position to give them an assurance that the object had been achieved. Mountbatten was struggling very hard to bridge the gap between Nehru and Liaquat by offering various alternatives on the situation prevailing in the State of Jammu and Kashmir.

Mountbatten requested Lord lsmay to draft a paper for discussion by taking the help of Mohammad Ali and V.P. Menon. These proposals were placed before the Council for discussion. They were the following:

1. Pakistan should use all the influence to persuade the so-called Azad Kashmir 'forces to cease fighting and the tribesmen and other invaders to withdraw from Kashmir territory as quickly as possible,

2. India should withdraw the bulk of the forces, leaving only small detachments of minimum strength to deal with disturbances,
3. The UN should be asked to send a Commission to hold a plebiscite and before it was held to recommend to the Governments of India and Pakistan steps which should be taken to ensure a free and fair plebiscite, and
4. Certain steps which were intended to take towards this objective such as release of political prisoners and return of refugees should be announced immediately.'[61]

In essence Lord Ismay proposals sought to reconcile the legal implications of Kashmir's accession to India with the requirements of Pakistan's expressed concern for a fair and impartial plebiscite. It implicitly acknowledged India's sovereign rights by permitting her to maintain a military presence in Kashmir after the withdrawal of the invaders and by recognizing the authority of the Kashmir administration. At the same time, it offered an assurance that the plebiscite would be free and fair by restricting the Indian army presence to a minimal level and by expanding the role of the UN by giving it an advisory role in the run up to plebiscite. It thus conceded Liaquat's demand for the induction of UN presence before the plebiscite but not his demand for reconstituting the state government.[62]

Mountbatten was very happy to note that by the course of discussion both Nehru and Liaquat had reserved their respective positions, neither having rejected the Ismay formula out-rightly. Mountbatten formed the impression that Liaquat Ali Khan was willing to compromise on total withdrawal of Indian troops and on a change of administration in Jammu and Kashmir. Nehru on his part had not rejected this implied linkage between the raider's withdrawal and an accord on conditions for a fair plebiscite. Nor had he dismissed the idea of a substantially expanded UN role. Mountbatten was hopeful that Ismay's Proposals would bring peace in the Kashmir valley. In fact Nehru got encouraged by the sincerity of Mountbatten and showed his desire to accept the Ismay proposals in a spirit of accommodation.[63]

Mountbatten took Liaquat Ali Khan into confidence and asked whether he could count on his support for the proposals. Liaquat reply was in affirmative and he readily agreed to cooperate. Having Liaquat approval in his kitty, Mountbatten sprung the proposal on Nehru when the meeting resumed and he requested both the parties to accept the Ismay proposals immediately so that peace could be restored in the State of Jammu and Kashmir. It was the only way to stop fighting, he argued, emphasizing that this must be the main objective. 'Liaquat gave Mountbatten his full support, stating that he would not mind in what manner the UN was approached, even if it should take the form of an accusation by India that Pakistan was assisting the raiders. Nehru remained adamantly opposed to the proposal, insisting that the first step was to drive out raiders. At one point he declared in an outburst that, in view of the Pakistan's position, the only solution was to clear Kashmir with a sword and that he would throw up his Prime ministership and lead the men of India against the invaders.'[64]

The meeting did not bear any fruit and Mountbatten was quite perturbed. It marked the end of Mountbatten's efforts of mediation between the two warring nations. Nehru in fact was more generous and offered significant concessions which were not reciprocated. The Indian Prime Minister had finally reached the end of his patience. Probably, Nehru was convinced that military solution was the only way out left. But Mountbatten had a different thinking. He was of the considered opinion that 'the only escape from war lay in an early reference to the UN.' In the initial stages Mountbatten was in favour of only the limited role, i.e. supremacy in nature of the UN. But when Pakistan did not agree on this, Mountbatten concluded that the UN should be called to find a way out of the impasse which he himself had failed to break.'[65]

When the hostilities in the Kashmir valley further flared up, Mountbatten wrote a lengthy letter to Nehru after the worsening of the whole situation. He expressed his concern over the proposal to send the army into Pakistani territory in order to strike of the bases or nerve centres from which the raiders were operating. He hinted at the international pressures, warning the Indian Prime Minister that the 'idea that a war between India and Pakistan could be confined to the sub-continent or finished off quickly in favour of India without further complication, is to my mind a fatal illusion' He urged the Prime Minister to broaden the terms of the reference to be made to the UN. 'Surely the main object should rather be to bring UN here at the earliest possible moment to get a team nominated to come out and deal with the business and help to stop the fighting, within a matter of days, he suggested.' Nehru sent a vigorous reply on the very next day, 'The invasion of Kashmir is not an accidental affair resulting from the fanaticism or exuberance of the tribesmen, he wrote', but a well-organized business with the backing of the state. We have in effect to deal with a state carrying "on an informal war but nevertheless a war, India had thus far followed a cautious defence policy which had presented Pakistan with an advantage." By carrying on operation in a weak defence way India could not produce an effective impression on the adversary. From a strictly legal and constitutional point of view, it is our right and duty to resist this invasion with all our forces.

From the point of view of international law, we can in self-defence take any military measures to resist it including the sending of our armies across Pakistan territory to attack their bases near the Kashmir border...Peace will come if we have the strength to resist invasion and make it clear that it will not pay. Nehru went on to say that the Government of India had accepted Mountbatten's suggestion too and would make a reference to the UN but it cannot ask the UN to arbitrate between raiders and the Dominion of India or to make a joint reference with Pakistan on mutually agreed lines. India as the aggrieved party would draw the attention of the UN to the invasion and to the fact that Pakistan was aiding and abetting it and she would ask the UN to call upon Pakistan to refrain from doing so. Meanwhile India must prepare for every eventuality we have taken enough risks already we do not care any more. We cannot even permit much longer the continuation of the use of bases in Pakistan to attack our troops and our territory in Kashmir. There is no question of small operations 'going on the Kashmir through the winter months, but of quick developments'. The Prime Minister concluded that the government should immediately proceed on the parallel lines of action.

1. Reference to the UN.
2. Complete military preparations to meet any contingency that may arise. If grave dangers threaten Kashmir or elsewhere on the West Punjab frontier, then we must not hesitate to march through the Pakistan territory towards the bases.[66]

On 22 December, Nehru in a letter to the Prime Minister of Pakistan had drawn his attention towards the aid which the raiders into Kashmir State were deriving from Pakistan. They had free transit through Pakistan territory and using it as a base for operating against Kashmir State. Their modern military equipment could only have been obtained from Pakistan sources, mortars artillery and Marh V mines were not normally the kind of armaments to which tribe-men possessed. Motor transport, which the raiders had used and the petrol required for it, could only be obtained from Pakistan. 'Food and other supplies are also secured from Pakistan; indeed we have reliable information that the raiders get their rations from military messes in Pakistan. According to our information, large number of these raiders are receiving military training in Pakistan, which could only be under officers of the Pakistani Army.' The forms of aid which the raiders were receiving constitute an act of aggression against India because they are being used against a state which has acceded to the Indian Dominion '... since protests have failed to bear fruit, the Government of India now formally ask the Government of Pakistan to deny to the raiders.

1. All access to and use of Pakistani territory for operations against Kashmir,
2. All military and other supplies, and
3. All other kinds of aid that might tend to prolong struggle.'

Nehru in clear terms warned the Pakistan Government that failing such response, they will be compelled to take such action, consistently with the provisions of the UN Charter, as they may consider necessary to protect their interests and to discharge their obligations to the Government and people of Kashmir.[67]

Liaquat Ali Khan replied back Nehru's letter on 30 December 1947 in which he had shown his disappointment regarding the referring of Kashmir issue to the UN. He strongly said that a reference of the UN therefore in my opinion must cover much larger ground and embrace all the fundamental differences between the two Dominions. They should see, it is neither Kashmir alone nor Junagadh and Manavadar, nor even the terrible tragedy of massacres of Muslim men, women and children in extensive area of the Indian 'Dominion, but a totality of these horrors and iniquities, indicating but one consistent, sinister pattern which should rightly form subject-matter of international investigations. There was a need to determine the root-cause which was vitiating the Indo-Pak relations and reinvented it, was much to be feared that fresh incidents will continue to threaten the peace not only between the two Dominions, but in a much wider field.'

He also made it clear that Pakistan Government had not accepted and could not accept the so-called accession of the Jammu and Kashmir State to India. As it was fraudulent and achieved by deliberately creating certain conditions, with the object of finding an excuse to stage the accession. It was based on violence because it furthered the plan of Kashmir Government to liquidate 'the Muslim population and could not be justified on any grounds whether moral or constitutional, geographical or economic, cultural or religious.' He refuted Nehru's charge of aid and assistance to the invaders.

On the contrary, the Government of India must answer the charge of conspiracy with the Maharaja of Kashmir repudiation of the very principles on which it had only one month before opposed Junagadh's accession to Pakistan. The plea that the accession was only temporary pending restoration of peaceful conditions is too flimsy to stand examination particularly in the light of recent negotiations in the course of which a perfectly fair and workable plan of withdrawal of opposing forces followed by a referendum under Government. He criticized the Indian Government's general attitude towards Pakistan ever since it becomes evident that partition was the only possible solution of the constitutional problems.

Liaquat, in the same tone, was critical of the Indian Government handling of the situation that formation after the emergence of the Dominions of India and Pakistan regarding the fate of the princely states. According to the Indian Independence Act, 1947, Indian states were further under no compulsion to join either of the two Dominions. Notwithstanding with this clear provision, the Government of India; by a combination of threats and cajolers, forced a number of states into acceding to the Indian Union.

The rulers of Junagadh and Manavadar were similarly threatened with dire consequences but they stood firm and exercised their right of joining Pakistan in preference to India. This was the signal for India to launch with full force her attack, using every possible weapon in order to force the states against their will, to change their affiliations. Protests were made to the Pakistan Government, pointing out that a state which had a Hindu-majority population could not accede to Pakistan and its accession to Pakistan was calculated to cause disruption in the integrity of India. Simultaneously with these protests, the Government of India had stationed Indian troops on the borders of Junagadh and encouraged the neighbouring Hindu states which had acceded to India, to do likewise. In clear violation of the Stand Still Agreement, the Junagadh state was subjected to an economic blockage involving stoppage of all vital supplies, communications, including railways and telegraph services, were operated in such a manner that it became impossible for the State or the Muslim population of Junagadh to communicate with the outside world. A strong press campaign, calculated to destroy the morale of the State administration and to create panic among the population was launched both inside and outside the state. In the interests of peace between the two Dominions, Pakistan refrained from sending a single soldier to Junagadh. The occupation by force of Junagadh, which was a Pakistan territory, was a clear act of aggression against Pakistan. The military action by which the occupation of Junagadh and Manavadar and other states was achieved, was an attempt of destroying the integrity and the very existence of Pakistan.

Liaquat wanted to know from Nehru, 'Now that you propose to take the case of Kashmir to the UN, you would be good enough to let us know why in spite of our clear request you have not withdrawn from the territories of Junagadh, Manavader and Hyderabad'.

Liaquat Ali in his communication to Nehru also raised the other issues which were awaiting solution. The Indian Government refusal to implement the financial agreement of all outstanding cases which had been referred to the Arbitral Tribunal and was deliberately withholding the payment of rupees fifty crore of cash balance which was the legal due of the Pakistan Government according to that agreement, in his opinion, that was the deliberate move of the Government of India to strangle Pakistan financially and economically which characterized the partition proceedings. In the case of the military stores, there was a similar refusal to implement the agreement. The Supreme Commander, who was appointed as a neutral authority under the (JDC) 'to carry into effect the partition of the armed forces and military stores was forced, despite the protestations of the Pakistan Government, to leave, by the Indian government long before he could complete his task. The (JDC) pledged the word of the India cabinet that Pakistan would receive her due share of military stores. This pledge like other similar pledges of the Government of India had not been honoured.

To sum up, Pakistan had levelled the following counter-charges against India:

1. That India at the time of partition had never wholeheartedly accepted the partition scheme but her leaders paid lip services to it merely in order to get the British troops out of the country,
2. That India was out to destroy the State of Pakistan which her leaders persistently continue to regard as part of India itself,

3. That there had been systematic sabotage against the implementation of partition plan, the stoppage of such essential requirements as coal and rail transport, the deliberate withholding of Pakistan's share of funds and arms and equipments. The massacre of Muslim population are all designed towards one aim namely the destruction of Pakistan, and
4. India forcibly occupied Junagadh, Manavadar and other states in Kathiawar which had acceded to Pakistan.[68]

In all the inundation of contradictory reports, mutual accusations and denials, it was not possible to ascertain true situation. It would appear that the Pakistani central authorities did not initiate the tribal invasions. On the other hand, it also appeared that the Prime Minister of NWFP himself a Kashmiri and his officers were at the back of the tribesmen and providing them overall support. Certainly, all Pakistanis viewed with open sympathies the struggle of the Kashmiri Muslims against the Maharaja and were ready to give them all political and moral support. When, however the Indian Army was sent to intervene and stop the tribesmen, an unknown number of Pakistani nationals joined the Azad forces for which the Pakistani Government was responsible. All the same when the Indian forces succeeded not only in stopping the tribesmen at the gates of Srinagar but began to push them back towards borders of Pakistan, the Pakistani Government became thoroughly concerned about the outcome of the struggle and helped them with military equipments, arms and ammunitions. Pakistan became alarmed that the intervention of the Indian army was not to be limited to Kashmir. She suspected that this was the beginning of an Indian onslaught against Pakistan herself. And it was this fear which perhaps was largely responsible for the extent of Pakistan's participation in the struggle, a fear which Liaquat Ali Khan expressed in a telegram which he addressed to Nehru: 'It is a matter for deep regret that even today, responsible members of the Government of India, including yourself, openly declare the intention or hope of bringing

Pakistan back into Indian Union, well knowing that this could be done only through conquest of arms... In other words, Pakistan's existence was never wholeheartedly accepted by India. Jawaharlal Nehru not only emphatically rejected Liaquat accusations but also hurled the counter-accusations that Pakistan's complicity in the Kashmir fighting was an act of aggression'.

Once again the real issue had broken through; it was once again the old issue of partition.[69]

In any case, as Jagmohan, a former Governor of Kashmir wrote, "If opinion of Kashmir's accession to India was being kept open, there was nothing wrong in it. India has never accepted the 'Two Nation's Theory'. It was justified in believing that if both the Maharaja and Sheikh Abdullah, who at that time had the support of the valley people, had expressed desire to join the union; it would have demonstrated the hollowness of the 'Two Nation's Theory'. The issue was largely one of ideology and the Indian perspective and not in territorial extension. The tragedy of India lay not in the conceptual framework, but in being wayward and impractical in executing.'[70]

The Indian Government lodged a formal complaint with the UN Security Council on 1 January 1948. 'Taking the case to the UN', Jagmohan, felt that was yet another mistake. 'The case got enmeshed in the international power-politics. At every stage, India faced a rough weather' and Kashmir became almost a permanent item on the agenda of the UN.[71]

Under Article 35 of the UN Charter, any member may bring any situation whose continuance is likely to endanger the maintenance of international peace and security to the attention of the Security Council. 'Such a situation existed between India and Pakistan owing to the aid which invaders, consisting of nationals of Pakistan and tribesmen, from the territory immediately adjoining Pakistan on the north-west, are drawing from Pakistan for operations against Jammu and Kashmir State which has acceded to the Dominion of India and is a part of India. The Government of India requested the Security Council to call upon Pakistan to put an end to the act of aggression against India. If Pakistan did not do so, the Government of India could be compelled, in self-defence, to enter in Pakistan territory, in extreme urgency and calls for immediate action by the Security Council for avoiding a breach of international peace.'

'The grave threat to the life and property of innocent people in the Kashmir valley and to the security of the State of Jammu and Kashmir that had developed as a result of the invasion of the valley demanded immediate decision by the Government of India... It was imperative on account of the emergency that the responsibility for the defence of the Jammu and Kashmir State should be 'taken over by a Government capable of discharging it'. But in order to avoid any possible suggestion that India had utilized the state's immediate peril for her own political advantage, the Government of India made it clear that once the soil of the state had been cleared of the invaders and normal conditions restored, its people would be free to decide their future by the recognized democratic method of a plebiscite or referendum, which in order to ensure complete impartiality might be held under international auspices.'

The Government of India filled their duty to respond to the appeal for armed assistance because:

1. They could not allow a neighbouring and friendly state to be compelled by force by others to determine its internal affairs or its external relations.
2. The accession of the Jammu and Kashmir State to the Dominion of India made India responsible for the defence of the State.

India also raised a number of points before the world body, the facts of Pakistan's active involvement in the tribal invasion. The facts mentioned below point indisputability to the solid conclusion:

(a) That the invaders are allowed transit across Pakistani territory.
(b) That they are allowed to use Pakistan territory as a basis of operations.
(c) That they include Pakistani nationals.

(d) That they draw much of their military equipments, transportation (including petrol) from Pakistan.

(e) Those Pakistan officers are trainning, guiding and otherwise actively helping them.

It should be clear from the foregoing recital that Government of Pakistan was unwilling to stop the assistance in material and men which the invaders were getting from Pakistan's territory and from Pakistanis, including Pakistan Government personnel both military and civil. 'This attitude is not only un-neutral but continues active aggression against India of which the State of Jammu and Kashmir is a part.'

The complaint in clear words stated that the Indian Government 'have exerted persuasion and exercised patience to bring about a change in the attitude of Pakistan. The invaders are still on the soil of Jammu and Kashmir and the inhabitants of the state are exposed to all atrocities of which a barbarous foe is capable... The Government of India has no option, therefore, but to take more effective military action in order to rid the Jammu and Kashmir State of the invaders.'

It was strongly felt that in order that the objective of expelling the invader from Indian Territory and preventing him from launching fresh attacks should be quickly achieved, Indian troops would have to enter Pakistan territory and the invaders be denied the use of bases and cut-off from his sources of supplies and reinforcements in Pakistan. Since the aid which the invaders are getting from Pakistan is an act of aggression against India, the Government of India is entitled under international law, to send their armed forces across Pakistani territory for dealing effectively with the invaders. However, as such action might involve armed conflict with Pakistan, the Government of India ever anxious to proceed according to the principles and aims of the Charter of the UN, desire to report the situation to the Security Council under Article 35 of the Charter. They feel justified in requesting the Security Council to ask the Government of Pakistan:

1. To prevent Pakistan Government personnel,

military and civil from participating or assisting in the invasion of the state of Jammu and Kashmir.

2. To call upon other Pakistani nationals to desist from taking any part in the fighting in the Jammu and Kashmir State.
3. To deny to the invaders:
   A. access to the use of its territory for operations against Kashmir;
   B. military and other supplies; and
   C. all kinds of aid that might tend to prolong the present struggle.

The Government of India approached the Security Council inspired by the sincere hope that, through the prompt action of the Council, peace may be preserved.[72]

Jawaharlal Nehru in a broadcast over All India Radio on 2 January 1948 to the people of India stated at length the complaint made by India to the UN Security Council. He also informed that the reference to the Security Council was thus limited to the issues related with the Jammu and Kashmir State. He also made it clear that the accusations and allegations levelled against the Government of Pakistan has been brought to cover up the Kashmir 'issue in a forest of other matters which have nothing to do with it.'[73]

The Government of Pakistan gives a detailed reply to the Indian complaint and presented its own complaint to the Security Council. It was a lengthy paper consisting of three documents. In document one, replying to India's complaint, Pakistan denied giving aid to tribesmen and thereby committing an act of aggression. On the contrary, the Pakistan government continued to do all in their power to discourage the tribal movement by means short of war. It admitted that 'a certain number of independent tribesmen and persons from Pakistan are helping the Azad Kashmir Government in their struggle for liberty, as volunteers.' In the document II, the Government of Pakistan raised numerous counter-complaints of its own.

1. It charged India with widespread genocide against the Muslim population, pursued by responsible

officials of the princely states and the Union of India in the period proceeding and following the partition.

2. It accused India of having forced by way of arms and occupation of Junagadh, a predominately Hindu state with a Muslim ruler, into accession to India, though the ruler had acceded to Pakistan. 'This action on the part of the Government of India amounted to a direct attack upon and aggression against Pakistan. Thus, Pakistan was entitled to repel by force. It maintained the Pakistan document is an obvious attempt to make the Indian accusations boomerang.
3. It gave the genesis of the Kashmir case and denied the validity of Kashmir accession to India. It protested against Indian forces being sent to Kashmir, 'without consultation with or even by notice to the Government of Pakistan with which the state had concluded Stand Still Agreement.' As to the Indian promise about a plebiscite in Kashmir, Pakistan expressed through this document the 'strong conviction that a plebiscite would be a farce if it was to be conducted in the presence of the Indian armed forces and proper conditions were not established to guarantee to the people of Kashmir complete freedom to express their will'.
4. It protested that India had failed to fulfil various agreements reached in connection with the partition, such as division of military stores, cash balances and other matters.

After summing up its complaints, the Government of Pakistan in this section of its replies requested the Security Council:

1. To call upon the Government of India to desist from acts of aggression against Pakistan and implement all agreements she had signed with Pakistan.

2. To appoint a Commission charged with the task of investigating all the accusations against India, arranging, cessation of hostilities in Kashmir, enforcing the withdrawal of all outsiders whether they came from India and Pakistan, facilitating the return and rehabilitation of Kashmir in refugees, establishing an impartial administration in Kashmir and finally conducting an impartial plebiscite.

In document III, Pakistan presented before the Security Council the detailed information on the preceding matters, stressing that 'even the Kashmir episode in all aspects is but one link in the chain of events which has been unfolding itself ever since it became obvious that there was no solution of Hindu-Muslim problem except the partition of India,' with which the Pakistan suspected, India had never recognised and as a consequence, harboured hostile intentions towards Pakistan. As to Kashmir, the document concluded 'the Pakistan Government has not accepted the accession of Jammu and Kashmir State with India. In their view, the accession is based on violence and fraud.'[74]

As both parties had presented their case to the Security Council, the differences were sharp between the two on the nature of the conflict but also on the way of solving it. The Indian Government strongly emphasized that the tribal invasion and Pakistan's participation in it, was the real cause. India therefore limited her presentation and defence of the case before the Security Council in these two acts. To Pakistan, however, the hostilities in Kashmir were only the part of the whole picture of unhappy Indo-Pakistani relations and her presentations were therefore an exhaustive account of all problems dividing the two countries.

After the presentation of the complaint by the Indian delegate before the Security Council, the then Minister for External Affairs Sir Zafarullah Khan, the Pakistani delegate presented his country's view point. In his lengthy speech which lasted for more than five hours, he went into the details of the 'story of Kashmir'. He 'linked it with the generally unsettled situation of the sub-continent, with the communal strife, the political struggle of Kashmiri freedom. He agreed with the Indian delegate with one aspect of the issue: 'That the situation is grave and urgently needed to be dealt.'

The Pakistan case was summed up by Sir Zafarullah Khan when he concluded what is to be done? All that we want to ensure is this 'everyone who has gone into Kashmir, should go out. Such bands, as the Rashtrya Sewak Sangh volunteers, other people who have gone in from the Muslim side and men from Pakistan, Muslims who are Indian nationals and who were refugees in Pakistan, everybody. They must get out including Indian troops.

Therefore by whatever means may be necessary, the condition to be brought about is this whether by joint administration under the two Governor Generals, by joint occupation of predominately non-Muslim areas in Kashmir, by Indian troops, by joint occupation in each place, by inviting the Commonwealth forces, non-Indian forces altogether, or whether through the UN, Kashmir must be cleared. Fighting must stop. Kashmir must be cleared of everybody. Normal administration must be restored. There should be no kind of pressure either from the Muslim Conference being in power and holding the reins of the administration. No kind of pressure should be brought upon the people. The people then should be invited to express the way in 'which they want to go and whatever they decide, they should be welcome to do it.'[75]

In its 29th meeting, Security Council on 17 January 1948 adopted a Resolution. It said that, 'realizing the urgency of the situation, taking note of the telegram addressed on 6 January 1948 by its President to each of the parties and of their replies thereof and in which they affirmed their intention to conform the Charter, calls upon both the Government of India and the Government of Pakistan to take immediately all measures within their power (including public appeals to their people) calculated to improve the situation and to refrain from making any statements and from doing or causing to be done or permitted any acts which might aggravate the situation, and further requests that each of those Governments to inform the Council immediately of any material change in the situation which occurs to appear to either of them, to be about to occur while the matter is under consideration, by the Council and consult with the Council thereon.[76]

India failed to present her case by not clearly stating that Pakistan had committed an act of aggression on India by allowing and helping the raiders to invade Kashmir and Pakistan was irrevocably hostile towards India, the diplomats of Pakistan were successful in convincing members of the Security Council that the Kashmir dispute was the direct outcome of and related to the partition of the Indian sub-continent on the basis of the 'Two Nation's Theory. Zafarullah Khan's handling of the case was clever and skillful. Though his attacks were too dignified, they put the Indian delegation on defensive. He was successful in winning over the members of the Security Council by presenting a gloomy picture of the mass killings in and around Delhi and in the Punjab, Alwar, Bharatpur, Patiala, Nabha, Jind and Kapurthala. In contradiction to India's legalistic approach, Khan brought in a 'human approach'. He said, 'the issues involved are not merely legal and constitutional or even political. There is a very large human background which it will be very necessary for the Security Council to appreciate before the members bring their minds to bear upon the concrete questions that need to be resolved and decided.'[77]

The Security Council on 20 January 1946 adopted a resolution keeping in mind the urgency of the situation. The Security Council, considering that it may investigate any dispute or any situation which might by its continuance, endanger the maintenance of international peace and security that, in the existing state of affairs between India and Pakistan, such as investigation is matter for urgency.

UN COMMISSION FOR INDIA AND PAKISTAN

It decided to constitute a three member Commission composed of the UN members, one to be selected by India and Pakistan each and the third to be designated by two. The Commission was to proceed on the spot as quickly as possible and was to act under the direct authority of the

Security Council in accordance with the directions it might receive from it. The Commission was invested with actual functions as mentioned below:

1. To investigate the facts pursuant to Article 34 of the Charter.
2. To exercise without interpreting the work of the Security Council any mediatory influence likely to smooth away difficulties to carry out the directions given to it by the Security Council and report how far the advice and directions have been considered. Speaking on the Resolution Noel Baker said: 'It is a first step of great value. I feel sure that both sides had to make concessions on some points to each other. That is right practice in an international authority. It is the 'way in which the litigants in a dispute uphold their points of view to arrive at an honourable result.'[78]
3. India wanted that the Commission must restrict its activities to the cessation of hostilities and should work for the holding of plebiscite by the Sheikh Abdullah Government. It was critical of inclusion of other issues in the purview of the Commission because Pakistan wanted to delay 'the consideration of one problem which might intensify and prolong Indo-Pakistan conflict by raising issues which were either already settled or about to be settled or which did not pose any threat to peace and security'. Secondly, widening the scope of UN investigation might mean expanding the possibilities of international interference.[79] Thirdly, it was an admission of defeat by both India and Pakistan.

The Resolution which the Security Council adopted on 21 April 1948 was considered to be very meaningful. Almost for four months, the Security Council heard the representatives of India in support of the complaint and the reply and counter-complaints of the representative of Pakistan.[80]

The Resolution clearly said that the Security Council was interested in the early restoration of peace and order in Jammu and Kashmir. It was required that India and Pakistan should do their utmost to bring about the cessation of all types of hostilities. It noted with satisfaction that both India and Pakistan had agreed to hold plebiscite in free and impartial manner. It also suggested that the membership of the Commission established by the Resolution of 20 January 1948, should be increased to five and instructed the Commission to proceed to the Indian sub-continent and there place its good offices and mediation at disposals of both the Governments, with a view to facilitating the taking of the necessary measures, both with respect to the resolution of peace and order and to the holding of a plebiscite by the two Governments, working in cooperation with one another and with the Commission and further instructed the Commission to keep the Council informed of the action taken under the Resolution.

It recommended to the two Governments a number of measures to be taken which the Council felt were appropriate to bring about the cessation of hostilities and to create proper conditions for a free and fair plebiscite.

1. 'Restoration of peace and order: The Government of Pakistan should undertake to use its best endeavours.
   (a) To secure the withdrawal from the State of Jammu and Kashmir of tribesmen, Pakistan nationals not normally resident there and who have entered the State for the purpose of fighting and to prevent any intrusion into the State of such elements and any furnishing of material aid to those fighting in the State.
   (b) To make known to all concerned that the measures indicated to this and the following paragraph provide full freedom to all subjects of the State regardless of creed, caste or party to express their views and to vote on the question of accession of the State and that therefore they should cooperate in the maintenance of peace and order.'

2. The Government of India should:
   (a) 'When it is established to the satisfaction of the Commission set-up in accordance with the Council's Resolution on 20 January that the tribesmen are withdrawing and that the arrangements for the cessation of the fighting have become effective and put into operation in consultation with the Commission a plan for withdrawing them progressively to the minimum strength required for the support or the civil power in the maintenance of law and order.
   (b) Make known that the withdrawal is taking place in stages and announces the completion of each stage.
   (c) When the Indian forces shall have been reduced to the minimum strength mentioned in (a) above, arrange in consulatation with the Commission a plan for the stationing of the remaining forces to be carried out in accordance with the following principles:
      (i) That the presence of troops should not afford any intimidation or appearance or intimidation to the inhabitants of the State.
      (ii) That as small a number as possible should be retained in forward areas.
      (iii) That any reserve of troops which may be included in the total strength should be located within their present base area.
3. The Government of India should agree that until such time as the Plebiscite Administrator (PA) finds it necessary to exercise the power of direction and supervision over the State forces and police.
4. After the plan referred to in paragraph 2(a) has been put into operation, personnel recruited locally in each district should so far as possible be utilized for the re-establishment and maintenance of law and order with due regard to protection of minorities.'

The Resolution also gave a comprehensive plan for the holding of plebiscite in the valley and gave detailed instructions to the Government of India. It suggested that Indian Government with the cooperation of the State Government should seek the help of the major political groups for the holding of plebiscite. It asked the Indian Government to establish a (PA) to hold the plebiscite as soon as possible on the question of the accession of the State to India or Pakistan. It also desired that the Indian Government should agree that nominee of the Secretary General of the UN would be appointed to be the (PA). The (PA) should be allowed to work independently and according to his wishes in order to establish a plebiscite administration. The Indian and the state governments should... declare and make known that all subjects of the State of Jammu and Kashmir, regardless of creed, caste or party, will be safe and free in expressing their views and in voting on the question of the accession of the State and there will be freedom of press, speech and assembly and freedom of travel in the State, including freedom of lawful entry and exit.[81]

Prior to the passing of this important Resolution, a debate was going on in the political as well as in the diplomatic circles in and outside the UN, whether the accession of the State of Jammu and Kashmir was provisional or final. Earlier, the President of the Security Council unilaterally changed the title of the issue from Jammu and Kashmir question to 'India-Pakistan question'. The Indian representative lodged his protest with the Security Council but ultimately accepted the change. Interestingly, the Soviet and British representatives supported the Indian delegation plea but the US attitude was different. Its representative did not see any difference whether the title 'India-Pakistan question' was used or whether the title 'Jammu and Kashmir question' be referred.

It seemed clearly that the UN Security Council was not much impressed with the Indian delegation presentation of their case. The change of the title resulted in the enlargement of the scope of the Kashmir issue. A renowned scholar Michael Breacher was of the opinion that, 'India conceded not only one of the cardinal theses of Pakistan's case but also provided the Pakistan's Foreign Minister with an opening wedge for the exploitation of his approach to the dispute.' It was considered to be a victory for Pakistan as Zafarullah Khan was successful not only in enlarging the scope of the Kashmir issue but also in diverting the attention of the Security Council from the Pakistani backed tribal invasion. Furthermore, Pakistan achieved what it cherished, the status of equality.[82]

The discussions at the Security Council in the initial stages were clearly going in favour of Pakistan. No doubt, 'the areas of disagreement were wide and since the reference of the Kashmir dispute to the UN, the gap between India and Pakistan on the Kashmir issue had widened considerably and it seemed, there was no change visible. The Security Council President on 28 January 1948 after lengthy discussions with the Indian and Pakistani representatives held that it was desirable at that moment to concentrate on the idea of plebiscite. He categorically stated that as the holding of plebiscite was agreed upon by both India and Pakistan and it was no longer matter of dispute. But Indian representative Gopalaswami Ayyangar vigorously opposed the holding of plebiscite first as it meant sidetracking the issue of the hostilities in the valley and restoration of law and order. He said, 'It would be putting the cart before the horse if the Security Council omitted that point at the very beginning but proceeded instead to deal with the question of a plebiscite, which if it is in fact a matter for discussion and decision by this body, should have come at the very end.'[83]

Pakistan immediately reacted positively and accepted the proposal of holding plebiscite immediately and Zafarullah Khan stated that Pakistan was really not to poke its nose into the matter concerning the legality of the Kashmir accession to India and various other issues. Plebiscite was to be held under the supervision of the Security Council. On the other hand, Indian representative while rejecting Zafarullah contention emphasized that the cessation of hostilities was the first requirement. He maintained that even if the accession was illegal, a demand and assumption of Pakistan which was not going to be conceded. Noel Baker's sympathies were with the Pakistan when he not only supported Pakistan viewpoint and said that: 'Of course, this would not exclude anything else which the representative of India may think relevant to the points which came up. We should not thereby put off the question of stopping the fighting. Perhaps we might be accelerating it because the plebiscite is part of that process. If we can create confidence in the plebiscite then perhaps all that the Indian representative desires may quietly follow.'[84]

The Indian Government was perturbed about the developments in the Security Council. India felt that Pakistan was not sincere and was adopting the delaying tactics.

The Hindu pointed out that, 'the Pakistan Government apparently thinks it necessary that the Commission should not arrive at these conclusions too easily or quickly as that might lead to a directive from the Security Council to the effect that Pakistan should immediately fortify through its territory to the Frontier raiders, stop giving supplies and other help to the invaders already on the soil of Kashmir and further actively aid to ejecting those'[85].

End of the hostilities was a genuine demand of the Indian Government but no one in the Security Council was paying any attention to it. Indian delegate felt that the Security Council resolutions did not raise the real problem; rather there was a vague reference to the core issue, i.e. the cessation of hostilities. He said:

> 'We put the issue (cessation of hostilities) in the forefront of our proposals for a settlement. What we tried to do has apparently been brushed aside. We attempted to propose something concrete, something which a Council of this composition and influence could issue as a directive to the parties concerned in order to bring about the stoppage of the fighting. That has been passed over.'[86]

Ayyangar was fed up with the various interpretations of the Kashmir issue. In order to correct the various versions, he said that, 'the Instrument of Accession is a document complete in itself. It does not contain any conditions. It does not state that the accession is provisional. The commitment which the Government of India made for themselves on the question of ascertaining the wishes of the people was contained in a letter accompanying the accepted Instrument of Accession. The Government of India is certainly bound by its commitment, but it would be wrong to call the accession itself a provisional.'[87]

India was very critical of 20 April Resolution and rejected it on the grounds that nothing had been clearly laid down in the Resolution regarding the territory to be evacuated by the tribesmen, that a coalition Government was not possible, that it was essential for India to keep troops sufficient not only to maintain law and order but also for defence against external aggression but that it was highly undesirable that the (PA) should receive advice from Pakistan in matters pertaining to plebiscite. It also opposed the provision regarding the appointment of special magistrates.[88]

Pakistan reaction was equally sharp and very critical. Zafarullah khan opined that the arguments and suggestions given by the members of the Security Council in the past were no where in the Resolution. He said that there was no logic in the retaining of the Indian forces for the maintenance of the law and order. He said that, 'the Security Council had for once let itself slip into a position of fairness and impartiality between the two contending parties which might help to restore to the UN, a fraction of the prestige that it was so rapidly losing in the eyes of the world. They therefore beat a hasty retreat from a position so unfamiliar and embarrassing and fraught with the possibility of such undesired consequences'[89].

The Economist of London, however, regarded the Resolution as a sound proposal in the direction of restoring peace in the State of Jammu and Kashmir. It considered it as a serious and sincere attempt to provide for a free democratic decision in Kashmir. But it had its own reservations concerning the holding of plebiscite in the valley. It said, 'a partition with pre-arranged and orderly transfers of population based on the lessons of the Punjab may still be the better way of cleaning up the Kashmir tangle and it is yet possible India and Pakistan will be able to agree on a boundary before the heat of plebiscite campaigning is turned on curiously enough, the political struggle would be likely to cause greater tension than the present military operations which have dwindled away into desultory skirmishing.'[90]

The Resolution was considered to be one-sided, as it contained elaborate provisions to safeguard the interests of Pakistan and Pakistan's backed raiders. India could not agree to the proposal to withdraw its army. There would have been serious repercussions for India. No guarantee or assurance was provided in the Resolution that the tribesmen won't return or re-enter Kashmir. It was naive on the part of the Western powers to expect India to let her be in the situation which existed in October 1947 and which forced her to airlift her troops to defend the State of Jammu and Kashmir. The provisions regarding the composition of the Government of Kashmir, i.e. huddling of two warring elements in one Government was tantamount to giving a place of responsibility to unlawful intruders. Again, a provision regarding drafting of Pakistani troops was designed to safeguard the position gained by the aggressor on Kashmir soil.[91]

The UN Commission, constituted under Security Council Resolution of 21 April 1948, arrived in Karachi on 7 July 1948. Soon after Pakistan Foreign Minister informed the Commission, 'that the Pakistan army at the time had three brigades of regular troops in Kashmir and that troops had been sent into the state during the first half of May 1948.' Joseph Korbel had analyzed the impact of this disclosure on the Commission. He said that the Commission preferred not to express its opinion openly about the most important element in the picture but to one another the members admitted that the presence of the Pakistani troops in Kashmir made of the situation something far graver and far more disturbing than what it had appeared to be to the members of the Security Council.[92] India could derive no satisfaction from the fact that the UN Commission had after eight months discovered the truth of India's allegations, for by now Pakistan had entrenched itself in Kashmir in flagrant violation of international law and morality. The predicament in which the Commission found itself was described by Korbel, 'it explained to the Pakistanis, the movement of these troops into foreign territory without the *invitation* of that territory'.

Government was in violation of international law, it had seriously aggravated the problem and had given India certain rights to explain. These complaints, it then further explained, must be reflected in any Commission's findings and moreover, the Commission would necessarily, on the same ground, have to give some expressions to the complaint. The Commission prepared a Resolution and adopted it on 13 August 1948, and it was carried unanimously.[93]

The Pakistan leadership and the people were under intense fear that the approach of the Indian army to the Pakistani border would spell the end of their independence. The Pakistani army intelligence service was in possession of reports indicating that the Indian army had a plan to finish the 'Kashmir campaign' by launching a general offensive. The plan was to reach strategic places in the Northwest and Southwest areas of the state very close to the Pakistani boundaries. Had the plan been implemented, it would have meant disaster for Pakistan. First the Indian Government have presented before the whole world the possession as an accomplished fact. Second, it would have inundated Pakistan with an additional several thousands of refugees who would have further crippled her economy. Thirdly, it would have placed the Indian army on the long Pakistan border and within thirty miles of the strategic railway line leading from Peshawar through West Punjab to Lahore. Pakistan would then have been at the mercy of India, which as people in Karachi were convinced, desired nothing less than to remove Pakistan from the map. Fourth, to break Pakistan from within, the Indian push towards the north would easily allow the Indian army to reach the boundaries of the Pakistani states, Chitral and Swat and further establish a physical link with the leaders of the anti-Pakistani movement for independence Pathanistan. Fifth, the occupation of the lower waters of three rivers flowing to Pakistan would have placed India in a position to strangle Pakistan commercially.

The latter economic threat was highly important in the minds of the people of Pakistan. The valets of six rivers, the Indus, Jhelum, Chenab, Ravi, Beas and Sutlej with their elaborate system of irrigation canals had been indispensable to the agriculture of the sub-continent. The partition brought the river Beas under the complete control of India. The Ravi and Sutlej flow through both India and Pakistan, but their headwaters are in India. The Indus begins in Tibet and flows through Kashmir. The Jhelum and Chenab headwaters are in Kashmir, a land of 35 million acres had been irrigated by 16 canals before the partition. Now the boundary line cut through both rivers and canals, but their waters would still irrigate 19 million acres of land in Pakistan. The occupation of these rivers and their dams by the Indian army and the eventual diversion of their waters through canals would have meant Pakistan's quick economic death.

The Government rejected the accusation of having ever planned such a project, pointing first to the physical impossibility of diverting these waters and to the financial burden of such an idea and second, to the enormous quantity of these waters, which are more than sufficient to satisfy the needs of the two countries.[94]

RESOLUTIONS AND MEDIATORY EFFORTS OF THE COMMISSION

Another important Resolution was adopted on 13 August 1948 which represented a significant landmark in the history of the Kashmir issue. The Commission submitted simultaneously to the Government of both the countries, after taking into consideration the views expressed by the representatives of India and Pakistan regarding the situation in Jammu and Kashmir and reached on the following conclusions.

Part one stated that both the countries would issue separately and simultaneously a ceasefire order to apply to all forces under their control in the State of Jammu and Kashmir. The High Commands of India and Pakistan forces had agreed to refrain from taking any measures that might augment the military potential of the forces under their control in the State of Jammu and Kashmir (forces under their control were to include all forces organized and unorganized fighting or participating in hostilities on their respective sides). Both Governments were asked to appeal to their respective peoples to assist in creating and maintaining an atmosphere favourable to the further negotiations.

Part II of the Resolution was regarding the Truce Agreement. It said that simultaneously with the acceptance of the proposal for the immediate cessation of hostilities as outlined in part I, both the Governments accepted the following principles as a basis for the formulation of Truce Agreement.

> "As the presence of troops of Pakistan in the territory of the State of Jammu and Kashmir constitutes a material change in the situation since it was represented by the Government of Pakistan before the Security Council, the Government of Pakistan agrees to withdraw its troops from the state.
>
> The Government of Pakistan will use its best endeavour to secure the withdrawal of troops from the State of Jammu and Kashmir or tribesmen and Pakistani nationals not normally residing there and who have entered the state for the purpose of fighting.
>
> Pending final solutions, the territory evacuated by the Pakistani troops will be administered by the local authorities under the surveillance of the Commission."

In the part B of the Truce Agreement, the Resolution made it clear that "when the Commission shall have notified the Government of India that the tribesmen from Pakistan nationals referred to in part A(i)(ii) hereof have withdrawn, thereby terminating the situation which was represented by the Government of India to the Security Council as having occasioned the presence of Indian forces in the State of Jammu and Kashmir and further, that the Pakistani forces are being withdrawn from the State of Jammu and Kashmir, the Government of India agree to begin to withdraw the bulk of these forces. Furthermore, pending the acceptance of the conditions for a final settlement of the situation in the State, the Indian Government was allowed to maintain, without the lines existing at the moment of ceasefire, the minimum strength of its forces which in agreement with the Commission were considered necessary to help the local authorities in the maintenance of law and order.

According to part III both the Governments were asked

to reaffirm their agreement that the future of Kashmir would be determined in accordance with the will of the people.[95]

On 20 August 1948, the Indian Prime Minister Nehru wrote a letter to the Chairman of the Commission in reply to the Commission's Resolution of 13 August 1948 when it visited Delhi, Prime Minister Nehru put to its member scores of questions as: 'will the Indian forces be permitted to occupy strategic points? Will they accept the ceasefire and give certain legality to the presence of Pakistani troops in Kashmir? Did the wording of the Resolution imply any legal change in the status of the Kashmir Government? Did the term 'law and order' imply sincerely external aggression? And the most important cardinal question. May the Government of India suggest change in these proposals? The answer to the last question was firm 'no.'[96]

Nehru in his letter also raised a number of more questions particularly regarding the paragraph A-3 of part III of the Resolution. He was of the view that these provisions should not be interpreted or applied in practice so as: (a) 'to bring 'into question the Sovereignty to Jammu and Kashmir Government over the portion of their territory evacuated by the Pakistani troops, (b) to offer any recognition of the so-called 'Azad Kashmir' Government, or to enable this territory to be consolidated in any way during the period of truce to the disadvantage of the state.'

From the Indian point of view, the effective insurance of the security of the State against external aggression, from which Kashmir had suffered so much during the last ten months, was of the most vital significance and no less important than the observance of internal law and order and that therefore, the withdrawal of Indian troops and the strength of the Indian armed forces maintained in Kashmir should be sufficient to ensure security against any form of external aggression as well as internal disorder. Nehru felt that as regards part III, should it be decided to seek a solution of the problem by means of plebiscite Pakistan should have no part in the organization and conduct of the plebiscite or in any other matter of internal administration in the State. As regards paragraph 3(2), the paramount need for the security was recognized by the Commission and the time when the withdrawal of Indian forces from the state to begin, the stages in which it was to come out and the strength of the Indian forces to be retained in the State, were matters for settlement between the Commission and the Indian Government.

Finally, Nehru said that part III, 'does not in any way recognize the right of Pakistan to have any part in a plebiscite.'[97]

In spite of these reservations, India accepted the Resolution. Pakistan made so many reservations that the Commission felt that it was tantamount to a *defecto* rejection. The Commission had spent 10 days in Karachi. Sir Zafarullah Khan, who was a hard taskmaster, harassed the Commission with number of questions which plainly revealed that Pakistan did not consider the Commission as an impartial body. His queries were so long and complex that the Commission took several days to answer. Zafarullah conversed with the members of the Commission for several hours daily and discussed almost every word and its exact meaning. Every eventuality was scrutinized by him what would happen? What would the Commission do? What is meant by local authorities? Evacuated territory? Surveillance? Could you specify the role of military observers? 'What do you mean by the future status of the State of Jammu and Kashmir and hundreds of other questions? They were armed in part at removing all doubts or possible misinterpretations, but they revealed as well a deep-rooted mistrust of India.'

Khan 'proved to be a master of brilliant judicial analysis' Korbel who was heading the Commission at that time said 'he hurled interrogations at me until exhausted.' Interestingly Khan emphatically declared his complete trust in the integrity of Commission 'but suspected India'. But he tried to convince the 'Commission that good faith in the intentions of the other party is the only possible basis for negotiations and that the Commission had no power to impose anything, only to mediate.'

On 6 September 1948, the Government of Pakistan accepted the Resolution 'with so many reservations, qualifications that the Commission had to consider its answer as 'tantamount to rejection'. Again correspondence was exchanged between the Commission and the Pakistani authorities but they did little to bring Pakistan closer to actual acceptance.' Among the main objectives Pakistan felt 'the absence of any detailed guarantee for a free plebiscite in Kashmir'. Korbel said that basically the Commission was having full agreement with Pakistan, but Resolution was mainly designed to stop hostilities and maintain peace in the region and later to chalk out modalities for the holding of plebiscite in the State. The Commission was not happy the way Pakistani authorities behaved and was bitterly disappointed. Its efforts seemed to be frustrated by Pakistan's fear of India, but at the same the profound hope of reaching some agreement made 'Pakistan's position seem unnecessarily recalcitrant.

In retrospect, two questions emerged as to the wisdom of the Commission's procedure in regard to the Resolution. The first of these was it wise to have presented the Resolution in the two parts as on such (as a member of the Indian Government phrased it.) Take it or leave it basis?' would it have been better to have presented it as a tentative proposal, subject to negotiations and modifications? Many worthy arrangements might be presented for either course of action, but in the mind of the Commission, the time had come when concrete proposals carefully prepared and based on clear understanding of the problem, should be rather unequivocal presented. Any other approach was to 'produce additional wrangling, consultation and postponements—but no action.'

The second question was the product of Pakistan's reaction, which was tantamount to the rejection of the Resolution under these circumstances, was it wise to leave the sub-continent? Should we not remain and try again? Once more it could be readily argued either way, but the subsequent developments had established that the decision was a correct one.

The Commission in order to get more information and examine the ground realities, landed at Srinagar. Its members met the general public, various special political groups and of course the towering personally Sheikh Mohammed Abdullah. Korbel met Sheikh personally. The latter spoke at length about the past history of the movement, his fight against the Maharaja and the problem of the accession. Korbel described Sheikh a secular Muslim leader who strongly believed that Kashmir would be better off with India, but what could be done if the sentiments of his people pushed them in a direction against his better judgment? Sheikh described Pakistan a reactionary country and he was convinced that a union of Kashmir with Pakistan would finally work against the interests of the people. Sheikh was very vocal and did not conceal his helplessness. He was having four possible solutions to the problems, accession to India or Pakistan through plebiscite. This could not take place in less than three years because of the destruction of the country and the dislocation of its populations. Even then, it would be difficult to ascertain impartially the wishes of the people scattered over large areas and possibly subjected to intimidation. Would such a plebiscite be democratic and would India or Pakistan accept the verdict?

Third, there was a possibility of independence under the joint guarantee of India, Pakistan, Afghanistan, China and Soviet Union. He was ready to meet the leaders of Azad Kashmir, Ghulam Abbas, with whom Sheikh was once tied by bonds of friendship and a common struggle. But even should Kashmir's powerful neighbour agree to give us a guarantee of independence, Sheikh was doubtful, that it could last for long.

'There in my opinion, therefore, only one solution open' Sheikh Abdullah concluded, 'that is the division of the country. If it is not achieved, the fighting will continue, India and Pakistan will prolong the quarrel indefinitely and our people's suffering will go on.'

When Korbel enquired from Sheikh whether the conflict could be settled by way of arbitration, he replied that he personally would be agreeable to such an attempt, but was convinced that neither India nor Pakistan would agree and most certainly not on the composition of an Arbitration Committee.

It was difficult to judge his rather 'melancholic reasoning' whether Abdullah was following the attitude of Nehru. As the Government of India was ready to accept the division of Kashmir between India and Pakistan, India was ready to divide the country as a realistic solution; Sheikh Abdullah saw in it an act of desperation and last resort.

Korbel and other members however were convinced that Pakistan would refuse to consider any division of the Kashmir which would give the valley with its over-whelming majority of Muslim to India. He felt that Pakistan could not abandon the fate of the people of Kashmir who were prepared (Pakistan was sure) to join Pakistan. The Commission was indeed convinced as far as Pakistan's attitude was concerned.

On 21 September 1948, the Commission left Srinagar for Geneva to prepare its report and present to the Security Council. It felt 'deeply disappointed that it had been unable to stop the fighting and thereby bring some degree of peace to the suffering of the Kashmiris."

All the more disturbing was, Pakistan's refusal to accept the Resolution in the present form and content, but even more so was the general attitude of both the governments towards the efforts the Prime Ministers of both the countries would say 'we want to assist the Commission' or 'we wish to facilitate your task' speaking as through the struggle in Kashmir were exclusively a UN affair in which India and Pakistan were only interested observers. Even more disheartening were such opinions as these expressed by the Indian Deputy Prime Minister Sardar Patel, who after the Commission had left the sub-continent, declared that the Kashmir conflict could be solved if India could be released from the embarrassment of the UN investigations adding his criticism the shocking comment that the Security Council, 'insecurity Council and a disturber of peace.'

As a result of Pakistan's virtual rejection of Resolution of 13 August, complete deadlock ensured. The Commission reported the matter to the Security Council, but however and as directed by the Council, the Commission continued its efforts for a solution on 11 December 1948, and the Commission formulated certain proposals in elaboration of part III of the 13 August Resolution. These proposals gave some recognition to the objections, India had voiced at the time of the adoption of 21 April Resolution. The (PA) under the new proposals was to be appointed by and to receive his powers from the lawful Government of the State of Jammu and Kashmir.

As for Pakistan's *locus standi,* the Commission completely excluded it from any role in the final disposal of the troops; and the Government of Pakistan was recognized as a lawful Government.

The Prime Minister of India requested certain clarifications. The Commission set those out in the two memoirs dated 20 and 22 December 1948. These were:

1. That Pakistan must implement the first two Parts of the 13 August Resolution before India could accept the proposal for plebiscite, to the Commission proposals of December 1948.
2. In the event of Pakistan not accepting these proposals or having accepted them not implementing parts I and II of the Resolution of 13 August 1948, the Government of India's acceptance of them should not be regarded as in any way binding upon them.
3. The (PA) would not usurp the function of the state Government in the field of normal administration and law and order.
4. That the term "freedom of speech during a plebiscite did not imply the right of Pakistan propagandists, to play upon religious fanaticism" as well as disbanding of the Azad Kashmir forces.
5. There should be large scale disarmament and disbanding of the Azad Kashmir forces.[98]

Another landmark Resolution was adopted by the Commission on 5 January 1949. The Commission received communication from Indian and Pakistani Governments on 23 and 25 December respectively, regarding the acceptance of the recommendations which were supplementary to the Commission's Resolution of 13 August, 1948.

The question of the accession of Kashmir to India and Pakistan would be decided through the democratic method of a free and fair plebiscite. It was also stated that a plebiscite would be held when the Commission would be convinced that the ceasefire and the Truce Agreements set forth in part I and II of the Commission's Resolution of 13 August have been carried out and proper arrangements for the holding of plebiscite have been completed. It was the UN Secretary General who in consultation with the Commission would nominate (PA). The (PA) would drive from the state powers he considered necessary for organizing and conducting the plebiscite and for ensuring the freedom and impartiality of the plebiscite.

It was the (PA) who was to be the sole authority to decide, of course, in consultation with the Government of India, would decide the final disposal of the Indian and State armed forces. But the creation of peaceful conditions was the first requirement. All the citizens of the state who had left it on account of the disturbances would be invited and be free to return and exercise all the rights. All the persons (other than the citizens of the State) who on or since August 1947, have entered it for other than lawful purposes would be required to leave the State.[99]

The Commission sent its member Alfredo Lozano and his alternate Hernando Samber to the sub-continent at the disposal of both the Governments for any explanation of the proposal. Nehru expressed concern as to whether the proposal did not include the possibility of seeking other methods for ascertaining the wish of the people if the holding of the plebiscite should prove to be impossible, though he made it clear that the Government of India was sincere and would help in holding it. He somehow did not like the idea of the appointment of (PA) before the full implementation of the Truce Agreement. He did not wish the (PA) to have powers which would imply any right of interference in the administration of the state, he insisted upon large scale disbandment and disarming of Azad forces, he regarded appeals to religious fanaticism as going beyond the scope of the legitimate activities, he emphasized on the supreme importance of the maintenance of the security of Kashmir and hinted that adequate Indian forces should remain in the country during the plebiscite period.

Zafarullah Khan on the other hand wished that the

(PA) be selected at the earliest and the organizing and conducting of plebiscite would be his sole responsibility. Despite these reservations, questions and dissents, however, both the governments finally accepted the proposal, as the first step, ordered on ceasefire in Kashmir effective one minute before midnight January 1949. The contribution made by commission was widely acclaimed by the leaders and peoples of the world. The Manchester Guardian regarded the ceasefire decision as an encouraging start to the New Year. 'The ceasefire would not have been possible if both parties had not decided to control their senses, but the work of the Commission made the process far easier and it is in this which is the UN proper job.[100]. The New Statesman and Nation paid a tribute to the wisdom of Indian and Pakistani leaders but had also shown its anxiety and note of warning to the West. That Asia is 'taking the initiative in setting higher standards for international morality and that if Europe and America fail to follow suit the prestige that remains to them in the East Asia will disappear'.

It is obvious of course that the ceasefire in Kashmir will not end all the problems, but it has already caused a marked lifting of tension between the two dominions and may help to develop the mutual trust between India and Pakistan which will make of them the most powerful association in South-East Asia. Their own conflict resolved, their influence among other Asiatic nations will be on a scale not yet realised in Europe.[101]

DAS GUPTA OBSERVATIONS ON KASHMIR

Since the signing of the Instrument of Accession to the acceptance of ceasefire by both India and Pakistan, a large number of developments took place in open and secretly which in fact were 'the roots of the Kashmir dispute'. C. Das Gupta has summed up this nearly one and a half years period in his famous work 'War and Diplomacy in Kashmir'.

Das Gupta felt that 'Mountbatten' role has been misunderstood in Pakistan as well as in India. Mountbatten was no doubt considered to be a friend of India but was in no sense a foe of Pakistan, but he was keen to pursue British interests. He rendered a great service not only to Britain but also to Pakistan 'by retaining Indian military initiatives on more than on one critical occasion.' He became worried when he learnt about the Indian military's plan to extend its operations in the Poonch and Mirpur districts, 'going to the extent of sabotaging his government's plan for creating a Cordon Sanitaire along the border by aerial action' also by prevailing upon Nehru to take the issue to the UN. Mountbatten in fact was not merely a constitutional head. His appointment as Chairman of the Cabinet's Defence Committee gave him 'very real executive authority in an area of vital importance to state.' As a consequence, Mountbatten 'manoeuvred himself into a position from where he could directly influence government policy where possible or undermine it, where necessary'. At the beginning of the Kashmir crisis in October 1947, the accession was the top priority of Mountbatten before providing any assistance to Maharaja. When the raiders were on the outskirts of Srinagar, and advancing towards the Srinagar Airport, Mountbatten 'insisted that military intervention was impermissible in the absence of accession.'

The final act in the first stage of the conflict was when General Gracy refused to carry out the orders of Jinnah, to send units of the regular Pakistan army into Kashmir as Gracy had acted in conformity with the secret 'stand down' instructions. Field Marshal Auchinleck, the Supreme Commander for India and Pakistan flew to Lahore to personally inform Jinnah that all the British officers would be withdrawn if Pakistan army sent into territory which belonged to the Indian Union by virtue of the Maharaja's accession.

It was a fact that in the outset of the Kashmir conflict, the British played a crucial role and its policy was largely elaborated by the men of that time Mountbatten, Auchinleck and the British Generals commanding the forces of India and Pakistan. By the beginning of November, 'Britain began to move away from a position based on legality and impartiality to a policy based on immediate political and strategic considerations. The British Foreign Office feared that antagonizing Pakistan might 'align the whole of Islam against them jeopardizing British interests in the Middle-East. As Pakistan was a potential ally and her proximity to the Gulf gave her great geo-political importance. Furthermore, Britain felt that the survival of Pakistan would be at stake and challenged if India were to gain control of the whole territory of the State of Jammu and Kashmir.

The prime motive of the Britain policy shift was carried out by Noel Baker, British Secretary of State. Baker in association with Mountbatten, played a crucial role, followed by Mountbatten mediatory role between India and Pakistan. It was a classic example in the 'annals of diplomacy where the bolder of the highest office in a country had attempted mediation between that country and another.' His mediatory efforts failed however miserably, despite several concessions made by India to Pakistan.

But in collusion with the service Chiefs, Mountbatten ensured that nothing came of the Government's decision for preparations to be made for a cross-border operation... Mountbatten was able to vindicate his boast that his presence in India as Governor General was the 'best insurance' against a full scale inter-dominion war up to the end of 1947; Britain was the only outside power, with 'a significant involvement in the Kashmir conflict.' Its first priority was to dissuade India from launching a counter strike across the border. Prime Minister Attlee even warned Nehru against such a move as it would invite UN censure. As India was free to initiate such move, British inspired Security Council Resolution of 17 January 1948, urging the two countries to refrain from any step which might aggravate the situation.

The British were quite active in the Security Council well looking after the Pakistan's interests. It was under British inspiration that the Security Council next turned its attention to the question of a ceasefire linked arrangements for a plebiscite, brushing aside the question of Pakistan's involvement in the invasion. Noel Baker was the Britisher's torchbearer in the Security Council. He 'persuaded the US to seemingly take the lead. For reasons of alliance solidarity, the US was prepared to offer the maximum possible support to Britain but it demurred when Noel Baker advanced proposals involving, the unqualified acceptance of Pakistan's demands and the outright rejection of Indian views'. When the British asserted that Kashmir was 'territory in dispute' the Americans disagreed, stating that they found it difficult to deny the legal validity of Kashmir's accession to India. The US Secretary of State, Marshall expressed 'grave doubts' about the plan which, he pointed out, excluded the possibility of a compromise solution acceptable to India.

Noel Baker initiatives were also questioned by the leading members of the British cabinet. He had far exceeded his instructions in extending unqualified support to Pakistan, India's Commander-in-Chief, General Bucher, sought a private understanding with his counterpart in Pakistan General Gracy, to observe 'an informal truce on the basis of his turning a blind eye to induction of Pakistani regulars into specified areas of Jammu and Kashmir'. The intention presumably was to pave the way for ceasefire on the terms envisaged by the British delegation at the UN.

Das has appreciated the role played by the United Nations Commission for India and Pakistan (UNCIP). No British was its member and London had no direct say in its proceedings. It consulted in the formulation on a set of proposals and recommendations for maintaining law and order calling for a True Agreement on the basis of withdrawal of all Pakistan forces. The British Government was behind the scene overtime. Secret assurances were given to Pakistan by a British minister that in the event of an Indian incursion into Pakistan, the Security Council could impose sanctions against India and London would not ask British officers in Pakistan to stand down. The British archives threw fascinating light on the ways in which the British offices, generals and diplomats in India and Pakistan coordinated their moves to contain the war. India's Commander-in-Chief General Bucher kept his colleagues in Pakistan informed about his military plans, giving them an assurance that he would not advance beyond specified positions.

Das while concluding the British role said that, 'in wars in the third world, secrecy, surprise and speed are essential requirements for adhesive campaign. In the absence of these factors, an offensive runs the risk of being aborted by external intervention in the shape of Security Council Resolution simply by a warning from one or more of the great powers unless a benign superpower is prepared to hold the ring, by exercising its veto against a Security Council Resolution or deterring intervention by other powers—secrecy, surprise and speed are of fundamental importance from a diplomatic as well as military point of view. These conditions were unattainable in a situation where Britons presided over the Defence Committee as well as all these services. It was after the Indianisation of Indian army and the military leadership that contingency planning could be undertaken for a counter-attack across the Pakistani border. Thus in August 1952, Nehru was in a position to inform the Indian Parliament that any further aggression or attack or military operations in regard to Kashmir, if such takes place by the either side, that would not mean an all-out confrontation in Kashmir only, but else where too. "That was the policy implemented in 1965."[102]

The Resolutions of 13 August 1948 and 5 January 1949 form the basic Resolutions for the settlement of the Kashmir dispute but there has been no movement towards their implementation since their formally adaptation. No doubt, a ceasefire came into effect on 1 January 1949 and a ceasefire line was established by mutual agreement on 27 July 1949 and on 22 March 1949, the Secretary General of the UN, nominated Fleet Admiral Chester, W. Nimitz, and an American as the (PA). Each side has blamed the other for the impasse. A Pakistani scholar felt that India had consistently refused to recourse to arbitration or adjudication and was not serious about solving the dispute.[103]

The Commission tried its best to implement the Resolution and returned to the sub-continent on 4 February 1949. It started with the implementation of the ceasefire, put into effect the Truce agreement and to prepare the ground for the holding of the plebiscite. It negotiated with the Indian and Pakistani representatives officially and conversed with them formally. It travelled extensively in Kashmir and constituted various sub-commissions to study specific issues. But according to its Chairman, Joseph Korbel, it ran into enormous difficulties which were partly due to its own lack of cohesion. The Czechoslovakia delegate sabotaged the Commission's efforts, encouraged intrigue among individual delegates and reported regularly to Sheikh Abdullah on its confidential meetings.[104]

The demilitarization was posing a great challenge. The Commission gave a free choice to prepare a plan of their own and submit it to the Commission, for the demilitarization of the State, but their proposals differed materially. The Commission then submitted its own proposal, which was prepared keeping in mind the spirit of the Resolution. Neither side agreed on it. The Commission started its efforts again, prepared another proposal for the demilitarization of Kashmir as envisaged in the Truce Agreement and asked for its 'unreserved acceptance' but to the Commission's surprise, there was no positive response from both the countries. The Commission made another attempt by sending its representatives to Delhi and Karachi to discover 'on what conditions they would accept the truce terms'. Again it was evident that India was principally pre-occupied with the control of the sparsely, populated areas in North and North-West of Kashmir, a control which clearly went beyond the stipulations of the accepted Resolutions. It also continued to insist upon the disbanding and disarming of the Azad forces as an act never envisaged at that stage by the Commission. Pakistan had its own reservations and its final answer elaborated on a number of points of the Commission's Truce Agreement, but principally her rejection was based upon the fact that indeed it did not give the schedule of the withdrawal of her troops from Kashmir. The Commission requested both the countries for a common meeting of their representatives, to sort out the differences on the demilitarization process, but they could not even agree upon the nature of the agenda and the Idea of a common meeting had to be abandoned.

INDO-PAK COMMISSION: FINAL VERDICT

After all mediation efforts were exhausted, the Commission felt that arbitration was the only way-out to bridge the gulf between the two countries. Prime Minister

Attlee and President Truman suggestion of arbitration was out-rightly rejected by India. Her contention was that the scope of the arbitration was not known in advance and the Government of India considered that 'this procedure was novel and without precedent and could hardly be justified' she could 'only express surprise and disappointment at the attitude of the Commission' as it was forgetting the past, namely the moral aspect of the Kashmir conflict.

Once again it was an old story. India was insisting on the legality of the accession, considered it her right and duty to defend Kashmir against the danger of renewed external aggression. She persistently refused to disclose to the Pakistan representatives the strength of her army in Kashmir, the bulk of which she had agreed to withdraw, this despite the fact that in negotiations between the two countries, she had repeatedly asserted her wish to establish friendly relations. Such a procedure could only strengthen Pakistan's suspicions as to India's real intention.[105]

The Commission, no doubt, seemed to be working very hard and was maintaining balance between the two countries. It also showed wisdom by separating the political and military issues. A military conference was convened at Karachi, which was able to conclude the agreement on the ceasefire line. The drawing of the ceasefire line set the stage for the opening of the negotiations for implementing the second part of the 13 August 1948 Resolution namely in Truce Agreement calculated to ensure a fair and free plebiscite. The Pakistan Government announced that it had, succeeded in withdrawing the tribesmen from Kashmir. In fact not only the tribesmen had been withdrawn from the State, but Pakistan deployed its regular army on the other side of the invaders. The withdrawal of the tribesmen, Pakistan's armed forces and the Pakistani nationals who had entered the State for the purpose of fighting, constituted the major road-block in the way of the Truce Agreement. Another difficulty that based a threat to the Truce Agreement was the setting up of a so-called Azad Government in the area occupied by the raiders and the Parkistan army. The 13 August Resolution contemplated the restoration of local authority in those territories after the withdrawal of the

Pakistani army tribesmen and Pakistani nationals. Pakistan maintained that the local authority meant the Azad Kashmir Government. The withdrawal was circumvented by constituting the so-called Azad forces, the army of the Azad Kashmir Government. The Pakistan Government was adamant on its stand. On the other hand, the Government of India was equally firm on the disbanding of the so-called Azad forces. It was unthinkable for the refugees to return to those territories to take part in the plebiscite, in the presence of such a large number of forces.[106]

Korbel pointed out that the problem of disbanding and disarming of the Azad forces was very acute and holding of plebiscite was to be implemented only after the demilitarization of the state. It was to be affected as the last measure preceding the actual act of plebiscite. But the circumstances had changed drastically in the summer of 1949. It was much different from what it had been at the beginning of that year. The Azad forces were reorganized and rearmed. Before they had been loosely-knit guerrilla groups, now they were a seasoned and well-equipped army of the thirty-two battalions.

India had valid reasons to be warned about these Azad forces. They were composed of soldiers who once had been considered among the best in the British Indian Army. India could by no means be sure of the ability of the Kashmir who lived in the Indian part of the country to resist the Azad people either politically or militarily, though they were in a numerical majority at a rate of two to one. Moreover, once the Indian army had withdrawn, it could be difficult to get them back over high mountains and long distances. On the other hand, should the Azad forces suddenly erupt into a holy war, Pakistani supplies, and weapons and perhaps once again troops could be easily and immediately available. According to Korbel, the problem of demilitarization was a real one and it could have been solved and implemented easily, because goodwill and mutual confidence were the requirements.[107]

Having exhausted all possibilities of mediation and facing the Indian refusal of arbitration, the Commission submitted another report to the UN Security Council. It concluded that, 'The reports of the Kashmir dispute are deep, strong under currents, political economic and religious, both the Dominions have acted and don't act against on an easy and prompt solution of the outstanding disputes between them. These currents, which at this early stage of national formations are often antagonistic, account to a considerable degree for the misgivings, reluctance and hesitancy.'[108]

On the whole, the Commission report was markedly critical of the Indian attitude. Earlier, the Commission was critical of Pakistan's behaviour. Korbel described the report 'balanced and impartial'. Commenting on the Commission's work, a British expert Sir Godfrey Devis wrote, 'Goodwill and devotion...could do no more. It is true that the Commission failed in its final objective, but the devoted labour of the members still is an asset to the cause of the peace.'[109] Korbel, further said that 'the Security Council burdened with many other and more burning issues, seemed satisfied with the cessation of hostilities and was reluctant to risk by more resolve, action possible, protect or overt defiance from either of the two principal contenders. Instead, it based all further deliberations upon the two Resolutions of the Commission already approved by the Government of India and Pakistan, the core of which was the conducting of a plebiscite in Kashmir.'[110]

Commenting on the failure of the (UNCIP), an Indian expert on Kashmir issue Surendra Chopra felt that it 'was doomed to failure because like the Security Council, it also ignored the core of India's complaint and equated the lawful army with a band of intruders. The (UNCIP) did not hold Pakistan responsible for illegal acts of planning, arming and leading an armed attack by irregulars.' However, it did criticize Pakistan for the deployment of Pakistan regular army units. The Commission was keen for a settlement between the two countries, it gave assurances to both India and Pakistan 'which were diametrically opposed to each other.' To India's favour, it recognized India's sovereignty over Kashmir but never accepted the legality of the presence of Pakistani troops in Kashmir. That was a reason why the Commission had ordered the total withdrawal of Pakistani forces, but on the other hand only requested India to withdraw a part of its forces making special provisions to maintain internal order.[111]

The Commission attitude was unreasonable in connection with the appointment of the (PA), which was considered to be a 'significant road block in the way of settlement.' India was not in favour of the appointment of a US citizen as an administrator a move which India 'rightly viewed with suspicion' for there was no reason why a member of the (UNCIP) who also acted Chairman of the Commission in turn and (PA) should be a US national. India very well knew the US under the influence of Britain was hostile to her on the issue of Kashmir. 'Ceasefire, however, remained a distinctive achievement of the (UNCIP) which helped in creating atmosphere of peace in the State of Jammu and Kashmir.'[112]

McNAUGHTON PROPOSALS

The Commission was of the strong opinion that a single person might be more effective to carry on further negotiations for creating a congenial atmosphere and solving the Kashmir issue. The Security Council asked its own President for the month, General McNaughton of Canada to try and resolve the deadlock. The principal considerations underlying the following proposals of the President of the Security Council were:

1. To determine the future of Jammu and Kashmir by the democratic method of a free and impartial plebiscite to take place as early as possible;
2. Thus to settle this issue between the Government of India and Pakistan in accordance with the freely expressed will of the inhabitants, as is desired by both governments;
3. To preserve the substantial measures of agreement on fundamental principles which had already been reached between the two Governments under the auspices of the UN?; and
4. To avoid unprofitable discussion of disputed issues of the past and to look forward into the future towards the good neighbourliness and constructive cooperation of the two great nations.

There should be an agreed programme of progressive demilitarization, the basic principle of which should be the reduction of armed forces on either side of the ceasefire line by withdrawal, disbandment and disarmament in such stages as not to cause fear at any point of time to the people on either side of the ceasefire line. The aim should be to reduce the armed personnel in the State of Jammu and Kashmir on each side of the ceasefire to the minimum compatible with the maintenance of security and of local law and order and to a level sufficiently low and with the forces so disposed that they would not constitute a restriction on the free expression of opinion for the purpose of the plebiscite.[113]

He also suggested that the programme of demilitarisation be supervised by a UN representative appointed by the Secretary General in agreement with the two Governments and that, upon the completion of their programme, the (PA) should exercise the functions assigned to him. Finally, he held that the Pakistan Government should give an unconditional assurance that tribesman would not be permitted to enter the territory of Jammu and Kashmir across the border.

These proposals were presented to India and Pakistan on 22 December 1949. While Pakistan accepted them, India proposed two modifications. It first desired the disbanding of the Azad forces alone and second reversal of the administration in Northern areas to the Government of Jammu and Kashmir of the so-called local authorities.[114]

McNaughton proposals were welcomed by the members of the Security Council. Except the Soviet Union, all other members of the Council favourably received the proposals. The British considered these proposals a pre-requisite for the holding of plebiscite in the State. The US representative described the proposals as 'fair and reasonable'. It was believed that the UN Security Council members had pre-planned everything in order to put pressure on the parties to accept the McNaughton proposals. McNaughton met the representatives of India and Pakistan. He announced on 3 February 1950 that his mission had failed and any further activity on his part won't serve any useful purpose. The Indian Government rejected the proposals.

India, however, insisted upon the complete disbanding and disarming of the Azad forces and the occupation of the northern areas of the State by the Indian army. 'On the other hand, surprisingly, Pakistan was almost ready to accept the proposals with some modifications'. Once again lengthy speeches were delivered by the representatives of India and Pakistan. Recriminations were repeated, reminiscent of the original diatribes, new accusations were exchanged and the atmosphere was heavy with bitterness and hostility. Sir B.N. Rau, the Indian delegate, objected to the McNaughton proposals, saying 'they completely ignore the legal and moral aspects of the question... in effect therefore in crucial respect of the new proposals are the old minus some of the small concessions made to Pakistan. It is a matter of surprise that India has been unable to accept them as they stand.' The Resolution containing McNaughton proposals was carried on 14 March 1950 by eight votes with two abstentions (India and Yugoslavia). It called upon India and Pakistan 'to prepare and execute within a period of five months from the date of this Resolution, a programme of demilitarization on the basis of the principles laid down in the McNaughton proposals'. It further decided to replace the UN Commission by a representative entrusted with arbitrary powers 'to interpret the agreements reached by the parties for demilitarization' in case they should argue in the most important matter. It also requested this representative to make any suggestion which would in his opinion expedite and offer an enduring solution to Kashmir dispute.

OWEN DIXON EFFORTS

In pursuance of the McNaughton proposals, Sir Owen Dixon of Australia, was appointed as UN Representative. At a conference of the Prime Ministers of India and Pakistan from 20 to 24 July 1950, Dixon discussed with both certain proposals for the solution of the Kashmir dispute. The discussion showed there were serious differences and obstacles for reaching an agreement concerning the holding of a plebiscite. The Prime Minister of Pakistan protested against the course proposed on the ground that it meant a breach on

India's part of the agreement that the destiny of the State of Jammu and Kashmir as a whole should be decided by a single plebiscite taken over the entire state. Dixon spent some time in Delhi for the purpose of obtaining from India a definite answer with respect to the suggested lines of settlement. After consideration, the Indian authorities informed Dixon that they would be prepared to discuss a settlement of Kashmir dispute on the basis of certain principles. The principles were first that the areas of the State of Jammu and Kashmir where there was no apparent doubt that as to the wishes of the people in those areas should go to India or Pakistan without a plebiscite. Second, that the plebiscite should be limited to those areas where there was doubt as to the result of voting; and third that the demarcation should give due regard to geographical features and to the requirements of the international boundaries. In the first place, there should be a plebiscite in the valley of Kashmir. The area should, however, include part of the Muzafarbad district to bring in what India regarded as the natural geographical feature provided by the river Kishanganga and its watershed on the north.

In the second place, India considered that the following should go to it:

1. The province of Jammu so far as it lies east of the ceasefire line subject to minor corrections; one correction was to reduce the bulge in the ceasefire line near Gulmarg.
2. In the district and the tehsil of Ladakh and Kargil, except approximately the area above the Suru River which should go to India or Pakistan according to the result of the plebiscite of the valley.

In the third place, India was willing that the following areas should go to Pakistan viz, Gilgit, Gilgit Agency, Gilgit Wazarat, political districts and tribal territory and Baltistan of so much of the Jammu province as lies to the west of the ceasefire fine as corrected.

It also appeared that India was prepared to include in

any such settlement a territory would not be any artificial works in the state, divert the waters of the Chenab River or reduce the flow substantially of the waters of the river, except that it might construct canals for irrigation confined within the State. Without reducing the waters of the stream, it might establish hydro-electric works for the production of electrical energy. The Indian Prime Minister was ready to meet its Pakistan counterpart, so that the possibility of a settlement on such principles might be discussed.

And with the Indian proposals Dixon went to Karachi. He met Pakistani Prime Minister and told his opinion that the territorial claims desired by India, were not according to the situation prevailing and also did not represent the division of the State to which in the end India might be expected to agree. But the Government of Pakistan declined to attend a conference on the footing, as proposed by Dixon, in the light of the position taken by India, the possibility of solving the dispute.

The primary reasons of the Government of Pakistan for refusing to accept the idea of conference laid in its unwillingness to depart at all from the claim that the fate of the entire State of Jammu and Kashmir should be decided by an overall plebiscite that India had earlier agreed measures for holding such a plebiscite. But as a second ground, it was said that India's position was too indefinite and if it wished to embark upon to discuss the possibility of settlement according to the suggested principles, it should make definite proposals. After knowing the views of Pakistan Government, Dixon continued its effect to persuade Pakistan. Dixon said by coming to the conference to discuss an alternative possible settlement, it could not be held to abandon its main contention. It was enough that the basis of the settlement to be discussed was a limited plebiscite and partition of the rest of the state, Kashmir valley being included in the plebiscite area. Dixon did not see why it should not be possible area, for the parties to argue the issue of plebiscite, the division of the remaining territory and the conditions for securing independence of the voting until either they saw they could not agree or else found some basis of agreement. Even on the assumption that the conference failed, Pakistan would come away from it better informed as so far, without suffered any real prejudice.

Dixon further said in the course of the discussion, he ascertained that if the basis of the suggested settlement had been simple partition, a solution having the advantages of being immediate in the operation and self-executing, Pakistan would consider the matter provided that it took the Kashmir valley. Dixon was convinced that India would not concede the partition of the valley.

Dixon, after meeting the Prime Minister of Pakistan, returned to New Delhi and informed Nehru of the position taken by Pakistan. As was expected, Nehru flatly refused to accept the partition of the valley.

The stand adopted by the Prime Minister had led Dixon to the conclusion that there no longer existed any possibility of bringing the two parties to any compromise. Dixon decided to prepare fresh proposals after its meeting with the two Prime Ministers. The plan would be one for holding a partial plebiscite in a limited area including or consisting of the Valley of Kashmir and for partitioning the remaining of State. Dixon proposed to call a conference and would decide to lay the plan before it for acceptance or rejection, or if independently the parties wished to modify it by agreement, Dixon told the Indian Prime Minister that Pakistan might take the view that it could have no cause for fear that, by complying with my invitation to take part in such a proceeding, it would be considered as departing from its stand on the overall plebiscite and as waiving its primary claim. After a little discussion of the chances of such a course proving successful, Nehru took time to consider the matter. Nehru, after discussion with his cabinet members, informed Dixon that it had decided to fall in with the suggestion.

Dixon returned to Pakistan and placed before the Government there, its proposals as a last resort: on the faith of the assurance by Dixon, Pakistan agreed to attend a conference to consider the Dixon proposals, notwithstanding that it was based on the alternative to an overall plebiscite. But Pakistan in its turn put a condition. The condition arose out of the insistence upon the view that India would not agree upon specific practical measures which would ensure the freedom and fairness of the plebiscite.

But India refused to accept any conditional offer and Nehru emphatically refused to accept any condition, Dixon on the request of Nehru rushed back to New Delhi and Nehru explained to him India's position, to avoid any possibility of misunderstanding, Nehru's main objections as conveyed to Dixon were:

1. Pakistan was an aggressor and it would be a surrender to an aggressor, to allow it to take part in any part of the plebiscite. For the same reason and because of the danger involved, Pakistan's troops could never be allowed to enter the plebiscite area.
2. The provision would mean that the Government of the State would be superseded and went far beyond what was necessary for the purpose in view.
3. Only those people belonging to the State of Jammu and Kashmir should be allowed in the campaign over the plebiscite. There won't be any equality of any right between India and Pakistan in this or in other relevant respects. The security of the State would be endangered.

These arguments, as Dixon said, appeared to overlook the real nature of the proposed partition plan and a partial plebiscite or else to make it completely impossible. The question whether Pakistan had or had not been aggressor, had Dixon felt nothing to do with the results of the partition and the fairness and freedom of a partial plebiscite. To agree that Pakistan should take under a partition, part of the State must be to agree that, independently of any such question, it took not merely an interest in but sovereignty of the territory. Dixon further said to agree that the territory not immediately divided between India and Pakistan should pass to one or the other according to the vote of the inhabitants at a plebiscite conducted by the UN must be to agree to a text involving an equal interest in both countries in the result. Further it was to agree to the ascertainment of the will of the people by an independent authority because that authority would see that the plebiscite was freely and fairly conducted.

Dixon had formed the opinion that it was not easy to exclude the danger that the inhabitants of the valley of Kashmir would vote under fear or apprehension of consequences and other improper influences. They were not the high spirit people of an independent or resolute temper. For the most part they were illiterate. There were large number of regular soldiers of the Indian army as well as the state military and police and more often than not they were under arms. The State Government was exercising wide powers by ordering arbitrary arrests. These were not matters that the Kashmiri inhabitting the valley could be expected to disregard in choosing between voting as the Government of Kashmir asked them and voting for accession to Pakistan. The freedom and fairness of the plebiscite could not be removed unless in the administrative hierarchy of the state so far it controlled the plebiscite area, the UN offices were interposed temporally. The authority of the Ministry over the rest of the State would not be affected. The ordinary working of the machinery of government in the plebiscite area would go on without change. The presence of number of troops, armed militia and police in the valley did not appear to be favourable to be free expression of the people's will and Dixon considered that the administrative body might be safely given powers to divide what was necessary to ensure the maintenance of order and to protect the area from external danger if it found that any existed.

Dixon came to the conclusion that it would be impossible to give effect to the doctrines formulated by India's objection to Dixon plan and at the same time frame a plan for partition and a limited plebiscite plan. Both the countries did not accept the views of Dixon.

It would be seen that two main lines were being pursued in the attempts which were made to settle the dispute between India and Pakistan about the State of Jammu and Kashmir. The attempt find a solution by taking a plebiscite over the whole State and to decide by a majority to which country the entire State would go was having its origin in the first proceedings before the Security Council. It should be recalled that by the Resolution of 2 April 1948, the desire of both the countries that the questions of the accession of the

State to one or other of them should be decided by a, free and impartial plebiscite. Once again issue of holding of plebiscite became a part of the Resolution of 5 January 1949. Indian insistence to ascertain the real will of the people, felt Dixon was just not possible. That conception of 'real will' was not shareed even by Pakistan. The Resolution provisions in relation to the holding of plebiscite and the antecedent steps and about those general provisions the parties were able to agree. But to apply propositions of this kind of a programme of practical acts and physical 'events must be agreed upon'. Without that, it was impossible for the (PA) to begin the extensive and difficult work of organizing the poll. It was the practical measures which had proved the obstacle, not the more general propositions.

Pakistan complained of India's failure to agree on the practical measures which must precede the preparations for the taking of poll and had maintained this failure was a result of deliberate policy. Moreover, the UN Commission failed in its efforts to secure an agreement upon them. Dixon also accepted his failure. Neither party put forward any other proposals nor did both appear to concur in the view that the possibility of an agreement hail been exhausted.

The contention of Pakistan that it was incumbent on India to agree did not advance the matter practically. These circumstances had compelled Dixon to turn away from a plebiscite of the whole state, an overall plebiscite, as a method of solving the problem of Kashmir and partition of the whole State between the two countries was the only alternative available. But Dixon also accepted that unfortunately the valley of Kashmir could not be partitioned. And it was an idea claimed by both the countries.

He strongly believed that no method of allocating the valley to one or other of the contending parties was available. The difficulty of using the expedient of a plebiscite appeared to lay entirely in the conflict between on the one hand, the necessity of ensuring that plebiscite could be held in conditions which made it an effective method to ascertain the real will of the people independently and freely expressed and on the other hand certain conceptions or perceptions of the Indian Government? These were based in part on what

India conceived to be the origin and cause of the fighting in 1947 and 1948 and in part of its unwillingness to have any interference with or restriction of the powers of government in the state whether in reference to the use of armed forces or in reference to the civil administration. A different conception also existed on the process of ascertaining the will of the people. India might come to realize that the necessity of practical measures which would really secure the freedom and fairness of a plebiscite must be paramount over these conceptions. India and Pakistan must accept the partitioning of the valley rather than an overall plebiscite. The State of Jammu and Kashmir is not really a unit geographically, demographically or economically. It is an agglomeration of territories brought under the political power of one Maharaja. That is the unity it possesses. If as a result of an overall plebiscite, the State is entirely passed on to India, there would be large movements of Muslims and another refugee problem would arise for Pakistan, which would be expected to receive them in very great numbers if the result favoured Pakistan, although not any such dimensions would arise for India, because of the movement of Hindus and Sikhs. Almost all this could be avoided by partition. Great Areas of the State are predominantly Hindus. There is a further area which is Buddhist. No one doubted the sentiments of the great majority of the inhabitants of these areas. The interest of the people, the justice as well as the performance of the settlement and the imperative necessity of avoiding another refugee problem all point to the wisdom of adopting partition as the principle of settlement and of abandoning that of an overall plebiscite. But in addition, the economic and geographic considerations point in the same direction. The difficulty in partitioning the State was to form a sound judgment where the line should be drawn.

The partition plan dealt broadly with State as a whole. It was by no means easy to fix the limits on each side. That was because it was necessary that the territory allocated to each other should be contiguous with that country, because there were pockets of people whose faith and affiliations were different from those people by whom they are cut off, because the change in the distribution of population as the result of the troubles could not be completely ignored, because geographical features remain important in fixing what might prove an international frontier.

So far the attitude of the parties was to throw the whole responsibility upon the Security Council or its representatives for settling the dispute, notwithstanding that, except by agreement between them; there was no means of settling it.

When actual fighting was going on between them, it was natural, if not necessary that the Security Council and the Commission as its delegate should intervene between them and propose terms to stop hostilities. But when this was done to the extent of stopping open hostilities and the question came as to how to settle the rival claims to Kashmir, the initiative was still left with the Security Council and the Commission. The whole issue has been discussed thoroughly by the parties with the Security Council, the Commission and the representatives appointed by the Security Council and the possible methods of settlement have been exclusively investigated. Dixon felt that the initiative passed back to the parties concerned. He was not ready to recommend to the Security Council for any further course of action for the purpose of assisting the parties to settle between them how the state of Jammu and Kashmir is to be disposed off.

Dixon in the end felt that the continued maintenance of two armies facing one another was a serious matter. A danger was in existence while this state of things continued. Except for mutual distrust and fear, one or another, there was no reason why the two countries should go on maintaining armies separated by check-posts and the line in the same was as any frontier between countries at peace. It was hard to believe that the Indian and Pakistan Chiefs of Staff would have any difficulty in arranging for a concurrent reduction of forces or in effecting the necessary change in the manner in which ceasefire was held, if they were instructed by their respective Governments to meet for the purpose.

He recommended the maintenance of UN military observers on the ceasefire line. They should be allowed to continue forever, but after the question of their withdrawal might be settled in consultation.[115]

Dixon, had examined the Kashmir issue in depth. He heard the views of both the parties very patiently and his observations were analytical and one could say they were objective. Interestingly, the partition plan he suggested was prepared after careful examination of every aspect. But the way both the countries raised objections it seemed were having stands without taking into consideration the ground realities prevailing in Kashmir.

Dixon failure was certainly because of the circumstances prevailing. His approach had been thoughtful, his alternative proposals many and varied, his authority unquestionable. But the method of mediation in this dispute revealed its own aridity. The concluding part of his report indicated something of the despair which this hardworking and conscientious man must have felt. There was no hope, it indicated, of solving the problem of Kashmir by agreement. So he suggested the partition of the State along the ceasefire line. This would bring about stabilization and peace, albeit forces and uneasy, a peace born of appeasement, a peace which neglected entirely the justice of determining from the people involved their will for their nation.

One cannot criticize Dixon motives in his concluding recommendations. He appeared sceptical of the ability of the UN to force upon India any just solution. On the other hand, he felt strongly that the UN could not be a party to any compromise which would cast any doubt on its integrity. Any solution short of a completely free plebiscite, he concluded that the only course open was for the UN to toss the responsibility for any further development in Kashmir back to the parties concerned, India and Pakistan. And perhaps, at least for the Kashmiri's, there was some value in the temporary armistice.

But one may criticize his conclusions, for the assumptions upon which they were based, were considered to be dangerous. The nationalist elements in Pakistan were increasingly impatient with the UN efforts and from time to time wanted to settle the problem by means of the sword. On the contrary people were acquainted with situation, they were afraid that the Council failure would tend to guarantee a renewal of war. Besides, had the Security Council adopted

Dixon's recommendation, it would have been a humiliating admission and a grave blow to the prestige and authority of the world organization.

Korbel felt that, even the immediate deadlock in the Kashmir negotiations seriously affected Indo-Pak relations and further widened the gulf between the two. The media and general public, leaders, politicians, etc. were critical of Dixon's way of functioning, but appreciated his efforts too. Even articles appeared asking for the withdrawal of the Kashmir issue from the UN and some extremists even called for the withdrawal of India and Pakistan from the UN.[116]

The idea of partition of the State however was not new.[117] In 1933, the British Government had planned its partition on communal lines. They wanted Hari Singh to part with a major part of his Muslim majority to be placed under Agha Khan as the ruler. The proposal stipulated the cession of Kangra district in Punjab in order to compensate Maharaja Hari Singh for the loss of Muslim majority area. The move however could not materialize. It was not mere coincidence that the British inspired and 'convinced at' the movement against the Dogra Raj started by Sheikh Abdullah at the same time.[118]

Dixon proposal for allocation of the different areas of the valley was misfired. It seemed there was no dispute about the areas under Pakistan's occupation and the province of Jammu easy of the ceasefire line but the question of the valley was a hard nut which could not be cracked. It would be reasonable to believe that the ideas sometimes thrown up for the independence of the valley, owe their birth to Dixon proposals to partition of the rest of the State. In retrospect, one can say that Dixon's suggestion could have been agreed to by both India and Pakistan if Dixon had pursued the matter further and had also come out with a face-saving device.[119]

The world press as whole was very critical of India's reaction. The London Times was always cautious while commenting on international affairs. It was of the view that, like most great men Nehru had also a black spot. In his case, it was Kashmir, the land of the forebears which he loved like a woman. Because he was not amendable to reason on this subject, but allowed emotions to get the better of common sense as Kashmir remains a stumbling bloc in the path of Indo-Pakistan friendship.[120]

And so, with India and Pakistan then at each other's throat with the world press increasingly critical and with the very authority of the UN at stake, the Security Council did not follow Dixon's advice of 'hands-off' and decided to resume its study of the Kashmir dispute.

Liaquat Ali Khan, the Pakistani Prime Minister, was keen to discuss the Kashmir problem with the members of the Commonwealth, at the conference scheduled to be convened on 4 January 1951. He threatened to boycott the conference, if his colleagues won't agree to include the Kashmir problem in their discussion. After getting an assurance that Kashmir would be discussed outside the conference, Liaquat landed at London on 7 January 1951, to participate in the conference. Accordingly Kashmir issue was discussed in two informal sessions. Nothing tangible came out of these discussions and the main issue continuing to be hold to demilitarize Kashmir, in the period preceding a plebiscite without exposing her to the danger of 'external aggression'. The Australian Prime Minister Robert Gorden Menzies suggested that the Commonwealth troops be stationed at Kashmir. Both India and Pakistan should be asked to constitute a joint Indo-Pakistan forces or the (PA) be allowed to raise local troops. Liaquat was ready to accept these three proposals.[121] Nehru rejected them and declared in the Indian Parliament on 12 February 1951, he failed to understand why the Commonwealth troops were to be dispatched to the State of Jammu and Kashmir because of the suspicions arising out of the recent past and those growing out of current international tensions, that the second solution would place Pakistan, the aggressor, on an equal footing with India and that although the third proposal could be considered. India must still be responsible for the security of the State and would continue to station troops in Kashmir.[122]

It looks Pakistan got more serious regarding the Kashmir issue as she was feeling confused as Indian attitude on the issue was getting harder. Nehru became vocal but was worried about Pakistan's moves to internationalise the issue in order to divert the attention of the people of Pakistan from the uncertain political environment. The gulf between India-Pakistan started widening and fear of insecurity was visible in the moves and counter-moves of the foreign policy-makers of both the countries.

The world was in the grip of Korean crisis and the cold war was getting colder. The emergence of People's Republic of China on the world scenario gave a new dimension to the US-Pak relations which were at that junction taking a definite shape.

Notes and References

1. Sangat Singh, *Pakistan's Foreign Policy: An Appraisal* (New Delhi, 1970), p. 78.
2. For details of the British Proposal see, Pendral Moon, *Divide and Quit* (London, 1961).
3. *Ibid.*, pp. 78-79.
4. S.M. Burke, *Pakistan's Foreign Policy* (London, 1973), p. 109.
5. For the text of the declaration see, Pattabhi Sitaramayya, *History of the Indian National Congress.* As cited in *Ibid.*
6. *Ibid.*, p. 110.
7. *Ibid.*, p. 110-11.
8. *Ibid.*, pp. 111-13.
9. Zulfikar Ali Bhutto, *The Myth of Independence* (London, 1969), p. 6.
10. *Ibid.*, p. 7.
11. *Ibid.*, pp. 7-8.
12. Herbert Feldman, *Omnibus* (Oxford, 2001), p. 406.
13. Lassy Goodson, "Foreign Policy Gone away: The Kalashnikovization and Talibanization of Pakistan", in Craig Baxter and Charles H. Kennedy, *Pakistan 2000* (Oxford, 2001), pp. 151-52.
14. Keith Callard, *Pakistan Foreign Policy: An Interpretation* (London, 1957), p. 9.
15. Jamil-ud-Din Ahmed (ed.) *Some Recent Speeches and Writings of Mr. Jinnah,* Vol. 2, (Lahore, 1947), p. 75.
16. Z.A Bhutto, *Political Situation in Pakistan* (Karachi, 1968), p. 25.
17. Stephen Philip Cohen, *India, Pakistan and Kashmir.* Paper Presented at the University of Texas, Dec. 2001.
18. *Ibid.*
19. Stephen Cohen, *The Idea of Pakistan* (Washington, 2004).
20. *Times of India*, 6 June 1966.
21. Sangat Singh, n. 1, pp. 43-44.
22. Mohammad Ayub Khan, "*Pakistan American Alliance: Stresses and Strains*", *Foreign Affairs,* Vol XXXIV January 1964, p. 32.

23. Sukhwant S. Bindra, "Continuity and Change in Indo-Pakistani Relations", *World Affairs*, Vol. X, No. 1, Autum 2005, p. 32.
24. K.K. Aziz, *The Making of Pakistan: A Study in Nationalism* (London, 1967), p. 184.
25. Humoanun Kabir, "Muslim Politics," (1942-47), in C.D. Philips and M.D. Wainwright (ed.), *Partition of India: Politics and Perspectives* (London, 1970), p. 404.
26. Maulana Abul Kalam Azad, *India Wins Freedom*, (London, 1960), p. 265.
27. *Ibid.*
28. Z.A. Bhutto, n. 9, pp. 162-75.
29. *Ibid.*
30. N.S. Gehlot and Anu Satsangi, *Indo-Pak Relations*, (New Delhi, 2004), pp. 5-6.
31. *The Statesman*, 27 September 1947.
32. Wayne Wilcox, "The Well Springs of Pakistan", in Lawrence Ziring, *et. al.* (ed.) *Pakistan: The Long View*, (Durban, 1977), pp. 25-34.
33. G.W. Choudhay, *Pakistan's Relations with India*, (Meerut, 1971), p. 50.
34. Sangat Singh, n. 1, p. 53.
35. Arif Hassan, *Pakistan: Its Ideology and Foreign Policy* (London, 166), p. 76.
36. G.W. Choudhary, n. 33, 54.
37. Mohammed Ayub Khan, *Friends Not Masters*, (London, 1967), pp. 123-24.
38. Varinder Grover, *The Story of Kashmir: Yesterday and Today*, Vol. I, (New Delhi, 1995), preface.
39. Sisir Gupta, *Kashmir: A Study in Indo-Pakistan Relations*, (Bombay, 1966), pp. 113-34.
40. S.M. Burke, n. 4, p. 18.
41. *Ibid.*, p. 21.
42. *Ibid.*
43. *Ibid.*, pp. 22-23.
44. Joseph Korbel, *Dangers in Kashmir* (Princeton, 1954), p. 25.
45. *The Dawn*, 5 November 1947.
46. Varinder Grover, (ed.), *The Story of Kashmir: Yesterday and Today*, Vol. III, (New Delhi, 1995), pp. 110-11.
47. *Ibid.*, p. 12.
48. *Ibid.*
49. Arif Hussain, n. 35, p. 76.
50. V.P. Menon, *The Story of the Integration of the Indian States*, (Bombay, 1961), pp. 368-91.
51. As cited in C. Das Gupta, *War and Diplomacy in Kashmir, 1947-48*, (New Delhi, 2002), pp. 36-37.
52. *Ibid.*, pp. 36-40.
53. *Ibid.*

54. *Ibid.*, pp. 40-42.
55. *Jawahar Lal Nehru Speeches*, Vol. I, (New Delhi, 1958), pp. 160-61. Also See, Attlee to Nehru, 3 November 1947, File L/P/S/13/1845b. India office record, Liaquat Ali to Attlee, 4 November 1947, File L/ P and S/13/1845b India office record as cited in *Ibid.*, pp. 74-75.
56. File LIP and SI 131 1843b, India office record as cited in *Ibid.*, p. 76.
57. Attlee to Liaquat Ali Khan 6 November 1947, File L/P and S/13/ 1845b. India Office Record as cited in *Ibid.*
58. C. Das Gupta, n. 50, p. 76.
59. As Cited in *Ibid.*, pp. 77-78.
60. *Ibid.*, p. 78.
61. *Ibid.*
62. See for more details, *Ibid.*, pp. 77-78.
63. *Ibid.*, p. 79
64. *Ibid.*, pp. 81-85.
65. *Ibid.*
66. Selected works of Jawahar LaI Nehru, Vol. IV (New Delhi: Publications Division), pp. 399-403.
67. Varinder Grover, n. 46, pp. 137-38.
68. *Ibid.*, pp. 139-46
69. Joseph Korbel, n. 44, pp. 95-96.
70. Jagmohan, *My Frozen Troublence in Kashmir* (New Delhi, 1993), p. 84.
71. *Ibid.*, p. 89
72. S/628, 2 January 1948.
73. *Jawaharlal Nehru Speeches*, Vol. 1, September 1946-May 1949 (New Delhi, Publication Division, 1958), pp. 169-73.
74. See for details, 8/646, 15 January 1948.
75. For more details see, S/P.V. 228, 16 July 1948 and S/P.V. 229, 17 January 1948.
76. S/651, 17 January 1948.
77. Sisir Gupta. *Kashmir: A Study in India-Pakistan Relations*, (Bombay, 1946), pp. 140-41.
78. S.P.V. 229, 17 January 1948.
79. S. 654, 20 January 1948.
80. Sisir Gupta, n. 77, p.151.
81. 21 April 1948.
82. Michael Breacher, *The Struggle for Kashmir* (New York, 1953), pp. 77-78.
83. S/PV 236, 28 January 1948, pp. 271-74.
84. *Ibid.*, p. 274.
85. *The Hindu*, 22 January 1948, p. 295.
86. S.P.V 237, 29 January 1948, p. 295.
87. S.P.V 242, 6 February 1948, p. 31.
88. S.P.V 285, 19 April 1948, pp. 12-18.
89. *Ibid.*, p. 26.

90. *The Economist,* (ed.) "UNO Proposals for Kashmir", 30 April, 1948, p. 667.
91. Surendra Chopra, *UN Mediation in Kashmir: A Study in Power Politics* (Kurukshetra, 1971), p. 53.
92. Joseph Korbel, n. 44, p. 121.
93. *Ibid.,* p. 140.
94. January 1948, pp. 139-40.
95. S/1100, 13 August 1948.
96. Joseph Korbel, n. 44, pp. 141-142.
97. S/1100, 13 August 1948, para 78.
98. Joseph Korbel, n. 44, pp. 142-51.
99. S/5 January 1949.
100. *Manchester Guardian,* (ed.), "Kashmir", 3 January, 1949.
101. *The Statesman and The Nation,* 5 January, 1949.
102. C. Das Gupta, n. 51, pp. 200-10.
103. S.M. Burke, n. 4, p. 34.
104. Joseph Korbel, n. 44, p. 154.
105. *Ibid.,* pp. 155-58.
106. *The Hindu* (Ed.), "Kashmir", August 1949.
107. Joseph Korbel, n. 44, pp. 158-60.
108. *Ibid.,* p. 160.
109. Sir Godfrej Davis, "Kashmir: A Sovereignty State", *The Artistic Review,* Vol. XLVII, January 1951, p. 35.
110. Joseph Korbel, n. 44, p. 166.
111. Surendra Chopra, n. 91, p. 166.
112. *Ibid.,* pp. 77-78.
113. S.C.O.R., 5th January-May 1950, pp. 14-16.
114. *Ibid.*
115. See for More details, *Ibid.,* supplement, Jan-May, 1980, pp. 4-6.
116. Joseph Korbel, n. 44.
117. Sangat Singh, n. 1, p. 57.
118. B.N. Mullik, *My Years with Nehru: Kashmir.* (Bombay, 1971), p. 28.
119. Surendra Chopra, n. 91, pp. 91-92.
120. *London Times,* 17 January, 1951.
121. *Ibid.*
122. *Hindustan Times,* 13 February, 1951.

Kashmir Issue: Formative Phase and Beyond

International milieu was marred with tensions because of the Korean War. Though India and Pakistan were not directly involved in the Korean Crisis but were in the grip of solving the problems that emerged out of the partition of British India.

Pakistan particularly was deeply involved in setting her house in order. There was a leadership crisis prevailing after the death of Jinnah and murder of Prime Minister Liaquat Ali Khan in 1953. The army and bureaucracy were working together in the hope of making inroads into the power structure of Pakistan.

Liaquat Ali Khan was trying his best to control the power structure. It was a diplomatic gimmick by Liaquat to cash the situation prevailing in the State of Jammu and Kashmir in order to strengthen his political position.

CORRESPONDENCE BETWEEN PRIME MINISTERS OF INDIA AND PAKISTAN, 15 JULY 1951 TO 29 JULY 1951

On 15 July 1951 in a telegram to Prime Minister Nehru, Liaquat Ali Khan pointed out the concentration of troops in east Punjab and in Jammu and Kashmir. The concentration of Indian troops 'constitutes a great threat to the security of Pakistan and to international peace.' He alleged that the main reason for the existing tension between India and Pakistan was due to the persistent failure by the Indian Government to settle disputes between the two countries by peaceful means. Pakistan was interested in solving the disputes by peaceful methods and it 'has no aggressive designs against anyone.' He also referred the need for the maintenance of a peaceful atmosphere in the State as Dr. Graham; the UN Representative is endearing to carry out his duties entrusted to him by the Security Council in its Resolution of 30 March 1951. He demanded the immediate end of the concentration of Indian troops and the movement Indian armed forces towards the Indo-Pakistan border.

Indian Prime Minister Nehru in his reply on 17 July 1951 informed his Pakistani counterpart that 'our apprehension regarding any threat to the Security of Pakistan is completely unjustified.' India did not want war with Pakistan and India had unilaterally reduced the armed forces last year in the hope that this might have some effect on Pakistan. On the other hand, Pakistan troops had been largely massed on the Indian frontiers. In addition to this, an intensive and astonishing campaign for Jehad and war against India was carried on not only by newspapers but by responsible authorities in Pakistan. Nehru made it clear that 'my government cannot ignore this continual talk and preparation for war in Pakistan and we would be failing in our duty if we did not take effective defensive measures.' The movement of troops on the Indo-Pakistan frontier was a defensive step and there was no intention whatever for any aggressive action on our part and any aggression on Indian territory would be resisted... The attitude and propaganda was to be felt the major impediment in the development of these relations. Nehru in order to clear Indian intentions reminded Liaquat Ali Khan of the proposal of a 'No War Pact' between India and Pakistan, offered by the Indian Government.

He urged him 'to stop the propaganda for Jehad and war against India in Pakistan. This will help more than anything else in improving the relations between our two countries.'

Liaquat Ali Khan had shown his disappointments after reading Nehru reply and sent another telegram to him on 20 July 1951. He said that instead of revoking the concentration of Indian troops on Pakistan frontier, Nehru made a series of allegations against Pakistan. He challenged Nehru's contention regarding his desire to maintain peace in the area by alleging that 'the continual denial to the people of Kashmir their right of self-determination and repeated threats to security of Pakistan by massing Indian troops against its borders were hardly 'indications of a desire for peace.'

He denied 'that there was any concentration of Pakistani troops on the border and this would be borne out by an independent observer. He made serious charges against Nehru and prominent Indian leaders for launching propaganda in the Indian press against Pakistan. They spoke of the 'liquidation of Pakistan... and to make attacks aimed at the integrity of Pakistan.'

He also made a reference to Nehru's proposal of 'No War Pact'. The proposal for a 'No War Declaration' could not be carried out to a conclusion only because of Nehru's refusal to agree that if disputes between India and Pakistan could not be settled by negotiations and mediation, they should be referred to arbitration. There could be no clear proof of Pakistan's desire for a peaceful solution of its disputes with India that all our disputes should be settled by negotiations and mediation and failing that by arbitration. Unfortunately India preferred threat or use of force in settling disputes in its favour whenever the opportunity arose.

Nehru had earlier admitted the concentration of Indian troops on Pakistani frontier for purely defensive purposes. Liaquat argued that 'the nature and magnitude of these movements and in particular the forward movement of your armoured division and a brigade would not lead anyone to feel that their presence so close to Pakistan's frontier is for defensive purposes.' As Pakistan had not concentrated any troops on the border, Indian action could not be justified on any ground. He described the concentration of troops as a have threat to Pakistan's security and urged him 'earnestly to withdraw these forces so that this threat to security of Pakistan and international peace is removed.'

Nehru sent the reply of Liaquat telegram on 23 July; describing the contents of Liaquat as 'propagandist'. He was of the view that there was no propaganda against Pakistan in the Indian press. On the contrary, threats of war over Kashmir in the Pakistani press had occurred almost daily for many months. He quoted a few extracts from reports of views publicly expressed by persons in Pakistan holding the highest offices.

You can take it from us that the day we became desperate and lose all hope of a just solution of the problem, not only the entire Pathan population of Pakistan and the tribal areas will rise up for the holy Jehad in Kashmir but our brothers from across the Afghan frontier will also throw in their lot with us for the cause (Khan Abdul Qayyum Khan, Prime Minister of (NWFP). 'So long as a single Pakistani is alive, no body dare snatch Kashmir from Pakistan by force... If the problem was not settled immediately, the whole of Asia would be engulfed in the flame of war which might lead to a world conflagration' (Sardar Abdul Sattar, then Governor of West Punjab).

"I say this with full responsibility that India has now over several months taken up the attitude with regard to Kashmir which deliberately blocks progress along peaceful lines, what does India desire? It has no right to complain if it gets something else (Sir Mohammed Zafarullah Khan, then Foreign Minister of Pakistan). Prime Minister Liaquat Ali Khan told a press conference in Karachi that the Kashmir question cannot brook any delay. He said there were only two courses open to Pakistan to settle the issue. One was to pursue the matter in the Security Council. The second I would not tell..."

The charge that India had persistently refused to allow a peaceful solution through a free plebiscite in Kashmir was as India repeatedly pointed out, was baseless. It was Pakistan which from the beginning had created obstacles in the way of holding plebiscite. It was the continuing presence of Pakistan armies there that was responsible for not holding the plebiscite. The posture adopted by the Pakistani leadership and press that Pakistan was preparing herself to seek the solution of the Kashmir dispute by fierce hiss and this alone is responsible for the precautionary measures that we have taken. Nehru once again assured Liaquat Ali Khan that 'military movements on our side have not been inspired by any aggressive intent or design on our part against Pakistan. India has no intention whatever of attacking Pakistan or of seeking the solution of any problem by force, but if Indian territory including Kashmir is invaded by Pakistan then India will take all measures in self-defence. If as you say it is Pakistan's policy not to attack India, I see no reason why peace between our two countries should in any way be threatened.'

Nehru repeated once again his offer of 'No War Declaration'. It was without any conditions and no strings attached, but Liaquat did not accept it. Nehru further emphasized 'what is needed to ease the present tension is a declaration by your Government that on no account will they attack or invade Indian territory. If the military propaganda against India and talk of war in Pakistan ease. I am confident that not only the present tension will ease but the way will be prepared for a calm discussion, in a peaceful atmosphere, of disputes outstanding between our two countries.'

Pakistan Prime Minister replied on 26 July regarding the 'No-War Declaration' offered by Nehru. Pakistan was of view that the fact of the matter was that you were not prepared to accept any effective 'No War Declaration' which would rule out the use of force in the various forms in the settlement of disputes and which would establish effective procedures for settlement of disputes. He denied that he had added any conditions. Liaquat wrote he was only in favour of accepting arbitration if negotiations and mediation fail to solve the disputes. No doubt, both the countries had pledged not to attack each other. These declarations had proved to be futile as India have threatened the security of Pakistan by demonstration of force. The first and foremost condition was the withdrawal of Indian armed forces from the frontier to their normal peacetime stations.

Liaquat also presented a Peace Plan to Nehru which he felt would establish a durable peace in the region. He made the following proposals:

1. The troops now concentrated on borders should immediately be withdrawn to their normal peacetime stations.
2. As soon as this had been done, both India and Pakistan should reaffirm their agreement that the question of the accession of the State of Jammu and Kashmir will be decided through the democratic method of a free and impartial plebiscite held under UN auspices. Both governments, should state their readiness to implement without obstruction or delay, the obligation undertaken by them under the (UNCIP) Resolutions of 13 August 1948 and 5 January 1949 which include the observance of the ceasefire agreement and the withdrawal of their armed forces from the State and to accept the decision of the Security Council in the event of any differences in regard to the interpretation and execution of these agued Resolution.
3. Both Governments should also declare their renunciation of the use of force as methods in the settlement of any other disputes and to refer such disputes to arbitration or judicial determination if they are not resolved by negotiations or mediation.
4. Both Governments should reaffirm their obligation undertaken by them in the Delhi Agreement of 8 April particularly in Clause (VIII) that they shall not permit propaganda in other country directed against the territorial integrity of the other or purporting to incite to war between them and shall take prompt and effective action against any individual or organization guilty of such propaganda.
5. Both Governments should make a declaration that they will on no account attack or invade the territory of the other.

Liaquat Ali Khan also invited Nehru to visit Karachi and discuss the efforts to be initiated by the two countries in the near future for the restoration of peace.

On 29 July 1951, Nehru sent the reply of Liaquat Ali telegram. He reminded Liaquat that Pakistan Government was continually saying or hunting that if you would resort to force to settle the dispute, India was compelled to take precautionary measures against the threat If Pakistan had no intention to attack India explicitly including Kashmir and the temper of the war so manifested in Pakistan was cooled, arid then the danger of the war between the two countries would ease. Nehru denied his charges that India was not committed to honour the 'international agreements for a free and fair plebiscite in Kashmir under UN auspices'. The delay in the holding of plebiscite was the non-implementation of the various clauses of these Resolutions; particularly the very first condition regarding the withdrawal of Pakistan army from the Jammu and Kashmir. As regards the peace plan, Nehru said that India had already initiated measures in this regard:

1. The withdrawal of our forces which have recently been moved towards the Pakistan border.
2. The settlement of Kashmir problem.
3. We are ready to affirm again that the Government of India renounce the use of force as a method of settling all (repeat all) disputes we have not rejected either arbitration or judicial determination as a method of settling disputes which are not resolved by negotiations or mediation. All that we have contended is that the question of arbitration or judicial settlement should be decided with due regard to the merits of each case. You will remember that we made proposals for the judicial determination of two of our major disputes, namely canal waters and evacuee property. But you did not accept these proposals.
4. We accept again the obligation undertaken by the two Governments about propaganda against the territorial integrity of both countries taking action we have to act within our own constitution and in

accordance with judicial pronouncements about freedom of expression which limit our action. Our Government's policy however is clear and has been repeatedly affirmed. In this connection may we draw your attention to the type of propaganda which has been and is taking place in Pakistan, propaganda often calls not only for war but the conquest of India by Pakistan? We are not troubled by these fanatic outbursts but inevitably they produce some reaction here...

5. I entirely agree with you that we should make a declaration that neither Government will on any account attack or invade the territory of the other. I must ask, however, that the declaration should cover the State of Jammu and Kashmir...the future of which must be decided by peaceful means.[1]

The efforts made by the two Prime Ministers to create a congenial atmosphere did not produce desired results. In fact, if we analyse the contents and tone of these telegrams, one aspect is clear that the chain of sending and receiving telegrams ended by levelling charges and counter-charges. Both parties accused each other for creating tension in the region and also creating obstacles in the way of the solution of the various bilateral issues.

If we take into consideration the atmosphere prevailing in both the countries in particular and in the State of Jammu and Kashmir in general, it was not proper time for the Prime Ministers of both the countries to indulge in the war of words and arguments. It further widened the differences between the two neighbours. The atmosphere in Kashmir was tense after the failure of the UN to clear the valley of the undesired elements and the illegal occupation of the large chunk of territory by Pakistan. The failure of General McNaughton and Dixon Mission and the way the leadership of the two countries reacted to these proposals, further established that the situation in the valley had been complicated for any investigation, interpretations or explanations. The political elites of both the nations were not on a right path. As political instability was prevailing in

Pakistan and it failed to provide any constitution to the people the issues raised by Liaquat Ali Khan in the telegram were of no importance. It was only to divert the attention of the people that such charges were made against India.

GRAHAM MISSION

On 21 February 1951, The UN Security Council once again took up the Kashmir issue. The British representatives Sir Gladwyn drew the attention of the Council to 'the developments in Asia have clearly demonstrated the urgent need for removing the obstacles to cooperation and mutual assistance between the Governments of India and Pakistan. Never was it necessary indeed than it now for the two great peace loving states to give practical evidence that these issues which divide them, are still capable of adjustment in accordance with the purposes and principles of the organization to which they belong.'[2]

The US and Great Britain submitted another slightly modified version of their earlier Resolution of 21 February, reaffirming the two original Resolutions of the Commission of 13 August 1948 and 5 January 1949 accepted by India and Pakistan. Once more, the UN appointed its representative after consultation with the Governments of India and Pakistan to complete the demilitarization of Kashmir within three months and in case of failure to report to the Security Council the points of difference between the parties in regard. to the interpretation and execution of the Commission's Resolution. It called upon the parties to accept in case of failure, arbitration by an arbitrator or a panel of arbitrations appointed by the President of the International Court of Justice after consultation with the parties concerned.

The Resolution had also shown its concern regarding the convening of the Constituent Assembly in the State of Jammu and Kashmir for the purpose of determining the future shape and affiliations of the State of Jammu and Kashmir. Reminding the Governments and the authorities which were behind such move, the principles embodied in the Security Council Resolutions of 21 April 1948 (S/426), 3 June 1948 (S/819) and 14 March 1950 and (UNCIP)

Resolutions of 13 August 1948 and 5 January 1949 that the final disposition of the State of Jammu and Kashmir will be made in accordance with the will of the people, expressed through the democratic method of a free and impartial plebiscite conducted under the auspices of the UN.

It affirmed that the convening of the Constituent Assembly in order to determine the future shape would not constitute disposition of the State in accordance with the spirit of the (UNCIP) Resolutions. The Resolutions further laid down that a prompt settlement of the Kashmir dispute would help in maintaining peaceful environment in the Indian sub-continent. Observing from Sir Owen Dixon's report the main points of difference preventing agreement between the parties were:

- The procedure for and the extent of demilitarization of the state preparatory to the holding of plebiscite.
- The degree of control over the exercise of the functions of government in the state necessary to ensure a free and fair plebiscite.

The Resolution was adopted and accepted by Pakistan but Indian Government refused to accept it as she was against the arbitration proposal, contained in the new Resolution. Frank P. Graham was appointed by the UN as its representative.[3]

Korbel was of the view that this was over clouding. It had never been recommended, nor can one seriously believe that Nehru actually thought it had been, that the final fate of Kashmir should be decided by a tribunal. The Resolution continued to insist and both parties to the dispute agreed, that the final fate of the Kashmir would be settled in one way by plebiscite. The Security Council, its Commission and Sir Own Dixon had repeatedly on every occasion confirmed this agreement. It was only the extent and procedure of the State's demilitarization which was to be submitted to arbitration, one could therefore expect that a country of such undisputed greatness, led by man of Nehru's stature and integrity, would have reacted more favourably to such a valid and under the

Charter of the UN, recommended technique of international cooperation.[4]

Meanwhile, the process of democratization was going on in the State of Jammu and Kashmir. Pakistan requested the Council to stop the convening of the Constitution Assembly. Accordingly accepting Pakistan's plea, the Council wrote a letter to the Indian and Pakistani Governments that such a step would involve procedures which are in conflict with the commitments of the parties. The Kashmir Government decided to hold elections for the Constituent Assembly in September 1951 as it was within the jurisdiction of the State to have its own Constitution and discard the out dated legal system enforced by the Maharaja. But the Government of Pakistan reaction was very sharp as it considered the move another calculated attempt by the Indian Government to further consolidate her position in the State. In Pakistan, cries of Jehad against India were raised frequently. Lot of tension was on the Indo-Pakistan frontier.[5] Times of India wrote 'If Karachi believes that by such tactics, it can intimidate the government and people of this country, it mistakes the temper of India. Delhi has always been willing to parley with reasons but sword will be met by a sword. If hostilities, unfortunately breakout again, they cannot be confined to the territory of Kashmir and will involve a full scale war between the two countries; neither of the two can afford this costly adventure. Pakistan is playing with fire.'[6]

Addressing the Annual session of the All Jammu and Kashmir National Conference on 1 July 1951, Sheikh Abdullah declared, 'The current problems of Kashmir are so complicated that I don't know where to begin and where to end. It is fairly well known to everybody how Pakistan has felt about our problems. But so far as the people of Kashmir are concerned, they feel they have waited long and it is very difficult on their part to live in uncertainty any longer. So they have decided to end this uncertainty once for all.' He further said that whatever Pakistan might think or like to do, the people of 'Kashmir are bent upon framing their Constitution and taking decisions on valid matters that have awaited their decisions.' He criticized the Draft Resolution introduced by the US and Britain in the Council on 21

February 1951, he said that, 'The attitude which the Draft Resolution reveals towards the Constituent Assembly comes as a painful reminder of all the dilatory means which had invaded our Country.' Criticizing the attitude of those who were advocating the Resolution, Sheikh felt that it 'appears as an attempt to stay the democratic development of the people who wish to build the framework of their government in a democratic manner.' It was the desire of the people of Kashmir to convene the Constituent Assembly. He without mincing words lashed out at the Anglo-US move and said, 'Surely any individual or institution that denounces such move cannot be sympathetic to the vital spirit of the democracy. The objection that our being in the Government while elections are held will be prejudicial, to correct expressions of the popular will, is not valid: can any democratic government, say England, the US, France or even Pakistan show any example when the Government in power came out of Kashmir being convened with the present Government in Office? Not only was that but objections being raised at the convening of the Constituent Assembly too. He asked: those who raise objections surely are sufficiently aware as constitutionalists that such an objection is an attack on the prerogative of the Government to seek the confidence of its people. Further, it is an anti-popular move which seeks to deny the people its sovereign right to self-determination, a right which is as inalienable as the soul of democracy.'

Sheikh the then leader of the House, made statements of objectives in his opening address in 1951 and clearly defined the issues being faced by the Constituent Assembly. He said that the Assembly was to decide about the accession. Sheikh asked it to 'declare its reasoned conclusions regarding accession. This will help us to channelize our energies resolutely and with greater zeal in the direction in which we have already started moving for the social and economic advancement of our country. He discussed the various alternatives and rejecting the possibility of the State's accession to Pakistan or its independence status, he observed that the Congress had always supported the cause of State's people's freedom. The Congress had ended the autocratic rule of the princes and representative Governments have been established and democratic process was already going on. He categorically said, naturally if we accede to India, there is no danger of the revival of feudalism and autocracy. Moreover, during the last four years, the Government of India has never tried to interfere in our internal autonomy. This experience has strengthened our confidence in them as a democratic state.'

Sheikh Abdullah also praised the Indian Constitution as it was really secular and based upon justice, freedom and equality for all without distinction. He considered it as the 'bed rock of modern democracy'. This should meet the argument that the Muslims of Kashmir cannot have security in India where the large majority of populations are Hindus. He felt that 'the artificial divisions between the religions and the Indian Constitution have amply and finally repudiated the concept of a religious state, which is a throw-back to medievalism.'

He further emphasized that economic development of the State must be given top priority for the well-being of the people of the state. The traditional markets for the goods produced by the State were centred in India. Industry was also very important for the State. As the State was rich in minerals and raw material for the industry and with the help of India, the industrial capability would be further strengthened. India being more highly industrialized than Pakistan could be more helpful to develop State's resources, could provide equipment technical services and materials. India could be more helpful in marketing as many goods which the State won't be in a position to produce, for instance, sugar, cotton, cloth and other essential commodities could be supplied by India in large quantities.[7]

In the initial years the issue was not so complicated and the process of democratisation which started with the convening of the Assembly was considered to be a healthy process, as India was committed to provide the people of the State of Jammu and Kashmir, a political system based on democratic values and traditions. The people of Kashmir were very excited, as was evident from their active participation in the elections held for electing the members of the Constituent Assembly. They were fed up with the interference of other forces in their internal affairs, were quite happy to be with India. As India was against sending of Frank P. Graham to the State of Jammu and Kashmir, the people of the State 'in tune with the Indian Government wishes, held demonstration against Graham when he arrived in Srinagar. The main political force in Kashmir, the National Conference, led by Sheikh Abdullah, was supporting the strengthening of the relations with India instead of Pakistan'. There was no talk of making Kashmir an independent State as it was not practically feasible and political parties, peoples and outside forces were well aware about this fact.

When Graham arrived in the Indian sub- continent on 30 June 1951, war hysteria and tension in the area was on the highest pitch, was clearly evident from the telegrams and letters exchanged between the Indian and Pakistan Prime Ministers from 15 July to 9 August 1951.[8]

On 7 September 1951, Graham sent a letter to the Prime Ministers of India and Pakistan. He was keen that both the parties must reach on some sort of compromise, by accommodating each other viewpoint and also according to the (UNCIP) Resolutions. He asked both the parties that they must reaffirm their determination not to resort to force and adhere to peaceful procedures and specially pledge themselves that they would not commit aggression or make war, the one against the other, with regard to the question of Jammu and Kashmir. Both the Governments must control those elements which were bent upon or issuing war-like statements.

He asked in his letter that both the parties must take steps for the process of demilitarization and it should be completed by 15 July 1952 and reaffirms their acceptance of the principle that the question of the accession would be decided through democratic method of free and impartial plebiscite.

On the Pakistani side of the ceasefire line, Graham asked for the immediate withdrawal of the tribesmen and Pakistani nationals not normally resident there, had entered the State for the purpose of fighting. The withdrawals of Pakistani troops and large-scale disbandment and disarming of the Azad Kashmir forces must be carried out.

On the Indian side of the ceasefire line, the bulk of the Indian forces in the State must be withdrawn and further withdrawal of Indian troops and reduction of Kashmir State forces.

The proposals also stipulated that demilitarization should be carried out in such a way so as to involve no threat to the ceasefire agreement. The Government of India was asked to appoint a (PA) not later than the final day of the demilitarisation period.[9]

There were serious differences between the two Governments regarding the process of demilitarization but it did not discourage Graham and he recommended to the Security Council that both the parties should be called on to refrain from building up military potential and avoid hostile statements and that negotiations be continued on the remaining differences.[10]

Altogether Graham submitted six reports to the Council. His work, as Joseph Korbel said, 'Revealed a pain-staking relentless effort to narrow, step by step, the differences between the Governments of India and Pakistan.' After thorough investigations, he prepared a plan containing twelve proposals, but most of them were of a general nature and 'did not present serious obstacles to acceptance.' But Graham found himself precisely where Sir Own Dixon had been in September 1951. In the conclusion of his Fifth Report to the Council, he expressed the hope that both the parties should enter into direct negotiations to bring about a solution, 'and reporting an agreement on Kashmir and thereby light a torch along the difficult path of the people's pilgrimage towards peace.' Once more a 'thoroughly frustrated negotiator had arrived at the same conclusion as Sir Owen Dixon that the inability of the two parties to agree under UN mediation left no solution except that they agree between themselves. It is difficult to envisage that any torches lighted under these circumstances would be for the purpose of illuminating the path to peace.'[11]

Graham's methods were somewhat different from Sir Owen Dixon's approach. Dixon's proposals had touched the crux of the problem moved swiftly and when rejected by one of the parties concerned, put the blame where he believed it belonged. Dixon, gave up after three short months of negotiations while he assumed .the role of the realist. Graham on the other hand was a patient mediator, who listened, ascertained the points of disagreement and until his Fourth Report abstained from recommendation of a concrete nature.' In the beginning of his mission, he concentrated on the minor issues of little importance in the hope that it would help in preparing the ground for a better understanding between the two countries on the crucial problem of demilitarisation. Before starting his mission, Graham had studied carefully the attitude of the Indian and Pakistani leaders and above all the happenings in Kashmir. Keeping in mind all these pressures and circumstances prevailing, he proceeded with his mission; he studiously avoided any possible statements or proposals that would increase these antagonism or destroy his mission. But even so, his every step was prejudged and his mission hopeless.[12]

With the presentation of the Fifth Report ended the first phase of the UN mediation in Kashmir which had been carried out by three mediators and continued for about five years. The UN mediation failed as its Security Council as well as all its three representatives failed to fix the responsibility for the aggression and treated the aggressor and the aggressed on the same footing. It was also believed that another factor which contributed for the failure of the UN efforts because 'it did not handle this dispute fairly and honestly. It seems that the UN worked as an Anglo-American alliance against India.' Both the US and Britain, since, India formally lodged her complaint with the Security Council were working with one single aim, to support Pakistan's position on Kashmir. The presence of an American on the (UNCIP) nominated by the President of the Security Council -the appointment of Admiral Nimitz as (PA), again an American, General McNaughton a Canadian, obviously toeing the Anglo-American line, the appointment of Dixon, an Australian, also representing the same alliance and finally the impression as if the American bloc was 'determined to force its verdict through these mediators'. That was behind the contention that why all the mediators could not evoke confidence of the Indian leadership. 'It is but natural for the

Indians to doubt the credentials of a representative of a state that had adopted an attitude in the Security Council which was anything but sympathetic. It is likely that the mediators, if they had been chosen from amongst emergent nation would have been more successful.'[13]

The debate on the Graham Reports established beyond doubt that 'the game of power politics had its full circle.' There was a change in the attitude after the KMT was pushed out of the Chinese mainland and its dependence on the US increased, it adopted an attitude which 'can be characterized as cheaper edition of the Anglo-American attitude. The Soviet Union started sympathy with the Indian Government and it 'came out in defence of India's action in convening the Constituent Assembly of Jammu and Kashmir to decide the future of the State. The US was supporting Pakistan because of its desire for bases in Pakistan occupied Kashmir also proved true.'[14]

After Graham abandoned his mission as per his observation, direct negotiations were held between the Prime minister of India and Pakistan. The internal developments in Pakistan also 'facilitated the appointment of Mohammed Ali Bogra, as the Prime Minister of Pakistan as earlier Nazimuddin was dismissed by Governor General Ghulam Mohammed. Bogra was a seasoned diplomat, a successful Ambassador to Burma, Canada and the US and had certain amount of boyish charm and optimism. He was conscious of Pakistan's lack of military strength and economic weakness and believed that she could best be strengthened by allying herself with the US.' At the same time, he also adopted a more realistic attitude towards India and expressed his desire to narrow the differences with India and 'establish good neighbourly relations' was his prominent objective. The days after taking over, Bogra described Nehru as the 'elder brother' and desired to meet him 'soonest'. The two Prime Ministers first met informally in London in June 1953. The occasion was Queen Elizabeth II 'coronation and were the guests of the British Government. On 25 July 1952, Bogra met Nehru for serious negotiations at Karachi. Nehru was 'spontaneously cheered' by the people on arrival. The joint statement issued after Nehru visit on 28 July, mentioned that the two leaders had 'talked together cordially' and the discussion had 'necessarily been of preliminary nature' and would be resumed further in Delhi.[15]

The dismissal of Sheikh Abdullah on 9 August 1953, replaced by Bakshi Ghulam Mohammad had generated a new controversy. Earlier Sheikh was showing signs of drifting away from Nehru and the Indian Government. On 11 March 1952, Sheikh appealed to the people of Azad Kashmir to struggle hard in order to get themselves liberated 'from the present Pakistani rulers whose attempt always is to mislead you and keep you away from knowing the true facts about US.'[16] Sheikh continued his campaign against India, sometimes criticizing Indian political setup and the communalism prevailing in India. Nehru was worried about the behaviour of Sheikh Abdullah and the speeches he was delivering in various parts of the valley. He warned India of applying the Indian Constitution to the State of Kashmir.

On 24 July 1952, Nehru announced in the Lok Sabha, the agreement signed between him and Sheikh Abdullah, giving special status to Kashmir which was not provided to any other Indian state. It was agreed that the hereditary ruler would be replaced by a Head of the State who would be elected for five years by the Constituent Assembly and would be recognized by the President of India. Fundamental rights that were guaranteed by the Indian Constitution would be applied to Kashmir, subject to the provision that, they won't encroach upon the programme of land reforms, including the appropriation of land without compensation, nor must they in any way or from hamper the security of the State. The Government of India further agreed that the Kashmir legislature 'shall have the power to define and regulate the rights and privileges of the permanent residents of State, more especially in regard to the acquisition of immovable property, appointments to services and like matters. That meant clearly that, Indian citizens were debarred from taking over immovable property in Kashmir, but the Kashmiri were free to acquire land or property in any part of India'.

The jurisdiction of the Indian Supreme Court was to be curtailed in the case of Kashmir, to inter-state disputes and to matters of defence, foreign affairs and communications.

Nehru Government wanted the Supreme Court to be the final authority but Sheikh Abdullah wanted to leave the question open. Furthermore, the Indian Tricolour (National Flag) was recognized by the Kashmir State as supreme, but it was allowed to maintain its own flag. In financial matter, the Indian Government wanted complete integration, but again Sheikh wished to again reconsider the matter.

The most important provision of the Nehru-Sheikh Abdullah Agreement was concerning the emergency powers of the President of India under Article 352 of the Indian Constitution the President has the right to declare a state of emergency in case of invasion, external danger or internal disturbances. The Agreement provided that in the latter case, the President's power could be applied only 'at the request or with the concurrence of the government of the state'. That would mean that in the case of a violent uprising in Kashmir, the President of India has no right to declare a state of emergency and to intervene unless the Srinagar Government asked him to do so.

The Nehru-Sheikh Agreement met with severe criticism in some Indian newspapers and parliamentary circles. They were concerned both with the fate of the Hindus in Jammu and to privileged position Sheikh Abdullah had managed to carve out for him. They wished to see the State integrated with India as were all other constituent units of the Indian Republic. Nehru, however, defended the Agreement and said that it was the need of 'the circumstances prevailing there. He had signed the Agreement with Sheikh in good faith pointing to the necessity of having confidence in Abdullah's friendship towards India.'[17]

Meanwhile, serious differences emerged between the leadership of National Conference on various political issues, particularly on the Kashmir accession to India. Sheikh did not consider that the accession was final. He said that though the accession to India was complete in all aspects yet it was conditional and temporary in the sense that the people were to decide its future through plebiscite. Sheikh even said that Kashmir's accession to India was imposed on us because of India's refusal to give any help without the signing of the formal Instrument of Accession. The other faction led by

Bakshi Ghulam Mohamad who was strongly in support of India 'advocated that Kashmiris would defend at the cost of their lives the State's accession to India and the special privileged position granted to the State under the Indian constitution.

In the numerous statements that Sheikh made in and outside Kashmir, he has been able to clarify his ideas and aims which had been blurred by somewhat contradicting and provocative utterances. But the foremost matter on which Sheikh had always laid much emphasis was the affiliation of the state with India and Pakistan. Once he said that 'the eyes of the world are seeing that the Kashmir people reject the Indian claim that the Kashmir's accession to India is final To repeat that Kashmir is an integral part of India is nonsense.' He warned that the people of Kashmir would not rest until they were given an opportunity to decide their future freely. As a corollary, Sheikh Abdullah repeatedly demanded that the right of self-determination for the Kashmiri. He called as the basic issue from which neither he nor his colleagues would budge.

Like all dispassionate students of Kashmir affairs, Sheikh Abdullah firmly advocated that there could be no peace or progress in the State until the accession issue was decided, finally keeping in mind the wishes of the people of Kashmir. 'Whatever is the legal arid constitutional arguments, the fact remains that the Kashmir is still an unresolved dispute and is causing much misery in both countries.' But he was convinced that the dispute could only be 'settled with the goodwill of India and Pakistan. He was of the opinion that the solution should be such as to satisfy all the three parties 'if India and Pakistan suffer, how Kashmir can prosper... so long as India and Pakistan are at logger-heads, the people of Kashmir will not enjoy freedom.'[18]

While considering different solutions of Kashmir Sheikh was by no means dogmatic nor was he unmindful of the tremendous difficulties with which it was beset. Finding the Kashmir's incessantly talking about accession, he reminded them. 'Accession after all was a means to an end; it is not an end is itself. Let us keep our ultimate goal before us and not get impatient.'[19]

What kind of solution did Sheikh Abdullah envisage? Though no well defined formula did emerge to this repeatedly asked question but he did not entirely cancel his demand. When asked of his view that the accession was a minor issue Sheikh Abdullah asserted that the people of Kashmir realised that the lasting peace between India and Pakistan was essential for them. He was confident that if some way of creating harmony in the sub-continent was in sight, the Kashmiri would not impede the settlement by demanding their pound of flesh. He also warned the Muslims in Srinagar on 23 April 1965 that in making up their choice they should bear in mind the possible repercussions of their decision on the Muslim minority in India and the Hindu minority in Pakistan. A solution I am working at, should neither give to India nor Pakistan a sense of victory. Sheikh also expressed firm faith in secularism and opposition to the 'Two Nations Theory.' Any solution of the Kashmir question should be such that while it should not weaken India's secularism, it should also satisfy aspirations of both India and Pakistan.[20]

For obvious reasons, Sheikh Abdullah consistently refused to outline a solution which he claimed to have involved after consultation with the Indian leaders and other friends in India. That was considered to be a wise step. He had however made a few unambiguous declarations about important matters thereby giving certain definite hints into the working of his mind. Interestingly on either side of the ceasefire line many people, taking clue from Sheikh Abdullah statements, were led to believe that he was for the independence of Kashmir. But that was also not entirely correct. He declared on 13 April 1964 what he said was that the Kashmir dispute should be settled to the satisfaction of India, Pakistan and Kashmir in accordance with the wishes of the Kashmiris. He made it clear that he stood by the views on this subject which he expressed in 1949 when he had emphasized that 'Independence was not only theoretical and academic but also meaningless.' There had been a talk of creating a confederation of India and Pakistan and Kashmir also can join as an independent unit. Sheikh Abdullah was of the view that 'I am thinking in term of a confederation of

India and Pakistan or any such proposal but I am not thinking in terms of peace and amity'. When on 10 May, *New York Times* reported that 'Sheikh Abdullah was advocating an Indo-Pak condominium as solution of Kashmir problem. But Sheikh Abdullah declared it as purely based on 'mere assumptions and speculators'.

But he was an able statesman and refused to be provoked when even responsible people made untimely statements calculated to irritate him.[21]

He worked hard for creating amicable atmosphere between India and Pakistan with the ultimate aim of finally resolving the Kashmir dispute. It was 'an arduous job' which Sheikh Abdullah had taken upon himself. But it would be a futile attempt if one overlooks or minimizes the difficulties and impediments in the path while proceeding towards the goal or not to clearly comprehend the reasons that he kept India and Pakistan apart, rendering it extremely difficult to end the deadlock in Kashmir. The antagonism which had been plaguing India and Pakistan was not something peculiar to this sub-continent. In the contemporary international politics, it was a worldwide phenomenon that the clash between the two nationalisms which stood irreconcilably poised over territorial claims creates difficulties. Unless a rational outlook is adopted and a sense of accommodating each other demands is not in existence, there can be no hope of agreement. But a rational mind refuses to move in narrow groves or to confuse itself to geographical limits, it considers the entire world as its homeland nationalism is lane of human culture and in certain respect it functions more stupidly than communalism, the horrors of which are visible in plenty in the Indian Sub-continent.[22]

Consciously or unconsciously, Sheikh Abdullah had realized that the deadliest foe to thwart his attempts was the unyielding spirit of nationalism. When he declared in Madras that 'we should accept Kashmiris as human beings and allow them to decide their own future otherwise they will be reduced to the position of animals.' He was indicating then as the only possible way of solving the Kashmir issue. When Sheikh Abdullah decided to visit Pakistan, it was contended that 'by making the settlement of the dispute which depend upon bringing the two irreconcilable nationalisms together in friendship and amity, Sheikh Abdullah had undertaken the reformist role of humanizing the politics.'[23]

About his mission to Pakistan, Prem Nath Bajaj, an eminent historian and analyst who had observed Sheikh Abdullah closely as a human being and as a political personality, wrote that 'Pakistan nationalism is narrower in outlook and more difficult to appease. As long as Sheikh Abdullah talks in terms of basic human values, the leaders of India as well as Pakistan will hear him with patience, be receptive, kind, suave and indulgent. But when he will like a proposal indicating any deviation from the posture publicly adopted by either side, it will be a different story.'[24]

The intervening period after the arrest of Sheikh saw two Prime Ministers (Bakshi and Shams-u-din) and the Chief Ministers (Sadiq and Mir Quasim) at the helm of affairs. The period 1953-66 under the Prime Ministership of Bakshi witnessed dramatic transformations in the socio-economic structure of the, state enjoying preferential treatment within it. The period witnessed impressive advancements in the sphere of education (including vocational), business, transport facilities, health services, tourism, industry, etc. creating enormous jobs and business opportunities. The role of Sadiq and Mir Quasim did not witness any further growth of development at activities to generate new jobs and business opportunities; Shams-u-din's tenure was too short to be of any consequence whatsoever. Within the system of governance, one parameter that rose unchecked was corruption in public life, through educational and other professional institutions including the judiciary were left untouched.[25]

On his release from jail in 1964, Sheikh on touring the inner- most parts of the State confessed that a Muslim of 1964 had materially changed beyond recognition from his predecessor of pre-1953 era. Another remarkable and politically significant act of various governments between 1953 and 1975 was to disallow emotional integration of Kashmiri Muslims even with the Hindus of Jammu. This was achieved by religiously transferring Muslim employee back to Srinagar after a brief stay at Jammu replacing them with Kashmiri Hindus.[26]

Despite the overall growth witnessed by the people in post-1953 era, Muslims of Kashmir always considered Bakshi a traitor and Sheikh a victim of circumstances. They considered the period without the Sheikh as transitory and awaited his release before he could lead them to the promised political set-up where they would be free. The man the people of Kashmir expected to struggle after having been set free ostensibly chose to occupy the seat of power in 1973. Sheikh was disgraced in the eyes of a common Muslim because their Sher-e-Kashmir had been assimilated into system, that is what at least they inferred.[27]

Much of what had been provided in the Article 370 had lost its relevance by the time Sheikh took over the Government in 1975. Some political analysts had concluded that Indira Gandhi brought Sheikh back into mainstream politics to put a stamp of legitimacy over the process of political assimilation of Kashmir within the Indian Union which had been initiated when G.M. Sadiq took over as the CM of the state. If the Indian political leadership had their plans *vis-a-vis* Kashmir, then the least that could be said here was that the National Conference leaders of post-1975 era had their own plan quite different from those of the former.[28]

The process of assimilation of Kashmir polity within the Indian Union had to be reversed if the right of self-determination had to become a live issue again among the people and dissent within Kashmir over the accession had to be covertly encouraged. Any formation any planned activity which looked promising in furthering the dissent had to be encouraged.[29]

The National Conference led by Sheikh Abdullah has always been an important political force beside the Congress. The internal situation in Kashmir on the political front, more or less remained calm as compared to the political environment prevailing in other states. The Central Government was always too cautious initiating any move or making any policy statements. Kashmir was a pampered child and was to always remain as long as any permanent solution of the Kashmir problem is found, which was unlikely in the near future. Pakistan had always analysed according to its own perspective whenever any important political development took place. There is no denying of the fact that a strong correlation was in existence between the Kashmir problem and the internal political environment. Since, the end of Maharaja rule, the Government in Kashmir State had always been pro-centre, it may be a Congress-led coalition or coalition led by any other political party. The money liberally provided by the Indian Government, for the various development projects and the various subsides provided in various forms, could be calculated in billions of rupees and there was never to be any shortage of finance for the State. But the various militant outfits and other political forces always cried for more development and other facilities to strengthen the infrastructure.

EFFORTS OUTSIDE THE UN AND THE KASHMIR ISSUE

The Graham Mission failed but it forcefully recommended that the Kashmir dispute be settled by sitting across the table. The direct negotiations were held in Delhi between Nehru and Bogra in the third week of August 1953. Before their formal meeting in Delhi, the political environment underwent a significant change in Pakistan. *The Dawn* of Karachi strongly suggested to Bogra that he should not undertake his planned journey to Delhi but pursue the question of Kashmir more vigorously in the UN. If Nehru could not tolerate his dear friend Abdullah expressing views which he (Nehru) does not like, how can he be expected to tolerate the ordinary man in Kashmir going to the polls and voting against Bharat 'in plebiscite?'

The tense atmosphere in the Kashmir emerged after the arrest of Abdullah which resulted in the killing of scores of Muslims. 'It was a stroke of lighting that had shattered the promising atmosphere of Indo-Pakistani relations.' The Pakistani Prime Minister rushed to Delhi because he wanted to avert the danger of a violent 'outburst of indignation on the part of Pakistanis, partly because he probably wanted to convince Nehru of the necessity of an early settlement of the Kashmir.' After four days of extensive consultation and negotiations, a joint statement issued contained the various unsettled problems discussed by the two Prime Ministers and of course, this Kashmir issue too. The part on Kashmir issue read:

> 'The Kashmir dispute was specially discussed at some length. It was their firm opinion that this should be settled in accordance with the wishes of the people of that State with a view to promoting their well-being and causing no disturbance to the life of the people of the state.'

The most feasible method of ascertaining the wishes of the people was holding of fair and impartial plebiscite. Such a plebiscite had been proposed and agreed to some years ago. Progress however, could not be made because of lack of agreement in regard to certain preliminary issues.

The Prime Minister agreed that these preliminary issues should be considered by them directly in order to arrive at agreements in regard to this. These agreements would have to be given effect and the next step would be the appointment of (PA).

In order to fix some kind of provisional time table, it was decided that the (PA) should be appointed by the end of April 1954. Previous to that date the preliminary issues referred to above should be decided. With this purpose in view, committees of military and other experts should be appointed to advise the Prime Ministers.

On the (PA) final appointment induction into office by the Jammu and Kashmir Government, he will examine the situation and report on it. He will then make such proposals as he thinks proper for preparations in the entire state and take such other steps as may be considered necessary there.

The joint comments marked a new phase in the direction of solving the Kashmir problem. In a way, it marked its new treatment. It no doubt confined the old agreement to let the people decide the fate of the State of Jammu and Kashmir by free and impartial plebiscite, but it also meant that the problem of demilitarization ('certain preliminary issues') would be considered by the Governments of India and Pakistan directly upon the advice of their experts and without any direct assistance from the UN or any other bodies. It further envisaged their implementation prior to the appointment of a new (PA) to succeed Admiral Nimitiz that was to take place by the end of April 1954'[30].

Interestingly, the communiqué did not mention the UN, though there was not reference of withdrawing it from the agenda, unfortunately, however, the proverbial ink of the common issue had hardly been dried. Its working instead of strengthening Indo-Pakistan friendship freshly established and still 'provoked critical reaction among the rightist parties in India and among all the newspapers'. The Azad leaders even declared at a press conference at Karachi that, 'It has been natural for Bharat (India) to devise some means to blanket her stark misdeeds and to camouflage the real situation in valley. It is our considered opinion, which we express with considerable pain that the Delhi Agreement has been used to serve exactly this end and no other... It has not brought the plebiscite about nearer than it was in 1949.'[31]

A number of commentators were of the opinion that the communiqué showed that India and Pakistan were well on their way towards the settlement of the Kashmir dispute and that it was Pakistan who 'foolishly upset the whole arrangements by accepting the US military aid.' A Pakistani scholar S.M. Burke was of the opinion that if we examine, the communiqué it was clear that it overlooked certain important implications. First, though it agreed that the Kashmir dispute to be settled according to the will of the people, the basic objectives were stated to be promoting the well-being of the people and to cause the least disturbance to their life. A favourable interpretation of these goals was that India being a progressive country and Pakistan a bigoted backward one, the well-being of Kashmir laid in joining hands with India and if they vote for in favour of Pakistan, the life of the Hindus and the Sikhs in the State would be in danger, setting of a fresh wave of communal frenzy in the sub-continent and this situation had to be avoided. Secondly, the joint declaration did not assign any future role to the UN Resolutions on Kashmir. The two Prime Ministers had vowed to resolve differences directly but it was not spelled out what would happen if the customary deadlock took place between them. The role of the UN on which weaker Pakistan had relied so much, was altogether discarded. Third, the (PA) who was previously a nominee of the Secretary General of the UN was decided to be 'appointed by the State of the Jammu and Kashmir Government. Fourth, the important question of conditions under which a plebiscite was to be conducted was not even touched in the statement. India remained adamant because first, the pro-Indian regime in the State should remain in power while the plebiscite was being conducted and second, no neutral troops should replace Indian troops to ensure freedom of the vote. Nehru also said publicly that (PA) should be a man from the neutral country and Nimitz should be replaced.[32]

The reason behind Nehru proposal as he had stated in his letter to the Prime Minister of Pakistan on 10 November 1953 was that the (PA) should not come from any major power or any country which was involved in the so-called cold war.

While rejecting Pakistan plea for a 'regional plebiscite', he said that any method that creates problems would be bad for the people of Kashmir. 'If a decision leads to large migrations that will upset the major character of the State and would also create ill feelings in Pakistan and India as well as in the Kashmir State.' Furthermore, it would be difficult to decide to divide the State into different regions. Also the mere definition of a region by some rough and ready way at this stage would create certain measures of upset at within that region. Nehru firmly believed that 'plebiscite should be for the State as a whole and the detailed result of the plebiscite would then be the major factor for the decision to be taken.'

Bogra replied Nehru letter on 1 December 1953 and stated in the beginning that as India and Pakistani both had already abandoned the idea of the regional plebiscite, the question of definition of the regions, therefore now no longer arises. He was somewhat confused what Nehru had said in his letter to him that after the declaration of the plebiscite results, the other factors would be taken into consideration. Bogra feared that such a course would not be feasible since it implied that even after the plebiscite had been taken there won't be automatic merger of the State with India or

Pakistan. In another letter, Nehru had drawn the attention of Bogra regarding the rumours that the US and Pakistan were in the process of signing military pacts. But the Government of Pakistan had denied that there was no such move. Nehru pointed out that any such pact between Pakistan and the US meant the alignment of Pakistan, both in regard to the foreign and defence policies, with a particular bloc of nations. So far India was concerned, it was her policy, to avoid any such alignments, because India believed that this would be undesirable from the point of view of peace in Asia as well as world peace. India hoped that the countries of Asia would keep free from these entanglements and an area of peace, whatever happened elsewhere. Some other countries in South Asia had independently followed the same policy. Apart from the danger of expanding the sphere of war, such alignments were highly likely to lead to progressive limitations in the independence of the country so entangled. The countries of Asia had only recently gained freedom and in India's opinion, it would be most unfortunate that any policy should be pursued which would inevitably bring in powerful influences, limiting that freedom.

Nehru said that he was pointing out in view of the developments appeared to be taking place, Pakistan's foreign and defence policies would become diametrically opposed to the policies of both India and Pakistan so consistently and earnestly pursued. He regretted that the area of disagreement between India and Pakistan would be extended over to wider field. India won't abandon its policy to pursue peace and nonalignment.

He feared that as reported in the US press that large-scale military assistance and equipment, arms and training would be given to Pakistan by the US. As reported by the *New York Times* that an army of a million men might be so trained in Pakistan. No doubt the US thought that these forces might be utilized for a possible war against the communist countries. It seemed to be rather an encouragement to war. Whatever the motives might be the mere fact that large-scale rearmament and military expansion taking place in Pakistan had adverse repercussions in India. The whole psychological atmosphere between the two countries would change for the worse and every question that was pending between the two would be affected by it. Indeed India was not at all in a mood in entering into any kind of armed race with Pakistan or any other country. But it was obvious that such an expansion of Pakistan's war resources, with the help of the US, could only be looked as an unfriendly act in India and one that was fraught with danger. It was not the people of India who thought so but people of other countries, because the result in any case was going to be the same.

The alignment with the US, Nehru wrote 'will affect the major question that we are considering and more especially the Kashmir issue.' The whole issue would change its face completely if heavy and rapidly militarization of Pakistan: it was to take place. In fact 'if becomes rather absurd to talk of demilitarization, if Pakistan proceeds in the reverse direction with the help of the US.'

Pakistani Prime Minister sent his reply to Nehru on 17 December and did not like India objection to strengthen Pakistan's defences and being descried it as an unfriendly act. India's military and economic potential as everybody was aware, was far greater than Pakistan. Since partition, India had spent large sum of money on strengthening her armed forces. Nevertheless, Bogra made it clear that Pakistan looked upon the additions in the Indian military strength, an unfriendly act. He ruled out war between the two countries as responsible leaders of India and Pakistan knew very well the implications of such a war, in terms of material destruction and human misery. India and Pakistan must pursue the path of peace, promote goodwill and cooperation between the two countries and to that end eliminate the disputes that were embittering their relations. He was surprised on the observations made by Nehru, regarding the possible implications of Pakistan's alignments with the US and its impact on the Kashmir issue. Bogra wrote to Nehru 'I am unable to understand how any proposal for the strengthening of Pakistan's or as a matter India's defences generally could have any bearing on the question of demilitarization of Kashmir State.' He also emphasized the need for the demilitarization of the Kashmir State in order to ensure that its people were able to vote on the question of accession of the State to Pakistan or India without any fear or pressure from the presence of armed forces within the State itself. The overall military strength of India and Pakistan outside the State won't in any way affect the Kashmir issue. He feared that if India or Pakistan were to stage a military come back in Kashmir after the State has been demilitarized, a conflagration would start which would not remain confined to Kashmir alone but might well engulf the entire sub-continent.

The chain of letters between the two Prime Ministers continued. On 19 January 1954, Nehru wrote back to Bogra that he was anxious to proceed with the Kashmir issue as speedily as possible. First, India and Pakistan were to settle the issue of the appointment of (PA). The issue of the appointment of (PA) was not in any way related with other problems which were awaiting solution. Nehru made it clear that there were differences between the two countries on various defence and foreign policy matters. The total 'differences in our outlook are exemplified when you say that such aid given to Pakistan will add to the security or India. Nehru felt that lining up with one of the power blocs brings insecurity and danger; apart from this being a step away from peace'.

Bogra it seemed was very serious to bridge the gap between the two countries. He had shown his willingness to proceed in agreement with 'Nehru to select a new (PA) in replacement of Admiral Nimitz'. When the Constituent Assembly of Kashmir endorsed the proposal that the State of Jammu and Kashmir be acceded to India, Pakistan was really surprised to learn of this decision, taken in contemptuous disregard of Indo-Pakistan talks, the Delhi Agreement and of India's international commitments.

Bogra was of the view that the decision of the Assembly must be repudiated. However, Nehru rejected the suggestion and demand of Pakistan Prime Minister. He described it an 'absurd'. Bogra felt that India had accepted commitments contained in the UNCIP Resolutions and the Delhi Agreement, here no such reservations were made.

Nehru expressed his views in clear terms once again that the US decision to give aid to Pakistan 'has changed the whole context of the Kashmir issue'. There was a basic difference between the military and economic aid, The consequences and implications of both were entirely different. 'More particularly if two countries have actually been conducting military operations against each other and aid given to either of them is an act unfriendly to the other and not in keeping with neutrally.'

Nehru reminded Bogra of his argument that the US military aid would help in solving the Kashmir issue. That meant that Pakistan had a wish to settle the issue by force of arms or by threat to use arms unless the preliminary issues, outstanding, such as the quantum of forces, were settled to the satisfaction of Pakistan. Similar reference had been made by others also, which indicated that was in connection with India. Pakistan had asked for and received the military aid. Nehru once again said that the issue of providing aid was a very serious matter as it would take it out the region of a peaceful approach for a friendly settlement by bringing in the pressure of arms. Now that the pressure of arms had taken the place of the previous peaceful and cooperative approach and an abundant supply of military aid was to be provided by the US to Pakistan what India at a previous stage said about the quantum of forces had left little relevance?

Nehru made it categorically clear that India was not prepared to take risks, as it had taken previously and India was at its liberty to keep such forces and military equipment in the Kashmir State as it felt necessary in view of the new threat.

Nehru showed his inability to appoint a (PA) as the preliminary issues were pending and awaiting solution and there was a little prospect of their settlement in the near future. The new series of events that had taken place in the Indian sub-continent had given a setback to India's calculations and prevented any future progress. It was not merely the Kashmir question that had become much more difficult, but a serious threat was clearly visible to India's security.

IMPACT OF US MILITARY AID TO PAKISTAN

There was a near storm in India when it was made known that Pakistan was all set to receive large quantity of military aid. President Eisenhower, in his personal letter to Nehru on 5 March 1954 said that military aid to Pakistan was not directed in any way against India and if the US aid would be misused by Pakistan in any way or form and directed against India, the President assured Nehru that action would be taken against Pakistan in accordance with the US Constitution. He in the same letter informed Nehru that the US would continue to provide economic and technical assistance to India. If India needed any military assistance for strengthening its already established military power, be assured that its request would receive most sympathetic consideration.[33]

Nehru made a lengthy statement in the Lok Sabha on 1 March regarding the possible repercussions of the US decision to supply military aid to Pakistan. He appreciated the US President letter and the assurances he gave to India. So far as the President Eisenhower was concerned, he was India's well wisher and he would not take any step to injure India.

It was not a question of motives but rather of certain results which inevitably would follow certain actions and it seemed that as regard the matter of military aid to Pakistan that the results would bound to be unfortunate. It was stated that the aid was merely meant to strengthen Pakistan so that it could defend itself against aggression and also to ensure security, and peace. It was not clear what kind of aggression and from what quarter Pakistan feared.

There was no danger of aggression on Pakistan from any quarter but as Pakistan's delegate to the UN, Ahmed Bukhari spoke in New York and made it clear that 'we want the guarantee that the two biggest countries in Asia will leave us none.' His obvious reference was to India and China. It was not clear how China was going to invade Pakistan, whether it was going to come over the Karakoram pass in to Pakistan.

So far as ensuring security and peace was concerned,

there was no need for any arguments. It was a fact that since the announcement of aid to Pakistan, there had been a greater insecurity and greater tensions. Whatever the motives might be, the result, the fact, was there, that there had been in India, Pakistan, an upsetting of things as they were and a sense of insecurity.

He also made it clear that India had offered a 'No War Declaration' to Pakistan. A 'No War Declaration' was like a 'Non-Aggression Pact' but in spite of India offering it repeatedly to Pakistan and it had rejected it for whatever reasons it might be. If such a Declaration would be there, obviously that would have eased tension between the two countries and its surroundings areas and produced a greater feeling of security in both the countries. It was in the context of this rejection of India's proposal of 'No War Declaration' that India had to view the military aid to Pakistan. It was not easy to imagine any aggression on Pakistan as things were, either from that great country China or from India regardless of motives about it. India was looking at the barest physical possibilities of the matter.

How then the question of aggression arose and, was made a pretext for the kind of military aid being given from Pakistan's side? Nehru said he would welcome the strengthening of Pakistan even militarily, economically in the normal course, if they build up themselves up. But Pakistan did not adopt that normal procedure, up-setting normality and so far as it upsets normality, it must be considered a step away from peace.

He did not agree with the US President contention that if Pakistan would misuse the aid, action would be taken against her. But if the past experiences were any indication, aggression took place and nothing was done to thwart it. Aggression had taken place in Kashmir, the US did not condemn it and India was asked by the US not to press the point in the interest of peace. Aggression would again take place as the conditions were being created, in spite of the US desire to prevent it. Later debate and arguments would be carried on as to whether it was aggression or not. The military aid given to Pakistan by the US would likely to create the conditions which facilitate and encourage aggression.

But Nehru said 'If we object to military aid being given to Pakistan, we would be hypocritical and unprincipled opportunists to accept such aid for ourselves.' The military aid given to Pakistan 'is a form of intervention in these problems which is liked to have more far-reaching results than the previous types of intervention.' He was doubtful whether the large number of American observers posted 'on the ceasefire line would 'no longer be treated by us as neutrals in this dispute and their presence there appears to us to be improper.'

While referring the wider aspects of this aid, which might affect the whole of Asia, Nehru pointed out that many countries in Asia got freedom after long years of colonial subjection. They prize their freedom and any intervention which lessons their freedom was considered to be harmful and a step away from both freedom and peace.

The Prime Minister of Pakistan had stated by the receipt of the military aid, a momentous step had been taken towards the strengthening of the Muslim world and the Pakistan had entered a glorious chapter in its history and was preparing herself for a significant role in the world affairs. How Muslim world was going to be strengthened through arms supplied by a foreign power and how any country was going to play a significant role in world affairs relying on military aid from another?

The Prime Minister of Pakistan had also stated that the military aid would help to solve the Kashmir problem. That was an indication of the way his mind was working and how he would utilize the military aid as military aid is usually only utilized in war or in a threat of war.

There was another aspect which Nehru also mentioned. The world, Nehru said, was suffering enormously with suspicion and fear and to be examined every matter from this point of view whether it added to suspicion and fear or lessened them. Could there be any doubt that the Pakistan joining of military pacts was a step which added to suspicion and fears and therefore the tension of the world instead of bridging about any feeling of insecurity?

He also informed the House that there was no progress in the field of demilitarization and no agreement had been signed or to be signed in the near future. Now the whole question had to be examined from an entirely different angel when across the border, across the ceasefire line, on the other side large additional forces were being thrust from outside in Pakistan and put at the disposal of Pakistan. It did make a difference because the military aid had changed the balance of things in India and Asia.[34]

In the fifties, the situation in the Indian sub-continent, particularly on the Indo-Pak relations and related issues was somewhat fluid, but the situation took a worst turn when the US decided to provide military aid to Pakistan, after it formally decided to join its sponsored alliances. There was some progress in their relations, after Mohammed Ali Bogra took over. Both the Prime Ministers tried to narrow down, the differences over the Kashmir issue particularly over the demilitarisation issue and the appointment of a (PA). It was looking after the direct negotiations between the two that considerable progress had been made as far as the demilitarisation issue was concerned. The Delhi Agreement was really a welcome sign in the relations of the two but the whole of the situation took a turn after the US decided to enter into the affairs of the sub-continent by luring Pakistan, in order to achieve its foreign policy objectives. The way the US behaved and tried to influence the Security Council proceedings from the very beginning in favour of Pakistan has further complicated the Kashmir issue.

The American nationals or its supporters were appointed members of various bodies and Commissions to probe the various aspects of the Kashmir issue. Indian Government from the very outset was warned about the US-UK Axis, as both worked together to tilt the balance in favour of Pakistan at every stage. No doubt this got considerable success too but the Indian Government was never demoralized as from 1952 onwards, the Soviet Union took up the Indian side in the Security Council and the issue became a hot issue for the two powers blocs which started getting complicated after each debate in the Council.

The implications of the US aid and Pakistan's formally joining of the US sponsored pacts have been dealt with considerably earlier. The situation underwent a big change in the sub-continent which in fact is responsible for what is going on even today regarding the Kashmir. The US was directly or indirectly involved in the affairs of the sub-continent always because it has strong stakes in the West Asia, Central Asia, and of course in the South Asia too. It is the US which could be held probably responsible for the sorry state of Indo-Pakistan affairs. No doubt, it sometimes worked behind the scenes to calm down both when they were on the verge of a war but its efforts can never be described as impartial.

The Anglo-American combine in fact was responsible for compelling the Soviet Union to adopt a pro-Indian attitude. In order to safeguard its security interests, the Soviet leaders could neither have agreed to the stationing of UN troops, which Anglo-American forces in Kashmir, so close to their frontier nor to the appointment of a US or a British official as a (PA). When the US had started giving military assistance to Pakistan, which was one of the parties to the dispute, these developments made it difficult for both the parties to the dispute and the UN to settle it. It was believed that had the US not agreed to give military aid to Pakistan, direct negotiations or the UN would have succeeded in resolving the dispute. The idea was to draw attention to the fact that the UN becomes helpless when one superpower lured Pakistan into its orbit and the other openly accepted India's viewpoint. When the two superpowers got interested in the parties to a dispute, it became rather difficult to solve the problem.[35]

The Pakistan's Government total alliance with the US by the end of 1956 became clear from its stand on the Suez Crisis which was in consonance with western thinking. Pakistan found the climate favourable to itself because of Israeli-British-French misadventure in West Asia. The Indian Government attitude towards the developments in Hungry was pro-Soviet and by taking the stand, it had incurred the wrath of the Western powers. It was the only non-communist nation which opposed the US sponsored Resolution calling for free and fair elections under the auspices of the UN.

Nehru in a statement in the Lok Sabha on 29 March 1956 while replying to the points made in the course of a discussion on demands for grants relating to the Ministry of External Affairs said that the holding of the plebiscite could have taken place, if Pakistan had taken certain steps like the withdrawal of armed forces from that part of the State on which it had committed aggression. That was a major fact to be remembered. There were certain other prerequisites for a plebiscite and many attempts had already been made but without any desired results.

Another important fact to remember was that Government of Jammu and Kashmir State could not remain continually in a state of suspended animation, something had to be done. Nehru informed the House 'that India was keen to solve the Kashmir issue while keeping in mind the new developments that had taken place in the Indian sub-continent, particularly the US promise to provide military aid to Pakistan, a promise which she had subsequently fulfilled'. That created not only a new military situation but a new political environment also and the ways and means adopted by India were outdated and had to be viewed afresh. Apart from legal and constitutional issues, India had to keep the environment prevailing in the valley and of course the well-being of the people, must be the top priority. India was to avoid any step being taken which would be disruptive, which would again lead to conflict with Pakistan. The creation of one unit in West Pakistan was also a matter of concern for the people of Kashmir. He wanted the Government of Pakistan to adopt a realistic approach towards the whole issue and they must take into consideration what had happened in the last nine years. Keeping in mind the past experiences of the Kashmir affair in all its changing phases, a problem that was affecting the people of the Jammu and Kashmir, affecting India in a variety of ways, affecting India constitution, sovereignty and India's vital interests, 'am I to be expected to agree to some outside authority becoming an arbitrator in this matter.'[36]

CONSTITUTION OF KASHMIR: PAKISTAN'S REACTION

A new Constitution prepared by the duly elected Constituent Assembly was to come into force on 26 January

1957 in Kashmir. On 2 January, Pakistan Prime Minister Feroz Khan Noon wrote a letter to the UN Security Council, to secure a stay order in respect of the new Constitution in Kashmir. As nine out of eleven members of the Council were either Pakistan's allies in military alliances or under the influence of Pakistan's allies, it was expected that the Western powers were likely to oblige Pakistan by talking a hard line against India. Nehru said at a public meeting in Calcutta that India would not tolerate any attempt which might spell doom into Kashmir and that Kashmir had advanced immensely and was going forward in every direction.[37]

Noon made a speech in the Security Council when his letter was tabled in the Council for deliberation referring to India's objections of the military aids and pacts. Noon said that they had 'no relevance whatsoever to the international agreement for a plebiscite in Kashmir.' He offered to conclude with India a 'No War Pact' after India's unfulfiling his promise of holding a plebiscite in the State. 'We are willing' said Noon's 'to enter into a pact which will say that an attack on India will be attack on Pakistan.' He requested the Council to call upon India to refrain from accepting the change envisaged by new Constitution adopted by the so-called Constituent Assembly. The Security Council under article 37 paragraph 2 of the UN Charter spell out the obligations of the parties under the terms of the international agreement for a plebiscite as embodied in the UN Resolutions. He also made a vigorous plea for the withdrawal of all troops from the State and for placing the local troops at the disposal of the Security Council. He also requested for the appointment of (PA) at the earliest.[38]

Krishna Menon, Indian representative in the UN devoted three meetings of the Council to furnish his lengthy statement in reply to the issues raised by Noon. He while elaborating the history of the partition and the Kashmir dispute strongly repudiated the charges of Noon that it was a spurious accession and that Pakistan should be asked to present the tribal's and Pakistan nationals from taking part in the fighting in Jammu and Kashmir. He made a well documented case to prove that Pakistan had committed aggression and created the circumstances in which India was to accept the offer of accession from the Maharaja of Kashmir. He also refused to accept the charges levelled by Noon that elections in the Kashmir State were unfair and reminded Noon that in the territory occupied by Pakistan, there had been no elections at all. He also made it clear that as far as the holding of plebiscite was concerned that it was 'a commitment given to the people of Kashmir' by India of its own. It was the wish of the Indian Government in fact Maharaja had never asked for it. It was in fact mentioned the term 'reference to the people' that might be any kind of reference a referendum, a plebiscite, a general election, it might be a 'Gallup Polls'. It might be anything of like wise Menon said that even if it were a plebiscite, it was conditional, i.e. when the soil was cleared of the invaders and peace and order was restored. He went on to say that expression of a wish was not binding in any equitable relations.

Menon pleaded that holding of a plebiscite was out of question since the circumstances had been changed, firstly because there was a complete transformation of conditions in social and economic areas and secondly Pakistan was a part and parcel of the US sponsored military alliances and got arms and military equipment form the US, which resulted into converting the small landing strips in the Kashmir territory into large air bases.[39]

In the UN Security Council, the constitutional remedies taken by India in the case of Kashmir were not well received and there was widespread resentment in Pakistan, but Pakistan's alliance partners were not happy with the Indian Government moves. The British, the US and the Chinese Resolutions in the Security Council had completely supported Pakistan. Gunnar Jarring of Sweden who supported the Resolution tabled in the Security Council felt strongly that *status quo* should be maintained and pointed out that the 'parties concerned should desist from taking internal legislative measures which the State of Jammu and Kashmir would be considered definitely incorporated in the territory of one of the two parties and which would prejudice Security Council's continued deliberation on this matter.'[40]

The Resolution was strongly opposed by the Soviet

Union. Its representative Sobolov while supporting the efforts made by the Indian Government, lashed at the US and her allies for complicating the issue. He said that 'the problem was created by certain powers which are using every means in their endeavour to formost discord between countries striving for their national freedom and independence...' These powers were guided primarily by their interests who were aimed at penetration into this region as one of the great strategic importance.[41]

Sobolov also mentioned the convening of the Constituent Assembly and its decision to endorse Kashmir's accession to India, an effort to put an end to the uncertainty of their position and to stabilize the situation. The Kashmir problem was thus settled by the Kashmir people themselves who consider them to be an inalienable part of the Republic of India. The Security Council cannot disregard this fact. He opposed the Resolution as it was 'in complete disregard of the radical changes which have taken place in the Kashmir valley.'[42]

GUNAR JARRING PROPOSAL

The debates in the Security Council continued from 761-775 meetings.[43] But nothing tangible came out of these Draft Resolutions.[44] The foremost four powers Resolution was tabled by Cuba, the UK, France and the US in February 1957 in the 768 meeting of the Security Council.[45] It was voted in favour and the USSR against.[46] The US criticized the Soviet Union could have only one purpose to perpetuate international conflict for using the veto power and said that the action of the Soviet Union had increased dissensions between two of Asia's great countries.[47] The Soviet Union had exercised veto power after giving a proper warning.[48] At the 774 meeting on 21 February, the Council adopted an amended Resolution with 10 votes in favour and none against and one absent, calling upon its President Gunnar Jarring to discuss with the Indian and Pakistani Governments any proposals which they deemed fit for the settlement of the Kashmir issue keeping in mind the Resolutions earlier adopted by the Security Council.[49] He submitted his report on

28 March 1958, suggesting .a conference at the Prime Ministerial level. It was accepted by Pakistan but rejected by India when Jarring suggested arbitration as another method for the Kashmir issue. The Government of India however did not feel that arbitration, as outlived by Jarring, would be appropriate. It explained that, while it was not against the principle of a arbitration as a method of conciliation and had, indeed, agreed to this procedure to arrive at a solution of certain other problems between India and Pakistan, it felt that the issue of Kashmir was not suitable for arbitration because such problem would be inconsistent with the sovereignty of Jammu and Kashmir and the rights and obligations of the Union of India in respect of that territory. It was furthermore, apprehensive that arbitration might be interpreted as indicating that Pakistan had a locus standi in the question. The offer of arbitration was accepted by Pakistan.[50]

Jarring wrote in his report that in dealing with the problem and investigating its various aspects, he failed to take note of the concern expressed in connection with the changing political, economic and strategic factors surrounding the whole of the Kashmir question together with the changing pattern of power 'relations in West and South Asia'. He reminded the Council that the implementation of international agreements of an adhoc character, which could not be achieved speedily might become progressively more difficult because the situation with which they were to cope has tended to change.

He had shown his inability to submit any concrete proposals to the Council. No doubt, a severe deadlock was going on between the two parties on the question of Kashmir but both the parties were in favour of solving the dispute with the help of the UN. At its meeting on 2 December 1957, concerning the Indo-Pakistan question the UN Security Council adopted a Resolution thanking Jarring for the care and ability with which he has carried out his mission. It considered the importance which Jarring Report had attached to the demilitarization of the state of Jammu and Kashmir 'as one of the steps towards a settlement.' Recalling its previous Resolutions and the Resolutions of the (UNCIP) on the India-Pakistan question; it requested both the parties to refrain from making any statements or permitting any acts which might aggrevate the situation and appealed to their respective people to assist in creating and maintaining an atmosphere favourable to the promotion of further negotiations. It made an urgent request to the (UNCIP) to make and recommendation to the parties for further appropriate action with a view to making progress towards the implementation of the (UNCIP). It also asked the (UNCIP) members to visit the sub- continent.[51]

EFFORTS OF FRANK P. GRAHAM

On the request of the Security Council, Frank P. Graham, had discussions with Prime Minister Jawaharlal Nehru assisted by Krishna Menon and M.J. Desai between 12 January and 13 February 1958 in New Delhi and with Prime Minister Malik Feroz Khan Noon assisted by Mirza Aslam Beg and Din Mohammad between 17 January and 15 February 1958 in Karachi. Graham was well aware of the whole issue and the various aspects related with it. His discussions with both the parties were fruitful. While talking about India's objections regarding the security of the evacuated territory and more particularly, the apprehension that the Pakistan army, after its withdrawal, might return to the territory, Graham took the matter very seriously and proposed that the feasibility of placing a UN force on Pakistan side of the Jammu and Kashmir border should be explored. He also examined various other suggestions and in his views 'the most immediate requirement of the situation, namely a resumption of direct negotiations under UN auspices'. In order to create proper framework for these negotiations, Graham asked the two governments should consider the possibility of a renewed declaration in favour of the Resolutions of the (UNCIP), under which they would appeal to their respective peoples to assist in creating and maintaining an atmosphere favourable for further negotiations and in which they themselves would undertake to refrain from statements and action which would aggregate the situation.

In the Second phase, Graham proposed that the two

Governments reaffirm that they would respect the ceasefire line on the ground and in the air, as established by the ceasefire agreement, signed by both the Governments on 29 and 30 July 1949.

On 15 February 1958, on the eve of the departure from the sub-continent, Graham submitted to the representatives of both the Governments the following recommendations. First two recommendations were of general nature. In the third recommendation regarding the withdrawal of Pakistan troops from the State pending a solution, the territory evacuated by the Pakistani troops was to be administered by the local authorities under the surveillance of the Commission. It further recommended that if progress was to be made in the settlement of India-Pakistan question, there was a need for an early agreement between the two Governments on the interpretations that should be placed on part -III of the 13 August Resolution and those parts of the 5 January Resolution which provide for a plebiscite. In this connection the Representatives would call attention to the Joint Communiqué of the Prime Minister of India and Pakistan issued following their meeting in New Delhi in August 1953, which recognized that a plebiscite had been agreed too and expressed the opinion that solution should be sought causing the least disturbances to the life of the people of the State.

Graham further believed that there was a need that negotiations could be undertaken at the highest level, proposed to the two Governments that summit conference of the Prime Ministers might be convened. The Government of India rejected Graham recommendation but informed him that there should be a constructive and peaceful approach while placing their deep faith in the UN and its Charter.

Graham also pointed out that, these unsettled and unsettling difference between the two great peoples have long corroded their relations, continuously drained off their resources and cut deeply into their development programmes for education, health, production and welfare.[52]

The Security Council debate from January 1957, to December 1957 was significant in many ways. No doubt, except the Soviet Union, all other 10 members of the Council sided with Pakistan, but it failed to get a directive in respect of integration of the State into the mainstream of national life. Second, the western powers wanted to induct a UN armed contingent to conduct a plebiscite, a new dimension to the UN Charter. It speaks of the use of force only for the purpose of maintenance of peace and security as was in the case of Korea to take enforcement measures and then in Egypt to supervise ceasefire and the withdrawal of the aggressor. Thanks to the Soviet Veto, the first ever exercised by the Soviet Union in respect of the Kashmir issue, an extra-legal use of UN force was prevented. The Soviet amendment to the vetoed four powers Resolution gave the western powers a chance to reconsider their proposal and the Soviet attitude in the Security Council was clear hints for any body to see that the Soviet Union would not accept the Resolution.

Another important feature of the debate was that the Indian viewpoint was upheld by Jarring when he emphasized that the circumstances had changed and the old Resolutions were outdated.

The Pakistan joining of military pact also figured prominently during the debate. In fact it was a deciding factor for the Soviet Union to support the Indian viewpoint. The change in the Soviet attitude on Kashmir could also be attributed to India's emergence as the leader of newly independent countries. Khrushchev emergence as the most important leader resulted in a change in Moscow's attitude towards the newly independent non-communist countries. Non-alignment emerged as a most important instrument of policy in the eyes of the Kremlin. It also became clear that unless both the superpowers agreed on a method of settlements of Kashmir issue, stalemate was likely to continue and the discussion and debates in the Security Council would be simply an exercise in futility. That might be reason why a debate on the Graham Report was shelved.[53]

Communing on the Security Council debate under review, Das Gupta, an eminent scholar on Indo-Pakistan relations, observed that 'the Soviet leader's unqualified support to India in her conflict with Pakistan had drawn heavily on whatever was left of the western reservoir of goodwill for India and Pakistan's successful conclusion of military alliances assured her of solid support in her struggle for Kashmir.' Voting pattern and the arguments advanced in the earlier debates show that it was not the Soviet support to India's viewpoint that influenced the Western support to Pakistan, was not a new phenomenon, but a strong Soviet reaction to the unreasonable attitude of the Western powers, was something to reckon with.[54]

In the meanwhile Sheikh Abdullah, having been released from jail on 8 January 1958, had immediately proceeded to criticise the decision of the Constituent Assembly to accede to India on the ground that the Assembly had become an unrepresentative body after he, its founder, had been arrested in 1953. He also stated that the Kashmir's original accession to India had been provisional, that the only solution of the Kashmir problem was a plebiscite and that the invasion of Pakistan had taken place after the oppression of Muslims in Jammu. He was again put behind bars on 29 April and silenced once more.[55]

The army took over the Civil Administration in Pakistan in October 1958 and it was felt that the situation might change. After signing the Indus Water Treaty, Nehru stayed in Pakistan until 23 September 1960 and discussed the Kashmir issue at length with Ayub Khan. When Ayub Khan lost all hopes of solving the Kashmir issue, he decided to seek the help of the US President and met him in July 1961. The Joint Statement issued after his visit affirmed 'the desire of the US to seek a satisfactory solution of the Kashmir issue.'[56] The US President John F. Kennedy wrote to Nehru and Ayub suggesting that they should accept Eugene Black, President of the World Bank as a mediator in the Kashmir issue. The proposal was accepted by the Government of Pakistan, But Nehru suggested direct negotiations instead of mediation.[57]

In 1962, again Pakistan's representative, Zafarullah Khan in a letter to the Security Council President said that there was a grave danger to the maintenance of peace in the Kashmir region because the recent 'pronouncements by responsible personalities in India have emphasized that the situation has changed with utmost gravity.'[58] The Indian representative C.S. Jha made a plea to the President of the Security Council to postpone consideration of the issue until the General Elections in India were held so that the new Government could fully participate in the discussions.[59]

The Pakistan representative again requested to the Security Council for an immediate session be convened. The issue was debated once again from 27 April to 4 May and from 15 June to 22 June.[60] On the last day of the second debate, Polish and Irish representatives moved a Resolution.[61] When the Resolution was put to vote, it was vetoed by the USSR.[62] The debates produced nothing.

DIRECT NEGOTIATIONS ON THE KASHMIR ISSUE

The relations between India and Pakistan were further strained after the Sino-Indian war of 1962 when the situation in the Indian sub-continent had changed drastically.[63] There was an improvement visible in Indo-US relations and the Sino-Pak ties were further strengthened after the signing of the Border Agreement between them in 1963. Direct negotiations were held again, spanning into six rounds from December 1962 to May 1963. But when the negotiations were in progress, the signing of the Border Agreement between China and Pakistan was described by the Indian Government as an act of direct interference by the Beijing Government in Indo-Pak relations. The Agreement manifested the Chinese desire to exploit the differences between India and Pakistan on the Kashmir issue. Nehru Government blamed the Chinese for intending to destroy the amity which had been developing between India and Pakistan, as a result of the joint talks between the two countries on Kashmir and other related matters.[64]

The Agreement stabilised Pakistan's position regarding Kashmir in the eyes of the Chinese compelling her to reject, unequivocally the contention that Kashmir belonged to India.[65] It seemed, China was happy to create a dent in the western system of anti-communist alliances by having sort of alignment with Pakistan which was considered to be the most allied of America's allies.[66] The Manchester Guardian weekly observed that 'the Pakistan may be excused for thinking that a bird in the hand is worth two in the bush. They got very little from talks with India over the past decade or so there was still no evidence that India was ready to concede their minimum demand. Certainly the agreement with China could be used by India as a justification if the negotiations failed. But the Indian Government has never been at a loss for such justification in the past.'[67]

It was generally believed that, Ayub Khan was somewhat flexible on the Kashmir issue when the ministerial level talks were about to begin. He stated that Pakistan would be prepared to consider a solution other than the plebiscite if Nehru had any in mind. Pakistan's attitude won't be rigid and that the Pakistan delegation would be guided by whether a solution was likely to be acceptable to the people of Kashmir and it must be according to the vital interests of Pakistan and also met legitimate demands of India. It was Nehru's implacability that had doomed the Indo-Pakistan negotiations on Kashmir to failure from the very beginning. The ink was barely dry on his Joint Statement with Ayub Khan that India and Pakistan would settle their dispute by making fresh efforts, when he publicly declared that anything which would upset the present arrangement would be very harmful to the people of Kashmir as well to the future relations of India and Pakistan. But he firmly continued to hold the positions that the only permanent solution acceptable to India would be the recognition of the ceasefire line as the border between India and Pakistan. In a revealing interview with Salig H. Harrison of the Washington Post, Nehru said that 'while India was prepared for adjustments in the present ceasefire line, which is not a very sensitive one, we are persuaded that any major change would be ruin of the vale. He also indicated that he did not attach much importance to statements of western spokesmen linking military aid against China with a Kashmir settlement and expressed the belief that even if a Kashmir settlement was not reached, it would not broadly affect the western military aid programme'. In the same interview, he also revealed that he really believed in the final solution of all Indo-Pakistan differences. 'Confederation remains our ultimate goal though if we say it; they are alarmed and say we want to swallow them. In fact there was no change visible in Nehru's attitude on the issue as he remained adamant and wanted that Pakistan must vacate aggression.'[68]

When the talks were in progress, Pakistan felt quite despondent after the fifth round, was hopeful that, the US and British delegates, who were visiting Karachi at the beginning of May to attend a meeting might be able to use their influence on India to save the situation. After the CENTO meeting, the British and the US delegates met and were joined by Mountbatten, a well known friend of Nehru. On 6 May, it was announced in Delhi that Indian Government had agreed to a low key mediation or good offices be an American or a British in the Kashmir dispute. It was observed that the acceptance of mediation by India in no way implies a fundamental change in the Indian claim to the disputed State of Jammu and Kashmir It has given Mr. Rusk something to take hope from his trip. Perhaps most important, it will give the Kennedy Administration a better position in its efforts to get an arms aid appropriation for India from the US Congress this summer, because India has made a concession.[69]

The proposal of mediation dragged on for sometime after the final session of the Kashmir discussion had ended inconclusively. Ultimately it came to naught as Pakistan could not get any hint that some concessions would be offered. There was no assurance from any quarter of any type, while India was open-minded and desired that the mediator would be asked to survey the entire gamut of Indo-Pakistan differences. Pakistan thought he should concentrate his efforts upon the Kashmir problem. Pakistan also required that the terms of reference for the mediator should mention the UN Resolutions on Kashmir, that the mediator must report his recommendations to the parties within a specified time, that the parties must undertake to abide by the mediator proposals and then the Western long-term military aid to India be frozen while the mediation was in progress, but some of these stipulations were not acceptable to India.[70]

Nehru once again ruled out the mediation and in his opinion, it was not a suitable course. In his statement in the Lok Sabha on 13 August, he alleged that Pakistan had made impossible demands in regard to mediator and referring to India's offer of a settlement by making adjustments in the ceasefire line, declared that the concessions which India had offered to Pakistan must be treated as withdrawn.[71] But some observers believed that Nehru agreed on talks and mediator offer not willingly but he was under constant pressure from the Americans and the British from where he was getting vital supplies. The talks had failed because India, the party in possession of everything that matters had felt strong enough to resist the concessions that any solution would require.

In the somewhat changed environment once again on the initiative of the Pakistan representative Z.A. Bhutto, Security Council discussed the Kashmir issue from 1087 to 1104 and 1105 and again 1112 to 1117 Council's meetings.[72] After the two fruitless debates of 1964 in the Security, Pakistan felt that 'without creating crisis in and around Kashmir, the West was not prepared to oblige Pakistan by supporting her cause.'[73] Meanwhile Pakistan started creating tension on the border on 28 May 1965 and indulged in border violations. India lodged a complaint with the Security Council about heavy concentration of Pakistan troops all along the Indian border which posed a serious threat to peace.[74]

The situation in the Indian sub-continent took a sudden turn when on 8 May 1965 Sheikh Abdullah, the only hope of Pakistan was arrested for the anti-Indian activities.[75] The Pakistan Government got irritated and it protested against this action to the President of the Security Council on 18 May 1965.[76] On 28 June Pakistan also complained to the Security Council about the heavy concentration of Indian troops on the Indo-Pak border.

As one surveys, the February and May 1964 debate in the Security Council one notices that there was a change in the arguments of the Indian delegates countering Pakistan demand for self-determination for a part of India. India was justified in demanding the same for Pakhtoons and the Baluchis who were also demanding self-determination. Indian representative M.C. Chagla put across his ideas with firmness coupled with politeness and humour. There was a change in the US and the British attitude towards India too. It was less hostile as compared to earlier. Around that period there was a diplomatic move towards a closer Indo-US relationship involving the possibility of a military pact between India and the US. India was supposed to have agreed with this move to help the US to contain China in Asia. On the other hand, Pakistan argument was that she had gained much from this debate. But it was clearly an exaggeration. The core of the Pakistani complaint that there was a threat in Pakistan from India and that Kashmir was in open revolt was hardly taken seriously by the members of the Security Council. Pakistan could not secure an injunction against the extension of the jurisdiction of the Indian Elections Commission in the State of Jammu and Kashmir. Only one obvious gain was visible, that was two African States, Morocco and Ivory Coast supported Pakistan's view point. The Soviet Union was unequivocal in respect of its support to the India's view-point as far as the speeches of the Soviet representatives conveyed. The Soviet attitude, outside the Security Council however did undergo a change and that was limited only to restraint on anti-Pakistan utterances. One thing may, however be added that Pakistan got a dangerous hint and that was unless there was crisis in and around Kashmir, the West was not prepared to oblige Pakistan.[77]

Since 1948, the Kashmir issue had been debated in the UN Security Council several times and several missions were sent by the Council. Instead of solving it, they complicated it. The crucial question however is why India did approach the UN and main reason behind the lodging of the complaint was India's faith in the Charter of the UN.[78] Her belief that the military was not always the most helpful and stable means of settling the issues. The Indian Government felt that armed conflict on the sub-continent immediately after freedom could complicate the situation.[79]

As far as the UN role was concerned one can say, it was biased and confusing. From 1966 onwards, no debates took place in the UN Security till present day. There was no role or initiated after the Indo-Pakistan of 1965, to solve the Kashmir issue. There were several factors which were partially responsible for creating such a situation. Probably, the most acceptable explanation for this state of affair was that the situation in the Indian sub-continent changed drastically in the mid-sixties, particularly after the Sino-Indian war of 1962. There were visible changes in the foreign policy priorities of both the USSR and the US led power blocs. The efforts of the UN were exhausted and Pakistani military and political elites were restless, hence, the Kutch Crisis and the war in the Kashmir valley erupted in 1965. The war gave clear indications that every body was tired of the Kashmir issue and the widening gulf between India and Pakistan.

Both the countries solved the issues that emerged out of the war first in the form of signing the Tashkent Declaration with the help of the former USSR. The years 1966 to 1970 saw many ups and downs in the Indo-Pak relations. Owing to their respective attitudes during the war, 'the Chinese ranked much higher in Pakistan's esteem than the US and the Soviet Union. There was a feeling emerged in the minds of the Pakistani foreign policy planners that they had not gained much by openly siding with the US and joining the military pacts. Pakistan had not yet relinquished her membership of SEATO and CENTO, but was only a formal member of this organization. Pakistan started attending the meetings only as an observer and not was taking any part in the military side of these pacts. Pakistan's interest in the organizations was confined to their cultural and economic activities. But the Soviet leadership was not much convinced with the Pakistani moves. It wanted the end of the US presence from Pakistan, totally dismantling of the US military bases from Pakistan. The Pakistani leadership was annoyed with the US also because its attitude was neutral in the war and moreover the supplies of arms were stopped when the war was in progress.[80]

REVIVAL OF THE KASHMIR ISSUE

But as far as the Kashmir issue was concurred, there was no activity from 1966 to 1989 in and outside which could be considered very important with far-reaching consequences. The Indian Government continued its political efforts to consolidate further its position in the valley by initiating various measures. In February 1975, an accord was signed between Sheikh Abdullah and the Government of India on the future set-up of the state. On 24 February, 1975, Mrs. Gandhi, then Indian Prime Minister announced in the Parliament the main features of the agreement formulated within the framework of the Indian Constitution. The Plebiscite Front was disbanded and National Conference led by Sheikh Abdullah was reviewed. In June 1977, elections were held in the State of Jammu and Kashmir. Sheikh Abdullah's National Conference got absolute majority.

Pakistan in the meanwhile continued raising the Kashmir issue whenever it got an opportunity. On 27 January 1980, K.S. Bajpai, Indian Ambassador to Pakistan walked out of the Islamic Conference of Foreign Ministers after lodging a verbal protest with Pakistan Foreign office against the reference to Kashmir in the inaugural speech of General Zia-ul-Haq who was reported to have remarked that, 'the people of Pakistan and Kashmir are yearning for the restoration of their rights.' On 1 October, President Zia in his inaugural speech at the UN General Assembly said that the process of normalisation of relations between India and Pakistan could be further accelerated with a peaceful 'settlement of the question of Jammu and Kashmir.' India's Permanent Representative to the UN reaffirmed that Jammu and Kashmir was an integral part of India. He asserted that Pakistan's action in repeatedly raising the issue in the UN and other forums constituted an attack on the territorial integrity of India.

It was believed in some quarters that the leaders of Kashmir in order to exploit their sentiments had always tried to maintain a sense of crisis and the threat of an external enemy. At times when Sheikh Abdullah felt that, the situation in Kashmir got out of hands, he did not hesitate in arousing the sentiments of the people against India, Kashmir National Conference has thus been in the form of a very broad-based national front including semi-communalists, reactionaries orthodox radicals, socialist and communists were held together by all powerful personality Sheikh Abdullah.

The pressing internal problem of the State, thus, arose due to the conflict of regional nationalism and due to the one of the 'most regimented undemocratic political setups.' All that is required is to make a suitable political and constitutional adjustment between Jammu, Kashmir and Ladakh and to guarantee the growth of democratic traditions.

INDO-PAK RELATIONS: AN ERA OF CONFLICT AND CO-OPERATION

In addition to the rival claims of New Delhi and Islamabad, there has been a growing and often violent separatist movement against the Indian rule since 1989. But both India and Pakistan reject the opinion of Kashmir becoming an independent State. Kashmir is considered to be one of the most dangerous disputes in the world. In 1998, both declared themselves to be nuclear powers with a string of nuclear tests. The year 2002 saw deployment of troops on both sides of the border as India reacted to an armed attack on the national Parliament in New Delhi in December 2001. In the worst case scenario, the Kashmir dispute could trigger a nuclear conflict. Aside from that, the separatist militancy and cross border firing between the Indian and Pakistan armies had left a death toll running into thousands and a population brutalized by fighting and fear.

There are several groups pursuing the rival claims in Kashmir. Not all are armed, but since Muslim insurgency began in 1989, the number of armed separatist has grown hundreds to thousands. The most prominent are the pro-Pakistan Hizbul Mujahideen. Islamabad has never accepted that she has been providing them with logistical and material support. The Jammu and Kashmir Liberation Front (JKLF) was the largest pro-independence group but its influence has weakened. Other groups have joined the umbrella of the All Party Hurriyat (Freedom) Conference which is for the peaceful end to India's presence in Kashmir. A number of times, attempts have been made to get talks going between the government and the separatist parties. Some groups are demanding that Pakistan should be included in the dialogue.

Religion is an important aspect of the dispute as partition in 1947 gave Indian Muslim a state of their own, i.e. Pakistan. So a common faith underpins Pakistan claims to Kashmir, where many areas are Muslim dominated.

There exists a Line of Control (LOC) in the State of Jammu and Kashmir. A demarcation line was drawn originally in January 1949 as a ceasefire line following the end of the first Kashmir war.

In July 1972, after the signing of the Simla Agreement by India and Pakistan, the (LOC) was re-established with minor variations on the earlier boundary. It passes through a mountainous region about 5000 meters high. The weather conditions are so extreme that in the North of the (LOC), the rival forces have been entrenched on the Siachin glacier (more than 6600 meters high) since 1984 the highest battle field on earth.

The (LOC) divides Kashmir on an almost two-to-one basis. Indian administered Kashmir to the East and South (population about nine million), which falls into the Indian controlled State of Jammu and Kashmir and Pakistan administered Kashmir to the North and West (population about three million) which is labelled by Pakistan as 'Azad' (Free) Kashmir. China also controls a small portion of Kashmir.[81]

For first generation of Pakistan's Kashmir had never been a territorial or strategic concern but later on 'Kashmir came to symbolize the idea of Pakistan as a homeland for South Asian Muslims.' Indian reluctance to give the right of self-determination to Kashmir seemed to demonstrate both the correctness and justice of the 'Two Nations Theory' and to demonstrate the continued antagonism towards all of Pakistan and the cruelty towards its own Muslim citizens.[82]

For the first generation of Pakistanis, Kashmir's captivity conjured up vivid images of oppression. Generally, the Pakistan's propaganda organs present a 'cruder and more virulent description of Kashmir'. The staunchest supporters of the 'Two Nations Theory' still feel that their identity is 'wrapped up in the fate of Kashmir, a region that reflects their own personal and political histories.' They feel that if India will vacate Kashmir, then Indian Muslims will migrate to Pakistan or would at least achieve a separate status within a restructured Indian confederation whereas India regarded the creation of independent Bangladesh as a death knell of the 'Two Nation Theory'. Many Pakistanis even now assume strongly the existence of two Islamic states in South Asian region. Compatible with the original Pakistan movement, a few hardliners are waiting for the disintegration of the Indian state, adding to the list of independence of South Asian states. In effect, they are in agreement with Chaudhry Rehmat Ali's vision of many Muslim states in South Asia-Pakistan being joined by Bangladesh (he called it Bangistan), a new Kashmir and perhaps an 'Osmanistan' (the former princely state of Hyderabad, now a part of India's Andhra Pradesh) and others. Interestingly, some of the staunchest supporters of Kashmir liberation are those political and military elites who suffered under various military regimes or at the hands of Z.A. Bhutto. For them, the liberation of Kashmir is a cause that 'justifies their uprooting and sufferings, their anger at Martial Law during the Zia regime could be channelled in to support for Kashmir. They usually establish a link between their own private agony with India's policies 'on Kashmir and the neutral and unhelpful attitude of the countries as the US.'[83]

To be sure, much of this vocal support is bravado especially when coming from civilians. The army leadership would not risk the future of Pakistan over, until the 1989 Kashmir uprising. Few thought that there was a little possibility of any change in the status of Kashmir (there is also a degree of cultural disdain, especially for Punjabi for the non-martial Kashmiri). Army officers no doubt talk openly of aid to the Kashmir liberation movement but 'basically see it as a guerrilla struggle, which must therefore be waged by the Kashmir, not outsiders. This feeling has never created any problem for Pakistan from supporting Kashmiri militants and facilitating the movement into Kashmir (and India) of Punjabi's and other who would like to join the fight against India, but the motive is as much to bleed India as to hope that Kashmir can be wrested from India.'[84]

For years, 'this seemed to be no losing position. If Kashmir failed to achieve their freedom' feels Stephen Cohen, then it was because they were insufficiently motivated, despite their just grievances against India. If Kashmiri are successful, then this can only be to Pakistan's advantage; it would validate the 'Two Nations Theory.' In fact, there has never been so serious thinking among the civilian people and leaders about the actual strategic consequences of an independent Kashmir. How it would affect Pakistan's relations with Central Asia, Russia, Afghanistan, China and India and possibly other potential new states carved out of India or Pakistan or how it would affect separatist demands from Sindhi or Baluch.[85]

Stephen Cohen feels strongly that 'Pakistan has had a military strategy for Kashmir but not a political one, except to embrass India in international forums.' It has tried to snatch Kashmir for several times and now it has adopted proxy war as a new method and 'militants to force India to come to the negotiating table'. These tactics did not produce the desired results and Pakistan leadership has yet to examine and pronounce the kind of compromise settlement on Kashmir that they would be wiling to accept.[86]

Cohen also feels that 'over the years, Kashmir has become part of the Pakistani identity, at least of those Pakistanis who focus on strategic and security issues, notably the arms and it raises deep passion and emotions, especially among the target Kashmiri population in important Pakistani cities. The obsession with Kashmir can be said to have seriously damaged Pakistan's prospects as a State, but it is a cost that several generations of Pakistani leaders have been wiling to pay and the same can be said of the Indian counterparts.'

In case of Kashmir and other important issues, a consideration of the role of external influences as inputs into national decision-making in Pakistan is very significant. Pakistan's position in international system and the regional system of South Asia has contributed to the kinds of decision taken by the national leadership. Likewise the policies implemented by the major powers of the international system (the US, the former USSR and the People's Republic of China) as well as the policies of regional powers (the Republic of India) have contributed inputs into the decision-making in Pakistan. No doubt, it is very difficult to isolate for the purposes of analysis, various exogenous influences on the decision-making in Pakistan and to indicate in any precise, cause and effect fashion, the relative contribution of these influences on decision-making process. It is widely considered that the US as the external source of influence on decision-making quite evident in number of important areas, particularly in the Indo-Pakistan relations and the related issues. Why the US? The precise answer is, it has provided the bulk of military and economic assistance extended to Pakistan since its inception in August 1947. During the 1950s and 1960s, decisions taken in Pakistan both in foreign and domestic policy areas were made within the framework of the opportunities and constraints posed by the US economic and military assistance. The role of the US was critical to both domestic and international activities in Pakistan.[87]

The particular bilateral relationship that developed between the US and Pakistan is considered to be unique and interesting as it was cyclical in nature with definite 'peaks' and valleys that did not necessarily confirm to the amount of public assistance from (1953-71) estimated to be 4,101 million US $, extended to the Pakistan. Although 1962 through 1965 was the period in which Pakistan received the largest amount of said per capita, the late 1950s and first two years of the 1960s have been described as 'the Zenith' in the US Pakistan cooperation and relations. In short, the US assistance (in $ or in military hardware), certainly a contributing factor to the relations between the countries, and has necessarily been the dominating factor.[88]

A certain definite downgrading of American involvement occurred between 1965 and 1970. The US did not provide significant amount of military equipment to Pakistan despite the willingness of the former USSR to send arms to Pakistan and Chinese also committed them to supply military hardware to Pakistan. Even the 1970 agreement to sell arms to Pakistan was quite small by comparison to the quantity furnished in earlier years. The US new commitments for economic assistance also have been declared considerably. There 'has been a substantial, though by no means total withdrawal of the US from the affairs of the sub-continent at the same time that the Soviet Union was expanding its activities and China was continuing its involvement.'[89]

The inclination of the US to play a reduced role in the sub- continent while the communist powers remained deeply involved represented to the extent that it was a calculated decision rather than one taken by default as a result of concern elsewhere judgement that India and Pakistani were less important than was once thought, less threatened by external aggression and more capable of dealing with the communist countries without conceding them much influence over internal affairs or foreign policy. In addition, the cuts in the US economy aid was probably motivated in part by declining confidence of the under developed countries generally to progress at a rate regarded as satisfactory.[90]

The US in its governmental activities directly and in the private sector indirectly has influenced national decision-making in Pakistan. All the same, there has always been an influence, but not dominance. At times, perhaps critical times, the US influence has tended to be dominant, especially during the 1950s and early 1960s. However, even at these points Pakistani decision-makers had attempted to maintain their latitude and had rejected the advice of the US officials. Although, members of the opposition in Pakistan over the years often use the charge of Pakistani 'submission' to the US interests against the regime in power, there is a little evidence that in fact those in power were the 'captive' of US Policy.[91]

There was a general consensus that decision-making in Pakistan was a 'closed' rather than an open process. In the initial years some, scholar and political elites portrayed Pakistan as a 'puppet' manipulated by the US decision-makers.[92] According to them, political decisions made by the Pakistan policy-makers were dependent or decision made by the US policy-makers in a cause and effect fashion. However, to say that the US exerted no influence on decision-making in Pakistan would as fallacious as to maintain that the influence was total.[93]

Certain geographical areas of the world have been considered vital to the US domestic and international interests and activities in these areas (late in America, for example) the US political and economic influence has been critical. South Asia and Pakistan, however, have become increasingly less vital to the US from a strategic point of view and in terms of the US economic activity neither the area nor the particular nation has been an attraction for the US private investment.[94] The US Pakistan relations developed out of mutual needs and shared attitudes regarding national security during cold war in a sense both nations used each other for; their own particular national interests. In doing so, dependency developed on both sides of the relationship.[95]

THE US AND INDO-PAK RELATIONS

Any influence or pressure exerted by the US and in turn accepted by Pakistan must be considered in the light of specific events, the vulnerability of Pakistan's political system during the event considered and the status of Pakistan's relations with other nations. If these variables are considered, the thesis of 'mutual benefit and need' is acceptable. In other words, Pakistan's willingness to be 'influenced' has been conditional, the major conditions being the absence of alternative sources of those goods and services which the US could supply and the incentives offered for such acquiescence. With regard to major political decisions, both external and internal, which were made by Pakistan leaders, it is evident that direct US influence has been limited.[96]

Even in the case of Indo-Pak relations, particularly the Kashmir issue, the US involvement behind the curtain has always been acknowledged and sometimes appreciated too. Some observers feel that whenever both the countries started dialogue or initiated various Confidence Building Measures (CBM's), it is not because of their own choice, it is only by extraneous factors or international pressure, such as in 1962-63, 1990, after May 1998 and so on. Both sides always blamed each other for the failure of the talks or any acceptable solution of the Kashmir.[97]

During 1962-63, India agreed to talks on Kashmir under the US persuasion at a time when relations deteriorated and the Sino-Indian war took place and it was necessary for India to protect its Western flanks with Pakistan. In 1994, India was hard pressed according to Pakistan's Foreign Affairs 'Ministry, again due to International pressure following the indigenous Kashmir, uprising at the end of 1989, under pressure from the US. Following the mission of the American President's Special envoy, India engaged in seven rounds of talks at Foreign Secretary level. The Pakistan blamed India for the failure of talks. But process further continued. In September 1998. Prime Ministers of both the countries met and declared that 'resolution of the Kashmir dispute is essential for peace and security.'[98]

After the nuclearisation of India and Pakistan, the international pressure to solve the Kashmir issue increased. The nuclearisation of South Asia had converted this area into a flash-point and the UN Security Council through its Resolution 1172 as well as the G-8 and P5 countries, number of world leaders, has expressed the urgent need for a dialogue to resolve the root-cause of tension between the two.

Pakistan Government felt that even though India agreed to the Lahore Declaration to intensify efforts to resolve the Kashmir issue, in February 1999, it adopted delayed tactics for holding the next round of talks. In May 1999, Pakistan dealt a severe blow to the dialogue process by launching military operations, involving air and ground forces, on the Kashmir Mujahideen fought fiercely in the Kargil Sector and across the (LOC) on Pakistan controlled areas, Pakistan Foreign Affair Ministry accused India of rejecting the suggestion to defuse the situation, including the proposal for immediate end of hostilities, mutual respect for the (LOC) and resumption of the dialogue in accordance with the Lahore Declaration.[99]

At the invitation of President Bill Clinton, Prime Minister Nawaz Sharif visited the US on 4-5 July 1999 and held in-depth talks with the US President on all aspects of the Kashmir dispute. According to the joint statement, the President of the US appreciated Sharif's views to expedite and intensify the process of resolving the Kashmir dispute. In order to find an early and just solution to the Kashmir issue, Pakistan has hesitation in accepting third party mediation. It encouraged the international community to play an active role and facilitate the peaceful solution of the Kashmir disputes.

The ministry emphatically said that, 'Pakistan will continue to extend full political, diplomatic and moral support to the legitimate Kashmir struggle for their right of self-determination as enshrined in the relevant UN Resolutions.'[100]

Stephen Cohen, a renowned analyst of Indo-Pak relations in an article in the *Financial Times*, appreciated the

US role, working secretly from time to time in defusing crisis situation. He appreciated Prime Minister Vajpayee efforts, as he 'takes the long-term view, in working for the eventual transformation of Pakistan.' Vajpayee won't be in a position to do it alone. The atmosphere created after the introduction of (CBM's) in the sub-continent, provided an opportunity to narrow the differences between the two Gen. Musharaff and Vajpayee. To clearly see this moment for a new approach, Vajpayee believed that he could bring a semblance of normalcy to South Asia. He knew India would never be counted among Asia's great states until it settled its affairs with the weaker Pakistan and was aware that hardliners in his own party regard talk of peace as just short of treason. In India, some believed that Pakistan will collapse eventually and there is no need to rescue it from this fate. Paradoxically, this approach has the practical results as of the Pakistan camp, which fears negotiating from a position of weakness and cites timings as the obstacle to negotiations. On the other hand, 'his improbable partner General Musharaff is harder to figure out. He lack of strategic vision and believed that ruling Pakistan is like running an army division, gave the orders and they would be obeyed.' He might have learnt that his approach did not work. One feels he was tired of water issues, sectarian rivalries and diplomatic double talk. Even his strategy of using militants to force the Indians to the negotiating table has failed. Then the militants were more interested in his death than victory in Kashmir, he was having second thought.[101]

Such doubts are not peculiar to Gen. Musharaff. He represented a large civil-military Oligarchy, dubbed the 'Establishment' in local circles. This 8000-10000 strong group includes senior army offices, bureaucrats, media leaders, politicians and even some Islamists. They knew that Pakistan was falling, that an economic and military race with an expanding India was a losing proposition and that Pakistan's friends are fair weather. Once Afghanistan stabilized and Al-Qaeda mopped up, the American will disappear leaving Pakistan without a major ally. The once reliable China, alarmed at Pakistan's support for Islamic radicals is moving towards an understanding with India over their border dispute even as Indo-China trade soars.[102]

Will India be able to provide Pakistan one reason its army desperately needs, a reason to accept a border drawn through Kashmir? ne words of one Pakistani officer 'the army understands it cannot wrest Kashmir from India, but, it cannot turn its back on six decades old struggle. At stake is its pride and it literally calls the shots.' Indians, understand this, but may still observe 'Chicago Rules' the best time to pick a man is when he is down. But they only postpone the problem. India cannot afford a radical Pakistan as its neighbour and Gen. Musharaff for all its shortcomings and bravado, represented the Pakistani establishment.[103]

Accepting Kashmir as human rights issue, rather than one of law and order, would maximize the interests of inhuman treatment of Kashmir people, even if they do not join Pakistan or become independent. The Indians will remove a blot on their own democracy and the Kashmiri of course will recover a semblance of normal life.[104]

The 1989-90 uprising was seen by Pakistan authority as a perfect opportunity to further their case with regard to Kashmir and to bring the Indian misdeeds in Kashmir to the international attention. It was precisely at that time that Pakistan initiated its current Kashmir policy 'moral' support for the Kashmiri natives and later, the insurgents that decided to take up arms for the Kashmiri cause. The Pakistan authorities saw this as a low cost, low risk policy that they hoped would raise the costs for the Indian side to the extent that it would abandon the Kashmiri's cause in due course. By bringing the Kashmir issue in the headlines, the Pakistani sought to establish moral legitimacy to their claim over Kashmir. Since the uprising, Pakistani authorities continue to hold the position that Pakistan only provides 'moral' and political support to the freedom-fighters for the liberation of their homeland from the oppressive Indian rule. India, on the other hand, holds Pakistan responsible for actively supporting the insurgents and their territorial activities and also maintains that Pakistani armies' personnel are involved in the insurgency.[105]

None of the desired goals of Pakistan's current Kashmir policy have been achieved. In fact in the last decade, India has managed to curtail Pakistan's alleged support for the insurgency and has been largely successful in selling its views to the world. Despite Islamabad's denials the world perceives a connection between the Kashmir insurgency and Pakistan's active support. To an objective analyst! it is somewhat hard to accept Pakistan's stance, though Indian claims may also be exaggerated. Pakistan's support of insurgents (if there is any) though having kept the issue of Kashmir alive has seen no positive results. The West is worried about the presence of extremist organizations and the radicals. The international community continues to be varying of Pakistan's nuclear capability. Moreover, the allegations of support to the Kashmiri insurgency that India described as 'terrorism' has witnessed fingers pointed towards Pakistan as a security threat.[106]

With regard to Kashmir, Pakistan today is seen as part of the problem, rather than a solution. This is itself a clear indication of Pakistan's failure to sell its views on Kashmir to the world. Pakistan has even lost support within the Kashmiri Muslim population. From the inception of the Kashmir issue, when a suggested plebiscite presumably would have seen Kashmir secession to Pakistan, Kashmiri now are likely to vote for independence. Just like the 1989-90 Kashmiri uprising was "a result of India's misadventure in Kashmir. The reversal of a Kashmiri opinion can be attributed to miscalculated Pakistan policy towards Kashmir, of course exacerbated by Indian exploitation."[107]

In effect, the Pakistani policy has neither produced any impetus for Kashmiri secession to Pakistan, nor has Pakistan been 'able to receive any international support for its stance. Most importantly, the Pakistani policy has seen no relief of whatsoever in the plight of the Kashmiri Muslims which officially is Pakistan's primary goal in Kashmir. On the contrary, India has largely been able to shrug-off the burnt of its own misdeeds against the Kashmiri population and had managed successfully to portray Pakistan as an aggressor. Kargil was a sombre reminder for Pakistan of the lack of international support for Pakistan's while its staunch ally China adopted a neutral posture.[108]

Even some Pakistani senior military officers feel that the problem of militancy in Pakistan was quite acute and that problem could be resolved if the US places heavy pressure on Pakistan, or more specifically, Pakistani-based militants groups and, their infiltration into Kashmir. The viewpoint tended to undermine the complexity of the situation at hand while also reflecting the agenda of New Delhi. As complex as the Kashmir problem is in its political context, the issue of militancy in Pakistan (which is also tied to the Kashmiri freedom struggle) is even more complex. To understand this controversy and realize the difficulty that Musharaff faced, it is important to examine the many faces of Islam in the region. At the outset, one has to come to terms with the fact that no doctrinally homogenous Islam has existed for many centuries, especially in the South Asian region A consistent play between varying levels of orthodoxy, each offering respective ways in which Islam doctrine can be understood and interpreted has always existed. Such variance in interpretation has had a large impact on the way in which Pakistan has approached the task of resolving certain modernization challenges. Generally there are two tiers of discussion that can be discerned in South Asian Islam. At one level there is the debate between the strict orthodox (legalistic) and the Sufi (or mystic) Muslims. This debate essentially puts rigid traditional principles but a tendency to preach different dogmas. The second level of debate revolves around certain modernization challenges and their impact on the essential faith. This debate, in particular, has a peculiar significance to the creation of Pakistan.[109]

Pakistan was created under the vision of the founders Iqbal and Jinnah, who subscribed to a modern progressive non- theocratic track that was meant to guide Pakistan into a pluralistic secular and prosperously democratic society. Until the time Zulfikar Ali Bhutto was removed in 1977, Pakistan remained on this track. In the decade thereafter, a series of events in the region took place including Zia-ul-Haq rule in Pakistan. The Soviet invasion in Afghanistan (particularly the role of Mujahadin in that war) affected Pakistan's society, pushing the countries and its institutions including the army, away from its original modernistic track and towards a definitely more conservation from the policy-making. The present situation prevailing in Pakistan is a legacy of this faction.[110]

Since late 1989, the Kashmir issue has become intimately linked to the larger question of war and peace in South Asia. The Kashmir dispute is the principal stumbling block on the tortuous road to a durable peace for South Asia as a whole, it is also problem for the rest of the world.' When the cold war was in full swing, it became its part and re-emerged as major global concerns when India and Pakistan became nuclear powers in May 1998. No nuclear war can be fought its having a profound effect on countries other than those obligations to come to the aid of victims or of the profound economic dislocations to which a nuclear war would lead. Some political and military strategists will argue that the risk of a nuclear war is slight, but even a 10% probability is unacceptably high. Hence, it is now entirely appropriate for countries outside the South Asian region, including those of Europe and the US to engage India and Pakistan cooperatively and constructively in working for peace and an honourable resolution of the Kashmir problem.[111]

The US has fully acknowledged the Pakistan viewpoint that the only cause of conflict between India and Pakistan is the Kashmir dispute which at any time can ignite the flames of war between the two countries. According to this scenario, a level crisis in Kashmir could trigger off a military response by either India or Pakistan then, the other side will overreact, leading to the direct clash between Indian and Pakistani forces, after that the world could escalate to an exchange of nuclear weapons. In a refinement of the scenario, it has been argued that even the suspicion of escalation might lead to a nuclear strike, presumably by the weaker or more vulnerable of the two countries (in this case Pakistan) since it would not want to risk having its small nuclear forces destroyed in an Indian pre-emptive attack.[112]

This scenario has led to great deal of activity much of it between the American officials and the Secretary General of the UN. There have been three stands to this diplomacy. First, the Kashmir problem has been addressed directly by several American officials. In a series of speeches and informal addresses, the traditional American approach on Kashmir was subtly altered, so that the US now openly declares all of Kashmir a disputed territory. In the past, the US has never publicly challenged the legitimacy of the accession of Kashmir to India, only its wisdom. Secondly, both India and Pakistan are urged to engage in additional (CBM's) that might prevent or slow down the escalation process. Third, both incentives and sanctions have been wielded in an attempt to get the two countries to talk directly about their nuclear programme. But none of these efforts have produced any significant results. The Kashmir problem is not closer to resolution. With the passing of each day, new (CBM's) have been introduced into South Asia, but it is generally that the old ones have fallen into a disuse or distrust. The crisis is for more complex than has been admitted by most of the American officials and therefore, Stephen Cohen argues that 'resulting the crisis and addressing the supplementary problem of nuclear proliferation and regional distrust require a more sophisticated than has hitherto been apparent.'[113]

(i) The Kashmir problem is a mixture of terrorism, state violence subversion and general horror that rests upon several layers of history. If the field, existed we could use the skills of political archaeologists to entirely unearth it. There are at least five different components of the Kashmir problem, each with its own origins, and each with its own consequences. Kashmir originally came into dispute because of a British failure of will when they divided and quit India in 1947. The mechanism by which the princely states were sorted out was inadequate. Each prince or ruler was to decide whether he could accede to India or Pakistan, presumably taken into account the make up and interests of the population. But there was no adequate mechanism for ensuring this, each ruler would make a fair or reasonable decision, or to ensure that 'third option' independence, would not be a temptation (the British, the Indian, the Pakistani) all agree that the further partition of the sub-continent would be wrong and that the princes had to go to one side or the other). In the case of Kashmir, a Hindu ruler governed a largely Muslim population, but was also considering independence. While there were other failures in the partition process, none so crippled the successor states as Kashmir, and the British were no longer around to repair the damage. Indian and Pakistanis have lived with the consequences, but now blame each other, rather than a faulty partition process.

(ii) The leadership in both the countries compounded the original problem when they turned the Kashmir problem into their national identities. For Pakistan, which defined itself as a homeland for Indian Muslims, the existence of a Muslim majority area under 'Hindu' Indian rule was grating, the purpose of creating Pakistan was to free Muslims from the tyranny of majority rule (and hence, of rule by the majority Hindu population); for Indian, their state had to include such predominantly Muslim region to demonstrate the secular nature of the new Indian state, since neither India nor Pakistan, so defined, could be complete without Kashmir, this raised enormously the stakes involved for both.

(iii) Subsequently Kashmir came to play a role in the respective domestic policies of both the states, especially Pakistan. For Pakistani leaders, both civilian and military, Kashmir was a useful tool which was helpful in diverting the attention of the people from the problems Pakistan was facing after independence. Further, there were and are powerful Kashmiri dominated constituencies in all of the major Pakistani cities, on the Indian side, the small, but influential Kashmiri Hindu community was over represented in the higher reaches of the Indian Government (not least in the presence of the Nehru family, a Kashmiri Pandit claim that had migrated from Kashmir to Uttar Pradesh).

(iv) Kahmir acquired an unexpected military dimension. After India crossed the ceasefire line during the course of the 1965, it became a strategic extension of international border to the South. Further China holds substantial territory (in Ladakh) claimed by India and New Delhi itself has made claims on regions which historically, had been subordinate to the rulers of the Kashmir (Gilgit, Swat, and Northern Territories) but which are now under Pakistani governance. More recently advances in maintaining techniques have turned the most inaccessible part of Kashmir, the Siachin Glacier into a battle ground, although more soldiers were cruelly killed by frost-bite than bullets.

(v) Finally, there is a contemporary dimension of Kashmir, the stirrings of a national self-determination movement among Kashmiri Muslims. Encouraged by neither India nor Pakistan, it burst into full view in late 1989 and threatened the integrity of both the states. There are two or three new generations of valley Muslims, educated and trained in India, but with a window open to a wider world. Angry and resentful at their treatment by New Delhi and not attracted to even a democratic Pakistan, they looked towards Afghanistan, Iran, the Middle-East and Eastern Europe for moral and to America, Britain and Canada for material support.[114]

As a strategic issue, Kashmir has waxed and waned. It was the central objective of the first two Indian wars (1948, 1965). But it was not an issue of high priority for either India or Pakistan from after the 1965 war until 1989 and the birth of a Kashmiri separatist movement what is striking how little a role Kashmir played in the large scale 1971 conflict (which was fought over the status of the separation of East Bengal from Pakistan) and even in the 1987 crisis that developed during a major Indian Military exercise along the India-Pakistan border operation Brass Tracks, It is believed that during the operation Brass Tracks, the two countries were much closer *to* war in January 1987 than in 1990 when Kashmir was the point of contention, yet Kashmir had little to do with the origin or evaluation of the Brass- Track crisis.

A major obstacle to peace-making in South Asia is that the key decision-makers have been guided more by considerations of domestic electoral politics, by the desire to control 'real estate' and international 'real politic' than by concern for the welfare of the ordinary people who will have to live with the consequences of their diplomatic failures. Thus funds that could much better be spent for education, health and other constructive purposes are diverted to 'support military establishments and 99% of the combined population of India and Pakistan, roughly more than people are in effect, hostages to 'control the destiny of the one percent who live in Kashmir'. This is morally unacceptable. Not until the needs of the people are made paramount, will a lasting peace be forged. While all Indians and Pakistanis bear the cost of confrontation in Kashmir, it is the Kashmiri who suffer most from its perpetuation and it is essential that they be given a significant voice in determining their own future.[115]

A second fundamental problem in respect to resolving the Kashmir dispute is the State's heterogeneity. In language, religion, culture, economy and terrain, the area of the erstwhile princely State of Jammu and Kashmir to use its proper name is exceedingly diverse. Yet India, Pakistan, a great many Kashmiri nationalists and even initially the UN have all been largely responsible to treat the area as an indivisible entity, assuming that the whole of world inevitably fall to satisfy a large population, was recognized as early as 1953 by UN mediator, Sir Owen Dixon of Australia, who proposed that portions of the State be assigned outright to India and Pakistan and the UN proposed plebiscite be limited to the valley and some adjacent areas.

In place of playing an essentially zero game, peace-making requires devising a solution in which all parties to the dispute gain significant portions of their most vital goals. It is also necessary to acknowledge the legacy of and depth of distrust between India and Pakistan.[116]

The Simla Accord of 1972 had offered a solution; defer a formal settlement, in the meanwhile bridge the gulf between the two countries. In both countries, the greatest hawks on Kashmir are journalists, politicians, academicians and other civilians and some of the intelligence services especially Pakistan's Inter Services Intelligence (ISI). Ironically both the regular armed forces are very cautious since both armies have calculated the risks of large-scale war and conclude that its outcome would be very uncertain that collective damage would be great and that the possibility of escalation to a nuclear conflict is unacceptably high. This was one of the lessons that both sides drew from their retrospective studies of the 1987 crisis over operation Brass Tracks.[117]

Many Pakistanis believe that India only responds to the main source of tension pressures and many Indians deny that Pakistan has only legitimate role in Kashmir except to end its support to the militants. Kashmiri—both Hindu and Muslim—however, tasted violence of a sort never experienced before as they undergo a terrible order. After 1971 Kashmir ceased to be a cause of bad India-Pakistan relations, but it definitely remained a cause. It is also a symbol of their inability to compose their differences and live in peace. Kashmir thus both cause and effect, which makes it definately so difficult to conceptualize as a political issue.[118]

Before we start thinking about solutions, there is a need to discuss the matter. Physicists approach a problem by first 'sizing it'. What are its parameters and contours? Here Kashmir assumes an unusual shape.

First, while the valley Muslims felt aggravated that they were dominated by outsiders from India, other Kashmiri group especially the valley Hindus and largely the Buddhist population of Ladakh, feared the dominance of the State by the valley Muslims. Thus a number of proposals have suggested the possibility of separating the valley from other regions (like Azad Kashmir, Ladakh, Jammu) and allocating parts of Jammu and Kashmir to India and Pakistan, leaving to the end the intensely disputed valley. Here, the appropriate analogy is the Middle-East peace process, where the overall strategy is to leave to the end such very contentious issues as the status of Jerusalem.[119]

Second, there are outside the propaganda mills of Delhi and Islamabad diverse views on Kashmir in both India and Pakistan. Kashmir is not viewed in the same light by all Pakistani and Indians. Anyone who travelled throughout South Asia during the height of the 1990's, the less passion there was about Kashmir in Chennai, Calcutta, Hyderabad, (Deccan) and Mumbai. Kashmir was, and is seen as New Delhi's obsession in Karachi, Quetta, Peshawar and Hyderabad (Sind), it is seen as a secondary issue, relations with Islamabad and the Punjab come first. Indeed the size of demonstrations on behalf of the Kashmir revolution to all Pakistan cities are in direct proportion to the presence of large Kashmiri population. Kashmir is neither a homogenous issue within the states of Azad Kashmir and Jammu and Kashmir, nor within India and Pakistan.

Third, it is important to recognize the crucial role of time, and timing in resolving the Kashmir problem. Ironically one of the obstacles to reaching a solution is the belief, on all sides of the dispute, that 'time is on our side' since the Kashmir dispute has been mismanaged by the two generations of Indian and Pakistanis and Kashmiri's must own responsibility also, for their own error of omission and commission there is no age group except perhaps among the newest generations of South Asians who believe that the time has come for solution, what should be taken second, third and which should be reserved to the last. Like proposals to resolve the Arab-Israeli dispute, 'solution' to the Kashmir must operate at many levels. This suggests both caution and flexibility, but it does not suggest that doing nothing is the best course. The examples of Middle-East, South Africa and perhaps of Ireland indicate that seemingly intractable disputes can be resolved or ameliorated by patience and outside encouragement.[120]

PERCEPTIONS OF HAQQANI AND TELLIS

Hussain Haqqani's and Ashley J. Tellis, leading experts on Indo-Pakistani relations, had raised key issues in their interaction, particularly on the prospects for improved relations between India and Pakistan.

Haqqani felt that 'the thaw in relations is just that a thaw rather than a break-through. We have similar developments in the past hailed as breakthrough, only to watch them and in breakdowns', but India and Pakistan are, once again approaching the peace process but with a totally different objectives. Indian purpose is to seek one end to terrorism in Jammu and Kashmir and start the process of moralization. India has given no indication that it would negotiate alternatives future for Kashmir, though it has accepted Kashmir as one of the crucial matters, the two sides need to address. Pakistan on the other hand has abjured the use of force but would like to link this step to substantive talks about the future of Kashmir. The willingness of both sides to start a composite dialogue has raised hopes that they are willing to back away from their entrenched position. But their willingness to talk does not necessarily signal willingness to on what each side considers being the real issue requiring resolution.[121]

Ashley J. Tellis was of the view that the January 2004 Summit Conference between A.B. Vajpayee and General Musharaff resulted in the resumption of bilateral dialogue, signalled an end to the 2001-02 crisis. It symbolized the substantive conclusion of the crisis—meaning that the root-cause which generated that confrontation in the first place, were then eviscerated—was not clear. But the fact that both sides had committed themselves to a wide ranging dialogue offered a ray of hope. It implied a beginning of a process whereby outstanding disputes could be addressed through diplomacy rather than coercion and force.

Tellis raised three issues of prime importance which he considered very significant. First, the summit primarily signified a bilateral commitment to a process and not an agreement about and particular outcome hence; one should not conclude that a resolution of the outstanding disputes between India and Pakistan was imminent. Second, that the two key elements that did appear in their joint statement (the bilateral communiqué that followed the January 2004 Summit)—the acceptance of all disputes, including Jammu and Kashmir, ought to be resolved only through dialogue and the acknowledgement that terrorism was unacceptable as a means of securing political aims—are vital to the eventual success of the process. Third, if both sides consistently abide by these substantive elements, the peace process could be success overtime because it would effectively pave the way for accepting the current territorial division of Jammu and Kashmir (with some modifications) as the basis for an ending political solution. Such a solution would also include *inter alia*, increased political economy for both sides of the divided State, easily cross-border transit for their further respective population and a reduction in the military presence maintained by India and Pakistan along the present Line of Control (LOC).[122]

There was clearly as Haqqani said even 'a feeling of relief that a peace process is under way, even though a solution is not immediately in sight. A significant, though a small body of opinion in Pakistan recognizes that the economic and military race with India is a difficult proposition and that Pakistan's friends such as the US are fair weather and cannot be counted on the contest with India.' Haqqani further said that Pakistan must turn its attention inward and focus on internal development and self sufficiency, instead of remaining engaged in military competition. Adherence to this view further argued that Pakistan would not be able to seriously pursue economic development if it continues along the path of militarism and military. Sustained economic progress would only be possible after relations with India were normalized. These people constitute the peace constituency in Pakistan. But the question in Pakistan is always, 'Is there a constituency for peace within the Pakistani militancy.' The thinking of civilians is seemingly less important in a country where the military is all powerful and holding the strings of administration. There was no Pakistani civilian constituency for supporting the Sikh insurgency in India during the 1980s. But Pakistan did it, nevertheless was there a Pakistan consistency for supporting the Taliban when it ascended to power in Afghanistan or for ending the support after 9/11. Pakistan made both decisions any way because the Pakistan military considered both strategically very important. How much of Pakistan military want for permanent peace? That's difficult to say. In the past, there had been moments when the military desired that peace was required. Gen. Zia ul-Haq repeatedly declared that he would never let a war take place with India while he was President and while Pakistan was making a nuclear bomb. The Pakistani 'military is the key and it is always the most difficult institution to analyze.'[123]

Haqqani strongly believes that Pakistani military always wanted to be having a share in the political process of Pakistan. It doesn't want to relinquish its position of privilege and power. One of the major unanswered questions of the peace-process of India and Pakistan is what to do with the huge military establishments of both countries one of which also controls political power. If the Pakistani military were not running covert operation against India and if it were not running the country, what would it do? Pakistan military has traditionally drawn its legitimacy from the fact that it is the defender of Pakistan against the external threat from India and that it is the institution that will get Kashmir for Pakistan. If the existing threats from India were acknowledged as no longer real and the issue of Kashmir already settled, the Pakistani military would loose its legitimacy as the arbiter of the nation's destiny. The praetorian ambitions of the Pakistani army must be channelled in some other direction if peace initiatives is to have a long-term future.[124]

It was also believed that Musharaff has had a change of heart about India, transforming from hawk to dove, but one could not be sure whether that change was forever or momentary. At a time when *Jehadi's* were trying to kill him and Americans were worried about Pakistan's involvement in nuclear proliferation in Libya, North Korea and Iran and Musharaff was having no domestic support it served him well to turn off at least one source of heat.[125]

We may also have to make a distinction between the General Musharaff the individual and General Musharaff as the Chief of Pakistan's Army. There is a tendency to think that speaks for the entire Pakistani elite and especially the military. The generals and their ranks, have for years, believed that by stoking the fires of rebellion in Indian controlled parts of Kashmir, they could force India to make concessions on the territorial *status quo* if that disputed region. Now Musharaff has more or less acknowledged that 'Kashmir is not necessarily going to fall in Pakistan's lap as a ripe apple from the tree, simply as a consequence of a sustained Jehadi activity.' Haqqani was of the view that the first thing Pakistan needs is to make sure that the Islamist militants, the *Jehadi's* are truly put out of business. Musharaff seemed to be serious about maintaining peace in the region. It was a general feeling that the US worked behind the curtain to put pressure on both the countries for maintaining peace in the region.[126]

Tellis was of the opinion that 'What the US should do at the moment is layoff simply. The India-Pakistan peace process will succeed only when New Delhi and Islamabad and not outsiders conclude that they must accomplish something of value. In this context, the US had an important but limited role and that consisted primarily of using its influence with both sides to ensure that the process of dialogue simply steps on track, and that both India and Pakistan persist with their conversation even when the going gets difficult. Obviously, Washington has separate and different interests in India and Pakistan those interests will be pursued even as the bilateral dialogue in the sub-continent proceeds.[127]

The biggest challenge, here, of course would be managing the US relations with Islamabad which are important to the success of operating and enduring freedom in a way that had the following three effects:

- Strengthening Pakistan (which people keep forgetting is not synonymous with strengthening the Pakistani military) not weakening it further.
- Not undermining the US interests in India, which possess greater geo-political weight in the sub-continent and is important to a stable balance of power in Asia?
- Assisting Pakistan in reconciling itself to the existing geographical reality in Kashmir rather than hardening its attitude to overthrow the *status quo* through continued conflict.

Haqqani felt that American role was essentially one of that which 'encourages and facilitates and that's about it'. The truth of the matter is that the Indian and the Pakistanis are quite capable of creating crisis and occasionally resolving them without American assistance. The US must provide sense of security to Pakistan, even if it is temporary. Otherwise Pakistan would feel much weaker when negotiating with India.[128]

The fundamental improvement in the US-India ties in recent years makes a major turning point. With more than one billion people democratic institution, a large defuses establishment and a 'steady growing economy', India represents a partner of great value. India will have one of the world's largest economies and will become an increasingly significant security factor in the Indian Ocean region and in Asia as a whole. Despite policy disagreements with the US (for example, regarding Iraq and international economic and trade issues), Indian government and people find increasing overlays between their interests and those of the American people. After six decades of cool, Washington and New Delhi are now actively and constructively engaged in the task over the medium-term, through 2010, to consolidate the 'transformed' relationship into a genuine partnership. To this end task, force recommended that the US and India:

- Work to expand political, security, military and intelligence cooperation,
- Intensify both official and non-official dialogue on economic and trade issues, and
- Negotiate a trade agreement in services.

The task force recommends that the US:

- ease restrictions on cooperation with India with civilian satellite sector,
- treat India as a 'friendly' country in granting export licenses for transfers of defence equipments,
- ease restrictions on the export to India of dual use items that have civilian and military users, and

- Encourage the US foundations, business and scientific and educational institutions to expand efforts to develop cooperative programme with Indian counterparts.

The task force recommends that India:

1. Make important domestic economic reforms with greater vigour to promote more rapid growth,
2. Open its economy further to the global market by reducing administrative restrictions and other barriers to foreign trade and investment, and
3. Modify policies and reduce administrative restrictions that impede cooperative, academic and foundation activities.[129]

In the wake of 9/11, bilateral relations between the US and Pakistan have dramatically improved. Pakistan has become a valued partner in the war on terrorism. But as in the past, the US and Pakistani policies only partially coincide. The US interests in pursuing the way on terrorism conflict with Pakistan continued support for Islamic terrorists engaged in Jihad against India in a disputed territory of Kashmir (Pakistan considers many of these militants to be 'freedom fighters') and Pakistan's failure to prevent pro-Taliban elements from using the Pakhtoon tribal area as a base to attack Afghanistan. Islamabad's dissatisfaction with the *status quo* in Kashmir continues to fuel dangerously high tensions with India and has caused concerns about reported nuclear commerce with North Korea.[130]

America has a major stake in friendly and long-term ties with Pakistan. A positive relationship however will be difficult to sustain unless Islamabad firmly turns its back on terrorists groups and plays by non-proliferation rules. President Musharaff said on 12 January 2002 that, 'he wanted to make Pakistan a modern progressive and dynamic state.' But achieving this laudable goal will not be easy given the Pakistan's instable political institutions, its weak social and economic development and uncertain commitment of its military leadership to reform. The task force believed that

Pakistan could pursue the reform agenda supporting this effect should be the principal aim of the US policy over the medium-term, Washington should, however, adopt a much more nuanced approach than that followed by the Bush Administration.

In the economic and security assistance arena, the US should:

- Obtain Congressional approval for a five year 3 billion assistance package, but the package should be revised so that-two thirds ($400 million) annually is allowed for economic and one-third ($200 million annually) for security assistance, instead of the fifty divisions as proposed by the executive branch,
- Conditional release of aid above a baseline level ($1.5 billion over five years, or $200 million of economic assistance and $100 million of security assistance annually) on Pakistan's progress in implementation of a political, economic and social reform agenda, its cooperation in war, on terrorism and its prevention of leakage of sensitive nuclear, technology material,
- Make education the principal focus of the US assistance with high priority also for projects to aid Pakhtoon areas,
- Boost economic and technical support for institutions on which good government rests the courts, parliament, police, democratic political parties and revenue collection,
- Continue to use appropriated funds to buy-back Pakistan's debt to the US, and
- Ease restrictions on Pakistani textile imports into the US and avoid new barriers.

To promote democracy, the US should:

- Urge publicly as well as privately and enhanced civilian and a reduced army role in governance, and

- Oppose continued involvement of ISI in the electoral process and provide increased assistance in bolstering civil society.

To promote regional stability, the US should:

- Press President Musharaff to make good on his pledge to stop infiltration across the (LOC), the *defacto* border between Indian administered and Pakistan administered parts of Kashmir permanently,
- Press Kashmir not to permit the use of Pakistani territory as a base for pro-Taliban attacks on Afghanistan, and
- Make clear that Pakistan's failure to do a better role of preventing the use of its territory by terrorists will reduce US assistance levels.

Indo-Pakistan differences over Kashmir still unresolved, lie at the heart of their rivalry. If the two countries are to live amicably with one another, they will have to address the issue, contain the dangers and pursue and eventually implement a settlement. Their festering hostility remains the greatest single threat to regional stability and therefore to the US interests in South Asia. Given the fact that India and Pakistan are now nuclear armed, the possibility of conflict involving the first use of nuclear weapons since 1945, remains all too real. Till date neither government appears to have made the political decision that its national interest would be served by movement towards general detente and a Kashmir settlement except on its own terms.[131]

The US policy in recent years over Kashmir has been of crisis management. Washington leaps into action whenever the alarm bells ring to signal a possible Indo-Pakistan war. At other times, the US has limited itself to rhetorical calls for dialogue. Notwithstanding other demands on Washington's attention, this approach is inadequate giving the dangers inherent in India-Pakistan hostility and the seemingly inability of New Delhi and Islamabad to achieve progress of their own what is required more forward learning and sustained US engagement. There should be a long-term US diplomatic effort to assist not to mediate and arbitrate India and Pakistan's intermittent efforts to bridge their bilateral process that will gradually lead to resolution of bilateral differences, ultimately including the dispute over Kashmir. To help get the process going, the US should stress with Pakistan the need to,

- Permanently prevent infiltration across the LOC, and
- Modify its present negotiating stance on, which makes progress on Kashmir a pre-condition for dealing with other Indo-Pak issues.

The US should stress India that it needs to:

- Do more to reach an understating with the elected Jammu and Kashmir State government that better address the aspiration of Kashmiri and increases the pace of economic development, and
- Reduce the level of activity of Indian security forces and improve their human rights record.[132]

Facilitation should be long-term effort, implemented under White House and State Department over-sight. The goal of diplomacy should be to help India and Pakistan develop a framework that will enable them to address more constructively than they have in the past issues such as nuclear (CBM's), de-escalation along the (LOC) and the Siachen glacier, expanded trade relations, easing movement of people and reducing hate propaganda. Although, Kashmir dispute itself cannot be ignored, the wide gap between India and Pakistani positions and the depth of mistrust make it counter-productive to put forward the US ideas about shape of settlement or how to get there.[133]

No doubt, Pakistan's hostile relationship with India impinges on short and long-term American interests. Besides a concern about preventing a new India-Pakistan crisis or Washington now has excellent relationship with India and this for the first time in decades that the US has good relations with both South Asian powers. Can the US have close ties with two states that are hostile to each other and are reportedly on the brink of crisis? Washington managed to do this for many years in the case of Greece and Turkey but these states were each part of a larger alliance framework, they did not have nuclear weapons and had not fought a real war with each other for many years. There is no over arching American strategic framework for South Asia and 'terrorism' does not provide one. The US approach to Kashmir and perception of its interest in the Kashmir problem have been varied markedly since the issue first took on international dimensions a few months after the partition of British India in 1947. At first, Washington felt that Kashmir problem as a dispute between the two countries friendly to the US. For Washington, South Asia in those early years of Indian and Pakistani independence was perceived largely as a British show. In 1948, when India brought the Kashmir issue to the UN, then it was a fledging organization, the best hope for a resolution of the dispute.[134]

Accordingly, Truman Administration joined the British Government as a prime mover in the UN Security Council passage of a Resolution establishing the (UNCIP). The Eisenhower Administration that was in power from 1953 to 1961 for some time entertained the idea of a Kashmir settlement that did not involve a plebiscite and urged the two claimants to resolve the dispute bilaterally, it soon reverted to Truman's support of the formula spelled out in various (UNCIP) Resolutions. Its inclination to do so was heightened when it established security relations with Pakistan.

The 1962 border war between India and China set the stage for a new bilateral Washington initiative to bring about a Kashmir solution, this time outside the UN framework. But India-Pakistan talks held under the US pressure proved inclusive, Washington came up with some specific ideas of its own. One of these would have awarded part *of* the Indian-held Kashmir valley to Pakistan. When the talks failed, as he had expected they would, Professor John Kenneth, the then US Ambassador to India, remarked that the only one thing the two sides could agree on was to denounce Washington proposals. These led 1962-63 talks paved the high water mark of the US involvement in efforts to resolve the Kashmir dispute. Until the 1998 India and Pakistan nuclear lists and Pakistan's armed attack on Kargil area of Indian controlled Kashmir, the following year led US policy-makers to focus on the issue. Washington preferred to remain largely on side-lines. It neither pushed for a settlement at international forums nor undertook any significant unilateral initiatives. The 1965 India-Pakistan war over Kashmir significantly contributed to the hands of the US attitude. It crystallized the feelings of many US policy-makers that the best approach to Washington's political and security relevance with India and Pakistan was a pledge on both their houses and on Kashmir as well.[135]

In this context, Washington hailed the agreement India and Pakistan had reached at Simla in July 1972. In this accord, they pledged to solve the Kashmir and other problems bilaterally. They also undertook to respect the (LOC) dividing their forces. The agreement gave the US an unassailable; thoroughly respectable rational for remaining on the sidelines. Unable to change the situation in Kashmir, it was quite prepared to let the contestants work out with the problem by them. India, Pakistan and the US choose to put the issue in cold storage and allowed the *status quo* to become a *defacto* settlement, that would be fine with Washington. Successive US administrations maintained this aloof position for the better part of more than two decades. Kashmir disappeared from the world's agenda and the Kashmiri people seemed to have become reconciled to their lot as Indian citizens.[136] The outbreak of the Kashmir insurgency in the end of 1989 quickly returned Kashmir to the US radar screens. If feared that this time, an India-Pakistan war could develop nuclear dimensions. It was only concerned with the human rights violations by Indian forces. And it was troubled by the terrorist's attacks favoured by some of the insurgents, especially those with Islamic credentials.[137]

Despite those concerns, the US has always declined to play the role of a mediator. It struck to the line that 'the best way to resolve the Kashmir dispute is through direct negotiations between the Governments of India and Pakistan as envisaged in the Simla Agreement.' After the insurgency worsened, it added to this formulation the point that in their bilateral discussions, the two Governments should take into account the wishes of the Kashmir people. Washington did not offer advice about how this should be done.[138]

The 1998 India and Pakistani nuclear tests however greatly magnified Washington's concerns about Kashmir. It felt that, Kashmir was a 'flash point' that could ignite a nuclear war and give high priority to the resumption of the stalled India-Pakistan dialogue, including on Kashmir. But it continued to insist it would not take a more direct role on Kashmir unless both sides agreed.[139]

Although Pakistan welcomed the internationalization of the dispute, a long time Pakistani goal, the tests strengthened the primacy the US gave to preserving stability in South Asia and lessened the importance it attached to the equities of the Kashmir issue. For the US and other members of the international community, the use of violence to change the *status quo* was not an acceptable opinion. President Clinton made the position clear when he pressured the Pakistanis to withdraw their troops from the Kargil area of Indian Kashmir that they had seized in a military operation.[140]

The Bush Administration has tended to see the Kashmir issue primarily as a terrorist problem. This perspective is an outgrowth of 9/11 and of the attack on the Indian Parliament a few months later. So far the Bush Administration has focused its efforts on persuading the Pakistan Government to terminate its support for cross-border terrorist activities. Its high level interventions at critical moments in India-Pakistan tensions have been designed primarily as fire-fighting operations. They have not dealt to any extent with the basic problems in India-Pakistan relations.[141]

This attitude has charged Washington of gradually adopting relaxed approach. It now seemed to be prepared to go beyond the sterile failed formula that calls for bilateral talks, with the US willing to play the role only if requested to do so by both parties. Although, it continues to insist that it does not want to be a let alone an arbitrator, it has edged forward to the point where even senior administration figures such as Secretary of State, Collin Powell, also talked about more US participation. The term of choice has become facilitator.[142]

Ever since 9/11 have made such a role more feasible and General Musharaffs willingness to join the US led war against terrorism has turned around the US-Pakistani relationship that had earlier seemed in a state of continuing decline. At the same time, the US-Indian relationship have vastly improved following the end of cold war and New Delhi economic reforms measures. The improvement is continuing, which now include degree of cooperation on security matters that was unthinkable earlier. The US now enjoys the best relations simultaneously with India and Pakistan than it ever has. Both countries are willing to accept a larger US role in helping them to resolve, or at least more effectively manage their dispute with one another including Kashmir.[143]

This represents an historical change for New Delhi; one of the basic tenets of the foreign policy had long been to discourage any third party involvement in South Asian affairs unless this promoted its own interests. As the most powerful country in the region and the *status quo* power in Kashmir, it preferred to deal with the neighbour bilaterally. But now it is coming to recognize that the focus on stability and anti-terrorism that now characterizes the approach of the US to the Kashmir issue suggests that the US role could be beneficial, not dangerous, to India, aspirations in the state. The US policy-makers and specialists in the region differ about how Washington could best go about playing this new and enhanced role, though all now seem convinced that without such outside participation, neither a settlement nor more effective management of the problem will be possible. Some specialists prefer to offer at least the broad outlines of a solution as a useful initial step. They recognize that the settlement they favour will not be easily adopted. They argue that spelling out some basic principles will move discussions along more swiftly. In this view, such an outline can also serve to mobilize South Asian public opinion in a positive way.[144]

A different approach is required to deal with the problem step by step, avoiding at the earliest stages an effort to outline and what a final settlement would look like some of the adherents of this position agree that any eventual solution will include two elements:

- The acceptance of the (LOC) or something geographically close to it as the international frontier between India and Pakistan, and
- A greatly improved governance of Indian and perhaps Pakistani held Kashmir, to include a sizeable dose of autonomy. The Kashmir Study Group (KSG) feels that it does not make any sense to advertise these proposals until negotiations have gone to some distance.

Supporters of this approach talk about the importance of building blocks that can pave the way to an eventual *defacto* or *dejure* settlement. Such building blocks begin with the launching of the (CBM's) by the two countries.[145]

The US Government has not made any decision at a responsible level about how to proceed. Indeed, one of the remarkable and hopeful aspects of the view from Washington is the deep knowledge of South Asia that responsible US leaders including George Bush have acquired after 9/11. To be frank, however, it seems unlikely that some of the immediate problems the administration now faces become less pressing until the India-Pakistan reaches a truly critical point, not much will be done other than the crisis management.[146]

Stephen P. Cohen in a prepared testimony before the senate Foreign Relations Committee on 28 January 2004 suggested various measures towards Indo-Pakistan rapprochement and the steps that the US might take to strengthen the fledging peace process then underway. The US could and should do more, it had mostly been a bystander, but Cohen has been of the strong opinion that 'it will be up to the Indians and Pakistanis to determine whether debilitating rivalry will continue for another fifty years. This rivalry is costly to them, but it also places important American interests at risk.'[147]

He recommended that the present thaw will not last. India and Pakistan have moved from crisis to detente and back again for many decades. He suggested that:

- India and Pakistan can reach agreement on

ancillary issues, including (CBM's), but not on the issue of Kashmir,

- The introduction of nuclear weapons has been accompanied by a learning process in both states and several of the crisis were exacerbated by the nuclear factor,
- Negotiations take place when the two countries are in political and strategic balance, they find themselves momentarily agreeing that talks are worthwhile, but sooner or later, one or the other side conclude that the risks of moving ahead are greater than the costs of breaking-off discussions,
- In both countries there are powerful forces that oppose serious negotiations,
- Outside powers have played little if any role in advancing dialogue, and
- The US has intervened several times in times of crisis, but never developed a strategy that might promote and sustain a real peace process.[148]

India has only two realistic choices in its relations with Pakistan. The first is a dialogue that might lead to a settlement over Kashmir and other issues (especially trade) without changing core Indian policies; the second is a long-term strategy of containment, which would attempt to promote change within Pakistan while resisting Pakistan military adventures. Two other stages are also debated in India but both seem unattractive, one is to completely ignore Pakistan, the other is to openly challenge Pakistan, forcing change and perhaps (as in 1971) its break up. There were senior Indian officers who advocated a 'limited war' to teach Pakistan a lesson. The 2002 crisis was a turning point. Indian Generals could not promise that a limited war against Pakistan would not 'go nuclear' and the political leadership concluded that the risks of such a war were too great.[149]

Since 1947, Pakistan had sought to change Kashmir's status or to bring India to the negotiating table by appealing to international opinion and through Resolutions in the UN, a formidable legal effort and the use of force usually through proxies. The Kashmir issue is embedded in the very idea of

Pakistan, but it also has a strategic dimension. Pakistan Generals are concerned that if India were not pressed in Kashmir, its conventional military superiority would be overwhelming.

There are other ways in which Washington could help. In short form, there are the six steps that the US could follow:

- We should not be over concerned about the stability of the Pakistani regime. Musharaff's death would not bring chaos in Pakistan. Pakistan's overall policies are not likely to change; they are rooted in the interests of establishment, especially the Corps Commanders who form an inner circle of the government.
- The US can enrich and influence the inner circle of the Pakistani debate on Kashmir's future, but only if it has a presence on the ground. We have abandoned the field to the radical Islamists and those who purport to see a 'Christian-Jewish-Hindu' axis directed against Pakistan and the Muslim world. We need to dramatically increase our information activities in Pakistan and exchange programme with key Pakistani institutions, especially the universities and colleges where anti-Americanism is deeply rooted.
- India itself needs to be encouraged to continue its policies of normalization with Pakistan and with its Kashmiri citizens. India's greatest asset is its own rich and vibrant society. The US should urge India to unilaterally expand access for Pakistani scholars, politicians and media persons.
- Washington should strengthen the fledging peace process by increasing its funding for regional dialogues that now take place in various SAARC institutions and the Regional Centre for Strategic Studies in Colombo.
- Washington should also consult closely with its most important allies. Besides, providing technical expertise in border monitoring and other (CBM's),

the US and its allies should use their aid programme to reward India, Pakistan and various Kashmiri groups for progress on negotiations, they should also encourage Western and Japanese firms to invest in plants and companies that do business, both countries further strengthening regional economic ties.

- Finally, the US should not take a position on the shape of a final settlement of the Kashmir dispute, but let such a settlement emerge after dialogue among the parties including Kashmiri on both sides of the (LOC). However, it should support the view that Kashmir is a human right issue, not merely one of territory or international law. This position maximizes the interests of all parties and would make a final settlement easier. Pakistan can claim their struggle resulted in more human treatment of the Kashmiri people, even if they do not join Pakistan or become independent, India will remove a blot on their democracy and the Kashmir, of course, will recover a semblance of normal life.[150]

A discussion held at Brookings Institute on 11 June 2002 in which Stephen P. Cohen, Navnita Chandra Behera, Brigadier Feroz Hasan Khan participated and James B. Steinberg, acted as a moderator. 'What Role Does the US have in the India-Pakistan crisis?' Was the issue on which these scholars expressed their views? In the past, India had rejected external mediation in the Kashmir dispute while Pakistan has sought outside intervention. In the changed environment, India had sought American help in pressuring Pakistan to cease border infiltration or militants into the disputed territory. The US has also gained significant leverage with the Pakistani government since Islamabad's decision to join the international coalition in the global war on terror. Should the US use its new found position to broker a Kashmir deal that stops the terrorism in India and satisfies Pakistan's demands in Kashmir? Initiating the discussion, Stephen Cohen spoke from the US perspective. He said that there have been three major regional problems that have bedevilled American policy-makers. These are negative interests. The first has been Kashmir, right from the very beginning the US was engaged in the Kashmir issue. By 1964-65, the US had really given up on Kashmir and since then, there had been no significant American initiative on Kashmir.[151]

The other issue was the question of nuclear proliferation. This was a growing concern in the Carter Administration. The Reagan Administration looked at it. The Bush Administration followed it. The US made this the central focus of its foreign policy in the Clinton Administration and the policy then evolved into the phrase "cap, rollback and eliminate" nuclear weapons. That really guided the US policy towards South Asia, towards India and Pakistan particularly.

More recently, there is a war on terrorism which has brought the US attention to South Asia and at the same time the US relations with both India and Pakistan have undergone a change. The US regards both India and Pakistan as its allies in this war on terrorism even though they have strong disagreements between each other.[152]

The evaluation of the so-called war on terrorism in South Asia has made the US vulnerable to pressure from both India and Pakistan. The Pakistanis for many years have argued that a nuclear war in South Asia could take place over Kashmir and Kashmir was officially declared to the flash point of South Asia by several American administrations. So the Pakistan have argued that the US must put pressure on India to resolve the Kashmir dispute or at least to get the Indians to talk about Kashmir. After 9/11, the Indians took that argument that turned it inside out. They argued that terrorism was the leading possible cause of war in South Asia that Pakistani supported terrorists in India and Kashmir could trigger war between India and Pakistan which could then lead to nuclear detonation by one or both the countries. India rejected any US role in South Asia but in 1999, it accepted the US pressure in Kargil.[153]

The US has really three options in South Asia. The first is the traditional policy in South Asia the good old-fashioned simply loves them and leaves them policy. There do not seem to be vital US interests in South Asia, that is nothing of direct threat to the US except that possibly events that might occur in Pakistan. The war on terrorism of course transformed that perspective and Pakistan became a frontline state in the war on terrorism not only for the war in Afghanistan but clearly for the evolution of Pakistan or the deterioration of Pakistan into a state which was itself the source of international terror. Pakistan has been a transit point and a training centre for a number of Al-Qaeda and other radicals. The first option was to pullout. The Second opinion was to remain engaged out but tilting towards India. A third opinion was to engage India and Pakistan but ignore Kashmir. As long as the US is in need of Pakistan as an ally in the war against terrorism, clearly there will be a military relationship and a political relationship with Islamabad and the US Administration still sees India as a rising major Asian State. Cohen was of the opinion that the minimum the US could do was having a closer relationship with India, the beginning of military cooperation possibility even nuclear cooperation in the future. As the Indian economy revived, there would be much greater US-India economic ties. And in the case of Pakistan, there was a possibility of liberal economic aid to rebuild its economic structure. There would be more military assistance to Pakistan if that was the price the Pakistani's wanted in order to keep their cooperation and keep the US forces in Islamabad.[154]

Navnita Chandra Behera, an Indian scholar felt that there was a dramatic change in the Indian position. India has traditionally been very rigidly almost opposed to any role players, national players or intervention in any bilateral issues, Kashmir being one in that 'over the years'. India not only accepted but sometimes even welcomed the role played by outside powers. There was an emerging strategic partnership between India and the US on a larger sort of Horizon (inaudible). India's policy of denying a role for international affairs was routed in 50s. India had a bit of experience in the UN but by the turn of the century, the whole situation changed. Now it's a whole new world, i.e. its post-cold war and past 9/11 era. In the Kargil Crisis, the US openly tilted towards India and publicly held Pakistan as an aggressor and forced the Pakistani forces, the intruders to return back across the (LOC). It also depends; she argued how you make the international community turn around you. During Kargil Crisis, India gained sanctity of (LOC) against territorial aggression. The permanent solution to Kashmir problem lay around the (LOC).[155]

Another important area is of nuclear proliferation in South Asia. There is whole defence parameter of the nuclear questions in South Asia. As proliferation has already taken place, now one has to look into the real threat of use of nuclear weapons. The US administration was also worried about the nuclear threat prevailing in South Asia. Nobody wants a nuclear war and that's where the US stakes are very high.

The third question is the war on terrorism, where the war on terrorism does go. There is a convergence of interests between India and the US on the war against terrorism. The differences made in approaches and in metrics of achieving this objective. In India, there was a realization that you need to cooperate with the US because the large goals of both the countries are the same. The US has also realized that it is not possible to eliminate Al-Qaeda completely.[156]

India has to take the help of the US in ending terrorism from the Kashmir valley. Initially, the movement in Kashmir started as an indigenous movement. It changed in its character and turned into a terrorist movement. Pakistan should be asked to cooperate fully. The Pakistan view was presented by Brigadier Feroz Hasan Khan. He was somewhat different in his approach to put that, he said, what you are seeing in South Asia is not something that suddenly emerged. It is a continuum of something that has occurred and depends on how you like to approach it, that this problem in the long-term perspective began from 1947-48, there was a mid-term in 1971 where the issue between India and Pakistan was not Kashmir. The people of Pakistan were worried more about their survival. The bilateral negotiations were between India and Pakistan with the active support of the US, Russia and China could really be helpful in maintaining peace in the area. They must impress upon the Governments and political elites of both the countries that the peace process should not be stopped. In the long-term, Khan suggested, India and Pakistan must solve at least four strings simultaneously. A political sustained dialogue for conflict resolution, a strategic dialogue which has two legs of nuclear missiles, on the one hand, conventional forces on the other because they all are linked and hyping up the situation. More emphasis are to be put on cultural and trade relations.[157]

The Kashmir issue has become so complicated that it seems the maintenance of *status quo* is the only best proposition. The (LOC) should be accepted by both the countries as a permanent border. The failure of diplomacy to address let alone the Kashmir dispute is remarkable, given the amount of attention paid to it. The most constant feature of great power influence on Kashmir problem has been its ineffectiveness. Beyond their cold war patronage, both the US and the Soviet Union have played significant, often parallel and cooperative roles in the sub-continent. Over the years, the US had considerable influence with both India and Pakistan, at one point the Soviet Union, generally regarded pro-Indian moved closer to Pakistan also. Yet neither superpower seemed to be able to make a difference. This suggests that any outside power should step in carefully if it seeks to end or even moderate this conflict. Kashmir was important only so far as it concerned their respective regional partners, yet both resisted being dragged into Kashmir issue by those same partners while India and Pakistan often based their regional calculations on the assistance of outside support, their position on Kashmir, their support has been limited and constrained. For years the Soviets provided with an automatic veto in the UN in Kashmir-related Resolutions and otherwise backed New Delhi diplomatically. The Pakistan became more dependent on the US for political and military support, but never got the US to commit itself to firm security assurance against India, precisely because Washington was afraid of being sucked in to Kashmir conflict. Both Washington and Moscow made several inconclusive efforts to mediate the dispute or bring about its peaceful resolution, but were wary of anything more.[158]

Divergent interpretations of Simla Agreement added

another layer of Indo-Pakistani distrust. While there is a formal text, but there are chances that there may have been verbal agreements between Indira Gandhi and Zulfikar Ali Bhutto that have never been made public. According to most Indian accounts, Bhutto told Mrs. Gandhi that he was willing to settle the Kashmir dispute along the (LOC), but a final agreement had to be delayed because he was weak politically. Pakistani accounts claim that Bhutto did no such thing and that in any case the written agreement is what matters. For India, Simla had supplemented the UN Resolutions as a point of reference for solving the Kashmir dispute. Both the parties had pledged to work directly with one another, implicitly abandoning extra-regional diplomacy. For Pakistan, Simla supplemented but did not replace the UN Resolutions.[159]

After the Simla Agreement, the Kashmir dispute seemed too subsidized. The Indian Government began to view the (LOC) as a more or less permanent border, but both sides continued to nibble away of it when an opportunity arose most spectacularly in the case of India's move to occupy much of the Siachin Glacier. For Pakistani diplomats, the Simla Agreement neither replaced UN Resolutions nor did the conversions of the ceasefire line into (LOC) produce a permanent international border. Guided by these varied interpretations, both sides continued to press their respective claims whenever the opportunity arose, but for nearly three decades, Kashmir was widely regarded outside the region as either solved or on way to resolutions, other regional issues displaced Kashmir that 1974, Indian nuclear test, Pakistan's covert nuclear weapons programme and the Soviet invasion of Afghanistan in December 1979. Between 1972 and 1994 India and Pakistan held forty-five bilateral meetings, in all of them Kashmir issue had been discussed.[160]

Over the years, many solutions have been proposed for the Kashmir problem. These included partition along the (LOC), "soft borders" between the two parts of Kashmir (pending a solution to the entire problem) a region by region plebiscite of Kashmiri's referendum UN Trusteeship, the "Trieste" and "Andosra" models whereby the same territory is shared by two states, or a nominally sovereign territory in fact is controlled by two states "revolutionary warfare, depopulation of Muslim Kashmiris and repopulation of Hindus from India, patience, good governance, a revival of human values and doing nothing. The dispute is awaiting solution because of a number of factors. Any comprehensive solution to the Kashmir problem would involve many concessions and changes in Indo-Pak relations (and within each state). It would require a change in Indian federal system. It might require changes within Kashmir between its constituent parts, it would necessitate a re-examination of the military balance between India and Pakistan and provisions that would prevent the two countries from again picking up arms concessions on the part of Pakistan and India might have to accept and accommodate some of the Pakistan's demands. There also would have to be incentives for Pakistani to cooperate with such ameliorative measures, since its basic strategy is to draw outsiders into the region and to pressurise India. In brief, India has to demonstrate to Pakistan that it would be willing to make significant concessions, but also pledge that if Pakistan ceased its support for Kashmiri separatists, Delhi would not change its mind once the situation in the valley had become normal.[161]

Doing nothing is likely to be the default options for Kashmir. At best there might be an arrangement that would ensure that the State does not trigger a war between the two countries. However, this does not do little to address grievances or the widespread human rights violations in the state, nor does it address the deeper conflict between India and Pakistan.

Both India and Pakistan regularly pass through a point where both sides momentarily agree that the time may be right for talks. Just as regularly, one or the other side decides that the risk of moving forward is so great. Often they believe that time will not be on their side and will weaken the case of the other side or strengthen its own. To some degree, both sides also believe that the other side will not compromise.

A regional peace process seems improbable given the difficulty of getting political acceptance in both countries at the same time on a problem so closely identified with their respective national identities. From India's perspective any such process cannot go very far without running of India's hostility towards the "Two Nations Theory"—a theory that as India claim is an incitement to revolt for India's large Muslim population and encourages other separatist groups, such as the Sikhs, Nagas and Mizos. If we take the Indian argument at face value, there can be no real peace process between India and Pakistan as long as either retaining its identity. Any peace process is bound to fail if it does not recognize these core differences, yet no peace process that does not address.

Such a peace process would eventually require a change in India's policies towards Kashmir itself. Indians are deeply divided on this question. Some favour absolutely no change in the Delhi-Srinagar relationship, other urge a degree of autonomy and a few are willing to see the State partitioned, perhaps along the (LOC). One reason for Indian disarray is the uncertainty over to the actual loyalty of Kashmiri Muslims if a measure of autonomy were granted to the State or at least to its more discontented elements would that not lead to the slippery slope of a renewed movement for a separate State. Given the profound attention of many Kashmiris and the growth of extremist Madrassas as in the State, some fear that Kashmir is irretrievably lost to a secular India and a few Hindu extremists have advocated the repopulation of the State by Hindu settlers. While Pakistan began as a landlord for Indian Muslims and justified this identity because Hindus and Muslims were "two nations", the debate over Pakistani identity has moved well beyond this. After the Punjabi dominated military assumed power, Pakistanis come to see themselves as "Fortess" Pakistan, a state (that happened to be a Muslim) threatened by India. This was a Punjabi centric view of Pakistan. Subsequently after the loss of East Bengal, Pakistan turned towards Islam as a way of asserting .a national identity. Punjabi finds it essential to agree on at least one point and that is unremitting hostility of India.

Besides some long-term efforts to change perceptions, build trust and clarify areas of disagreement and agreement, the prospect of a major transformation of the India-Pakistan relationship cannot be ruled out. There are several scenarios, some of these seem far-fetched at the moment but all are worth at least a brief mention:

- Pakistan could collapse under the weight of its own contradictions and cease to exist in its present form perhaps splitting into several states. This seems to be the formula of many Indian strategists who expect the Kashmir problem will be solved in the same way that East and West Berlin were merged the smaller simply ceasing to exist. Such a Pakistan might continue as a united state (few Indian would welcome the addition of a hundred million Muslims to the Indian union) but it certainly would not be able to stand up militarily and politically to Delhi.
- India could cause Pakistan to change its identity or cease to exist in its present form. One precedent is the creation of Bangladesh, an Islamic State which is unwilling to challenge the India in significant way. However, India could alter Pakistan's national identify by other means. New Delhi could support dissident ethnic and linguistic groups in Pakistan, especially, those who were less "Islamic" or less anti-Indian than the Punjabi.
- Some RSS and Hindu fundamentalists believed that India's "Civilization Pull" will triumph over the idea of Pakistan and Pakistan will simply succumb to India's great cultural and social power. They don't expect Pakistan to necessarily merge with India, although many Indians who hail from towns and villages that are now in Pakistan would like to second parts of Sind and West Punjab reincorporated into Indus. This school is prepared to wait Pakistan out and think in terms of generations and decades, rather than months or years.
- India might underestimate Pakistani nationalism and power and take some action which would lead Islamabad to actually use its nuclear weapons as a last attempt to defend Pakistan and if that

fails to bring India down with Pakistan by attacking Indian cities.

- A no less dramatic transformation in the relationship could come about if Pakistan itself changed its priorities, putting development ahead of Kashmir at least for a while. This would confront India with a peculiar situation, a former enemy seeking peace. The questions whether India would or could not, respond in a positive fashion and be willing to negotiate a long-term settlement of the Kashmir dispute after Kargil seems less likely.
- India could accept Pakistan's identity as an Islamic State. It would declare that it disagreed with this identity that it rejects such a theory of religion-based statehood for itself it could point to the accomplishments of a secular democracy and the general willingness of Muslim and other religious and ethnic minorities to live in such a state but it could acknowledge that on this irreconcilable point Pakistan choose and have the right to continue to choose to live a different life. It could then move to cooperate on a whole range of shared economic, cultural, strategic and political interests.

Name of these extreme outcomes seems likely, but together they add up to a possibility that the Indo-Pakistani relationship could take a dramatic and even dangerous turn.

The most likely outcome to this dispute is one of continuing stalemate. The future is likely to be one of hesitant movements towards dialogue, punctuated by attempts on both sides to unilaterally press their advantage in Kashmir and in international fora. This is a conflict that India cannot win and cannot lose a true hurting stalemate without some fundamental social or political changes in India and Pakistan, the stalemate is likely to continue indefinitely.

Reinforcing this proposal is the fact that stalemate is more attractive to each side that some solutions that have been put forward. From the perspective of Pakistan military which has an absolute veto over any policy initiative regarding Kashmir, the ability to tie Indian forces down in Kashmir is an important consequence of the dispute. Cynically, it could be said that Pakistan is willing to fight India to the last. As long as Pakistan sees itself as militarily disadvantaged, it will try to equalize the military balance by any means possible. This includes the nuclear programme, but also a strategy at forcing India to divert important resources to a military front (Kashmir) where the time and political situation are in Pakistan's favour. For India, Kashmir has so many links to India's secular order especially the place of Muslims one settlement which appeared to compromise this orders unacceptable. Clearly, Kashmir is linked to broader issues of the military balance between India and Pakistan and the very identity of the two states and while more could be done to ease the suffering and paramilitary forces on the Indian side and some, reduction in support for extremists coming from the Pakistani side no settlement is possible without dealing with these larger strategic and ideological concerns.

Both sides will continue to acquire and probably deploy nuclear weapons. India is likely to remain resistant to outside mediation or facilitation of the Kashmir dispute. As for the domestic political turmoil in both countries will make it even more forge a relationship that is not grounded on distrust, hostility and now the threat of nuclear holocaust. There may be limited agreement between, New Delhi and its western neighbour, but the most problematic issue is not whether Indians and Pakistanis can be treated to fulfil obligations incurred in agreements where they had little incentive to comply, but whether, under the influence of pessimistic vision of the regional destiny, they cannot be trusted in cases where it is in their self-interest to comply. At best the Pakistani Generals may conclude that some normalization with Pakistan is necessary for India to play a wider role in the world. This is the basis for a truce between the two countries but not the basis for a peace. For that to occur, there will have to be more profound changes in their deeper relationship, otherwise there will remain two states allergic to each other without the development of strong economic cultural and political ties.

Notes and References

1. For the Complete text of the telegrams exchanged between Prime Minister of India and Pakistan, see, A. Appadorai, Select *Documents on Indian Foreign Policy, 1947-72,* Vol. I, (New Delhi, 1982), pp. 216-26.
2. S.P.V./523, p. 3.
3. S/20/7/Rev, 30 30 March 1951.
4. Joseph Korbel, *Danger in Kashmir* (Princeton, 1954), pp. 178-79.
5. S/2119, 4 May 1951 and S/2.45, 10 May 1951.
6. *Times of India,* 6 July 1951.
7. Diwan Chaman Lal, "The Kashmir Story", in Varinder Grover (ed.), *The Story of Kashmir: Yesterday and Today,* Vol II, (New Delhi, 1995), pp. 376-93.
8. For the text of letters and telegrams see, *White Paper on Indo-Pakistan Relations,* 15 July 9 August 1951, (New Delhi, Ministry of External Affairs, Government of India).
9. Letter dated New Delhi, 7 September 1951 from the UN Representative, Addressed to the Prime Minister of India and Pakistan Regarding proposals for an agreement.
10. S/2375, October 1950, para 67.
11. Joseph Korbel, n. 4, pp. 187-88.
12. *Ibid.,* pp. 188-89.
13. Surendera Chopra, *UN Mediation in Kashmir* (Kurukshetra, 1971), pp. 113-14.
14. *Ibid.,* pp. 114-15.
15. S.M. Burke, *Pakistan's Foreign Policy: A Historical Analysis* (London, 1973), p. 37.
16. *National Standard,* Bombay, 12 March 1952.
17. Joseph Korbel, n. 4, pp. 223-25.
18. Prem Nath Bazaz, Sheikh Abdullah, "Kashmir Democracy and Indo-Pak Relations", in Varinder Grover, (ed.) *The Story of Kashmir: Yesterday and Today,* Vol. 3 (New Delhi, 1995), pp. 272-73.
19. *Ibid.,* p. 274.
20. *Ibid.*
21. *Ibid.,* p. 276
22. *Ibid.,* pp. 277-78.
23. *Ibid.,* p. 279.
24. L.K. Kaul, "Sheikh Abdullah: Ambition and Polities", in *Ibid.,* p. 289.
25. *Ibid.,* p. 290.
26. *Ibid.*
27. *Ibid.*
28. *Ibid.,* pp. 290-91.
29. *Ibid.*
30. Joseph Korbel, n. 4, pp. 192-93.

31. Associated Press of Pakistan 20 August 1953 as cited in *Ibid.*, p. 193.
32. *Ibid.*, p. 194.
33. See, A. Appadorai, n. 1, pp. 249-64.
34. For Nehru Statements in the Lok Sabha see, *Ibid.* pp. 264-70.
35. Surendra Chopra, n. 13, pp. 131-32.
36. Nehru Statement the Lok Sabha, A Appadorai, n. 1, pp. 270-74.
37. *Hindustan Standard*, 17 January 1957.
38. For the text of the Feroz Khan Noon Speech. See S/PV, 761, pp. 2-21.
39. For detail see, S/PV, 762. 23 January 1957, pp. 1-39. S/PV/763, 23 January 1965, pp. 1-52 and S/PV. 764, 24 January 1967, pp. 1-96.
40. S/PV. 765, 24 January 1957, pp. 2-25.
41. For the text of the Resolution See, S/3739, 24 January 1957 (S//RES/122 (1957), 24, January 1957.
42. S/P.V. 765, n. 149, pp. 2-26.
43. S/P.V. 761 to 779, 16 January 1957 to 21 February 1957.
44. See S/3779, 24 January 1957 and S/3787, 14 February 1957.
45. S/3787, 14 February 1957.
46. S/PV. 773, 20 February 1957, pp. 28-29.
47. *Ibid.*
48. Surendra Chopra, n. 13, pp. 172-73.
49. S/3793, 21 February 1957.
50. S/3984, 28 March 1958.
51. SCORS April, May-June 1957, pp. 13-16.
52. SCORS, January, February and March 1958, pp. 38-46.;
53. Surendra Chopra, n. 13, pp. 172-73.
54. J.B. Dass Gupta, *Jammu and Kashmir*, (The Hague, 1968), p. 249.
55. Sisir Gupta, *Kashmir: A Study in Indo-Pak Relations* (Bombay, 1966). p. 385.
56. *New York Times*, 14 July 1961.
57. *The Hindu*, 30 January 1962.
58. For the full text of the Zafarullah Khan's letter, S/5068, 26 January 1962.
59. S/PV 1007, 27 April 1962, SP/V 1008, 2 May 1962, SP/V/1009, 3 May 1962, SP/V 101.0, 4 May 1962 SP/V 1012, 15 June 1962, SP/V 1016, 22 June 1962.
60. That was because of the decision of the US to supply arms to India.
61. For details see, S/5134, 22 June 1962.
62. S.P/V 1016, 22 June 1962, p. 19.
63. *The Dawn*, 3 March 1962.
64. See *Sino-Pakistan Agreement: Some Facts* (Government of India, n.d.), p. 22.
65. Anwar Syed, "Sino-Pakistan Agreement: An Overview", *Pakistan Horizon*, Vol. XXII, No. 3, 1969, p. 111.
66. Surendra Chopra, "Sino-Pakistan Border Agreement", *Journal of African and Asian Studies*, Vol. 1, No. 2, 1962, p. 237.

67. *The Dawn,* 27 May 1963.
68. *Washington Post,* 10 December 1962.
69. Christian Science Monitor, 17 May 1963.
70. *New York Times,* 7 May 1963.
71. *Times of India,* 14 August 1963.
72. For the text of the India and Pakistan letters see S/5522, 24 January 1964 and 8/5511, 16 January 1964 and for the views of Indian and Pakistani representatives and other members of Security Council see, S/PV 1104 to 1105, 17 and 20 March 1964; 8/PV 1112 to 1117, 5 May to 18 May 1964.
73. Surendra Chopra, n.13 , p. 215.
74. For the text of the letter of Indian representative see, S/6389, 28 May 1965.
75. *The Statesman,* 18 March 1965.
76. For the text of the Pakistani letter see, 8/6367, 18 May 1995.
77. For the text see, 8/6481, 28 June 1965.
78. Surendra Chopra, n. 13, pp. 214-15.
79. Verinder Narain, "Kashmir and Major Powers- A Study of Myths in Retrospect", *Political Science Review,* Vol. VIII, No. 394, July-December 1968, p. 422
80. Sisir Gupta, n. 55., pp. 138.
81. S.M. Burke, n. 15, pp. 358-60.
82. News.BBC.w.uk/1/hi world/South Asia/273993 http.
83. Stephen Philip Cohen, *The Idea of Pakistan,* (New Delhi; 2005), p. 52.
84. *Ibid.*
85. *Ibid.,* pp. 52-53.
86. *Ibid.,* p. 54.
87. *Ibid.,* pp. 53-54.
88. *Ibid.,* p. 55.
89. Robert Laporte Jr., *Power and Privilege: Influence and Decision-making in Pakistan,* (Bombay, 1976), pp. 142-43.
90. *Ibid.,* p. 143.
91. William J. Barnds, *India, Pakistan and the Great Powers,* (London, 1972), p. 261.
92. *Ibid.*
93. *Robert Laporte, Jr.,* n. 89, pp. 147-48.
94. *Ibid.,* p. 166.
95. *Ibid.,* p. 167.
96. www.pakistan.gov.pp/foreignaffairs_ministry/kashmirissue/kash_issue.j&k.
97. *Ibid.*
98. *Ibid.*
99. *Ibid.*
100. *Ibid.*
101. *Ibid.*

102. *Ibid.*
103. *Ibid.*
104. *Ibid.*
105. *Financial Times*, 16 January 2004.
106. *Ibid.*
107. *Ibid.*
108. *Ibid.*
109. www.brookin.ed/views/op-ed/fellows—200306/3
110. www.brooking.ed/views/details/fellows/khan 20020801
111. Joseph E. Schwartz Berg, "An Agenda for peace in Kashmir and South Asia", see, www.kashmirstudygroup/con/statement/103_ agenda. html.
112. The exact status of Indian and Pakistani nuclear capabilities remains uncertain. See, George Perkovick, "A Nuclear Third Way in South Asia", *Foreign Policy*, Summer 1999, pp. 85-104 and Devin Haderly "The Powers of Suggestion: Opaque Proliferation, Existential Deterrence and the South Asian Arms Competition", *Security Studies*, 20/3/4, Spring/summer 1993, pp. 256-83.
113. Stephen P. Cohen, "Kashmir: The Road Ahead", www.brookings.ed/ views/articles/cohens/Kashmir.
114. *Ibid.*
115. *Ibid.*
116. Joseph E. Schwartzberg, n. 111.
117. *Ibid.*
118. *Ibid.*
119. Stephen P. Cohen n. 113.
120. *Ibid.*
121. A Conversation between Hussain Haqqani and Ashley J. Tellis on "India and Pakistan: Is Peace Real This Time?" See, www.ceip.org/ files/pd61/indopakistan
122. *Ibid.*
123. *Ibid.*
124. *Ibid.*
125. *Ibid.*
126. *Ibid.*
127. *Ibid.*
128. *Ibid.*, New Priorities in South Asia: US policy towards India, Pakistan and Afghanistan, See www.crf.org pdf/indiasouthasia.
129. Howard Schalfer, "US Government Approaches to Kashmir Problem", www.kashmirstudygroup.com/statements
130. *Ibid.*
131. *Ibid.*
132. *Ibid.*
133. *Ibid.*
134. *Ibid.*

135. *Ibid.*
136. *Ibid.*
137. *Ibid.*
138. *Ibid.*
139. *Ibid.*
140. *Ibid.*
141. *Ibid.*
142. *Ibid.*
143. *Ibid.*
144. *Ibid.*
145. *Ibid.*
146. *Ibid.*
147. www.brookings.edu/views/testimony/cohens/20040128.pdf
148. *Ibid.*
149. *Ibid.*
150. *Ibid.*
151. Stephen P. Cohen, India, Pakistan and Kashmir, www.brookings.eduj viewjspeechesjcohen2001120/pdf.
152. *Ibid.*
153. *Ibid.*
154. *Ibid.*
155. *Ibid.*
156. *Ibid.*
157. *Ibid.*
158. *Ibid.*
159. *Ibid.*
160. *Ibid.*
161. *Ibid.*

5

Pakistan: Some Realities

The British India was divided on the basis of religion; the areas whose inhabitants were mostly Muslims were combined to form Pakistan. The North West Frontier Province (NWFP), Sind and Baluchistan, became part of Pakistan, Punjab was divided into two East and West Punjab being part of India and Bengal was also split—this division provided "the key to Pakistani politics." The reasons and circumstances for the partition were many and varied and a proper explanation of them would require a lengthy analysis. But the geographical peculiarities of Pakistan until 1971 were crucial to an understanding of Pakistani politics.

The political party which first put forward the demand for Pakistan was the Muslim League. It was difficult to assess whether the demand was initially meant as anything more than a mean of putting pressure on the Indian National Congress and British on behalf of the "landed Muslim interests and at later stage on behalf of the rising Muslim bourgeoisie." Plainly speaking, one of the reasons for the creation of the League was the pressure of the British imperialism. A large number of those present at the founding conferences belonged to landowning families from different parts of India and their influence as the poodles of British imperialism was exerted towards making the Muslim League to adopt as its main objective. This is to foster a sense of loyalty to the British government amongst the Muslims of India. It could not have been spelt out more clearly than that. Sprinklings of Muslim lawyers were also present; they concerned themselves with the interests of the Muslim landlords and British civil servants and in the first decade of its existence, it was to remain a loyal upholder of British interests. Any fears that middle class elements in the League might gain preponderance were soon dispelled.[1]

It was quite obvious that the British policy of "divide and rule" had fallen on fertile ground and its pernicious efforts were to be felt in the following years. In discussion with the Muslim leaders, Lord Minto used to stress that the aim of Muslim political activities should be to combat the increasing economic power of the Hindus. The Agha Khan was only too pleased to agree and send directives to League branches asking Muslims "to apply all their energy to furthering British prestige and instilling respect and affections for the British in the public mind."

The feudal lords continued to retain their grip on the Muslim League, but they realized that they would never be able to make the League a powerful political force, at least not on their own. So they began to welcome members of Muslim bourgeoisie, the limping bourgeoisie of India. Unlike the other Muslim League leaders, Jinnah had no belonging to the Ismaili community, he received his legal training at the Lincoln's Inn at London and the first political party that he joined was the Indian National Congress. He was well-versed in English. He was a reputed lawyer and championed the cause of the business community with whom he was associated in Bombay. When he joined the Muslim League just before the First World War, his reasons have nothing to do with religion, Jinnah was completely secular in outlook.[2]

TWO NATIONS THEORY AND CONSTITUTIONAL BEGINNING

It is the first reality on which the creation of Pakistan is based. Events in the late 1920s and 1930s led the Muslims to think that their destiny might be in a separate state, a concept that developed for partition. Moti Lal Nehru convened an all party conference in 1929 to suggest changes that would lead to independence when the British took up the report of the Simon Commission. The majority of the delegates demanded the end of the system of separate electorates. Jinnah in turn, put forward fifteen points that would satisfy Muslim interests—in particular, the retention of separate electorates or the creation of "safeguards" to prevent a Hindu controlled legislature. Jinnah proposals were rejected and from onwards cooperation between Hindus and Muslims in the independence movement was rare.

In his Presidential address to the Muslim League session at Allahabad, Sir Mohammad Iqbal (1936-38), described Asia in miniature, in which a unitary form of Government was in conceivable, religious community rather than territory was the basis for identification. Therefore, he demanded the establishment of a confederated India to include a Muslim state consisting of Punjab, NEFP, Sindh and Baluchistan. In subsequent speeches and writings, Iqbal reiterated the claims of Muslims to be considered a nation based on unity of language race, history, religious and identity of economic interests.

Iqbal gave no name to the projected state. That was done by a group of students at Cambridge in Britain who issued a pamphlet in 1933 entitled "Now or never." They opposed the idea of federation, denied that India was a single country and demanded partition into regions, the North-West receiving national status as a "Pakistan." They explained the term as follows, "Pakistan is composed of letters taken from the names of our homelands that is Punjab, Afghania (North West Frontier Province) Jammu & Kashmir, Iran, Sindh, Afghanistan and Baluchistan. It means the land of the Pakistan, the spiritually pure."

In 1934 Jinnah returned to the leadership of Muslim League after spending sometime in London, but found it divided and without a sense of mission. He set about restoring a sense of purpose of Muslims and he emphasized for the implementation of the "Two Nations Theory". Under the 1935 Government of India Act, elections to the provincial legislative assemblies were held in 1937. Congress gained majority and took a strictly legalistic stand on the formation of provincial ministries and refused to form coalition governments with the Muslim League, even in the United Provinces (Uttar Pradesh in contemporary India) which had a substantial Muslim minority and vigorously denied the Muslim League claim, however, was not substantiated. Because the Muslim League had not done well in the elections, especially in the Muslim majority provinces. The conduct of Congress governments in the Muslim minority provinces permanently alienated the Muslim League with the Congress

By the late 1930s, Jinnah was convinced of the need for a unifying issue among Muslims and Pakistan was the obvious answer. At the annual session in Lahore on 23 March 1940, the Muslim League resolved that the areas of Muslim majority in north-western and eastern India should be grouped together to constitute independent states—autonomous and sovereign—and that any independence plan without this provision was unacceptable to Muslims. Federation was rejected. The Lahore Resolution was often referred to as the "Pakistan Resolution", however, the word Pakistan did not appear in it.

An interesting aspect of Pakistan movement was that it received its greatest support from areas in which Muslims were in minority. In those areas, the main issue was funding an alternative to replacing British rule with Congress, that is, Hindu rule.[3]

When Pakistan emerged as independent nation, Jinnah was the supreme authority. An accomplished politician, he won independence for Pakistan within seven years of the Lahore Resolution and was hailed by his followers as Quaid-i-Azam (Great leader). As Governor General, he assumed the ceremonial functions of head of state while taking an effective power as head of government, dominating his Prime Minister, Liaquat Ali Khan (Quaid-i-Millet) and the office of the President of the Constituent Assembly. Although Jinnah had led the movement for Pakistan as a separate state only for Muslims, he was appalled by the communal riots and urged equal rights for all citizens irrespective of religion. Jinnah died in September 1948—only thirteen months after independence—leaving his successors to tackle the problems of Pakistan identity.

Jinnah acknowledged lieutenant, Liaquat Ali Khan, assumed leadership and continued in the position of Prime Minister. Born to a Punjabi landed family, Liaquat used his experience to draft a constitution along the lines of the British Westminster System of parliamentary democracy. He failed in large part because neither the Muslim League nor the Constituent Assembly was equipped to resolve in a parliamentary manner the problems and conflicts of the role of Islam and degree of autonomy for the provinces. Liaquat term of office ended when he was assassinated in October 1951.

The Muslim League unlike Congress had not prepared itself for a post-independence role. Congress had constitutional economic, social and even foreign policy plans in place before independence and was ready to put them into effect when the time comes. The Muslim League was so pre-occupied with the struggle for Pakistani that it was poorly prepared for effective government. Its leadings were largely urban whose political base was mainly in areas that were in India. In the areas that had become Pakistan, its base was weak. Landlords with inherited privilege were uncomfortable with procedures of decision-making through debate, discussion, compromise and majority vote. The Muslim League was a party with little grass-root support, a weak organizational structure, powerful factional leaders and decisions made at the top. Although, Ghulam Mohammed tried to exercise the "Viceregal" power that Jinnah had used powerfully as Governor General, concern for office and the fruits of power were more important to most of the politicians that the evolution of ideology or the implementation of mass programs. The effect of this lack of direction was shown more clearly when the Muslim League was routed in 1954 elections in East Pakistan by the United Front—mainly a coalition of the Awami League.

The Muslim League was held responsible for the deterioration of politics and society after independence and had to answer for the failure to fulfil people's high expectations. There was a rising level of opposition and frustration and an increasing use of repressive laws inherited from the British or enacted by Pakistan that included preventive detention and rules prohibiting the gathering of more than five persons. The armed forces also posed a threat to Liaquat government which was less hostile towards India than some officers wished. In March 1951, Major General Mohammad Akbar Khan, Chief of General Staff, was arrested along with fourteen other officers on charges of plotting a coup.

Pakistan's first Constituent Assembly (CA) was made up of members of the pre-partition Indian Constituent Assembly who represented areas that had gone to Pakistan. As a constitution-making body, the Assembly's only achievement was the Objective Resolution of March 1949 which specified that Pakistan would be Islamic, democratic and federal. But the Assembly could not reach agreement on how these objectives would take form raising fears among minorities and concern among East Bengalis other important matters remained equally problematic—the division of executive power between the Governor General and the Prime Minister, the distribution of powers between centre and provinces, the balance of power, especially electoral, between two wings and the role of Islam in the government.

During the years after Liaquat assassination, none of these problems were resolved and a major confrontation occurred between the Governor General, Ghulam Mohammed, and a Punjabi from the Civil service and the Prime Minister, Nizamuddin. Ghulam Mohammad, who relished the trappings of dominance earlier held by Jinnah, asserted his power by declaring Martial Law in 1953 in Punjab during disturbances involving the Ahmadiyas, a small but influential sect considered heterodox by orthodox Muslims and a year later by inspiring Governor's rule after the Muslim League defeat in East Bengal, not permitting the United Front to take office when Nizamuddin attempted to limit the powers of the Governor General through amendments to the Government of India Act, 1935—then the basic law for Pakistan—as altered by the Indian Independence Act, 1947—Ghulam Mohammed unceremoniously dismissed him in April 1953 and the following year appointed his own "cabinet of talents" dismissing the Constituent Assembly.

The so-called cabinet of talents was headed by Mohammad Ali Bogra, a minor political figure from East Pakistan who had previously been Pakistan's Ambassador to the US. General Mohhamed Ayub Khan became Minister of Defence while retaining his post-as Commander-in-Chief of the Army. Major General Iskander Mirza, was appointed Governor of East Pakistan. Ghulam Mohammed imposed Governor's rule in East Pakistan and became Minister of Home Affairs. Ghulam Mohammed was successful subordinating the Prime Minister because of the support of military and civil officers as well as the strong landed interests in Punjab. The façade of parliamentary government crumbled exposing the military's role in Pakistan's political system to public view. The cabinet thus provided an opportunity for the military to take a direct role in the political system of Pakistan.

The revived Constituent Assembly convened in 1955 was different in composition from the first assembly because of the noteable reduction of Muslim League members and the presence of the United Front coalition from East Bengal. Provincial autonomy was the main plank of the United Front.

In 1956, the Constituent Assembly adopted a Constitution that proclaimed Pakistan an Islamic Republic and contained directives for the establishment of Islamic state. The lawyer turned politician who led the Pakistan movement used the principles and legal precedents of a non- religious British parliamentary tradition even while they advanced the idea of Muslim nationhood as an axiom. Many of them represented a liberal movement in Islam, in which their personal religion was compatible with western technology and political institutions. They saw the basis for democratic processes and tolerance in the Islamic tradition of *Ijma* (consensus of the community) and Ijithad (the concept of continuing interpretations of Islamic law). Most of the Pakistan's intelligentsia and westernized elites belonged to the group of Ijama modernists.

In contrast stood the traditional *Ulema* whose position was legalistic one based on the unity of religion and politisation of Islam Islam. The *Ulema* asserted that the *Quran*, the *Sunna* and the Shariat provided the general principles for all aspects of life if correctly interpreted and applied. The government's duty, therefore, was to recognize the role of the *Ulema* in the interpretation of law. Because the *ulema* and the less learned mullahs (Muslim clergies) enjoyed influence among the masses, especially in the urban areas, because no politician could afford to be denounced as anti-Islamic, nor dared publicly to ignore them. Nevertheless they were not given powers of legal interpretation until the regime of Mohammed Zia-ul-Haq which lasted from 1977-88.

Another interpretation of Islam was provided by an Islamist movement in Pakistan which was regarded in some quarters as fundamentalists. Its most significant organization was the Jammait-i-Islami, which gradually build up support among the refugees, the urban lower middle class and students. Unlike the traditionalist *Ulema*, the Islamic movement was the outcome of modern Islamic idealism crucial in the constitutional and political development of Pakistan; it forced politicians to face the question of Islamic identity.

Shariat courts were established under Zia and under Prime Minister Mian Nawaz Sharif in the 1990s; the *Shariat* was proclaimed the basic law of the land.[4]

Despite the shared religion of over-whelming Muslim population, Pakistan has been engaged in a precarious struggle to define a national identity and evolve a political system for its linguistically diverse population. Pakistan is known to have over twenty languages and over 300 distinct dialects. Urdu and English are the official languages but Punjabi, Sindhi, Pashtu, Baluchi and Seaili are considered main languages. This diversity has caused chronic regional tensions and successive failures in forming a constitution. Pakistan had also been burdened by full scale wars with India, a strategically exposed NWFP and series of economic crisis. It has difficulty in allocating its scarce economic and natural resources in an equitable manner. All of Pakistan's struggles underpin the dilemma they face in reconciling the goal of national integration with the imperatives of national security.[5]

The post-1971 situation which created a new political country Bangladesh, out of Pakistan's territory, epitomizes the most dramatic manifestations of Pakistan's dilemma as a decentralized nation, political developments in Pakistan continue to be marred by provincial jealousies and in particular by the deep resentments in the smaller provinces of Sindh, Baluchistan and the NWFP against what is seen to be a monopoly by the Punjabi majority of the benefits of power, profit and patronage. Pakistan's political instability overtime has been matched by a fierce ideological debate about the form of government should adopt, Islamic or secular. In the absence of any nationally based political party, Pakistan has had to rely on the civil service and the army to maintain the constituents of government.[6]

Mohammed Ali Jinnah had always envisioned democratic Pakistan and many of his successors have struggled towards these goals but not more than maintaining their own platforms of power. It is ironic that such political instability plagued a country whose number one objective of its leaders was to secure their own power. May be it is a time for a new equation. The actions of both civil and military leaders have exhaustively tied the Pakistani people and their struggle as a nation. Pakistan faces the unenviable task of setting government priorities in accordance with the needs of its diverse and unevenly developed constitutional units. Regardless of the form of government—civilian or military, Islamic or secular—solutions of the problem of mass illiteracy and economic inequalities on the one hand and the imperatives of national integration and national security will also determine the degree of political stability or instability that Pakistan faces in the decades ahead.[7]

Shortly after the 1999 coup, then "Chief Executive" General Parvez Musharaff was advised to transfer power to civilian as quickly as possible. But his response was firm 'no' on the plea that "the system had to be cleansed, once and for all and thoroughly recognized to ensure that the military civilian balance was maintained and the civilians would never again lead Pakistan to disaster. "He had a few ideas to how this might be done, beginning with a commitment to the appearance of democracy, as long as checks and balances prevented a dominant political force from emergency other useful measures would be to discipline the politicians, give the military a permanent and constitutional role, rely upon technocrats and build a new system of government that would effectively link Islamabad to "the people of Pakistan." Not only the military regime disciplined the politicians and declared an attack on corruption, it launched a transformation of Pakistan's government's structure and its law and order mechanism, ensuring that the military would have a seat in any future government. Musharaff came to power intent on bringing about a fundamental change in Pakistan's political order but with no clear ideas about what had to be done.[8]

The then US Secretary of State Rice Condoleeza has toughened up American policy regarding Pakistan's democratization but it would be difficult to persuade the Musharaff government to democratize. She has publicly stated that the US expects the elections of 2007 to be a turning point. The military afraid that a return to complete civilian government means loosing grip over the civil administration. Nevertheless, the US should insist that the Pakistani government allow maintaining political parties (the Pakistan's People's Party and the Pakistani Muslim League) to function freely. There should be a spectrum of moderate parties, Islamic and secular, who are willing to operate within a parliamentary context and who are tolerant of sectarian and other minorities.

Those who argue against democratization are placing their bets on the army and Islamist parties. The former cannot effectively govern Pakistan and the latter may see democracy as a short-cut to absolute power, but their capacity to govern is questionable and their antagonism to the west is palpable. The army needs the radical Islamist as the "threat to hold up to its western supporters, the Islamists are building their own infrastructure in the form of chains of madrassas throughout the country. Unless Pakistan democratizes, what is likely to emerge is a coalition of the army and Islamist forces and the potential radicalization of Pakistan."[9]

The thrust of Pakistan's Army's military strategy build up during the 1990s onwards keep the fire burning in

Kashmir thus turning the territory into a liability for India. Hence military and religious extremism found sponsors in the Pakistani political parties that were willing to train people to wage a religious war on different fronts. New training outfits were opened in different parts of Pakistan and old and newly established militant groups were encouraged to take part in Jehad. The 1980s was a period when religious sectarianism was also on rise in the country with the Sunnis (orthodox Muslims) fighting against the Shias bringing a new increase of violence in the country. The military machine however approached both groups to participate in a greater objective of fighting Jihad against India. The unofficial declaration of war against India to liberate Kashmiri Muslim, brethren provided a common ground to a majority of religious parties and militant groups that otherwise had diverse agenda.

This does not mean that bisect Arian hostilities diminished. Infact, they intensified as these groups got weapons and trained manpower and were given free leverage by the government of Pakistan. It must be noted that the radical parties/groups in Pakistan are essentially driven by sectarian agendas rather than shared religious philosophy, the war in Kashmir, however, provided them with a common objective of ousting Indian forces and having control over a territory that could be used to implement their vision of Islam.

Also the understanding was that once this goal was accomplished they could then attempt to convert Pakistan into a theocratic state. Their alignment with the military for this purpose was also the basis for developing a symbolic relationship with state that was usually interpreted to turn a blind eye to the militants expanding their war to other fronts such as Chechnya or Bosnia or battle against each other. A noticeable factor is that these militant groups re-interpreted the meaning of Jehad tailoring it to their respective needs.

The definition of Jehad found in *Quran* the Muslim holy book, is for more limited in context and content than what was prescribed by these zealots. Jihad, according to *Quran,* is mainly a defensive war. The militants however, have interpreted it as a war fought against evil and intriguingly the definition of evil is extended to even include rival sectarian groups. Given the new interpretation, the militants were comfortable with the idea of fighting a war with no end in the foreseeable future.

The new militants produced in Pakistan were eager to move from one front to another for bringing justice to the Muslims of the world. During the 1990s, one observed a dramatic increase in the number of militant groups. According to an estimate, seventy-two militant groups were operating in Pakistan. The state machinery provided them all logistic support, training and equipments. Sources interviewed revealed that this large number denoted a particular strategy of the military intelligence, to keep the militants divided. In this manner, it was difficult for the later to pose a threat to the state. Interestingly, these groups were operating in isolation from the civil society that continued to be fairly moderate. The reason for their success in inducting warriors was mainly due to the peculiar economic and political conditions of Pakistan.[10]

The political instability prevailing in Pakistan was considered to be menace of militancy. The continuous manipulation of the political system by the armed forces to remain in power politics and conflict among the political leadership are two factors that generated political chaos. One of the painful realities of life in Pakistan is that since its creation, the state could not get rid of the predominant feudal system. Nor only the feudal class was a significant stakeholder in politics, it also helped proliferating feudal attitudes into the greater social failure of the society. For instance, the newly-developed industrial class shared the same attitudes as the landed class; discouraging dissent and eager to protect interests. The same can be said about the bureaucratic elite that have followed a tradition of protecting self-interests with no concern for commonman.

Wanting in liberal thinking, the elite of Pakistan has been extremely authoritarian in its behaviour. Hence, communication and dialogue to understand each other's perspective is not a forte of Pakistan's political and administrative system. These factors have led to confusion, chaos and political instability, thus allowing the military to grow into a key actor in power politics. Due to its corporate interest, the military acquired a similar attitude and used its power to gain political influence that, in turn was used to destabilize the political process.

A weak democratic system or government that did not question the military was an obvious corollary of the civil-military imbalance. Not only had that it established a pattern in politics of arbitrary removal of the governments. The political chaos in the early days hampered the creation of a sound political system and a constitution. The sore point is that the country had to wait for nine years for its first constitution adopted in 1956. Even that did not last long. It was abrogated by the military as General Ayub Khan imposed Martial Law in 1958.[11]

The political instability, incessant corruption of the political and bureaucratic elite and poor governance gave birth to public's skepticism of the prevalent system. This was reflected in the gradually decreasing turnout of voters in elections. This decrease however was caused by the inability of political parties to mobilize its voters and have strong political debate at the grass-roots. Although Musharaff presents himself as a harbinger of democracy and has promised to restore democracy, the continued aggressive involvement of the armed forces in politics as well as in administrative, the state is hardly a recipe for democracy.

The political instability, armed forces manipulators of the political system and feudal character of politics caused endless crisis. The growing ethnic and sectarian rivalry resulted in the fragmentation of the society, poor governance and diverse agendas of the political leadership caused the breakaway of Pakistan. The war with India was infact, just the culminating point.

Unfortunately, the policy-making elite failed to learn any lesson from the tragedy of East Pakistan. No efforts were made to minimize or eradicate the grievances of the smaller provinces against the bigger province Punjab. The main explanation of the anxiety of the smaller provinces is that the major source of resources is taken by Punjab.[12]

Interestingly, all the political parties were increasingly resorting to use Islamic ideology to prove their credibility. Unable to solve the core problem of poverty, under development and regional divide, it was considered politically expedient to revert to a theme that was considered non-controversial and a unifying force. The idea was to use whatever method available to muster political support of the masses. This behaviour, however, increased the blackmailing power of the religious parties and gradually created an impression of a phenomenal increase in ideology fundamentalism. Another trend which emerged after 1980's has been that political governments enjoyed lesser and lesser control over curbing extreme elements. As the official policies on Afghanistan, Kashmir and India were dealt with by the military—creation of militants being a corollary of these policies—the political governments were not permitted to debate in these areas.

The result was that while the governments were getting blackmailed by religious parties to formulate policies that projected a peculiar image of Pakistan, their supporters were unable to draw a mass support from the general public. This situation reflected by the political parties inability to attract voters in elections. Finally, the militant groups that grew under state patronge had opted for a change in the socio-economic system. They tried this by turning Pakistan into a theocratic state through the power of gun and not by electoral process to a great extent. Their pre-occupation with Jihad, did not allow them to disturb the political process to a great extent. Moreover, the majority of people continued to believe in bringing change through the electoral process rather than force. Hence militant groups continued to operate on the sidelines without having a major impact on the political process.[13]

The policies of military regimes to counter-political opponents had encouraged ethnicity and sectarianism thus adding to the chaos. For instance, General Zia-ul-Haq sponsored the creation of the Muhajir Qaumi Movement (MQM) to encounter the popular Pakistan's People's Party, in the southern province of Sindh. The MQM, an ethnic party accused of spreading violence in the province was the brainchild of military's prime intelligence agency: the Inter-Services Intelligence (ISI). It was in the same fashion that the ISI later created sectarian and militant groups in the country.

These developments not only denote the myopic approach of the military but also indicate military top brass failure to understand the negative impact of such policies on the political environment of the country. The growing political leverage have led to further fragmentation of the political system and society increasing frustration of the masses. The common man started to consider options that were not regarded as before in respect to political stability. The increased popularity and street power of the religious parties is clear evidence on this account. For example, Deobandi, the orthodox school of thought, has indeed, gained more popularity over the past ten to fifteen years.

The official support of extremism runs the risk of transforming the character of the society. In this case, it would tantamount to negative change. Even common people with an understanding of Pakistan's policy-making environment agreed that such a policy would have negative implications, particularly in a medium to long-term. However, there is also an understanding that this course of action would be pursued until the military changes its approach.

The problem, nonetheless, is that the military does not appear willing to change its mindset. Unfortunately, in the inner circles of the military, there appears to be little willingness to deviate from the traditional stance of using religion and militants in a tactical mode for short-term political and military gains. The extremists' area cornerstone of the Army's tactical plans of Kashmir and combating India. This does not seem to have changed drastically even after 11 September.[14]

Although Islamabad's official statements indicate an about-turn in its approach towards non-state actors/militants, there is hardly any evidence of a fundamental change. Of course, the pressure from the foreign governments can not be ignored, however, one feels that the Army High Command still believes that it could continue with its peculiar tactical approach. The Pakistani government is currently engaged in a three-pronged approach:

- Use the threat or fear of extremism to get support for the military regime from abroad;

- Save militants for future use; and
- Use external pressure as a ploy to get rid of groups problematic for the establishment.

The strengthening of democracy and democratic institutions are essential for any potential transformation. This would not only increase communication between different stake-holders in the state and the civil-military relations imbalance at this point, is strongly titled in the military's favour. Such a change would allow the political leadership and democratic institutions to monitor and control the activities of the armed forces. This may be a long-term approach, but this is the sure way to ensure that the state and society remains moderate and on track without further devastation.[15]

But interestingly one of the leading political parties, *Jamaat-e-Islami Pakistan,* committed itself to Islamic ideology and principles have challenged the working of democratic institutions in Pakistan. The central Shura of Jamaat which was busy in political deliberation at that time in Lahore when Musharaff took over made well considered observations concerning the army action and the problems the nation was facing. It is said that "after having destroyed or controlled all the important constitutional organs of the state, the Nawaz Sharif government embarked upon dangerous game of political interventions intending to create rift and division within army. This game had culminated in the sad but logical consequences and the army having dismissed the federal and provincal governments of Nawaz League. The ousted government it was felt, which because of the anti-*Shariat* and anti-constitutional activities, staking the country's integrity in the name of friendship with the US and India and its taking the country to the verge of bankruptcy as a result of mishandling the economic affairs and lost any constitutional, moral and political right of governance.... Protection of the institution of the army was necessary for the security of the country; but side by side, it is also essential that the country's ideology was upheld and according to the aspiration of the people Islamic constitutional system, full regard for basic rights and the rule of law was also ensured."[16]

The most important question in Pakistan is why the democratic system fails again and again and why a situation emerges after a given period that army steps in and winds up the political chess mat. When Pakistan came into being, Quaid-i-Azam and his companions could not get enough time which was required to reconstruct the new state on fresh foundations and according to the objectives in sight. Both Jinnah and Liaquat Ali Khan were soon snatched away by the cruel hands of death. No leader of calibre was available on the political scene of Pakistan to fill the political vacuum. In a matter of few years, the true representatives of the Muslim masses were deprived and state authority was taken in hand by the bureaucracy and the self-seeking elements. They were only suspending governments, abrogating constitutions, silencing the press, strangling political freedom in the name of Safely Act and fanning regional bigotry and prejudices. The party leadership got transferred to landed elites, capabilities and the civil and military bureaucracy. This is that "Qualize group" that got hold of Muslim League and its derivatives like Jinnah League, Awami League, Convention League, People's Party, Nawaz League. "This is the mimic group that every now and then changes the garb and controls the country politics."[17]

Political analysts estimate that there are a few thousand individuals from hardly a few hundred families who have been mastering not only the politics, but trade, industry, banking, administration, police and military during the more than half century political history of Pakistan. Democracy thus got hanged at the altar of family politics and governance based on self-interest. The political parties had never established any political organization based on people's strength, which could ensure participation and position for all eligible and work within a system of consultation and accountability that makes the essence of democracy. Constitution was drafted, but never respected.[18]

Along with these political realities, another cause of decay is the rebellious deviation from the objectives and vision, which made the moving force for the creation of Pakistan. More than a territory, Pakistan provides the sign of an ideology and a way of life. The struggle made by the

Muslims of the sub-continent was for the revival of their religion and to frame fresh their lives in accordance with their faith, values and Islamic culture and civilization. Islam and democracy were the dynamic forces that gave life to the freedom movement. In the post-1985 period which was considered to be a new democratic era "all assemblies and governments have trampled mercilessly the very roots of democracy. This post-1985 leadership did all what it could only to establish personal or family kingdom, all done in the name of democracy, overlooking the peoples' rights, being disloyal to national aspiration and considerations, destabilizing the constitutional state organs and plundering national wealth mercilessly and unhesitatingly." The leadership during this period did not initiate any measures to establish welfare state based on Islamic principles, nor to strengthen the democratic base. Both the leading political parties PPP and Muslim League followed the same strategy. In both cases, the power was centralized in one family, which tried to be master of every fact. Both the families were created by the Martial Law regimes and were also heavily pampered and favoured. They spared no effort to strengthen democracy. The constitution was badly deformed and its built-in balance of power was upset. They never believed in the constitution or rule of law. Every institution was crushed. The external forces got so much involved in the affairs of the state and politics that Pakistan's security and freedom were at stake.[19]

The experiments of democracy have failed in Pakistan but same has been the fate of Martial Laws. To correct the affairs, military leaders stepped three times before the present regime, but failed. General Ayub Khan gave the slogan of economic progress and sought the country's modernization through capitalistic liberalism. The result was dictatorial governance, limitations of freedom, increase in economic inequalities and a wave of regional hatred that could not sustain the powerful Chair. He did not transfer power to the Speaker of the National Assembly as envisaged in his own drafted (1962) Constitution and gave the reins to the army Chief General Yahya Khan—who was getting restless to grab power. General Yahya Khan's period came to a sorrowful end by breaking Pakistan in two pieces. General Zia-ul-Haq apparently came into power after toppling the civilian regime of Z.A. Bhutto, pledging to conduct elections in 90 days. As against Ayub's liberal capitalism and Bhutto's socialism, he chose the name of Islam. All these experiments bitterly failed and could not bring about any improvement.[20]

The real cause of these failures is that while the military action counters immediate danger, the army cannot solve through shortcut, the most complex issues of social life. Military is trained and prepared for specific purpose. That special capability and expertise is useful only in the battlefield. But it proves ineffective in addressing the issues of common life. The military discipline which is the best resource, cannot exactly, which provides the strength in war, become misfit and hindering in the consultative democratic process.[21]

Pakistan's people have generally not shared the wisdom of Pakistan's establishment. Each of Pakistan's military patriarchs have based their claim to power on grounds of the US support and their own ability to provide good governance. But good governance is not merely about some good guys making the right decision. It is also about showing ordinary people the right to appoint and remove those that govern them.

The British Viceregal System in India was based on the notion that the major decisions about choice of rulers could not be left to the illiterate natives. The patriarchal wisdom of the colonial structure rested on the notion that British trained generals and administrations were allowed to elect local officials for local functions but the Sahibs were to chase the highest echelons of government.

Ayub Khan's basic democracies, General Zia-ul-Haq's *Majlis-e-Shura* and the Mushrraf's regime's development schemes are all adaptation of the colonial patriarchal model. The people can choose members of the National Assembly, Councilors but they are not allowed to elect or remove the central governing authority in Pakistan.

The patriarchal model of governance has done little to unify Pakistan or provide a lasting system of governance. Democracy may not be as neat and methodical as the patriarchs might want but it is the only true empowerment of the people.

Musharaff's proclaimed hopes of creating a new breed of politicians while dispensing with the "old discredited lot" are unlikely to be fulfilled. If the objective of the exercise is to perpetuate the patriarchal notion of power, then it will only continue to hold at bay the creation of a self-sustaining Pakistani democracy.

Most of Pakistan's problems can be traced to its failure in creating a viable, self-sustaining political system and built-in checks and balances. There has never been a normal transfer of power in Pakistan, which in turn breeds constant insecurity on the part of rulers and the ruled.

A stable political system, with well defined rules of the game in all crucial areas of life, would end this insecurity and the consequent corruption and lawlessness.

ROLE OF ARMY IN PAKISTAN: A HARD REALITY

In the third world countries, the role of army in the political development is considered to be an important issue. The western outlook has advocated complete isolation of Army from politics whenever and wherever the Army is politicized and has established strong foothold in the political set-up of a country, it may help in maintaining order, it won't be helpful in the long-run to strengthen the roots of democracy.

The military is considered to be a general purpose interest group in many countries, either as a single group or somewhat divided into several services. As the military is to perform its duties in an altogether different circumstance as compared to the bureaucracy, the former emphasizes on more defence spending and the acquisition of more powerful weapons. In many countries countenances for the acquisition of nuclear armaments, a more authoritarian posture in domestic polities and a more pressure of national, territorial or ethnic claims against neighbour.[22] Bruce Russett and Elizabeth Hansion in a careful survey of over 1000 high level business executives and military officers, the members of the National Committees of the Republic Party and the businessmen in that order, all the three were more consistently more hawkish than a general sample of voters.[23]

There is a need to examine the role of general purpose interest group like the military in relatively domestic and authoritarian systems which ultimately leads to its politicization. In an authoritarian system the policy-making apparatus is generally centrally controlled and directed and thus in many ways it is relatively imperative to pressure. Nevertheless, the policy-makers are sometimes forced to tap the outside sources for certain kind of specialized information, a certain degree of expertise and some cooperation in the implementation of decisions. Because often there are groups (or groupings) that possess these special characteristics, they usually become associated with the top brass and whenever get an opportunity, exercise their influence. Though, it is somewhat difficult to gauge the influence, but the degree of influence is proportional to the policy-maker's sources, need for their expertise in handling various matters and the extent to which their cooperation is necessary for the effective implementation of decisions. There are differences from system to system but basically there are divergences in degree, not kind.[24] There is another aspect of the activities of the military to be considered with respect to authoritarian systems namely, the fact that various groups often strive to protect their particular interest by forcibly or otherwise taking control of the policy, making apparatus. In such an atmosphere, the objective is not to influence certain specific policies but rather to attain decisive influence within the policy-making organs themselves.

With respect to more democratic system, it is necessary to distinguish between those in which policy-making is relatively centralized and those which it is not. India provides us with an example of heavy concentration of power in the hands of the ruling party. With its parliamentary system and fusion of powers, policies are framed and made by ruling political party rather than via any kind of inter-party bargaining and compromise. In this kind of situation, there is precious little room for interest group like the military. Beside variety of groups do seek to influence policy-makers both at the executive and parliamentary levels, but they do so primarily by working through and in connection with the parties themselves, middlemen and bureaucrats. In some democratic systems like Sri Lanka, the decision-making is much more diffused with an intermingling, checking and balancing of functions and powers, the policy-making is difficult. But there are a multitude of points at which one may gain access to the policy-making process. The interest groups investigate these constantly, trying their best to impress the key policy-makers. India and Pakistan are spending billions of dollars on defence. More and more groups are becoming involved not only because of the size of the pie but also as a result of the two other factors; (1) the distinction between foreign and domestic policy is becoming increasingly obscure; and (2) more and more sectors of economy are being geared specifically to defence and its related activities.[25]

It has been universally acknowledged that the military is very much a part and parcel of a country's political set-up and tends to play an important role. Over the years, with fast changes that are taking place in the political, social, and economic and other related fields, the armed forces active participation has been legitimized and is a part of political culture at present. The military is bounced to take interest in politics. It is not a new phenomenon. If we scan the pages of history the instances of the military taking interest in the political affairs are numerous. Before 1917, nearly 40% of the states in existence witnessed in one way or the other the emergence of military power. There is no change in this trend and military whenever circumstances allowed, had dethroned the popular governments. The military coups are more frequent in the developing countries as compared to the developed.[26]

A number of scholars like Samuel P. Huntington[27], S.E. Finer[28], Morris Janowitz[29], Fred R. VanDer Mehden[30], A.R. Luckhan[31], Sang Seck Park[32], P.J. Vatikiontis[33], Moshecissak[34], Clande E. Welsh Jr. and Arthur K. Smith[35], J. Stephen Hoadley[36], etc. have analysed the various factors and trends which from time to time developed as a result of the civil-military relationship and have outlined five broad factors or their absence mainly responsible for the intervention of military in polities. They are:

- The internal organization of the military establishment,
- Socio-economic development,
- Level of political institutionalization,
- Professionalism and civilian control of the military, and
- Foreign influence and proximity of other military coups.[37]

The political power of armed forces reaches its nadir in countries which dispense with them altogether. The politicisation of the military begins when the armed forces offer their advice with a threat of sanctions if the advice is not given the due preference. Finer has discussed this aspect at a great length and summarized the high- handed techniques sometimes used threats to resign to withdraw support to announce disagreement publicly to demonstrate disdain for the regime, to refuse to execute its orders or to rise up in arms whenever the civil administrator surrender ultimately to these techniques, the armed forces become more ambitious and start ruling covertly, either by exercising a veto or by substituting policies and personal of their own choice for those of the *dejure* government. To further strengthen their positions, they manipulate to get the elections delayed, deploy the troops to intimidate to those opposing or to seize the key position and the arrest or assassination of politicians. In military intervention, the armed force usually acts alone or in collaboration with the civilians. They may take the initiative or respond, more or less eagerly to please the politicians. There are important distinctions.[38]

The military organization and personnel's play crucial role in determining the social, political and economic conditions of a large chunk of the global population. For many living in developing nations, military has been the most pivotal institution shaping the quality of their existence. In some nations, the military role is explicit and public-military elite controls the governmental organizations by occupying positions and considers it legitimate to openly dictate national policy, dominating the mass media of communication both public and private decisions and military dictated priorities supersede competing goals and policies. In other nations the military role is less obvious but important nonetheless. Military leaders may have effective access to the highest levels of national policy-making groups. Military budgets receive top priority and generally approved without any hitch regardless of other considerations or demands on limited national resources. Civilian political leadership may hold its position tenuously, dependent upon continued support for military leaders. To maintain their political positions, it is not possible for the civilian leaders to alienate the opinion, while taking major political decisions. However, obvious or inconspicuous the relationship to national life, there is little doubt that the military institution is inextricably involved not only in politics but in determining the outcome of every major social process.[39]

As far as the politicisation of armed forces in Pakistan is concerned, it started much earlier and has grown fully. It is adequate to lump the Indian and Pakistan armies together and assume that their behaviour will be similar because they share a common origin in the British Indian Army. But still there are important differences between Indian and Pakistani armies. First, the periodic political involvement of the Pakistani Army has affected its relationship with the social system, when a uniformed army strides into a room of civilians, the latter buckles. The social status and power of the Pakistan Army are radically different from those of the Indian Army. It is not all clear, however that its greater status has meant an improvement in fighting ability. Second, the Pakistani Army was created from scratch in 1947. It inherited very few training institutions, it was seriously deficient in most stores, supplies and weapons and it received far fewer officers with Staff College or advanced training than did the Indian Army. This meant that it was dependent on British officers for its first four years and this led to a mixed legacy of pride and bitterness at having to create a virtually new army in the face of alleged Indian hostility. Third, Pakistan was created on the basis of "Two Nations Theory." The army was supposed to follow and adopt Islamic principles and practices, while the Indian Army was not bound to adopt any such practices based on religion or otherwise. Fourth, upon partition, India was bound to change its entire strategy outlook because of the shedding of its responsibility for the defence of the north-west frontier. It inherited the much quieter northwest frontier Ladakh and other areas.

Fifth, in the early fifties, the Pakistani Army had developed a close relationship with the foreign military establishments as it was totally dependent on them for the supply of military hardware, whereas the Indian Army did not maintain any such contacts because of the non-aligned policy adopted by the Government of India. Sixth, in the 1950s, the Pakistan Army was completely reorgnised which led to a distinct and special approach to strategy and war. The Indian Army underwent on equivalent reorganization after the Sino-Indian war of 1962.[40]

Pakistan's armed forces, particularly the Army and Air Force are perceived as the bedrock upon which the existence or survival of Pakistan rests and as the primary institution influencing the nation's development as a modern state. Discipline, professionalism and national pride remain key features of the military establishment despite its deep involvement in politics.

Politics however has affected the army's professionalism and ability, particularly to the top ranks. Some lower ranking officers are embittered by their failure to get promotions because of political considerations. Dismemberment of Pakistan and the humiliation by India, was another cause for bitterness. The Officer Corps are derived from families with military traditions dating back to the British colonial and Mughal period. The majority of officers are Punjabis and Pathans. The other ranks are also mainly derived from these ethnic groups, especially from the rural areas, the Baluchis have sizeable contingents in the armed forces but the number of Sindhis and Muhajirs (refugees from India) is very small.

No doubt, Pakistan's Army had suffered a humiliating defeat at the hands of Indian Army in December 1971, the former still retain its reputation as a first-class fighting force.

-It is highly regarded in the Middle-East and elsewhere thousands of Pakistani soldiers and airmen have been sent abroad to bolster the forces of other Muslim countries, particularly in the Persian Gulf region. These deployments not only increase Pakistan's influence in the region and contribute to the nation's balance of payments, they also help to defuse tensions within the military by providing opportunities for faster advancement for some and distance postings for other, potentially disruptive offices.[41]

The armed forces of Pakistan constitute the largest single public employer nationally and one of the largest public employer globally. Prior to the emergence of Bangladesh, the military and particularly army was a highly prestigious force there. It is however, difficult to ascertain the damage done to the prestige of the armed forces as a result of the 1971 Indo-Pak war.[42] Nevertheless, the armed forces suffered both tangible and intangible loss of prestige, influence and control over the Pakistani polity and decision-making process as a result of this war. Z.A. Bhutto who took over as the President of Pakistan immediately after the end of war, successfully replaced several top ranking military offices, indicating that top military leadership lost its grip over the civil administration and was not as strong, organized or confident as it once was.[43]

No doubt, the military was demolished for sometime, but it remained an important political institution or very close to the top. In short, the influence of the military because of its traditional role and dominant position in the Pakistani social milieu, its priority with regard to public expenditure and its able top leadership, still remained strong, if not as openly dominant as in the past. The army role in the decision-making process was strong if not dominant and its participation in both defence and civilian affairs was relevant.[44]

Since independence, the army has played a definite role in Pakistan and it is considered to be highly politicized. The analysis of this phenomenon will be very interesting in the sense that the Indian and the Pakistani armies emerged as a result of the partition, are assuming altogether different positions as far as this aspects is concerned. This trend demands some explanation. Stephen P. Cohen has rightly pointed out that there are armies that geared their nation's borders, there are those that are concerned with protecting their own position in society and there are those that defined a cause of an idea. The Pakistan army does all three. Moreover, it has always regarded itself as the special expression of the idea of Pakistan and a few officers have advocated an active role in reforming or correcting the society, where it has fallen below the standard of excellence set by the militants.[45]

Pakistan's top military officer admire the Indian political set-up, but quite typically as in the case of an armoured division commander who said, "India had a very big advantage over Pakistan in the leadership of Pandit Nehru who ruled over these twenty years. You have seen that in spite of the fact that his daughter had a reverse and the Janata Party has seen her out, the people of India, because of the outstanding leadership of Pandit Nehru, once they saw that the other party is not good, then they ran back to her. So they have a very big advantage whereas we are a little unfortunate. You know at the time of partition, we had a reversal Quaid-i-Azam (M.A. Jinnah) had died, Prime Minister Liaquat Ali Khan had died, the other Prime Minister had gone away and then the cult was mediocrity, the politicians were not trained and we had political confusion for ten to twelve years. People thought that the country is gone and that is the reason this professional army was called in, because there was some leadership in it. These martial laws have come in and they have been very hard on the army, but there was no way out. Gradually now these politicians know that to be a leader, you have to be a leader—but there have been lapses on its part. But India has had a family; God Almighty was very kind to them."[46]

During the period which immediately followed Jinnah's death, there developed a fierce competition for influence, wealth, power and prestige among the various interests and personalities which made up political life. The arena in which this competition has first manifested itself was the organization for framing the constitution which was to give formal expression to Pakistan's policy.[47]

It was nonetheless true that the politicians, comprising the wealthy landlords, the lawyers and the journalists who between them, dominated the Central and Provincial Assemblies formed not very commendable group of people. Everyone knows that political activity has no purpose unless it is the acquisition of power and sometimes, the spoils that may go with it. Certainly, not everyone is concerned with spoils and in some countries, they don't amount too much. The point here is that one group of people, in politics, accuses another group of seeking power or being hungry for it, they are accusing themselves at the same time. There is only the instated assumption that "we want it for the good of the country, where, as they want it for the good of themselves. In Pakistan, in those days, there was unending bad image of this sort, but it was mostly a case of the pot calling the kettle back. The wealthy landlords were concerned with retaining both land and wealth."[48] The national political scene has largely been dominated by the landed aristocracy and the feudal lords, in and outside the legislatives. This large and powerful group has always been opposed to legal, political and agricultural reforms that may weaken its control on the rural areas where 70% of the population lives. The dichotomy between urban and rural population sections of the population is striking.[49]

Pakistan's political parties are also barely democratic. Few have held to House elections on a regular basis or have only nominally performed the rituals. Pakistan is rich in family controlled and autocratic parties in which the genes and means take precedence over competence and the accident of birth provides sure ladder for leadership. The feudal system negates the concept of democracy in the same way as the military rule does consequently the political system that has taken root in Pakistan is the anti-thesis of democracy. It is feudal in character and practice and in democratic in name only. There is no change in the situation since 1947.[50]

In any system of parliamentary representation, political parties form the primary unit of democracy. As such, they are instrumental in moving the process forward and determining the particular shape it assumes in a given socio-economic framework.

Unfortunately, in Pakistan, the role has not always been effectively played by more than 100 or so registered political parties. In addition, administrative intervention in the working of the parties and attempts made through a series of constitutional changes to diminish their significance alongside of an elected parliament, can act only to make political parties a still less significant force.

One of the major political parties, the PPP and the Pakistan Muslim League (PML) led by Nawaz Sharif, have come under sustained assault from the military regime, which has been accused of restoring to harassment and victimization directed against their leaders. However, the previous record of the two parties and their leaders is not impressive either, with multiple accusations of corruption and abuse of power levelled against them. The bar placed on electoral contest by the leaders of the two parties, under the rules in place for the 2002 elections and actions taken in an apparent attempt to weaken the two parties that have dominated general elections since 1988, has inevitably brought about significant changes on the political scene. The most important of those is the emergence of a new faction of the PML, known as the PML-QA, which is seen as the party backed by the regime and the largest PML faction in Pakistan.

The forging of opportunist alliances, with parties once divided sharply on the basis of ideology now united mainly in an attempt to create a strong front against parties backed by the military authorities signifies too what a limited role political conviction plays as far as parties in Pakistan concerned.[51]

Jamaat-I-Islami (JI) has been able to conduct regular, internal elections, within most other parties, leadership has remained limited to a particular coterie, sometimes based on kinship networks, articulating only a narrow range of interests. Internal power struggles in the absence of party elections have led frequently to the fragmentation of political parties into factions or splinter groups and this process has contributed in part to the steadily increasing number of political groupings present in Pakistan.[52]

Hasan Askri Rizvi, a Pakistani scholar and a keen observer of the politicization of military in Pakistan strongly felt that the major responsility "falls on the shoulders of the political leadership." He has identified five factors for an increasing participation of the military in non-military governance of the state: (i) in the sense of the insecurity of the new state following the partition riots and demographic shifts, the military moved with determination to provide stability, (ii) the weak social base and disarray of the political leadership and erosion of political institutions, (iii) discipline and cohesion of the military and bureaucracy, (iv) utility of skills for civil purposes, (v) the high prestige of the military as a competent, impartial and effective organization.[53] The gradual deterioration of conditions inside Pakistan gave rise to two closely related trends in Pakistan. First, the calls to the army to help the civil government in the maintenance of law and order gradually increased. Second, the military became an important factor in the decision-making of Pakistan. President Ayub Khan in his autobiography made it clear that the "unprincipled" behaviour of Pakistani landlords, lawyers and civil servants—turned politicians led directly to the October 1958 coup. Leporte feels that military bureaucrats in league with "President Iskander Mirza chose to move and perform the coup in the name of parliamentary corruptions and immorality was undeniable. At any rate, the instability of this period and out of parliament to appease the military civilian bureaucratic coalition did contribute to the abandonment of parliamentary democratic façade."[54]

For a brief period from January 1972 to July 1977 Pakistan saw the civilian rule, headed by Z.A. Bhutto. He was able to inject a new enthusiasm in the political scene of Pakistan and strengthen his position, concluded an Tripartite Agreement with the National Awami Party and *Jamial-ul-Ulema-e-Islam* on 6 March 1972 and by promulgating an interim constitution for Pakistan.[55] But after sometime, he started facing rough weather of home. His PPP was also in trouble as left was being purged and the old conservative forces surfaced. Bhutto's own behaviour disillusioned many. He was working in an authoritarian way and "over centralization of decision-making, not delegation of authority" was his style of functioning. He perceived himself as personifying the political system of Pakistan and was convinced that the country's stability correlates with his longevity in office.[56]

Bhutto, a seasoned politician was well aware of the politicised nature of Pakistan army to what it should be in democratic set-up. To army, namely defending the borders of the country from external invasions and render assistance to the civilian administration in the maintenance of internal law and order, when specifically asked to do so. The army when Bhutto took over was depressed and stood discarded. He planned to further discredit it by propagating through government media that it was the army which was responsible for the disintegration of Pakistan and thus, absolving himself of a responsibility for the session which was attributed to him by his opponents. To further tighten his control over the army, Bhutto eased out several top officers early in 1972. To establish upper hand of civil administration, Bhutto Government issued a white paper of defence in the middle of 1976. The objective behind issuing the paper was to tell the armed forces that entire decision-making was concentrated in the hands of the Prime Minister. He was to Chair the Defence Council also. He was responsible for coordinating defence with home and foreign affairs.[57] One of the prime objectives of Z.A. Bhutto in initiating and vigorously pursing the nuclear weapons programme was believed to reduce power and influence of the Army by having a more potent weapon system directly under civilian control. It is here, he seems to have miscalculated badly, Benazir Bhutto during an interview to the BBC in December 1992 admitted that the Prime Minister had no control over Pakistan's nuclear weapons programme.[58]

With the change of political climate in the country, Bhutto realized that it won't be possible for him to run the country and maintain his constitutional and increasingly unpopular rule, with the absolute support and loyalty of the armed forces. Bhutto otherwise maintained the armed forces in good humour, by allocating more funds and equipping them with modern weapons. Deep-rooted internal problems become his compulsion in the later part of his rule.[59]

Benazir Bhutto, the former Prime Minister of Pakistan, was of the view that in collusion with the right Islamic reactionaries who launched an agitation against his father regime, the military staged the coup on 5 July 1977. The reactionaries were astonishingly so naive as to expect the army to share power with them after it had overthrown a functioning democratic order.[60] It was once again the fast deteriorating political situation after the March 1977 elections, which the opposition blamed was totally rigged considered to be the main cause of army rule in Pakistan. The people of Pakistan were not stronger to the army rule. From 1958 periodically, the army itself or some politicians playing the game had thrown over board the so-called constitution and ruled the country. The total claim with which the people of Pakistan had accepted the coup was not surprising at all. No one was prepared to accept when Bhutto announced that he had put an end to "Bonapartism" after the proclamation of Constitution in 1973 and henceforth there would be no coup.[61] Once in power, the military, after a symbolic reprimand of the corrupt and inefficient public bureaucracy collaborated with the civil service of Pakistan in pursuit of the effective neutralization of the traditional politicians.[62]

The army has always been regarded as politically incompetent by a wide cross-section of public including professionally devoted armed officers who strongly feel that prolonged interference of army in the civil administration and internal security duties paved the way for determining the competence and discipline in armed forces and lays them open that sap morale. General Zia-ul-Haq had found it difficult to transfer power to the politicians, hold elections and return to barracks because he was duly worried about his and his associate's future.

The military in Pakistan, during Zia period "did contemplate institutionalizing its role in politics by creating an entirely new Islamic system of political life which implied drastic constitutional changes and uprooting or intimidation of all independent centres of power including the press, the judiciary, student unions and Pakistan's already enfeebled intellectual class.[63]

General Zia tried to legitimize his rule by projecting himself as a true follower of Islam, particularly changing the political, economic, social, cultural and educational structure of Pakistan according to the teachings of Holy *Quran* and *Sunna*. He seemed to be a popular leader among the masses and the sharp differences between the political parties particularly, those associated with the Movement for Restoration of Democracy (MRD) had convinced the people in Pakistan that only General Zia could provide Pakistan a stable political set-up.

Furthermore, there was no broad-based political party having mass following at the grass-root level. A leader of Bhutto's stature who with the help of some powerful army Generals could overthrow Zia regime. It was a general impression that "Pakistan for quite sometime to come was likely to be saddled with a military regime."[64] In sharp contrast to two earlier regimes of Ayub and Yahya, the military was considered to be Zia's constituency, more than any other section of society. It was described as a true military regime in Pakistan. Zia had considered the army as the first and fundamental pillar of the regime but also wanted to assign pivotal position to the Army in the Constitution as the final custodian of the country's integrity.[65]

The tragic death of Zia in a plane crash in August 1988 put an abrupt end of military rule in Pakistan. The greatest legacy he left behind in his death than anything else is the primary role for the armed forces. Never before has the army been able to dictate effectively and so much clout after relinquishing power, as in the case of Benazir Government. It was for the first time even with the political order undergoing a change; the military-civilian equation was more unfavourable to a democratic leadership.[66] Elections were held in Pakistan in December 1988. Benazir Bhutto became the first woman Prime Minister of Pakistan. She was to head a minority government and face the President Ghulam Ishaq Khan sympathetic to Islamic Democratic Alliance. Benazir had to strike political compromises in order to assume the Chair of the Prime Minister. To the army, she assured that they would be free to run their own affairs and there won't be cut in budget allocations. To acting President, Benazir promised her support in his election as the President. The Chief of the Army Staff, Gen. Aslam Beg was wielding strong influence. In Benazir's own words, realistically speaking, given the present situation, it would be very difficult for any government in Pakistan to survive without the critical backing of the armed forces."[67] She over-emphasized the link between the people's mandate and the return of democracy forgetting that in Pakistan which is still affected by feudalism, the powerful institutional business and landed classes were able to determine the success and longevity of any government. It was evident that the Army was not happy with the functioning of the Benazir Government.[68] President Ishaq, of course, by taking the top brass of the army into confidence, dismissed Benazir Bhutto Government on 6 August 1996 provided an opportunity to Islamic Jamoori Ithad. It had (ISI) to run the government, the differences between the Prime Minister Nawaz Sharif and General Beg over domestic and foreign policies became well known, had led to the speculation of an army take over. The conflict between the Army Chief and the fledging civilian government took a serious turn in January 1998 when General Beg publicly criticized the Government for supporting the US-led coalition forces in the Gulf War. But, Nawaz Sharif had successfully demonstrated that he was well aware of the predominant position of the Army in the power structure of Pakistan.[69]

The Army had become a part of the political process of Pakistan. The then Pakistan Army Chief Lt. Gen. Asif Nawaz Janjua was considered as "liberal and pro-US officer. The appointment of General Nawaz had ended months of political uncertainty in the country where the army had repeatedly seized power. In choosing General Nawaz, President Ishaq had rejected the favourites of many in ruling circles, including Lt. Gen. Hamid Gul, the former Intelligence Chief who was opposed to the US military aid to the Afghan rebels.

It is very difficult to sideline the army in Pakistan's politics. If at all, any attempt made is to displease the military in Pakistan, it may take another century. During this period, strong party system with the industrial workers, intelligentsia, etc. is to be developed which could challenge the army intervention effectively.

After the October 1993 elections in Pakistan, the army

supremacy in the political system of Pakistan had taken a different shape. The top brass of the army did not interfere in the elections and watched the show from the barracks. The elections had convinced them that they should not take undue interest directly, but must control the levers of power and defence policy while actively staying out of politics.[70] It was widely well known that Benazir and Sharif had accepted the army's anxieties on foreign policy and security issues. The Army, at that time was determining policies in the areas most important to them without getting into the mess of day-to-day governance.[71]

Mrs. Benazir Bhutto's second stint as a Prime Minister was from (October 1993-November 1996) abruptly ended when she was unceremoniously dismissed on 15 November 1996 by the President exercising the powers vested with him under VIIIth amendment of the 1973 Constitution. Benazir had maintained close liaison with the Army top brass but rampant corruption which resulted in an almost collapse of the Pakistan's economy were cited as some of the reasons which had compelled the President to take such a drastic step.

The gross mismanagement of the economy put Pakistan into an economic crisis. Pakistan economy was dominated by black money of $2.5 billion. Annual evasion was said to run into $16 billion. Rising inflation, worsening balance of payments positions, a crushing foreign debt burden and low foreign exchanges had all combined to make it vulnerable both internally and externally. It was even feared that Pakistan deficit might shoot beyond $5 billion. Its foreign debt serving had reached then $2.25 billion. An estimated trade deficit was put at $28 billion. Amidst these harsh realities annual expenditure on defence and debt servicing accounted for more than the total revenues and nearly 2% of gross revenue.[72]

The severe economic crisis had even prompted the IMF to withhold the $600 million stand by assistance package. The IMF also had argued that the worsening economic conditions should make Pakistan either cancel or at least postpone some major defence programmes, such as the $2.4 billion deal for 30 Mirage 2000. Going by the IMF conditions, some experts suggested that the axe might fall on the proposed $550 million deal with Ukraine for 300 T-80 UD main battle tanks and three submarines from France, estimated to cost $950 million. As things stood at that time, Nawaz Sharif, the newly elected Prime Minister of Pakistan could not be able to touch and cut the defence expenditure. The Army Chief Gen. Jahangir Karamat had given his mind in this regard, the day Sharif was sworn as the Prime Minister.[73] Notwithstanding Sharif's massive mandate, and one had to constantly keep in mind the Army's predominant position in Pakistan politico-administrative set-up. Few days before the elections, the President of Pakistan had announced the formulation of a National Security and Defence Council (NSDC). There were speculations that whether the Sharif Government would allow NSDC to function or his own Government would be under the scrutiny. Would the armed forces continue to be the final arbiters or would Nawaz Sharif be able to free himself from the extremely powerful group. All these were extremely complex and intricate issues and such speculations kept on going.[74]

A serious situation could however, arise if and when Sharif joined issue with the President on NSDC abolition or its functioning. It would have been tough fight as all three Chiefs and Chief of General Staff were the Council members. Moreover, its authority extended to defence, economics, law and order problems. He had also argued for economic ties during his pre and post-election speeches. But could he achieve that before settling the Kashmir problem, would the armed forces allow him? Infact chalking out a line which won't take into account the army, was desirable for democracy to take roots in Pakistan. But it was very difficult for Nawaz Sharif to pursue.[75]

Pakistan remained politically polarized during 1988-99. Successive governments lacked a healthy working relationship with the opposition. Such dearth of mutual trust created political instability and slowed down the growth of democratic traditions, corruption became a malignant disease and economic mismanagement was criticized at home and by the international aid-giving agencies. Politics became a quick buck business. The dismissal of four governments in quick succession was a set back to democratic values.[76]

The genetics of military intervention also differed from a blood bath, to a completely peaceful transition of authority. The psyche of the people, political culture and the country's experience are considered to be very important. For example, all military coups in Pakistan were peaceful and smooth transfer of power. These were preceded by political chaos and had polarized the country and the public anticipated that the military would no longer remain a silent spectator.[77]

At various stages and varying degrees, the Pakistani military has always been very important determinant of national politics. Some military top brass nourished political ambitions. All the army Generals starting from Ayub to Musharaff became deeply involved in politics and tried their best to legitimize their regimes by not only launching popular measures, even making use of the Islam. The military in Pakistan got sucked into political whirlwind by the force of circumstances, goaded and abetted by the politicians themselves. Power intoxicated all the army Generals. They started riding high and were unwilling to get off the power saddle.[78]

It is simplistic to judge a dictator by the yardstick of democracy. The military rulers did not topple the civilian governments to demonstrate their love for democracy. Their reasons and explanations were always different while some had political ambitions too; others were alarmed by threats posed to national security. They declared that they could not stay aloof, watching the country erode from within. Whether such acts were legally or morally justified, has always been a million dollar question to answer. They all claimed to be staunch nationalists. However, "repeated military role has established that within the defence hierarchy those political issues can be solved amicably only adopting democratic methods. Even military in Pakistan is aware that its intervention in civil matters has not helped in finding a durable cure for the ills of the state. Not only do the disadvantages of military action outweigh their gains, but the national image suffers. Furthermore the professional performance of the military has had a setback."[79]

It is not always desirable to drag the defence services into the political arena. The two respective players, the politicians and the military top brass, work according to their suitability. Some politicians had always their own agenda in politicizing the armed forces. This was understandable too. Also a couple of military commanders since 1988 misused their position and indulged in political activities and manipulations. The public in Pakistan has got them exposed. Such activities of army have always tarnished the prestige of the Pakistani armed forces.[80]

After the departure of Zia from the political scene in Pakistan, it became somewhat evident that the military had slowly receded into the background and maintaining a posture of neutrality and non-interference in political controversies. This discernible change was publicly applauded and appreciated by the political leadership in Pakistan Prime Minister Nawaz Sharif's two acts—the 13th Amendment in the Constitution and premature retirement of the Naval Chief in 1997—illustrated the growing political supermany.[81]

It is instructive to review the relationship between Nawaz Sharif and military during Sharif's second stint as Prime Minister. During the contempt proceedings against Nawaz Sharif, the Chief Justice wrote a letter to the Chief of the Army Staff General Jahangir Karamat, seeking protection and safety of the Supreme Court building and his own person. Karamat preferred to send the matter to the civilian government, to provide the necessary protection. It was understood in the political circles of Pakistan this non-intervention attitude by the Chief of the Army Staff led finally to the resignation of Farooq Ahmed Khan Leghari as the President of Pakistan and Sajjad Shah as Chief Justice.[82]

On 6 October 1998, newspapers in Pakistan prominently carried some answers that General Karamat gave to the questions put to him during his address at the Pakistan Navy War College at Lahore. A report of this session was released by the public relations office of the Ministry of Defence, which said that, "A National Security Council or Committee at the apex would institutionalize decision-making if it was backed by a team of credible advisors and a think tank of experts. The other tiers would be at the joint staff ministry and services level. We also needed neutral, competent and secure bureaucracy and administration at the federal and provincial levels. Institutions needed to be strengthened through professional leadership and autonomy with emphasis on results."[83]

When the government of PPP was dismissed in 1996, President Leghari and the caretaker cabinet in November 1996 issued a notification on the formation of a Council of Defence and National Security (CDNC). This was done by bringing changes in the Rules of Business of the Government. This Council was to consist of the President, Prime Minister, the three Services Chiefs, the Chairman of the Joint Chiefs of Staff Committee and Secretaries of Defence, Interior, Finance and Foreign Affairs. However political circles assailed the formation of (DNC) as a needless innovation. The only party that supported it was PML, headed by Nawaz Sharif. When Jahangir Karamat referred to the creation of a National Security Council (NSC), the Prime Minister reached a different conclusion and after a short meeting between Nawaz Sharif and General Karamat, the latter submitted his resignation on 8 October 1998. The idea of National Security Council was mooted when Zia was in power. He included in it the Provisional Constitution Order and latter in his revival of Constitutional order at the time of the framing of Eight Amendment, which contained an article on the NSC. However, this idea was fundamentally dropped. There exists a body called Defence Committee of the Cabinet (DCC).[84]

The Musharaff's military regime had also launched a transformation process of Pakistan's governmental structure and its law and order mechanism, ensuring that the military of Pakistan would have a legal authority to share power in any future government. Musharaff had National Reconstruction Bureau (NRB) and come up with a scheme that "would rebalance Pakistan's politics." No specific guidelines were given to (NRB), except that Musharaff placed a great emphasis on "checks and balances" and the need to moderate the excesses of the politicians.

The NRB was described as a think-tank by some political analysts, but it started working in its own style and conceived the idea of new distinct government (Nazim) system, which remains its major achievement. Nazim were to operate in apolitical vacuum, executing national and provincial legislation and Pakistan's own services from local government. Interestingly, politicians and bureaucracy opposed the system. The Nazim and the elected assemblies, on the other hand, were promised autonomy and were content with an arrangement that delivered money directly to them, bypassing the bureaucracy and the provincial legislatures. One level "with its discussion of transparency, openness, accountability, devolutions, responsibility and public accessibility, the new system is a mélange of contempt theories of public administration." Nazim system has its importance: First, it further weakens the power of the bureaucracy, much destructed by the army and given only an "ancillary role in the new system." It is different to analyse the purpose of the reforms or whether the bureaucracy was merely "road killer—an incidental causality. Second, by providing block grants at the local level or no fiscal control over what happens in the districts, perhaps the real motive behind this move was to carry political favour by creating class of local notables who owe their position to Army Headquarters.[85]

Musharaff felt strongly that "the role of the armed forces in government had to be constitutionally regulated—they had to be brought into the system to prevent them from having to take it over again under a new order put into effect in 2004. The military has been given formal constitutional role by providing membership in the NSC. Those who appreciate the role of military in the political process of Pakistan felt relieved as this arrangement will once and for all regulate Pakistan—civil-military dilemma—keeping the military's "random interference in civil affairs. This open, overt role is necessary they insist, because the army's rule as a "silent partner" in governance did not guarantee that it would stay out of politics owing to the politician's venality and incompetence." People close to Musharaff claimed that, "he eventually figures out that policies adopted on impulse and without careful analysis are not enough. The hope of such supporters is Musharaff." Combination of political naiveté, secularism and realism will get Pakistan through the next few years.[86]

Jahangir Karamat was the only Army Chief who

voluntarily resigned from his post-acknowledged that the army in Pakistan has been assertive and interventionist but strongly felt that the historical circumstances were responsible for strengthening the role of the army in politics. He appreciated Benazir Bhutto for better understanding. But other Generals were critical of the politicians as they branded them as "incorrigibly corrupt, venal and incompetent and eagerly compare the army's own high standards of integrity with the politician's abysmal record." Karamat also appreciated the fellow army offices and lamented that "the politicians have let the army down." There is a tendency among army to veto any civilian decision that it feels effects NSC policies budgets and domestic issues. Karmat tried to institutionalize the role of the army but Sharif punched "Pakistan thus has real chicken egg problem when it comes to civil-military relations. Under present circumstances, it is impossible for politicians to master the arts and science of domestic politics, to grow and mature in their profession. Once in office, it is equally difficult for them to govern without fear of army's encroachment or blank armies take over."[87]

In the foreign policy sphere, without taking army into confidence, no civilian government can take any bold step. The army is over sensitive to foreign and defence policy matters. The issues like Kashmir and relationship with India are considered to be very sensitive and a "government that fails to work out a strategy in concert with the armed forces will run enormous risk. The army, on the other hand, will have to understand the limits of its capacity to govern."

Pakistan has, so far seen four times military intervention, military government, military misrule, a return to civilian government, civilian floundering and renewed intervention. It does not mean that the future must look towards the past. "The only civil-military strategy that will work in Pakistan, short of a revolution, military defeat or ideological transformation, is one in which a staged transfer of power and authority takes place over a period of years spanning the tenure of more than one Prime Minister and one Army Chief. Unless that happens Pakistan's democracy will always be qualified or limited. In this case, "stages are meant both in the sense of a time schedule and a theoretical event: at each stage both the symbolic and substantive accouterments of power have no gradually shift from the armed forces to the political parties."[88]

Not much change is expected in Pakistan as far as the civil-military relationship is concerned as Pakistan has inherited weak institutions dominant by strong personalities. The self-perpetuation approaches of the political leadership further weakened the institutions. Their frailty caused military interventions. This vicious cycle has impaired domestic growth. The inability of the political leaders to check the national downward slide brought the military into the political scene. At times they overplayed the national security concern for genuine and selfish reasons always portrayed the defence establishment as "holy cow." Military rule, a one person act, is neither designed to promote democracy nor to develop institutions. This is unlike a representative government which is perceived to function on the concept of collective responsibility. The institutions of the state weakened under Martial Law. A democratic government may or may not be a good government. But its preference lies in its checks and balances and in the process of accountability.[89]

PAKISTAN: A NUCLEAR POWER

Earlier the decisions regarding strengthening military capability were considered to be the privilege of the top level experts in most of the developing and developed countries. The general public was not at all in the picture, but with the passage of time and the sweeping changes that took place on the world political scene has injected a number of new dimensions, particularly about the public awareness about the military and strategic matters. In the contemporary world, it is not possible to take broad military decisions without any public debate.

The political elites in order to put a seal of legitimacy on their policies and programmes in fact, encouraged the public to initiate debates and discussions on important matters of all types which directly or indirectly are concerned with national security or military set-up. In Pakistan, three major "overlapping elite groups", political, economic and social are in operations: The political group include, (a) leaders of various political parties, (b) top level military and air force offices, since in the third wing of armed forces, i.e. navy, has not been able to attract ambitions of the land-owning class, therefore, it has not exercised a great deal of power and influence relative to the armed forces (c) the central elite civil services (in particular the civil services of Pakistan and the Pakistan Foreign services), (d) other members of the land owing family, belonging to Punjab and Sindh who have adopted other professions outside civil service and military. But in the economic elite group, major importance is attached to industrialists. The decision-making process in Pakistan has usually been highly centralized and personal. No doubt, the continuity has been maintained through civilian and military bureaucracy in respect of domestic foreign policy, military and strategic matters.[90]

The strong desire to go nuclear in Pakistan emerged in the seventies and eighties. A number of factors which include strategic, military or security calculations, quest for regional or international status, to demonstrate national viability, to fortify military, scientific or bureaucratic morale, to meet the requirements of military industrial complex, to strengthen domestic moral or divert domestic attention from financial pressures. But there are, all the more important some possible precipitants or trigging events like deep-rooted involvement in external crisis or reduction of any alliance credibility or nuclearization of neighbouring or other fellow countries and possible elimination of international constraints or domestic crisis and political change or easy availability of necessary material components or knowledge and last but not the least the changed perception of nuclear weapons utility.[91]

The shattering impression, the public mind of those climatic moments of twentieth century history came from the revelation of the two inextricable dimensions of nuclear weapons, the first relating to its incredible power and the second to the unconscionable destruction and unimaginable suffering that they embody and symbolize. Nuclear weapons emanate wonder and horror. They have continued to do so ever since.[92]

The most ardent advocates of nuclear weapons have constantly sought to invest these weapons with a virtually religious authority and importance and to give them an accepted and respectable place in the most popular culture of the contemporary world. What better way is there to legitimize their existence than to do one or both these things? If nuclear weapons can come to acquire the same "profound value as the sacred symbols that supposedly condense the meaning and purposes of a religion and of the surrounding then can be seen as arcane and complex as the higher reaches of religious philosphy can be for the ordinary believer or the uninitiated, then we have surely succeeded in making the politics and ideology of the possession of nuclear weapons virtually incontestable"[93].

The other approach also seeks to make the presence of nuclear weapons and the discourse that justifies it contestable, but it does so, not by seeking to place it on a pedestal to be reversed from a far or below. Rather, it so immerses in the web of everybody life and values of a mass society that their presence is "normalized" and considered unexceptional and unobjectionable. These two approaches, the religious and the cultural—popular may appear to work at cross purposes, but they don't. Indeed the greatest success is delivered when the two can be fused, when the religious—sacred is both reversed and seen as an unproblematic and normal part of every day life.[94]

The great dilemma for the advocates of nuclear weapons and the good hope for those who unreservedly oppose them is that despite all efforts to either sanctify or popularize these arguments and the attention ideology of support, these efforts have never been able to gain anywhere near as much ground as its purveyors have wished. This has certainly not been for want of trying. Ever since such weapons were invented, pro-nuclearists have been trying to make them into desirable icons, to build glorious myths and weave attracting images around them, to routinize and domesticate their meanings. Yet there is this relative failure.[95]

Peace and threats to use force have persistently been a part in international relations and developments in military technology have often had an important impact on structures and processes of political systems. Thermo-nuclear weapons and long range ballistae missile systems are not merely quantitatively different from those that preceded them. They also possess qualitative attributes that have led, and will continue to have a significant impact on the international system, its member units, and the nature of relations between them. This is not to say that the conventional weapons are obsolete, indeed most nations, military forces are still limited to such weapons, and even the nuclear power have found it expedient to maintain conventional forces to deal with limited provocations.

It is not only the destructive capacity of the nuclear weapons that has had an impact on the international system. The development of long range ballistic missiles has provided the means for the delivery across continents at speeds that have reduced warning time, almost to the vanishing point. Space and time which once provided protection against divesting surprise attack have all but lost their defensive edge in the nuclear missile age. Since world war second, the policies of nations aimed with nuclear weapons have clearly dominated the international system, but acquisition and deployment of military instruments is by no means limited to the major powers. Thus, although nuclear ,weapons are of undeniable importance, several important points should be kept in mind: (1) Virtually all the nations maintain armed forces; (2) the intensity of violence in military actions may vary across a wide scale, but force is rarely used in an unlimited manner; (3) sources of international instability are by no means confined to the actions and conflicts between nuclear powers, and (4) many observations about force as an instrument of policy are equally void for nuclear and for conventional weapons.

Military strength has traditionally been one of the attributes distinguishing the so-called great powers from the small powers. Since the second world war destruction has tended to give way to that between the nuclear powers and those not so armed. The high cost of developing and procuring nuclear capabilities initially prohibited all but a few industrial powers from developing them. At present, nuclear technology has tended to create two clauses of international citizenship. In the long-run, however nuclear capabilities may tend to dilute the importance of traditional bases of power—population, territory, industrial capacity and the like—and therefore, reduce rather than expand the difference between large and small nations. To be sure, a nation with a large population, vast territory, and widely dispersed industrial capacity may be in a better position to survive a nuclear attack—and is thus capable of employing threats more effectively than in a nation with limited population and territory. In the pre-nuclear era, it was unlikely that a minor power could inflict an unacceptable level of damage on one of its large neighbours, much less threaten its existence; it was not inconceivable, however, that in the not too distant future, a small nation armed with nuclear weapons may be in a position to inflict such damages. This is precisely the reasoning that underlies the French "force de dissuasions." The ability to tear off an arm is assumed to be sufficient to deter even a much more powerful adversary.[96]

However, for most nations, nuclear power is currently only indirectly relevant to the conduct of their foreign policies. Although possessed of weak and crude military capabilities in comparison to those of the nuclear nations, these countries also enjoy the advantage of being unlikely direct targets of any nuclear exchange. It is thus one of the many paradoxes of the nuclear age that the threat of destruction hangs most heavily even on those states with the greater military power; in some respects, than security is inversely rather than directly related to military capabilities.[97]

The nuclear weapons, whose destructive power was so convincingly demonstrated at Hiroshima and Nagasaki in 1945, became a symbol of power and prestige among the nations of the world, and their possession gave a special status to the possessor in international power hierarchy.[98] Since 1945, various measures to freeze, limit or abolish certain categories of weapons, to prevent certain military activities, to regulate development of forces to prescribe the transfer of certain military important items, to construct or prohibit use of certain arguments to build up international confidence through greater openness in military field have come to be included in the rubric of arms control. It was consistently upheld that 20 to 25 nations might acquire nuclear capability around 1985 and the scenario would be that of more or less a "Nuclear Armed Crowd."[99]

This did not become a reality because the spread of nuclear capability was contained efficiently to an extent by others and the nuclear weapons states like the US. It tried to arrest the spread of nuclear weapons to other countries and regions where they did not exist.[100] This proliferation within a political lexicon came to be understood as the concern of some (states, intellectuals, media) with others possession of nuclear weapons because of those other's alleged willingness to play by the rules of the game.[101]

The evaluation of international order over the past sixty years has been radically different in a variety of respects from the way international events had unfolded with two hundred years of building of colonial empires. The onset of the nuclear age ushered in an era where nuclear weapons were to become instruments of furthering the hegemonistic ambitions of the states, which possessed these as instruments of mass destruction. The process of horizontal nuclear proliferation itself can be viewed as a historical process where adversary threat perceptions lead to a kind of chain reaction or a struggle against nuclear hegemony which results in more nations going nuclear. Thus the US nuclear weapons programme capitalized the former USSR nuclear weapons programme. The Chinese nuclear deterrent was directed at both the US and the USSR. Chinese capability spurred towards it.[102]

South Asia has long been an area of considerable instability and unrest. The inability of its states to remove the threats perceived within the region has reinforced traditional assumptions and fears about each other. A number of factors have encouraged this sense of insecurity. First, the Hindu-Muslim divide, together with deeply ingrained memories and experiences of exploitation and suffering have been more powerful barriers to accommodation and reconciliation between the two major states. Between India and Pakistan these historical realities have generated attitudes that are not conducive to innovative thinking in the region. Second, the dictates of "negative substances", which constantly emphasized the dissimilarities between cultures in order to preserve the justification for the partition of the sub-continent in 1947, have largely determined the policies of those in power, particularly in Pakistan and Bangladesh. While this too is receding the new reference points what can guide the present generations, are still evolving, making the present leadership in the region quite difficult.[103] Third, in the sub-continent different sets of arrangements have been evolved. The dissimilarities in the structures and aspirations of the elites in each country, the parliamentary, military and monarchical rulings that are prevailing in the region are responsible for the development of self-serving system of values and attitudes *ipso facto,* preliterate to seemingly irreconcilable conceptions of security. Fourth, keeping into considerations, the differences in size and potential between the states of South Asia, India which has common borders with each country although none of the neighbours border on each other inevitably emerge as the predominating factor in the security parameters of the region, the domestic as well as other.[104]

And lastly, post-1947 developments such as six major wars involving China, Pakistan, India and Bangladesh, the dismemberment of Pakistan, creation of Bangladesh, merger of Sikkim into India, the explosion of nuclear devices by India and Pakistan, demographic aggression (from Bangladesh to India), the trade war between India and China, India and Nepal, cross-border terrorism and its direct and indirect impact on South Asia to name only a few have created a security environment that raises more doubts and concerns than hope and optimism. There has emerged in the sub-continent a pattern of thinking in which there are only two adversaries India and its neighbours, with each accusing the others as the primary course of regional unrest and security.[105]

The threat perceptions of a nation in a given span of time are manifested to the geo-strategic environment of the area of its physical location. Threat perceptions are relational and emanate from the capabilities and threatening behaviour of a real or perceived by groups or parties in power and with changes in the ruling party or group, the threat perception often change, sanctions the changes and differences are perception in only marginal even though radical transformation may have taken place at the decision-making level. Dissimilar political units or ruling groups are likely to generate different perceptions of the threat.

Threat perception, in fact determines the level of security and defence to be strengthened. Threat is however, difference between the two concepts. The concept of defence is basically a concept that is responsive to an offence committed due to aggression. It medicates attack by defending and guarding the borders. The policy formulated is an offensive or defensive policy and is generally regarded as defence policy, security, on the other hand, is not merely confined to defending territory. Its real meaning is securing the state from threat perceptions. These threats may or may not be just limited to territory. Security therefore is a much wider term than defence. It includes in its fold both the internal and external threats to a state of all kinds. In the recent years, the concept of security has also become to include the concept of deterrence, i.e. that ability to deter against a threat. It requires an element of power and capability that will be able to thwart threat perceptions that may be generated. It encompasses the capacity to nullify (deter) the intentions of an intended aggressor to the extent that the aggressor will not commit aggression. And if an aggression was committed, loss to aggressor would be more because he will make use of the attacks. Thus a state's aim should be making it totally infeasible for only enemy to launch an attack.[106]

Each country's security needs a strong economic and indusial base and a cohesive social structure imbued with an idealism of its own. There is the relationship with other nation's foreign policy to influence those nations to further or at least not hinder the country's programmes. Then there is also the defence apparatus whose functions to withstand any attempt by other nations to resort to force or to deflect the country from the course of action the country has set for it.[107]

In the context of South Asian Security, M.G. Weinbanm says, "the new kinds of threat currently being faced by South Asian States call for an expansion of the term security to include not just security for military threats, but also from economic, social and ecological threats, all of which have emerged as factors affecting the validity of the contemporary nation-state system.[108] The most comprehensive views on security particularly in the Indian and its neigthbours context, have been expressed by noted Indian defence analyst K. Subrahmanyam. He feels that those familiar with western literature will define the concept of national security as the ability of a nation to protect its internal values from external threat." Walter Lipman's security definition says that a nation has security when it does not have to sacrifice its legitimate interest to avoid war. Subrahmanyan feels that while these definitions adequately cover the concept as applied to the stabilized nation-state of the industrialized West, these are inadequate to encompass the entire area of the problem faced by such a heterogeneous and developing nation like India. For a developing country like India, one of the most populated in the world, with the potential to develop into a major power, national security does not mean merely safeguarding territorial boundaries. It means also ensuring, that the country is in fact developing rapidly and has a cohesive egalitarian and technological society. Any thing that comes in the way of its development internally or externally is a threat to India's national security.[109] In short, we can define security as exclusive of threat—both internal and external dangers to a nation and perception, i.e. the art of perceiving these threats. It has various pre-requisites:

- Maintenance of sufficient military capacity in a world based on concept of power.
- Balance between defence and development.
- The appropriate strategic doctrine for the armed forces.
- The ability to deter.[110]

Furthermore, national security is the ability of a nation to use its national power for the preservation, protection and furtherance of its core values or national aims and objectives what most people do not understand is that the concept of national security is much wider than the defence of the borders or territorial integrity. It is the total preservation of state, a country's political, social and economic well-being, and the involvement of territorial boundaries and the maintenance of national interest. A realization and comprehensive approach to national security therefore includes economic strength, internal cohesion and technological capability besides the strategic aspects. The security spectrum is very complex these days. It is no longer visualized in narrow military terms, conventional threats as well as non-military threats, arising out of economic backwardness, poor governance; international and national terrorism, ethnic conflicts, fundamentalism, communal disturbances, migration and environmental pollution, all impinge upon the security of a nation. All the more, a secure national environment is the need of the hour which is considered to be a multidimensional phenomenon, where the totalities of political, economic, technical, social, cultural and defence activities nurture an atmosphere of political stability and national progress.[111] There are certain parameters of security which are well recognized and play an important role in determining security and threat perception. Geography and geo-strategic location of a country determines to a great extent the kind of a security and defence policy a state has to adopt. Geography includes land borders, territorial ranges, terrain, river sources, power, nature of territory, long coastline, etc. Geo-strategic location highlights the importance various territories occupy *vis-à-vis* its threat perception at global and regional level. Oceans and islands that a state possesses are also sometimes crucial for its strategy and security. The economic power, i.e. the infrastructure available and possession of strong labour force having its own importance for the industrial capability of a nation's trade and agricultural development are regarded as the backbone of a nation. Strong and stable political system, supported by political elite of repute, provide extra support to national security. Military power and possession of nuclear weapons increases the importance of state tremendously. Nuclear power gives the ability to deter against a threat which is an important dimension for state. A strong and effective communication system is a must for national security.

Satellites, space, radar and missile technologies are essentially to build a strong security system. Last but not the least, insecurity perceptions one has to look at the ability and capabilities of neighbouring states in overall security terms and security perceptions have to be continuously fed with information it has regarding the requirement and upholding the security needs.[112]

Pakistan's nuclear programme was principally influenced by security considerations. Pakistan had indigenously built its nuclear capability to neutralize the conventional asymmetry *vis-à-vis* India, and not transfer its nuclear technology to other states. Hence, the proliferation of nuclear technologies, that too to the axis of enemy states, like Iran and North Korea is obviously not the policy objective of Pakistan. Rather, it is against the national interests of Pakistan. Pakistan's nuclear policy inherently is security-centric with the perception of a dominant security threat emanating from India's conventional and nuclear programmes. Pakistan's nuclear potential fundamentally as claimed by the Pakistani government is designed to erect a credible minimum deterrent against aggression and to safeguard the country's independence and sovereignty, and not to use nuclear weapons, or to threaten to employ them against any non-nuclear weapons state.

The genesis of strengthening of Pakistan's nuclear programme can be traced back to the vision of Z.A. Bhutto who immediately after assuming the office of the President of Pakistan had called the meeting of the top Pakistan's nuclear scientists and desired

> . . . that nuclear bomb must be in Pakistan's possession, fixing a three years deadline. He was aware of limitations of Pakistan in respect of the huge expenditure involved in producing a bomb and the possible reactions from the US and others. He had planned to raise money for the project from the Islamic countries and in this way to mother an "Islamic" bomb (as distinct from a purely national Pakistan bomb), the wrath of the world would not be directed against Pakistan.[113]

During the decade of the 1950s, the US nuclear policy was guided by cold war imperatives. The US, therefore, assented the nuclear weapons programmes of chosen cold war partners, ignored the nuclear ambitions of other potential cold war allies. In the South Asian context, the US provided training, technology, and materials for India's nuclear energy programme under the Atom for Peace Programme. Aimed at promoting the peaceful use of nuclear energy, the programme placed effective curbs on the diversion of technology and hardware to nuclear weapons programme by states such as India. By the 1960s, more concerned about the spread of the bomb, Washington employed incentives to persuade states to adjure nuclear weapons, making such inducements conditional on acceptable non-proliferation behaviour. The 1968 Nuclear Non-proliferation Treaty promised access to nuclear technology in returns for non-proliferation pledges. However, this emphasis on conditional incentives was not linked to stringent sanctions. The only sanction imposed on non-signatory states was a denial of nuclear technology and material assistance.

India was among the states that refused to sign the NPT. Neither promised incentives nor the threatening sanctions contained in the NPT influenced India's decision-makers, since their nuclear weapons programme was underway. India's political leadership and its scientific bureaucratic state were determined to attain a nuclear weapon capability.[114] India's humiliating defeat in its war with China in 1962 and the Chinese acquisition of nuclear weapon strengthened India perceptions that nuclear weapons confer both military security and political prestige.

The US response to India's nuclear ambitions was shaped by geopolitical considerations. Democratic India did not pose a threat to the US national security. The US was disinclined to exert non-proliferation' pressure since India confronted communist China,[115] the US officials therefore, chose to overlook India's fast expanding technology and materials for India's civilian nuclear programme even after India's refusal to join NPT. Neighbouring Pakistan also acquired a nascent nuclear infrastructure as the result of the US assistance under Atoms for Energy Programmes. A cold war ally of the US and thus the recipient of the US preferential arms and economic assistance, Pakistan's political dominant/ military was initially expanding nuclear weapons infrastructure and continuing hostility between the two countries motivated Pakistan to explore the nuclear weapons options. Nuclear weapons were perceived as a means of matching India's technological powers, countering India's conventional superiority, and offsetting its regional influence. The first signs of Pakistan's nuclear ambitions became evident when it refused to join the NPT. In subsequent years, as Pakistan embarked on a nuclear weapons programme after defeat in the 1971 war, its nuclear choices were influenced by theUS policy towards India.

Neither country had signed the NPT, although Pakistan insisted that, it would do so if India did. It was a safe stance taken by her. India insisted that it would not sign the NPT or entertain a regional accord so long China retained its nuclear capability. Both countries still object to what they characterized as discriminatory aspect of the NPT, which allows the five acknowledged nuclear states to keep their weapons but bans others from joining the club. In addition, while both countries did not admit of seeking nuclear weapons, strategists in both countries had pronounced, the years after NPT was formally launched that they wanted to use nuclear weapons as a deterrence similar to those popularized during the US-Soviet cold war, and argued that nuclear weapons could be stabilizing rather than the reverse.

In response to India's nuclear explosions on 18 May 1974, the US non-proliferation strategists shifted from incentives to denials regimes and sanctions. The US Congress enacted Symington and Glenn Amendments and the 1978 Nuclear Nonproliferation Act (NNPA), requiring full scope safeguards for the transfer of nuclear hardware and material, and threatening military and economic sanctions on any state attempting to acquire or supply unsafe guarded nuclear technologies. Sanctions were also to be imposed on any non-nuclear weapons state that conducted a nuclear explosion. The US did not however, "develop or implement tangible targeted and sustained sanctions against India's nuclear weapon programme." On the contrary, the US agreed to reschedule India's external debt increased its economic assistance to India, and for a few years continued to supply nuclear fuel to India's nuclear reactors.[116] India was exempted from Congressionally managed sanctions, since these were only applicable to states that conducted nuclear explosions after the enactment of the legislation. The modest measures that were eventually employed—halting the transfer of nuclear weapons materials and technology—failed to change the cost benefit analysis of India's nuclear decision-makers since the cost imposed were insufficiently large, the US backed multilateral strategies to curtail the diffusion of unsafe guarded nuclear technology did slow the pace of India's weaponisation. India's nuclear weapons programme suffered as a result of the suspension of foreign technology transfer and assistance.[117] But these sanctions did not reverse India's nuclear development. India was capable of sustaining its nuclear weapon programme through indigenous means and it continued its efforts to achieve nuclear weapons status.

Had the US opted for either a formal or an *ad-hoc* multilateral regime, targeted somehow against India, it could have decisively influenced the nuclear policies of both India and Pakistan. Although its close ties with the Soviet Union would have helped India to circumvent some of the pressure of a US led sanctions regime such sanctions would have sent a strong signal of international disapproval, strengthening nuclear opponents in the internal Indian debate. In the Pakistani context, where the military was still hopeful of reviving its previously close strategic and economic relationship with the US, the economic and diplomatic costs of a US sponsored sanctions regime against India could have dissuaded Pakistan from following the suit.

India's 1974 nuclear explosion and the US failure to impose sanctions against India motivated Pakistan to accelerate its nuclear activities import some components from France. Although the US dissuaded France from going ahead with the sale, Washington failed to reverse the course of Pakistan nuclear proliferation. Exploiting the absence of an international consensus on countering nuclear proliferation and the gaps in the non-proliferation legislation of supplier states, Pakistan acquired nuclear technology and know-how through alternative sources of supply or through clandestine means.[118]

The Indian test marked the beginning of a long and unresolved struggle between successive US administration and Congress over how best to deter proliferations. For the most part, the US policy has concentrated on denying access to nuclear materials and technology, both through export controls and threats to withhold the US foreign assistance.

For a number of reasons, this strategy has fallen more heavily on Pakistan. *First,* India's nuclear programme was largely sufficient, whereas Pakistan needed to obtain nuclear technology from abroad. *Second,* while India's blast was an accomplished fact, the Ford and Carter Administrations, and non-proliferation activities in Congress and outside, wanted to nip the Pakistani effort in the bud and thereby to prevent nuclear arms race in the regions. *Third,* Pakistan's Prime Minister Bhutto talked of a "Islamic Bomb" and it gave greater urgency to preventing the development of technology that might be shared with Middle Eastern states, although many analysts judged that threat unlikely. In the mid to late 1970s, the Ford and Carter Administrations put strong pressure on France and suspended aid to Pakistan in order to get the French government to cancel a contract to build a large plutonium reprocessing plant in Pakistan. During the same period, the US Congress enacted several landmark non-proliferation provisions. This included the Foreign Assistance Act of 1961, amended (FAA), the body of law that governs the US and arms sales policies, Section 669 of FAA bars the US aid to enrichments improvement, materials or technology not under international safeguards Section 670 bans aid to countries that acquire plutonium reprocessing material, or that acquire, detonate, or transfer a nuclear explosive device.[119]

In one respect, India did fall foul US non-proliferation legislation. In 1980, the US terminated nuclear cooperation with India as a consequence of passage of the 1978 Nuclear Proliferation Act (NNPA), which required countries receiving the US nuclear materials or technology or materials to accept the so-called "full scope safeguards" by putting their entire national facilities has under international inspection. This action ultimately led to the termination of sales of fuel and spare parts to the US built Tarapur Atomic Power Station, which was already under safeguards and which had played no role in India's underground explosion. In order to gain India's commitment to maintain safeguards on the Tarapur Rectors and spent fuel, the Reagan Administration concluded a Tripartite Agreement with India and France in 1983, under which France agreed to supply needed fuel and spare parts. This made the US action largely symbolic in effect.

In 1979, the US cut-off aid to Pakistan under section 669 after it had learned that Pakistan had secretly begun construction of a uranium enrichment facility. Following the Soviet invasion of Afghanistan, the US Congress passed a new Pakistan specific provisions to the FAA section 620 E to provide a legal frame work for the reestablishment of the US assistance to Pakistan, thereby bolstering that country against Soviet pressure and facilitating the US aid to the Afghan resistance movement based in Afghanistan. The new sections gave the US President the authority to wave the applicability of section 669 in the national security interest, even through Pakistan had not abandoned its uranium enrichment programme. The legislative change set the stage for a six years $3.2 billion programme of economic and military aid to Pakistan, including the sale of F-16 Fighter Bombers.[120]

Throughout the 1980s actions by Pakistani repeated challenged the premise advanced by the Reagan Administration that support of Pakistan's conventional security requirements would reduce its incentives to pursue the nuclear options. By the mid-1980s, it became unmistakably clear that Islamabad would spare no effort to acquire a nuclear weapons capability, even to the context of violating the US export control laws to acquire needed technology and materials. In response the US Congress began progressively to circumscribe the President's authority to provide aid to Pakistan.[121]

Frustration over Pakistan's resistance to the US pressure led Congress in 1985 to end section 620 E(L), the so-called "Pressler Amendment" that required the President to certify annually that Pakistan did not possesses nuclear weapons as a condition of continued US assistance and arms and technologies transfers. President Reagan and Bush made several annual certifications, but each successive year's funding was more hedged with qualifications than the previous one. Due to reasons, known only to the Bush Administration, President failed to make the necessary certification on or about 10 October 1990, the beginning of fiscal year 1991 leading to a cutoff of most new US aid. As a result of the President's failure to certify for FY 1991, all new economic assistance and all military aid and foreign military financing (FMF) sales were stopped. At the time of the cutoff, about $700 million in economic aid remained in the "pipeline." This money continued to flow at the rate of about 200$ million per year until the previously obligated funds expended or projects were terminated in an orderly manner. More than few years after the inception of the cutoff, it continued to extract additional penalties. In late December 1998, the US Government asked Pakistan to return eight frigates and a supply ship that had been leased to Pakistan Navy. The 1950s and 1960s vintage ships, account for more than half of Pakistan's total of fourteen major surface combatants.[122]

The aid cutoff left a number of loopholes for the Bush Administration that apparently was not anticipated by the US Congress when it adopted the Presseler Amendment. In controversial actions, the Administration continued to allow commercial sales and spare parts for cash on a cash by cash basis, on grounds that there was precedent in similar situations for doing so. As of mid-1992, the State Department repeatedly had issued export licenses totaling more than 100$ million since the aid cutoff, including spare parts for F-16 fighter planes and Cobra attack helicopters.[123]

Critics of the US Administration's policy of continuing to sell Pakistan spare parts, including Senators Lary Presseler, John Glenn, and Claiborne Pell, among other considered that it undermined the aid cutoff and costs about on US determination to pursue a regional and global non-proliferation policy. The Senate Foreign Relations Committee held a hearing as the statutory meaning of the Presseler Amendment on 30 July 1992, without any apparent result in term of Administration's interpretation of the disputed section. The Congress itself had shown concern about the consequences of total end of aid to Pakistan and on several occasions had made amendments that had explicitly ended or relaxed the aid ban. In September 1992, during action on the FY 1993 Foreign Operations Appropriations Act, PL 102-391, the Congress adopted a little noticed Senate Appropriations Committee amendment to the Foreign Appropriations Act that appeared to have the effect of relaxing somewhat the development assistance to Pakistan.[124]

Although the new section does not mention any particular country, some Congressional sources suggested the change was adopted specifically to apply to Pakistan. It did not follow any policy debate and it was doubtful if most members voting on the Senate Bill or the conference report were aware of its significance. Both the US Congress and the administration in the late eighties and early nineties had agreed upon the need for a regional solution to the threat of nuclear weapons proliferation, thereby implicitly acknowledging that if Pakistan has felt the main force of the US anti-proliferation policies, India and Pakistan were equally part of the problem. Both branches of the US Government had endorsed a proposal by Pakistan for five power talks (India, Pakistan, China, Russia and the US) on nuclear non-proliferation in South Asia. P.L 102-391, the Foreign Assistant Appropriation Act for FY 1993, added a new section 620 F to the Foreign Assistance Act that established a regional accord as a US policy goal and required the President to report to the Congress every six months the progress in this direction. All the parties except India had conveyed their desire to accept the five-power proposal. India had opposed any such regional agreement that would allow China to keep its own weapons. (As envisioned China would only be guarantor of a regional accord but would retain its nuclear weapons) conscious of how strong the US concern about this issue, India engaged in a high level dialogue with the US in New Delhi in mid-June 1992, but no new ground was broken. As of late 1992, the State Department was seeking to initiate an indirect dialogue between India and Pakistan, with the US as go between, somewhat along the lines of Middle East peace talks.[125]

The US Administration had taken a serious view of the efforts made by the Pakistan Government to strengthen its nuclear weapons programme. Though, it was just not possible for the US to compel Pakistan to abandon its nuclear programme because in the early nineties it was on a very advanced stage that it was not easy for the Pakistan Government to cap its nuclear programme, mainly because of its domestic and security compulsions.

On the other hand, as judged by its actions and reactions, Pakistan was determined to produce nuclear bombs. It was believed in the end of sixties that if India becomes a nuclear power, the security assurance given to Pakistan under the alliances and pacts were of no avail at the time of Indian nuclear attack.[126] It was very much clear after Pakistan stand on NPT that if India would take steps to strengthen its nuclear programme, Pakistan government would like, if possible, a step ahead. Z.A. Bhutto, the main architect of Pakistan's nuclear programme wrote that "it is vital for Pakistan to give the greatest possible attention to nuclear technology, rather than to allow her to be deceived by an international treaty .... India is unlikely to concede nuclear monopoly to others and judging from her own nuclear programme and her diplomatic activities... It appears that she is determined to proceed with her plans to detonate a nuclear bomb. If Pakistan restricts or suspends her nuclear programme, it would not only enable India to blackmail, Pakistan with her nuclear advantage but would impose a crippling limitation on the development of Pakistan's science and technology."[127] He made it clear that Pakistan won't mind in producing nuclear device but everything depends upon India. Indian nuclear programme was built with foreign assistance, and she would be getting technical know-how in the future also. He further said, "Pakistan must therefore, conceive a similar programme, although a nuclear weapon will be a real deterrent."[128]

It was believed that a nuclear deterrent, if at all was the goal of Pakistan, would not check Pakistan from strengthening its military capability by collecting conventional arms. The conventional deterrent was the need of the hour, and in its absence Pakistan won't mind to respond to any attack or incursion with massive retaliation to aggression. Pakistan's bomb would not necessarily provide greater deterrence to an Indian attack than effectively conventional weapons, although it would surely have Indian perception of risk. Pakistan is already having the air strike capacity to deeply penetrate and has sufficient strength to inflict serious damage and thus to deter possible (though unlikely) Indian attack. Pakistan does not, however, have the strength and capability to defeat, Indian military, nor would nuclear weapons give it that strength.[129] The nuclear Pakistan would qualitatively change the strategic environment of South Asia.[130]

The Indian detonation of a nuclear device in May 1974 was accepted by the government of Pakistan as a challenge as "it generated new fear possible of future black mail. Z.A. Bhutto's often quoted remarks that Pakistan people "will eat grass if necessary to match the Indian nuclear capability in fact, reflected the intensity of helplessness and insecurity."[131] It stepped up activities in erecting sufficient infrastructure for the nuclear weapons programme. Indian government had categorically declared that it had no programme of producing nuclear weapons and would like to use nuclear energy for peaceful purposes. The nuclear explosion by India had created near panic in Pakistan. Bhutto, then Pakistan's Prime Minister warned that "if India builds the bomb, we will eat leaves or grass, even go hungry but we will have to get one."[132] At a press conference on 19 May 1974, Bhutto said that we will never let Pakistan be a victim of nuclear blackmail."[133] He also explained the steps Pakistan was going to take in response to India's nuclear explosion. He demanded nuclear umbrella from all the "five great powers."[134]

A number of other factors also contributed a lot and encouraged Pakistan to develop its nuclear programme. An American analysts Shirin Tahir Kheli, who was once related with Reagan's National Security Council felt that "the Russian invasion of Afghanistan, the exit of the Shah of Iran and emergence of fundamentalists, the subsequent election of Reagan as President of the US were some of the developments which boosted the Pakistani nuclear programme. Had these regional and international events not taken place, the situation would have been altogether different as substantial political and economic costs might have had to be paid by Pakistan for its current nuclear posture and it could not have continued its nuclear programme with such vigour."[135]

If we go through the history of Pakistan's nuclear programme, it would not be unfair to conclude that a covert purchasing activity of Pakistan to acquire ultracentrifuge technology was quite long.[136] It not only pointed to the lacuna in the export laws governing nuclear technologies but also to how existing laws could easily be by-passed. It also showed up Pakistan as master manipulator in the nuclear black market and its ability to step ahead of the law. At the centre of purchases was a German trained Pakistani nuclear scientist Dr. Abdul Qadir Khan. He was asked to prepare a blue print for strengthing Pakistan's nuclear structure. He worked in the Netherlands from 1972-75 for FDO, a subcontractor of URENCO, the British–Dutch–West German Uranium Consortium. From mid-1974, Khan was believed to have passed on URENCO classified enrichment know how to Pakistan. By mid-1975, he had been banned by such authorities from further enrichment related work. Subsequently he fled to Pakistan and was made in charge of Centrifuge Enrichment Programme.[137]

If one analyses the press reports and statements of mid-eighties, it could be easily assumed that Pakistan, if desired so could, produce nuclear bomb within no time. Dr. Khan, in an interview with Kuldip Nayar, an Indian journalist gave the impression that Pakistan was having a nuclear bomb in her kitty. He said, "the US know it what the CIA has been saying about our possessing the bomb is correct and so is the speculation of certain foreign newspapers" when enquired by Nayar, "why do not you announce that you have a bomb", he replied, "Is it necessary?" Regarding its testing he said, "the testing does not have to be on the ground. It can be done in a laboratory through a simulator. Planes are flown after testing their capability in simulators" India's nuclear programme, according to Dr. Khan, was not for peaceful purposes. Infact, he was very critical of India. "It is you who have forced us to go nuclear. The super-powers had to because of mutual fear, China being a big country had to make the bomb because both the Soviet Union and the US had it, why should you have done it? India had no such serious security problems. It had a friendship treaty with the Soviet Union. This was meant to threaten us, to establish its hegemony in the region, we were left with no alternatives. In fact, it was as a result of the Indian betrayal of trust that the Canadians abruptly cutoff all cooperation with us.[138]

On the very next day after the publication of the interview, Dr. Khan denied having granted any interview to any Indian Journalist and described the words attributed to him as mischievous, false and concocted and an attempt to malign Pakistan. He reiterated that Pakistan's modest nuclear research and development programme was solely for peaceful purposes.[139] The US Government was sharing Pakistan's view point. The then US Defence Secretary Weinberger in a nationwide TV programme on NBC said that Pakistan was no where close to having a nuclear weapon. Dean Hinton, the then US Ambassador to Pakistan said that "India is closer to a much bigger nuclear weapons capability than Pakistan."[140]

The question arose why Pakistan was not accepting the fact that it was capable of making a nuclear bomb? *First*, "the Pakistani leaders may want to remain close to nuclear weapon capability, is to hedge against Indian production of nuclear weapons." Furthermore as India is militarily superior to Pakistan in terms of conventional military forces, possession of a nuclear weapon would deter conventional attack by India. This competition had definitely provided incentives to Pakistan to strive for a nuclear capability, it had on the other hand given Pakistan a reason not to assemble or test a nuclear device, India would definitely resume its own nuclear testing. As India had strong base as far as its nuclear capability was concerned, it was quite doubtful that Pakistan could hold its own in a nuclear arms race with India. That was the reason adopted for an ambiguous position regarding its nuclear programme and intentions.[141] *Second*, as the US laws do not permit economic and military aid, those who are in the process of producing nuclear weapons, the Pakistan Government knew these actions would cause considerable damage to the economic and military aid programme, and such a cutoff would have severe consequences for Pakistan's security. Pakistan was the fourth largest recipient of the US aid, after Israel, Egypt and Turkey.[142]

Third, the Soviet presence in Afghanistan had influenced the thinking of those who were in favour of strengthening the nuclear capability. They felt that nuclear capability was required to deter Soviet military action.[143] The Soviet Union might in a swift move destroy Pakistan's nuclear installations. This fear had also compelled Pakistan to adopt a dubious attitude on her nuclear capability.

Fourth, it was an open secret that Pakistan's nuclear programme was heavily financed by the Arab world because it was believed that the Arab states would like to use Pakistani nuclear bomb "as a counter-weight to Israel's suspected nuclear capability as an affirmation of Islamic technical powers." But in the same way, Pakistani authorities were aware that if they demonstrated their nuclear capability, this would invoke a pre-emptive strike by Israel against Pakistan nuclear facilities similar to the Israeli air strike against Iran's nuclear reactor.[144]

While making the case for Pakistani nuclear capability and other allied matters related with it, one must keep in mind the arguments about the stability of nuclear deterrence. They are:

- Would it be in Pakistan's interest to stimulate India to develop and deploy nuclear weapons?
- In what circumstances, if any, could nuclear weapon rationally be used?
- Would the existence of such capabilities be stabilizing or destabilizing?
- What exceptional command and central measures would be required to avoid mistaken use of nuclear weapons?
- Are there other policies and other uses for resources that would better advance Pakistan's national interest?
- Would Pakistan be better or worse-off if it gained international cooperation and support for its peaceful nuclear programme by permitting international inspection of all its facilities?

These questions were raised by Dean Hinton on 16 February 1987 while delivering a lecture at Institute for Strategic Studies in Islamabad.[145] These issues raised by Hinton were quite relevant. Keeping in mind the changing international environment and the political scenario in South Asia region, there was no second opinion that if Pakistan goes nuclear, India would definitely take effective steps to contain Pakistan's nuclear threat. It might be in the form of producing nuclear weapons, for which India was quite advanced or to seek a guarantee from the Soviet Union in case of Pakistan's nuclear attack, the latter would be on her side with full strength. To avoid this type of situation, Pakistan must convince the world political elites that its nuclear programme was for peaceful purposes.

As India had shown too much concern towards Pakistan's nuclear programme, in the late nineties, there were speculations of pre-emptive strike by India against Pakistan. At that time there were the following nuclear facilities available in Pakistan:

- Kahuta Uranium Centrifuge Plant.
- Chesma Reprocessing Plant.
- Islamabad Reprocessing Plant.
- Karachi Nuclear Power Plant.

Kahuta would probably be the most critical single target in destroying Pakistan's capacity to develop a nuclear weapon. Kahuta however, is underground and well-protected. An Indian air strike or commando raid would have no guarantee of success. A pre-emptive strike, either by Indian or by a third power with Indian collaboration, would carry high costs for war with India. It would draw international sanctions and possible embargo of Middle Eastern oil, and expulsion of Indian worker from the Gulf. But beyond the risks of failure, strike against Pakistani nuclear facilities involve the danger of released plutonium and the deadly efforts of radiation poising over a wide area including northern India. A pre-emptive strike against Pakistan would also likely to bring Pakistani action against Indian nuclear reactors India was not likely to bring such destruction upon herself.[146] To make the record clear, Pakistan had put forward a series of proposals to India to diffuse the tension. These were:

- Signing of the NPT.
- Bilateral inspection of each other facilities.
- A collective and therefore, binding joint declaration by India/Pakistan renouncing the acquisition or manufacture of nuclear weapons.
- Agreement on a South Asia Nuclear Weapons Free Zone.[147]

Nuclear Weapons Free Zone

Between 1970 and 1975, there was an increasing interest in creating Nuclear Weapons Free Zones (NWFZ) in various regions of the World similar to that established for Latin America under the 1967 Treaty of Talelolco. At the request of the Pakistan, an item concerning the establishment of a NWFZ in South Asia was included in the agenda of the General Assembly's 29th session. In its explanatory memorandum, Pakistan indicated that it envisaged a regime of security for South Asia which had become necessary and urgent in order to ensure the proliferation of nuclear weapons.[148]

During the debate in the First Committee, Pakistan stressed that there was no difference between a peaceful nuclear explosion and the explosion that was conducted by India in May 1974. He felt that India's test would encourage nuclear proliferation in South Asia. India responded that it had no intentions to develop nuclear weapons and that it would use nuclear energy and technology, including underground use of nuclear explosions for peaceful purposes. India also held that South Asia could not be considered a distinct zone, as it was an integral part of the Asia and Pacific region which was surrounded by nuclear weapon states or countries belonging to the other alliances.[149]

In the debate on the proposals India stated that, in the past it had supported NWFZ in Latin America and Africa. Weapons conditions were suitable for the establishment of such zones in those areas and because the countries in each area had agreed to join their common efforts. That, it maintained, was not the case in South Asia, where no prior consultation had taken place and no agreement had been reached in a matter having a bearing on the vital interests of each country in the area. Pakistan, on the other hand, held that its Draft Resolution as far as possible had accommodated India's legitimate preoccupations and concerns sincerely NWFZ in South Asia. Afghanistan, Bangladesh, Bhutan and Mauritius agreed that the countries of the region should first consult among themselves on question concerning the creation of NWFZ before seeking endorsement of the Assembly. Sri Lanka endorsing the principle of such a zone, held that the concept should be defined through consultation with the all other states concerned.[150]

Pakistan's suggestion for the creation of NWFZ in South Asia amounted to the creation of such a zone at the cost of India and to the benefit of China. These moves were strongly opposed by India. With regard to the proposal for NWFZ, India pointed out that no consultation regarding its implications, possibility and all out ability took place before item was inscribed in the agenda of the 29th General Assembly Session. India was of the opinion that such arrangements could only be developed and matured from within the region concerned. For this purpose, South Asia could not be treated in isolation. It is a sub- region and an integral part of the region of Asia and the pacific. It is necessary to take into account the security environment of that region as a whole. A genuine NWFZ in the region could only fall in the total absence of nuclear weapons.[151]

As the world was marching towards nuclear non-proliferation, and the US, Russia and China had decided to cut their nuclear arsenal, India was from the very beginning demanding these cuts, but the US and Russia had refused to link the cuts to an ultimate goal of universal and complete disarmament to India's expectations. New Delhi was perturbed by the trend towards American Chinese cooperation. Probably, the Americans started treating China as the fast emerging number two power in the world with the new Sino-US partnership. It "became increasingly clear that traditional strategy of rallying the world's forces to create an alternative to the super power sponsored nuclear order offered few payoffs and entitled growing risks."[152]

With the Soviet withdrawal from Afghanistan in early 1989 and the suspension of the US aid to Pakistan in late 1990 over Islamabad's resumption of enrichment of weapon grade uranium, the Bush Administration concluded that the time was ripe to solve the increasingly dangerous South-Asia nuclear issue. During the 1990 India Pakistan's confrontation both countries had readied their "basement bombs" moving substantially close to outright weaponization. Washington's solution proposed in spring 1992 was to concern a meeting of India, Pakistan, Russia, China and the US to establish and guarantee a NWFZ. India did not agree with the proposal. New Delhi argument was that it meant India would accept permanent nuclear inferiority to China and assume a status equivalent to Pakistan, with completely surrendering the national interest and foreign policy objectives to Washington, Moscow and Beijing. In order to counter the proposal, New Delhi advocated a call for global efforts to put restrictions on nuclear weapons and their proliferation.[153]

An argument put forward in this context was that as creation of NWFZ in South Asia meant that India should renounce its right to develop operational nuclear capabilities but such remunerations should not be neutral, instead the nuclear proliferation in this region should be managed in such a way that it should "reduce the threat of three participating countries—India, Pakistan and China—posed to each other and to the degree possible, reduce the cost of potentially open ended arms race, especially between India[154] and Pakistan. This alternative which has been conceptualized as viable" in conjunction with some definite moves on the global scale towards substantial nuclear arms reduction and disarmament required negotiated and verifiable agreements committed both by India and Pakistan to eschew the development of nuclear weaponry while simultaneously constructing both the pattern and type of Chinese nuclear deployment in proximity to the sub-continent. Such a limited nuclear arms race control regime could consist of either multiple bilateral arrangements that would be man made for the three states to the maintenance of NWFZ support if necessary, by arranging the security guarantee like concluding "No War Pact" or getting other political commitments from the other nuclear powers. Strictly speaking, the NWFZ would resultantly in India and Pakistan eschewing the production and deployment of nuclear weapons. China would remain a nuclear weapon state but would undertake binding obligations that would diminish the nuclear threat it posed to India in the context of overall resolutions of the current Sino-Indian territorial dispute, China's residual nuclear capabilities would then by implications be reserved only for contingencies involving US and Russia. They would be treaty bound allies within while a NWFZ of this sort has never been formally tabled for discussion at the diplomatic level.[155]

PAKISTAN'S NUCLEAR WEAPONS PROGRAMME: SOME FACTS

In 1985, Pakistan crossed the threshold of weapons grade uranium production, and by 1986, it seemed to have produced enough fissile material for a nuclear weapon. Pakistan continued advancing its uranium enrichment programme and according to Pakistani sources, it acquired the ability to carryout a nuclear explosion in 1987.

On 28 May 1998, Pakistan announced that it had successfully conducted five nuclear tests. The Pakistan Atomic Energy Commission reported that the five tests conducted on 28 May generated a seismic signal of 5.0 on the Richter scale, with a total yield of up to KT (equivalent TNT). Dr. A.Q. Khan claimed that one device was a boosted fission device that the other four were sub-kiloton nuclear devices.

On 30 May 1998, Pakistan tested one more nuclear warhead with a reported yield of 12 kilotons. The tests were conducted at Balochistan, bringing the total number of claimed tests to six. It was also claimed by the Pakistan sources that at least one additional device, initially planned for detonation on 30 May 1998, remained emplaced underground ready for detonation.

Pakistan claims concerning the number of yields of their underground tests could not be independently confirmed by seismic means, and several sources, such as the

Southern Arizona Observatory Laboratory. Seismic observations had reported lower yields than claimed by Pakistan. Indian sources had also suggested that as few as two weapons were actually detonated, each with yields considerably lower than claimed by Pakistan. However, seismic data showed at least two and possibly a third, much smaller test in the initial rounds. The single test on 30 May provided a clear seismic signal.[156]

Device	*Date*	*Yield (announced)*	*Yield (estimated)*
[Boosted device?]	28 May 1998	25-36 kiloton	Total 9-12 kiloton
Fission device	28 May 1998	12 kiloton	
Low yield device	28 May 1998	Sub-kiloton	--
Low yield device	28 May 1998	Sub-kiloton	--
Low yield device	28 May 1998	Sub-kiloton	--
Fission device	28 May 1998	12 kiloton	4-6 kiloton
Fission device	28 May 1998	12 kiloton	

Note: This table lists the nuclear tests that Pakistan claims to have carried out in May 1998 as well as the announced yields. Other sources have reported lower yields than those claimed by Pakistan.

Southern Arizona Seismic Observatory reports that the total seismic yield for the May 28th tests was 9-12 kilotons and that the yield for the May 30th tests was 4-6 kilotons.

According to a preliminary analysis conducted in Los Alamos National Laboratory material released into the atmosphere during underground nuclear tests by Pakistan in May 1998 contained low levels of weapon grade plutonium. The significance of Los Alamos findings was that Pakistan had neither imported nor produced plutonium indicated by the US Intelligence wings. But Lawrence Livermore National Laboratory and other agencies later contested the accuracy of this finding.

These tests came slightly more than two weeks after India carried out five tests of its own on 11 and 13 May 1998 and after many warnings by Pakistani officials that they would respond to India.[157]

Pakistan's tests were followed by February 1999 Lahore Agreements between Prime Minister Vajpaee and Sharif. The agreements included CBM's such as advance notice of ballistic missiles testing and continuation of their unlimited moratorium on nuclear testing. But diplomatic advances made that year were undermined by Pakistan's incursion into Kargil.[158]

Pakistan's nuclear programme is based on Highly Enriched Uranium (HEU), which is produced at the A.Q. Khan Research Laboratory of Kahuta, a gas centrifuge uranium enrichment facility. The Kahuta facility has been in operation since the early 1980s. By the early 1990s, Kahuta had an estimated 3000 centrifuges in operation and Pakistan continued its pursuit of expanded uranium enrichment capabilities.

In the 1990s, Pakistan began to pursue plutonium production capabilities with Chinese assistance, Pakistan built the 90 Mwt (megawatt thermal) Khusali reactor at Joharabad, and in April 1998, Pakistan announced that the reactor was operational. According to public statements made by the US officials, this unsafeguarded Heavy Water Reactor generates an estimated 8-10 kilotons of weapon grade plutonium per year, that is enough for one to two nuclear weapons. The reactor could also produce Tritium if loaded with lithium-6. According to J. Cirincione of Carnegie, Khusali's plutonium production capability could allow Pakistan to develop lighter nuclear warheads that would be easier to deliver with a ballistic missile.

Plutonium separation reportedly takes place at the New Labs reprocessing plant next to Pakistan's Institute of Nuclear Sciences and Technology (PINSTECH) in Rawalpindi and at the large Chasma Nuclear Power Plant, neither of which are subject to International Atomic Energy Agency (IAEA) inspection. The Natural Resources Defence Council (NRDC) estimated that Pakistan has built 24-28 HEU-based nuclear warheads, and Carnegie reports that they had produced 585-800 kg of HEU, enough for 30-35 weapons. Pakistan nuclear warheads are based on an implosion design that uses a solid core highly enriched uranium and requires an estimated 15-20 kg of material for warhead. According to Carnegie, Pakistan has also produced a small but unknown quantity of weapons grade plutonium which is sufficient for estimated 3-5 nuclear weapons. Pakistani authorities claim that their nuclear weapons are not assembled. They maintain that the fissile cores are stored separately from the delivery systems. In a 2001 report, the Defence Department contended that Islamabad nuclear weapons are probably stored in component form and that "Pakistan probably could assemble the weapon fairly quickly. However, no one has been able to ascertain the validity of Pakistan's assurances about their nuclear weapons security."

Pakistan's reliance priority on HEU makes its fissile materials particularly vulnerable to diversion. HEU can be used in a relatively simple gun-barrel type design which could be within the means of non-state actors that intend to assemble a crude nuclear weapon.[159]

The terrorist's attacks on 11 September raised concerns about the security of Pakistan's nuclear arsenal. According to press reports, within two days of the attacks, Pakistan's military began relocating nuclear weapons components to secret locations. Shortly, thereafter, Gen Pervez Musharaff fired his intelligence Chief and other offices and detained several suspected retired nuclear scientists, in an attempt to root out extremists elements that posed a potential threat to Pakistan nuclear arsenal. Concerns have also been raised about Pakistan as a proliferation of nuclear materials and expertise. In November 2002, shortly after North Korea admitted to pursuing nuclear weapons programme, the press reported that Pakistan had provided assistance in the development of uranium enrichment programme in exchange for North Korean missile technologies.[160]

Since November 2003, two episodes have highlighted some of the external dangers that threaten the safety and security of Pakistan's nuclear deterrent as well as reasons that the country remains a serious source of proliferation concern. The first was acknowledged by the Pakistani government that it was conducting an internal investigation into the activities of some of senior programme—for possibly proliferating nuclear technologies, technical knowledge, and technical know-how to Iran, in violation of Pakistani laws. And second, there were two nearly successful assassination attempts on the life of President Musharaff.

The KPL investigation comes amidst mounting evidence of Pakistan being one of the key sources of Iran's, North Korea's and Libya's centrifuge-based uranium enrichment programmes and that its nuclear entities and scientific personnel constitute the hub of an international cartel that has been engaged in such clandestine trade for nearly two decades.[161]

These disclosers had raised alarming questions about the credibility of Islamabad's non-proliferation assurances to the international community; the priority and ethics of proliferating weapons of mass destruction technologies in pursuit of narrow geo-political and domestic corporate interests, and the possibility that Pakistan entities and scientific personnel were allowed to operate with little governmental oversight. Furthermore, this emerging evidence combined with some of the accusation of cooperation between Al-Quaeda and senior Pakistani nuclear scientists suggests that Pakistan is confronted with serious personal reliability and dependability issues, and that Pakistani scientists might be willing to share secret concerning the nuclear arts with foreign governments or terrorists groups out of personal ideological and financial motivations. One could also surmise that if the Pakistan Army cannot guarantee the security of its Chief in its own citadel, the security cordon surrounding Pakistan's nuclear warheads is not impenetrable. Equally disturbing is the consensus among South Asia Regional security analysts that has given the army's dominating presence in domestic Pakistani politics, the absence of robust political institutions and the technique of inter-institutional consensus on major policy issues, the successful decapitation of the Army Chief would put a question mark on the political stability and future direction of Pakistan.[162]

Rumours have long been persisted that KPL transferred drawings, designs, starter kits, and facit knowledge for centrifuge-based uranium enrichment as well as information about procurement networks to Iran, Libya and North Korea. When Pakistan embarked on a nuclear weapon programme in the early 1970s, Prime Minister Z.A. Bhutto framed Pakistan's aspirations in civilization terms as they quest for an "Islamic bomb." Since then knowledgeable observers of Pakistani politics have dwelt on the linkage between Libyan and Saudi funding for Pakistan's nuclear weapons programme and potential Pakistani nuclear technology or weapon transfers to regimes in Middle-East.[163]

However, from the 1980s onwards, Pakistani government officials have denied Bhutto's formulation, and portrayed the nuclear weapons programme as a national enterprise driven by the strategic necessity of safeguarding their countries against a conventionally more powerful India. Equally significant, the nuclear enterprise was not the creation of radical Islamists. Rather, it was led by secularists in the Pakistani military and the scientific and technological community; and more driven by aspirations of professional excellence, national glory, and monetary gains than religious fervour. The Pakistani government denied that it ever authorized state to state transfers to Iran, Libya, or North Korea. However, Pakistani government sources have admitted that scientists from KRL likely shared technologies and know-how with Iran for personal monetary and career gains. But most foreign observers are skeptical that individual scientists and labs, which have powerful ties to the military and its intelligence agencies, could have pursued their agenda independently without either tacit or formal approval from their patrons and clients in the Pakistani state. Given the logistics of any technology and equipment transfers, the presumption is that the military authorized nuclear technology sales, as a means to finance the expansion of Pakistan's nuclear weapons and ballistic missile programmes, or exchanged with technologies for ballistic missiles and other relevant technologies.[164]

However, Pakistani observers suggest that the relationship between nuclear labs and the military has been far more complex than is generally perceived abroad. During the development phase of Pakistan's nuclear weapons programme, which lasted for the mid-1970s till the nuclear tests in 1998, the nuclear scientists and labs enjoyed considerable financial and organizational autonomy, and were only nominally answerable to the military. During this period, the end goal of acquiring a nuclear weapon capability gained precedence over the means to achieve it. Most probably, the nuclear labs and scientists who are distinguished for their entrepreneurship, could have conceivably engaged in unauthorized nuclear trades in pursuit of personal professional and organizational gains, not known to the Pakistan government.[165]

According to these observers, the Pakistan military only firmly established control over all levels of the nuclear weapons programme in the period following the nuclear tests in May 1998. Iran's efforts to revamp existing control, to coordinate the creation of development programmes with strategic policy and to plan the operational use of nuclear weapons, the Pakistani government formally constituted a National Command Authority with separate organizational sub-units to oversee policy for the nuclear scientists, labs, intelligence agencies and military. And finally in March 2001, General Musharaff was fed up with the public feuding and grant standing of senior scientists such as Dr. A.Q. Khan and Dr. Samar, as well responding to specific US complaints about KRL proliferation activities, eased both scientists out of leading positions and appointed them to advisory posts. Thus for, the Pakistani government official complicity in the nuclear trade with Iran, Libya and North Korea had proved beyond doubt. But the evidence that the Pakistani nuclear labs and scientists engaged in nuclear trades unknown to Pakistani military and intelligence agencies was equally murky. If the IAEA investigations on the sources of Iran's and Libya's centrifuge-based uranium programmes proved Islamabad's official complicity, it would also establish that past Pakistani governments had acted irresponsibly."[166]

Until very recently, Pakistan's nuclear programme was believed to be a secular enterprise. However, the nuclear analysts believed that in the wake of the US invasions of Afghanistan, it was suggested that senior Pakistani nuclear scientists such as Sultan Bashiruddin Mahmood and Mazid may also have Islamists leanings; that they discussed basic information concerning weapons of mass destruction and provided Osama Bin Laden and his top lieutenants and preliminary information on such weapons and their use; that they were probably approached to try and recent other scientists in Pakistan's nuclear establishments to help Al-

Qaeda in the nuclear quest, and that they professed their desire to help other Islamic regimes to develop nuclear weapons. Pakistan's support for the Taliban regime in Afghanistan prior to joining the US global war against terror in the fall of 2001 and the promotion of Islamization laws and cultural practices within Pakistan starting in the 1980s have also raised concerns that the security of the country's nuclear arsenal might have been compromised by Islamist sympathizers in sensitive positions within its military and intelligence agencies. Some of these concerns were highlighted by assassination attempts on the President Musharaff himself, and suggested the existence of insider information.[167] However, the assassination attempts on Musharaff do highlight the problem of political instability in Pakistan, largely because of the military's over developed status in comparison to other institutions of state such as parliament, judiciary and the civil services. Furthermore, power within the country is highly centralized and personalized. Both factors act against the emergence of an inter-institutional national consensus on critical policy issues, which in turn raises the question whether Pakistan's domestic and external policies and governmental commitments are likely to outline individual or groups within existing regimes. Though most of Pakistan's history heads of government have either been dismissed or violently removed from power pending the completion of constitutional terms in office. The legacy has contributed to the creation of a political system that is inherently unstable in nature, and spawned political cultures of intrigue, corruption, and illegality. The absence of a history of peaceful and constitutional succession arrangements also makes physical force the ultimate political arbiter in Pakistan society, a condition that creates scope for recurring constitutional breakdowns, institutional clashes, fragmentation of authority, absence of legitimacy and potential for loss of political control.

Furthermore, the army's frequent interference in domestic politics has exposed it to political compulsions, with the result that it is now not an impartial force that was originally created to defend Pakistan's sovereignty from external aggressions. Rather, as some observers have regrettably noted that army has emerged as the largest political party in Pakistan, all be it an armed one. And also of great concern is the army's reluctance to retreat from domestic politics, which not only detracts from its professional goals, but also exposes it to the likelihood of corruption and serious internal divisions over domestic and external policy, which in the long-run has the potential to create serious internal divisions within its ranks.

Indeed in the past five and half decades, the Pakistani Army has emerged as a state within a state, accountable to no one but its own corporate interest. Its frequent coups, institutional contempt towards politicians and civil services and increasing control of government and quasi-governmental organizations and corporations have begun to create a gap between the military and society at large, with the latter resenting the military, domination of the civilian domain. Despite the army's self-perception of being the sole institution capable of safeguarding Pakistan's unity, the growing perception among civilian elites in Pakistan is that the military has transformed Pakistan into a garrison state, that the military commanders determine the country's national security policies in pursuit of its narrow corporate interests, and is in essence the root of some of the pathologies that affect the Pakistani state. The widening civil military schism is thus setting the stage for a future showdown and possible constitutional breakdown between civilian and military authorities—factors that are working against Pakistan's political stability—in the medium and long-term.[168]

The first and most important issue on which the US should focus is preventing the diffusions of Pakistan's nuclear technology and the loss of control over Pakistan's nuclear weapons. The problem affects the US security directly and in an area in which the US assistance can make an important difference.

In short, the US should secure a full accounting of the A.Q. Khan's Network activities regarding nuclear proliferation from the Pakistan government, including details about what was transferred and to whom. It also should ensure that Pakistan implements the appropriate technical organizational and procedural safeguards to prevent a recurrence of illicit proliferation. The Bush Administration began discussions with Islamabad on both these issues, but the US and international concerns are far from being fully assuaged.

Over the medium-terms, the US should help Pakistan to improve the physical protection, and the oversight of its critical materials at each of its strategic sites. This effort entails providing assistance to develop security related exercises, transferring appropriate materials from military handbooks on nuclear weapons security; providing technology for more sophisticated vaults, access doors, portal control equipments, surveillances gear, and advanced instrumentation for material accounting, helping Pakistan's Strategic Plans Division develop effective personal reliability programmes, and helping to develop procedures to reduce the likelihood of sensitive information leaks. Given the relatively large size of Pakistan, it will take time before it can be fully implemented. The Bush Administration conducted preliminary discussions with Pakistan on these matters, but Islamabad's suspicion about the US intentions and its fear about compromising the security of its nuclear assets imply that the US technical assistance may not be fully utilized for sometime. In any event Washington should continue and even accelerate this endeavour.[169]

In addition to improving passive protection, the US should also help Pakistan eliminate the threat of unauthorized use of its nuclear weapons. Confronting this challenge contributes both to increasing regional security and mitigating another possible danger to the US. Despite significant public fears globally, the likelihood of unauthorized use stemming from theft or rogue launches is relatively low in peace time because Islamabad's nuclear devices are stored in component form, in relatively secure facilities. Under conditions of crisis, however, when these components are integrated with complete weapons and then dispersed into the field, the threat of loss, capture or unauthorized use increases.[170]

To the maximum degree possible, the US security interests demand reducing the prospect of these threats, materializing, consistent with Pakistan's own regiments these goals in incorporating technical controls, which in turn implies that the US should consider providing Pakistan with early generation "Permission Action Links" (PAL), which ensures that the weapon could never be used without authorization even if they were for any reason lost or compromised. This issue will require amending the present US commitments to international regimes and possible to its domestic laws, but such exceptions are necessary given that iron-clad technical control on Islamabad's nuclear weapons. It will advance interests on both sides as well as increase regional security.[171]

Over the long-term, and as Pakistan confidence in the US grows with respect to the security of its nuclear stock-pile, Washington should work with Islamabad to develop plans for cooperative action in case of a nuclear emergency. Such plans could cover a variety of contingencies, including attempts to steal fissile material or nuclear weapons, a successful theft of sensitive items, and protection systems at particular facilities. As a matter of prudence, the US should plan for dealing with such contingencies.[172]

Ashley Tellis feels that to solve the problem of terrorism, nuclear proliferations, creation of democratic institutions, there is a need of complete transformation and the US must play a major role in it. Assisting the transformation of Pakistan, to avert its continued threat to the US security in particular and to western interests more generally, therefore represent a difficult challenge for the US. Pakistan has accommodated a complex set of strategic, economic, political and social problems throughout his troubled statehood that are not only individually challenging but also mutually and viciously reinforcing. Successive Pakistani leaders have shied away from promoting serious reforms because the daunting nature of their country's crisis has inevitably implied that even partial ameliorations would require revolutionary change. They have therefore traditionally settled either for half baked or sham efforts at reforms, none of which survived their terms in office.[173]

Musharaff has infact done little to develop institutions that will promote a democratic temper or provide moderate political force in Pakistan an opportunity to prosper. To the contrary, his political maChinations have resulted in Islamist political parties rising to prominence in Pakistan's rising to prominence in Pakistan's highest legislative bodies for the first time, while his strategies from preventing Islamist control of the state in the long-term all hinge on continued military supremacy in Pakistan success story have to be undertaken and led by Pakistan themselves outsiders including powerful allies such as the US, can only play a supporting role. Successful transformation will require Pakistan leaders to make difficult choices, including subordinating immediate, after important institutional interest for larger national gains. Few, however, have historically appeared capable of meeting this challenge, and the current military leaders hip despite being well intentioned, is unlikely to prove exceptional in his regard. Musharaff's refusal to implement an agreement previously reached with Pakistan's major political parties to retire as Chief of the Army Staff is the latest example of how short-term, sometime personal, interests still trump larger concerns of public importance.[174]

Assisting the transformation of Pakistan into a stable, non-threatening state will also require important allies such as the US to demonstrate a willingness to sacrifice key short-term interest to realize long-term benefits. Such a transformation demands that Pakistan serves a fully democratic regime in which the military functions as the guardian, not the master of the state. The key question is whether the Washington and other capitals have the foresight skill and political will actively to pursue policies that push Islamabad in this direction while still cooperating in fighting the war on terrorism.

Pakistan's Nuclear Doctrine

Several sources, such as Jane's Intelligence Review and Defence Department maintain that Pakistan's motive for pursuing a nuclear weapon programme is to counter the threat posed by India, which has superior conventional forces and nuclear weapons.

Pakistan has not signed the NPT and CTBT. According to the US Defence Department Report 2001, "Pakistan remains adamant in its refusal to sign the NPT, stating that it would do so only after India joined the treaty. Consequently not all of Pakistan's nuclear facilities are under IAEA safeguards. Pakistan officials have stated that signature of the CTBT is in Pakistan's best interest, but the Pakistan will do so only after developing a domestic consensus on this issue, and have disowned any connection with India's decision."

Pakistan does not abide by a no-first use of doctrine, as evidenced by President Musharaff's statements in May 2002. He said that Pakistan did not want to conflict with but that if it comes to war between the nuclear armed rivals, it would "respond with full might." These statements were interpreted to mean that if pressed by an overwhelming conventional attack from India, which has superior conventional forces, Pakistan might use its nuclear weapons. Beside from these public declarations, Pakistan has not issued an official nuclear doctrine. The organization was authorized to make decisions about Pakistan's nuclear posturing in the National Command Authority (NCA) established in February 2002. The NCA is composed of two committees that advise Gen. Musharaff on the development and employment of nuclear weapons; it is also responsible for wartime control and command. In 2001, Pakistan further consolidated Atomic Research Corporation under the control on of one Nuclear Defence Complex.

The command and control of nuclear forces of Pakistan is vested with the President, and it functions through a robust NCA. The NCA is assisted in its functions by Strategic Commands within the Armed Forces to maintain a dynamic command and control system of its strategic forces.

It would not be out of context to mention here the cardinal principles of Pakistan's nuclear policy. They are premised on the following rules:

- Deterrence against all forms of external aggression which could otherwise jeopardize Pakistan's national security interests.
- Deterrence to be achieved through the development and maintenance of an effective combination of conventional and strategic forces at adequate levels in accordance with Pakistan's resources.
- Deter Pakistan's adversaries from endeavouring a

counter force strategy against Pakistan's strategic policies.

- Bilateral stabilization of strategic deterrence in the sub-continent.
- Pakistan as a matter of policy would not use or threaten to use nuclear weapons against any NNWS.
- Pakistan would continue to refrain from entering into any arms race.
- Pakistan would not transfer nuclear weapons or weapons related material or technology to any other entities or states which of course also include the Muslims states as well.
- Pakistan would endeavour to realize the ideal of a strategic restrain regime in cooperation with India, and also adopt other nuclear risk reduction measures in the region.
- Pakistan would constantly support the international arms control and disarmament initiatives if they were of universal and non-discriminating character.[175]

The political brinksmanship, conflicting civil military relations, weak economy, fragile social cohesion ridden with fundamentalist ideologies, not so credible sustenance of nuclear command and control mechanism—together they all raise vulnerability to Pakistan. Also, the deceptions and ambiguities of Pakistan as a nuclear weapon state actor imply various unpredictable threats, though not unperceivable. The existing realities of nuclear Pakistan require attention of the international community for the long-term regional and international peace and stability.

Potential pilferage of sensitive nuclear technology, design, equipment, materials and vital information may only strengthen the imagination and planning of unscrupulous non-state actors or terrorist groups both inside Pakistan and their outside networks, the probable leaks could be either intentional or inadvertent. The incidence of worst scenario draws upon the willingness of the state itself to indulge in proliferation nuclear terror.

The increasing trends of trans-border Islamic affiliations and solidarities in the international security and economic system raise numerous speculations concerning possible use of Islamic card for terrorists' activities. The potential Islamic card that Pakistan can play in the Muslim world remains significant for the policy-makers and analysts who have been facing the challenge to devise mechanisms to prevent nuclear terrorism throughout the world. The case of concern is to tackle the threatening claims worldwide from terrorist's outfits of using nuclear explosives or to blow nuclear facilities and power plants at regular intervals.

In one of the interviews with Al-Jazeera television, while supporting Pakistan's nuclear capability, Osama Bin Laden was quoted endorsing that he was actively looking to collect more nuclear weapons chemical and biological arms.

India Abroad reported that "quantities of enriched uranium for making nuclear bombs were intercepted earlier this year by Uzbek border guards and handed over to the authorities in Tashkent." This shipment was intended for "the leader of a former *mujahideen* pro-Pakistani group who fought against the Soviet occupation in Afghanistan."[176] Pakistani scientists Sultan Bashiruddin Mahmood and Abdul Majid were arrested on 23 October 2001 in connection with their possible contacts with *Al-Quaeda*. The revelations concerning connections between senior Pakistani nuclear scientists and the Taliban had established that Pakistan does not have adequate control over its sensitive nuclear information.

Jane's Intelligence Digest reported that "relations between the country's self-appointed President General Parvez Musharaff and those scientists who actually developed the bomb for the world's first Islamic nuclear power raise a number of awkward questions."[177]

Pakistani officials maintain that the scientists did not pass important information or secretes to Al-Quaeda, but they have not disclosed that Mahmood failed multiple polygraph tests about his activities. Most disturbing to the US intelligence was another leak from Pakistan's nuclear programme that has been mentioned in media.

The historical motivations of Pakistan towards developing nuclear weapons have travelled over more than three decades. The claims that had long been sought for developing non-conventional capabilities are now running dangerous for the acquired assets. We know that Israel and South Africa have full nuclear capability. The Christian Jewish and Hindu civilizations have this capability. The Islamic civilization was without but that situation was about to change,"[178] wrote Z.A. Bhutto before his death from prison in 1978 prior to his execution.

Bhutto's assertion was turned with the Islamic zeal and the possible lead role that Pakistan expected to assume in the Muslim world by being the first to acquire nuclear weapons. This was later reinforced by General Zia ul-Haq in July 1978 who outlined his perception as China, India, the USSR and Israel in the Middle-East possess the atomic arm, no Muslim country has any. If Pakistan has such a weapon, it would reinforce the power of the Muslim world.[179]

The situation may become more precautious when close nexus between state institutions like military, ISI and Jehadi groups try to dominate over the ideologies of democratic norms and agencies. It is an acknowledged fact that Pakistan has a history of close collaborations with the Jehadi groups to help Pakistan achieve political goals both inside and outside Pakistan. But it was seldom realized that one day this opportunist convergence could also have negative impact for the state itself in Pakistan. The combined ties of fundamentalists groups and their sympathizers in civil and military leadership pose considerable threat to the social system of Pakistan, prevailing weak economy of the country for the odds to the possibility of getting ignorant individuals falling into the trap of quick money by supporting the mafia groups who operate on behalf of the fundamentalists entities and terrorists networks. Such domestic vulnerabilities in Pakistan widen the scope of theft or of attack to country's strategic assets, mainly nuclear devices and materials. The physical security of nuclear installations and storage of radio active materials may become more prone to the reach or attack of disaffected groups even within the country.

Pakistan's inability to solve international problems as well as its relentless support to hardliners in the name of Jehad not only destabilizes the Asia security environment but also may adversely affect the future of regional and international nuclear security. The existences of nuclear weapons in Pakistan have become vulnerable to international security than ever before.

Transparency often lacks in the issues related to nuclear and missile development programme of a country. Safety and security of the strategic capabilities lies primarily on the wisdom of the possessor state. In Pakistan, the vulnerabilities to the overstretching desire of acquiring non-conventional capabilities have achieved multi-dimensional threatening postures.

The world community needs to ponder over the potential risks of nuclear threats they may emanate from nuclear Pakistan. Only an appropriate revision and consequent suggestive policy adoption could deter any mass destruction in future.[180]

Pakistan's Nuclear Proliferation Activities and the US Policy Constrains and Options

The US interest in preventing nuclear proliferation is closely linked to an interest in promoting regional stability. Although India's nuclear and missile programmes can be partly attributed to other factors such as prestige and competition with China, Pakistan-India rivalry has given the South Asian nuclear proliferation threat its greatest flip and danger. India and Pakistan have fought four major wars with each other and continue to exchange brickbats at the diplomatic levels and in international forums on various issues which are evading solution. Both maintain first strike air and armour units in a high degree of readiness and from time to time conduct provocative exercises.

Despite the rivalry, low priority of South Asia in the US security policy, the India-Pakistan rivalry has absorbed significant the US policy attention since the creation of India and Pakistan as independent states in 1947. South Asia remains a region that is susceptible to a variety of US source of influence, including the ability of the US to fill the military balance, the region's dependence on the US market, and the direct and indirect US influence over aid flows. In a region where no outside power has gained significant economic or military foot-hold, the attitude of the US still counts heavily despite the passionate nationalism of all the regional states.

The diverse nature of US interests in South Asia inevitably suggests a long list of policy issues and options. Typically, the US policy has been marked by a considerable number of either conflicting policy objectives or contradictions in the means used to pursue them. For instance, past support for Pakistan's security arguably helped promote competition in military technology between India and Pakistan and thereby to endanger stability. Broad agreement exists on the basics of the US policy goals such as deterring nuclear and missile proliferation promoting stability, democracy and adherence to internationally recognised human rights standards, encouraging economic liberalization, etc. In the beginning of nineties, both the Congress and the executive branch have concluded that getting India and Pakistan to give up what they have already achieved may be unrealistic, but that capping their nuclear programme, stopping the continued production of fissile material and preventing the deployment of nuclear arms and ballistic missiles might be achieved. The US remained better positioned than any other power or grouping of countries to act as an even handed but forceful broker on proliferation and regional stability issues. This required a careful balance of pressures as well as positive incentives to maintain mutual confidence and advance negotiations.

The US efforts to reduce India-Pakistan tension over territorial disputes and to discourage interference in each other's regional dissidence situations would provide positive support to the good of a regional non-proliferation accord, though not necessarily enough to bring the parties to an agreement on several grounds; some observers felt that the Pressesler Amendment has outlived its usefulness. It had failed to move Pakistan, it arguably had reduced the US influence and, ironically, it gave India added incentive to oppose talks on a regional non-proliferation accord, since keeping Pakistan in the dock with the US over its transgressions served to weaken defence capabilities of Pakistan. The main drawback in removing the sanctions was that the post-policy of accommodating Pakistan's conventional defence recruits did not achieve the desired objective either and the aid cutoff remained the main source of the US leverage.

Earlier while critics have often dismissed claims by India and Pakistan that their nuclear programme were to meet pressing civil power needs, and not for military purposes, these needs did exist and meeting them was critical to the efforts of both countries to attract more foreign investment.[181]

A former Pakistan External Affair Minister, Abdul Sattar, was of the view that the non-proliferation efforts might be more effective if the Security Council were to establish a pattern of prompt and effective collective action to frustrate aggression. Such an action on demand side strategy would assuage apprehension of states falling with real threats to their security, neutralizing the urge to acquire independent deterrence. This urge has frustrated the supply side strategy, however, restrictions on the transfer of nuclear materials and technology have failed to dissuade insecure states from the pursuance of nuclear weapons. Such economic sanctions applied on a country on specific basis have failed to coerce the targeted states.[182] While a serious doubt remains in the minds of Pakistan scholars who are concerned about the US duplicity pertaining to the nuclear proliferation regime. It is said, "Washington's policies and diplomatic manoeuverings take a variety of directions and ambiguities... South Asia being a classic example that shows that the US policies are contradictory, ambiguous and inconsistent."[183]

The US Administration shows serious concern for the security of the region, and proliferation of nuclear weapons. The US foreign policy analyst has once again realized that it was not possible to ignore the defence needs of Pakistan in view of its strategic location and the menace of terrorism which is spreading like a wild fire. In June 2004, President Bush declared Pakistan to be a Non-NATO ally of the US, a move that may be more symbolic than practical. The close US-Pakistan securities of the cold war era—which had come to near halt after the 1990 aid cutoff—appear to be in the process of restoration as a result of Pakistan's role in the US led anti-terrorism campaign. In July 2002, the US began allowing commercial sales that enabled Pakistan to refurbish at least part of its fleet of American made F-16 fighter aircrafts. One year later, the US Ambassador to Pakistan announced that Islamabad will purchase six C-130 military transport aircraft from Lockheed Martin for approximately $75 million under a Foreign Military Financing grant. The US Congress was also notified of another pending Foreign Military Sale arrangement with Pakistan reportedly worth 155$ million. Under this deal, Pakistan was to receive six Aerostat Surveillance Radars. These marked the first major arms sales to Pakistan in more than a decade and were intended to bolster Islamabad's counter terrorism capabilities. In September 2003, the Pentagon notified the Congress of three pending major arms sales to Pakistan potentially of $78 million worth of Military Radio System meant to improve Pakistan communication capabilities and to increase interoperability between Pakistan and the US-led counter-terrorist forces. The US also had undertaken to train and equip new Pakistan Army Air Assault Units that could move quickly to find and target terrorist targets. The Pentagon reported Foreign Military Sales Agreements with Pakistan with $27 million in FY 2002 and $167 million in FY 2003. Islamabad continued to seek increased arms imports, especially in an effort to bolster its air forces. Pakistan officials were eager to purchase major US weapons platforms, including F-16 Fighters, P-3 Maritime Surveillance Aircraft, and Harpoon Anti-ship Missiles. A revived high-level US Pakistan Defence Consultative Group (DGV)—moribund since 1997—met in September 2002 for high level discussions on military cooperation, security assistance, and anti-terrorism. A September 2003 meeting had set a schedule for joint military exercises, discussed how the US military could assist Pakistan in improving its counter-terrorism capabilities and included a US vow to expedite future security assistance.

The US analysts considered the arms race between India and Pakistan as posing a serious challenge to the security of South Asia region. The 1998 tests by both the countries had created a near global storm of criticism, and gave a serious set back to the two decades of the US nuclear non-proliferation efforts in South Asia. Both countries have aircraft capable of delivering nuclear bombs, which may number 35-100 each side. Indian army has inducted short and medium range ballistic missiles while Pakistan itself possess short and medium range missiles (allegedly acquired from China and North Korea). All are assumed to be capable of delivering nuclear warheads over significant distances.

Press reports in late 2002 suggested that Pakistan assisted Pyongyang's covert nuclear weapons programme by providing North Korea with uranium enrichment materials and technology beginning in the mid-1990s. Islamabad had described such reports as "baseless" and the US Secretary of State Powell was assured that no such transfers were occurring. If such assistance was confirmed by President Bush, all non-humanitarian US aid to Pakistan might be suspended, although the President was empowered to waive any sanctions that he determined would jeopardize the US national security. In March 2003, the administration determined that the relevant facts "do not warrant in position of sanctions under applicable US laws." Press reports during 2003 suggested that both Iran and Libya benefitted from Pakistani nuclear assistance, Islamabad denied any nuclear cooperation with Tehran or Tripoli, although it conceded in December 2003 that certain senior scientists were under investigation for possible independent proliferation activities. Those investigations led to the February 2004 "public humiliation of metallurgist Abdul Quadir Khan, when he confessed his involvement in a proliferation network. Khan and at least seven of his associates were said to have sold crucial nuclear technology and uranium enrichment materials to North Korea, Iran and Libya. President Musharaff issued a conditional pardon for Dr. Khan. The US assured that the Islamabad government had no knowledge of such activities and indicated that the decision to pardon is an internal matter of Pakistan. Musharaff had promised to share all information about the Khan's proliferation investigation.[184]

In May 1998, following the South Asia "nuclear tests, President Clinton imposed full restrictions on all non-humanitarian aid to both India and Pakistan as mandated under Section 102 of the Arm Export Control Act. In some respects, Pakistan was less affected by the sanction as compared to India, as most of the US assistance had been cutoff in 1990. At the same time, Pakistan's smaller and more fragile economy was more vulnerable to both negative effects of aid restrictions. However, the Congress and the President acted almost immediately to lift certain aid restriction and, after October 2001, all remaining nuclear-related sanctions on Pakistan (and India) were removed. In April 2004, the US Assistant Secretary of State for Proliferation urged Pakistan and India to join the NPT as non-nuclear weapon states, saying that the US does not accept either country as nuclear weapon state under NPT.

During the later years of the Clinton Administration, the US set forth non-proliferation "benchmarks" for India and Pakistan, including halting for the nuclear testing and signing and ratifying the CTBT, halting fissile material production and pursuing Fissile Material Control Treaty negotiations, refraining from deploying nuclear weapons and testing ballistic missiles and restricting any and all export of nuclear materials or technologies. The results of the US efforts were mixed at best, and neither India nor Pakistan are signatories to the CTBT or NPT. The Bush Administration made no reference to the benchmark framework. Senator Richargd Lugar, Chairman of the Senator Foreign Relations Committee, had called upon the US to promote nuclear—(CBM'S) in South Asia, including "assistance on export controls, border security, and the protection, control, and accounting of nuclear weapons and nuclear power plants, but Pakistani officials insisted that Pakistan would not accept any demand for access to or inspections of its nuclear and strategic assets, materials and facilities. Concerns about onward proliferation and fears that Pakistan could become destabilized by the US-led counter-terrorism efforts in Afghanistan have heightened the US attention to weapons proliferation in South Asia.[185]

Through a series of legislative measures, the Congress incrementally lifted sanctions on Pakistan and India resulting from their nuclear proliferation activites. After the 2001 September terrorist attacks on the US, policy-makers searched for new means to provide assistance to Pakistan President Bush's September 2001 issuance of a final declaration, removed remaining sanctions on Pakistan (and India) resulting from the 1998 nuclear tests, finding the restrictions were not in the national security interests of the US. Some members of the 108th Congress had urged reimposition of proliferation-related sanctions in response to evidence of Pakistani assistance to the North Korean, Iranian and Libyan nuclear weapons programmes. The Nuclear Black-Market Elimination Act (HR 4965) authorized the President to impose three minimum sanctions on any "foreign person or entity" that was determined to have been involved in the illicit transfer of nuclear weapons or technologies. Title III of the Act would require the President to determine that Pakistan had verifiably halted all proliferations activities and was fully sharing with the US all information relevant to the A.Q. Khan proliferation network.[186]

Foreign Assistance and Pakistan Nuclear Programme

The Chinese role in providing technological assistance to Pakistan in building and strengthening its nuclear weapons programme is an open secret. The nature of Pakistan-China nuclear, scientific and technological cooperation, which dates back to the mid-1976, was known to the US also. It was in 1976, when both the countries had formalized nuclear, science and technology agreement. This accord had nothing to do with the supply of centrifuge uranium enrichment technology. On the contrary, it was purely for peaceful application, science and technology, including for research and development.[187]

Equally important in the Chinese missile exports and assistance to Pakistan have been a serious proliferation concern for the US over the years and remain a contentious issue in Sino-US relations. The US intelligence reports revealed that China had transferred complete M-11 missiles, missiles-related technology and manufacturing assistance to Pakistan. The US was concerned that Chinese Missile transfers could lead to instability in South Asia as India and Pakistan continue to engage in a regional arms race, heightening the risk of military confrontation between the two countries. In that context, proliferation of ballistic missiles in to this region was particularly destabilizing, more so in the aftermath of the nuclear tests of May 1998. Chinese missiles and other technology might also be retransferred to third parties, further under cutting international non-proliferation efforts.

The US has made and continue to make serious efforts to dissuade China from transferring missiles components, and missile-related technology to Pakistan. Washington has engaged Beijing in a series of negotiations, seeking to obtain Chinese pledges to abide by the Missile Technology Control Regime (MTCR) guidelines and eventually to become a member of the regime. For these purposes the US has applied consistent diplomatic pressure, offered economic incentives and even imposed economic sanctions on China. China while made pledges in 1991 and 1994 to the US promising to comply with the main provisions of the MTCR and halt all sales of complete MTCR-class missile systems. It has tended to interpret these pledges narrowly and has continued missile technology transfers and manufacturing assistance to Pakistan, including a second missile factory. China has also implicitly linked its MCTR commitments to issue of increasing salience to its own security concerns, namely, Theatre Missile Defence (TMD), the US arms sale to Taiwan, and the US intentions to deploy National Missile Defence (NIM) and amend the ABM Treaty.

Because of the weak scientific base, Pakistan had to rely heavily on outside help for its nuclear and missile development programmes. The Space and Upper Atmosphere Research Commission (SUARC) formed in 1961 gave a boost to the Pakistani missile development programme. The western countries, in the initial stage provided critical support as some of the technical know-how acquired under (SUARC) was used for the development of Hafts. Even when it became well known that Pakistan had embarked on the path of missile development, sensitive and prohibited materials kept flowing from the western countries including the US, Norway, France and West Germany. However, China has been Pakistan's most important and predominant source of foreign technological aspect for its missile development effort.[188] Pakistan missile programme had attached the US sanctions on both Pakistan and China following transfer of M-11 missiles and their associated technology. This was held by the US to enforce the MTCR guidelines despite strong objections being raised by the Chinese that the M-11 were only short-range missiles.[189] For the western definition of a medium range missile was one with range nomenclature equations of short range (1000 km), medium range with (1000-3000 km) long range (3000-8000 km) and Inter Continental Ballistic Missile (ICBM'S) beyond 8000 km. Thus stay on the right side of the MTCR which prohibited export of missiles having more than 300km and payload of above 500 kg.[190] India analysts perceived M-11, with a range of about 300-350 km, a border line case safer as restrictions under MTCR were concerned.[191]

The first report on the transfer of M-11s received attention of the international media in April 1991. In May, the American newspapers provided details on the transfer of these nuclear capable missiles and earlier dispatch of mobile launchers and missile frames to Pakistan. The initial induction appeared to have taken place in 1992/93 because satellite photographs in the spring of 1994 reportedly showed canisters at Sargodha (Pakistan) that were identical to those seen at the Chinese M-11 production facility.[192]

The sale clearly represented violation of China's November 1991 agreement with the US on foreclosing the option of selling M-11 or M-9 missiles. It transgressed the MTCR guidelines and posed a security challenge for India. There are various strategic, commercial and foreign policy rationals behind Chinese missile exports and assistance to Pakistan. China and Pakistan have enjoyed a solid strategic relationship since 1960s. Over the years, China has provided Pakistan with wide range of major conventional weapon systems and the three countries have also developed a close partnership in various defence cooperation programmes. While this strategic partnership initially grew out of the mutual needs of China and Pakistan in countering the Soviet and Indian military threats respectively, it continues to serve the two countries national security interests in the post-Cold War era. Pakistan relies on China as a trusted ally in dealing with India from a position of military weakness; Beijing valued its close ties with Islamabad both to extend its influence to South Asia and to balance against India.

Commercially as China began its economic reform and opening up of the early 1980s, defence industries and arms exporting companies were under tremendous pressure to tap into the lucrative international market. Pakistan becomes a valued customer for Chinese arms. Finally, the US had great concern about and emphasized on missile proliferation issues, Beijing found it useful to exploit them as bargaining leverage in dealing with Washington on issues important to China. The US arms sales to Taiwan, TMD deployment in East Asia, among others.

In April 1991, the US announced that it had discovered the transfer of an M-11 missile even though China insisted that it had never shipped the system to Pakistan.[193] In May 1991, the US imposed sanctions against China. In November 1991, the US Secretary of State, James Baker reached an agreement with the Chinese Foreign Minister Qian Qichen in which Beijing virtually agreed to abide by "the guidelines and parameters of the MTCR" in exchange for the lifting of sanctions imposed. After China sent Washington a letter in February 1992 affirming its earlier MTCR assurance in writing the sanctions were lifted in March 1992.[194]

But by December 1992, reports had again surfaced that China had transferred M-11s to Pakistan in violation of the agreement to abide by the MTCR guidelines. China and Pakistan both denied that the transfer had taken place, but in August 1993, the United States against imposed sanctions against China. China denounced these sanctions, calling the US decision "a wrong judgement based on inaccurate intelligence" and threatened to scrap its promise to abide by the MTCR.[195]

The US and China finally broke the impasse in October 1994 when the two countries issued a joint statement on missile proliferation. The US agreed to lift sanctions, in returns for which the Chinese promised not to export ground to ground missiles featuring the privacy parameters of the MTCR[196] that is, whereby capable of reaching a range of at least 300 km with a payload of at least 500 kg, which would cover the M-11's. The Beijing also agreed to the concept of inherent capability. The sanctions were waived in November 1994.

However, in early 1995, reports once again surfaced that China had transferred M-11 components and production technology to Pakistan, and Pakistan again denied that any such transfers had taken place, and China went further, denying that China had ever cooperated with Pakistan on M-11 missiles. Since then China has repeatedly sought to assure the US and especially India that it is not selling M-11 missiles to Pakistan. President of the US efforts since 1994 have also led China to clarify its MTCR commitments. Beijing has also reaffirmed its obligations to permanently curtail its missile cooperation with Pakistan and indicated that it is actively studying joining the MTCR as a full member. However, serious questions about China's missile export control remained a matter of concern. Although China had promulgated regulations conventional arms transfer in 1997, it was not clear if they had covered missile and missile-related technology transfers while an internal control list restricting missile exports exists, Beijing has not revealed its scope contents, and the extent to which it approximates various factors had contributed the meager progress that had been made between the US and China on various issues related with MTCR. The release of the Cox report, the US bombing of the Chinese embassy in Belgrade, and the US intentions with regard to National Missile Defence (NMD) Theater Missile Defence (TMD) have effectively put any prospects of China's joining the MTCR on hold. Beijing is demanding a linkage between its MTCR membership and broader issues of the US arms sales to Taiwan, and the development, and future deployment of TMD in North-East Asia. China's continuing transfers of missile technology to Pakistan and Iran may be a means of gaining leverage over the US. However, if China feels its fundamental security interests are threatened, it might step up these activities.

The Sino-US disagreements over China missile-related activities and missile proliferation is still continuing. China has not accepted the MTCR annex and the US efforts to get China to adopt legally binding export controls MTCR items have yet to lead to the publication of regulations on missile exports (although Chinese officials insist they have an internal control list). In addition, suspicion of continued Chinese assistance to Pakistani missile production facility at Rawalpindi persists and this raises serious questions of Beijing sincerity in abiding by its pledges. During and immediately after the Sino-US Summit of June 1998, Beijing indicated that it was "actively studying 'MTCR' membership, and removed once more its missile non-proliferation pledge on curbing its missile technology transfers and assistance to South Asia in the Jiang-Clinton Joint Statement."[197]

Chinese missile transfer to Pakistan has raised a number of issues for the US non-proliferation policy and Sino-US relations. First, China's missile exports and assistance can undermine international missile non-proliferation efforts, in particular the objectives of the MTCR. China's most serious confrontation with the US over ballistic missile proliferation have involved Chinese transfers of complete M-11 missiles and missiles-related technology to Pakistan. The M-11 is a single stage, solid fueled missile with a reported range of 290 km and a payload of 800 kg while technically M-11 missiles do not fall within the MTCR parameters, they have the inherent capacity of being able to deliver a 500 kg payload over 300 km. The fact that China has resisted joining the MTCR for quite sometime as formal member, coupled with its ambiguous interpretation and implementation of its bilateral commitments, raises questions as to the seriousness of Chinese commitment to arms control and non-proliferation.

The US concerns over Chinese missile exports to Pakistan focus mainly on regional stability and the potential of further proliferation to other regions, the Middle-East and Persian Gulf. The introduction and improvement of ballistic missiles could result in a fierce arms race between India and Pakistan, which in turn could be highly destabilizing given the potential animosity between the two countries, and the short distances between major population centres of the two countries, poor intelligence, and short warning time would be a great temptation to launch pre-emptive strikes in crisis situations. A more serious concern is the making of nuclear warheads and other WMD with missiles, the further proliferation of ballistic (and cruise) missiles to countries such as Iran, Syria and Libya could enable these countries to seriously threaten the US interests with regard to the Middle-East and the Persian Gulf.

Furthermore, China's missile export to Pakistan represent a major bone of contention in Sino-US bilateral relations and has the potential to limit and undermine bilateral cooperation in other areas. Over the last decade, the Chinese proliferation behaviour, bilateral trade issues, Taiwan and human rights controversies have been the four key obstacles to better the US-China relations. The US efforts to change the Chinese behaviour through both economic incentives and sanctions have achieved noticeable but limited results. While the US has made strong efforts to persuade China to join the MTCR, China continues to resist and remains critical of the regime, in particular to charge that the regime is discriminatory in nature and its exclusions of high performance aircraft continued controversy over Chinese missile-related transfers and assistance to Pakistan points to serious differences between Washington and Beijing with regard to regional security. While the US tends to compartmentalize non-proliferation issues on their own merits, the Chinese have insisted that proliferation issues cannot be separated from underlying security courses.

Finally, the differences in interests exist and this may account for the difficulty for a final resolution of the issue. Washington seeks to stem proliferation of WMD's and their delivery systems to the Middle-East, the Persian Gulf and the South Asia out of its interests for secure supplies of oil, the security of Israel, and stability on the sub-continent. Beijing on the other regards its nuclear and missile exports as an important source of foreign exchange as well as a means of gaining influence in these regions. China's refusal at the adaptation of IAEA Full Scope Safeguards (FFS) might be due to concerns that such measures would deprive it of potential nuclear markets. Regarding continued missile technology transfers and assistance to Pakistan, Beijing motive may be more strategic than commercial. Islamabad has remained as an important factor in Beijing's strategic calculations regarding South Asia and a useful over weight to India.

Three issues confronted the Clinton Administration, the credibility of Chinese commitments to missile non-proliferation, whether the US should impose sanctions on China as required by domestic laws, and balancing the management of bilateral relations and the enforcement of non-proliferation legislations. The charges about renewed Chinese missile technology cooperation with Pakistan occurred at a particularly sensitive movement as Beijing and Washington were resuming both the security and arms control dialogues, as the Senate was to begin debates on PNTR on China, with some serious concerns proposing the "China Non-proliferation Law" bill seeking to amend the bill with provisions requesting annual review of Chinese missile proliferation activities, and as the deadline of a task force investigation of the 1992 Chinese sale of 34 M-11 missiles was approaching and might have already been passed. While both China and the Clinton Administration were having the incentives to reach a compromise to avoid sanctions, but the reason for such an outcome remained limited.

The suspicions also persisted regarding China's continued missile cooperation with Pakistan. It was speculated that the Shaheen—ICBM, which Pakistan had tested in April 1999, was actually modelled like Chinese M-9 missiles. A February 1999 CIA report stated that "Chinese and North Korean entities continued to provide assistance to Pakistan ballistic missile programme during the first half of 1998 to produce ballistic missiles ... China's involvement with Pakistan was to be continued to be monitored closely." A September 1999 National Intelligence Council (NIC) report stated that "Pakistan had Chinese supplied M-11 short range ballistic missiles." That was the first time the US government had publicly verified that China actually supplied missiles to Pakistan. The NIC report referred to the transfer of 23 M-11 missiles delivered in November 1992, but there was no evidence that China has resumed the transfer of complete missile systems to Pakistan. However, an unclassified CIA report to the US Congress released in February 2000 suggested that "Some (Chinese) ballistic missiles assistance (to Pakistan) continues."[198]

Following the September 1999 NIC Report Republican Senator Jesse Helms, Chairman of the Senate Foreign Relations Committee, threatened to block the appointment of Acting Assistant Secretary of State for Proliferation Affairs Rohnert Einkorn to a permanent position unless the Clinton

Administration formed a task force to impose sanctions on China. The US and Chinese reportedly had been meeting to reach a compromise to avoid sanctions. Chine was unlikely to become a full member of the MTCR, but a compromise on strengthening China's nuclear export controls might be possible.[199]

The intelligence reports suggested that despite pledges to the contrary, China continued to provide Pakistan special guidance regarding systems and technical expertise in the latter's effort to develop long range ballistic missiles. These and other allegations have apparently led to the proposal by Republican Senator Fred Thenupson and Democratic Senator Robert G. Torricells of legislation aimed at monitoring Chinese nuclear proliferation activities and mandating automatic sanctions should "credible evidence" indicate that specific Chinese experts and transfers have taken place.[200] The US Assistant Secretary of State for Non-proliferation travelled to Beijing in early June 2000 to seek commitment from China not to export missiles and missile technology to Iran and Pakistan.[201]

China, for all practical purposes, had directly interfered in the South Asian Affairs by supplying and transferring missiles and its related technology to Pakistan. This Chinese move had altered the strategic balance in the region. It was generally a strong view of the nuclear analysts that all the missile nuclear programmes of Pakistan are Chinese in origin.[202]

China and Pakistan's Nuclear Programme

Covert Chinese assistance to Pakistan's nuclear programme started after India detonated the nuclear device in May 1974. According to a report by the US Defence Intelligence Agency, sometimes before October 1974, China assigned twelve nuclear scientists to assist Pakistan's nuclear energy programme. The Chinese government assumed that "a nuclearised Pakistan might also reduce the danger that China itself would have to choose between going to war with India to uphold Pakistan's subordination by India." In 1965 and 1971 Indo-Pak wars, the Chinese had witnessed such situations and had also faced unpleasant choices. Chinese were warned about Indian superiority in conventional armed forces, were well aware that in the case of another war, Pakistan would be ruined totally. "In such an eventuality Beijing would face the unpleasant choice of intervening to save Pakistan, thereby assuming the cost of .another war with India or doing nothing while its key South Asian ally was reduced to importance. Support for Pakistan's nuclear programme averted such a choice by diminishing the likelihood that India would opt for a decisive war against Pakistan."[203]

In fact, the real co-operation between Pakistan and China for developing Pakistan's nuclear programme was initiated by Prime Minister Z.A. Bhutto. A top level Pakistani scientific delegation led by Z.A. Bhutto visited China from 26 to 30 January 1976. Two public agreements resulted from this visit one on military cooperation, the other on the scientific cooperation. A high level Chinese scientific team also visited Islamabad in June 1976, resulted in the signing of a secret nuclear technology cooperation agreement between the Chinese and the Pakistani governments.[204]

In fact Bhutto himself had confirmed the existence of a mysterious agreements concluded in June 1976 which he declared was of utmost importance for Pakistan's security and territorial integrity. In his death cell testament, Bhutto refers cryptically to "the agreement of mine concluded in June 1976", which in his words was his: "single most important achievement which I believe will dominate the portrait of my public life" and which "will perhaps be my greatest achievement and contribution to the survival of our people and nation." Bhutto did not specify the content or even the parties of the "momentous agreement", but he did say that negotiations of the agreement took "eleven years" thus tracing back to 1965, the year after China tested its first nuclear device. "Bhutto's last statement is a rambling document, as befits a manifesto written in a "tiny death cell" by a man facing imminent execution. Bhutto argued in his testament that the various nuclear energy programmes he pursued was the reason for his over- throw, which he implied was inspired by the US: "I have been actively associated with the nuclear programme of Pakistan from

October 1968 to July 1977 (when Bhutto was over thrown by a military coup) ... when I took charge of Pakistan's Atomic Energy Commission (in the 1950s) it was no more than sign-board of an office. It was only a name. Assiduously and with granite determination, I put my entire vitality behind the task of acquiring nuclear capability for my country."[205]

Bhutto insisted that the nuclear capability he had sought for Pakistan was "peaceful" but at the same time, he asked: "what difference does my life make now when I can imagine eighty million of my countrymen standing under the nuclear cloud of a defenceless sky? It is clear that what Bhutto meant by "peaceful" was that the nuclear capability he sought was meant to deter India from launching a war against Pakistan. It is also an open secret that the "mysterious June, 1976 agreement" had played a permanent role in that process. The Chinese assistance, no doubt had helped Pakistan to foil US-led western efforts today Pakistan's having nuclear weapons. It was the Chinese who were responsible for supplying Pakistan critical centrifuge equipment for the enrichment plant. Because the US thwarted Pakistan in its quest for a reprocessing capability to export plutonium from spent reactor fuel, Pakistan then turned to uranium, enrichment via gaseous diffusion at a facility at Kahuta, East of Islamabad. The Chinese scientists had given enough training and technical know-how to Pakistani scientists to master the technical difficulties associated with the production of the highly enriched uranium at the Kahuta plant.[206]

The following circumstantial evidence seems to support Bhutto's statement: *Firstly,* Dr. Abdus Salam, Bhutto's Scientific Advisor had been part of his team during his third visit to Beijing. The 1977 Noble Laureate, Dr. Salam was the brain behind Pakistan's nuclear efforts until Dr. A.Q. Khan replaced him. *Second,* close on the heels of Bhutto's China's visit, a high level team of Chinese scientists visited Pakistan in October 1974, and another team in March 1977, another team of Chinese scientists toured a number of places in Pakistan and had discussions with Pakistan nuclear scientists. Such reports of Chinese nuclear scientists touring or working in Pakistan's facilities continued to come in. *Third,* towards the end of 1973, Dr. A.Q. Khan returned from the Netherlands to Pakistan to take up an ultra-centrifuge enrichment project known as Project 706. Since Khan had stolen important blueprints from Dutch laboratories, the Chinese scientists worked on centrifuge technology, could have benefitted from useful information provided by the Pakistanis for the design and fabrications of the ultra centrifuge technology based on manufacturing of enriched uranium which the European nuclear Consortium (URENCO) had developed. *Fourth,* on 29 January 1977, Pakistan and China signed a protocol on scientific and technical cooperation. Chinese assistance for the development of nuclear energy was implicit in the protocol. Pakistan, in fact, had begun playing the Chinese nuclear card when the US economic military aid was terminated in 1977 and in 1979 by the Carter Administration in the hope that the Pakistani nuclear programme could be brought to halt.[207]

Ever since China declared itself a nuclear power in October 1964, it started considering itself as a "benevolent leader of the Third World, had shown its desire to protect the interest of the downtrodden, backward countries lacking in technical capability and political prowess, to withstand the discriminating international order. But May 1998 Indian tests have altogether changed the Chinese perception, mainly on two major counts. *First,* the nuclear tests by India had given a major setback to Chinese position as a sole leader of the developing world in the global arena. *Second,* "it had compelled the Chinese military analysts to think and revise their strategic perceptions. It would definitely compel the Chinese to have a fresh understanding of Indian military capability and in other spheres also.[208]

There is considered to be a change in the Chinese nuclear doctrine after May 1998. The evaluation of Chinese nuclear non-proliferation can be roughly divided in three stages: (1) Emphasis on the national right to develop nuclear weapons (1949-1959); (2) Acceptance of the non-proliferations norms; (3) Gradual integration with international community.[209] What has been China's rationale for maintaining a cooperative relationship in lethal technologies with Pakistan? The most obvious would be the armed

Pakistan as a potential counter to Indian predominance in the sub-continent and the collusion between India's most probable adversaries sure to divide Indian attention as well as keep its political military decision-makers off balance. Chinese help in crucial weapons related technologies have allowed Pakistan to leap frog the knotty details in design and production of advanced defence engineering. What surprises however, China's continued adherence to its nuclear and missile technology supply contracts with Pakistan at the risk of explicit threat of sanctions and world-wide criticism. Probably, the Chinese government weighted the impact of sanctions against the core preferences of other important powers, the international system and then decided that sanctions did not pose any threat worth the name of its economy. Another factor was the sheer profit-making for China's fastest growing defence industrial corporations.[210]

Some analysts argue that the Chinese are the ultimate realists. China's proliferation and non-proliferation policies are governed by strategic and commercial interests. Even more significantly, China celebrates its proliferation behaviour and compliance with global arms regimes and cartels to gain bargaining leverage in negotiations with the US over Taiwan.[211]

Pakistan is China's all-weather friend in South Asia and the two countries are united by their rivalry with India. In negotiations with the US, China has described Pakistan as its "Israel" and is committed to its security. In the context of the nuclear arms, competitions in the region China views Pakistan as the under-dog and has therefore accepted the task of under writing Pakistan's security against advance in the Indian nuclear and missile programmes. The Chinese have also calculated that aiding Pakistan with nuclear and missile technologies will divert India's military attention and prevent it from focusing on China. This goal might have assumed added priority after May 1998, when India decided to deploy a minimum deterrent with China as a primary target.[212]

Another argument most frequently advanced is that China sees in Pakistan "a strategic counter weight or balance to India" and that is the reason a nuclear weapons capable Pakistan is required. But this argument has raised a number of awkward questions. If we take into consideration the overall superiority of China to India at both conventional and nuclear levels, how much does Pakistan's military prowess matter in an India China balance. The Chinese are possessing near 500 nuclear weapons. On the other hand, India, by all account, has less than 100 and Pakistan not more than 50. If so, it is difficult to see what Pakistan is going to do in strengthening the military might of China. Indian nuclear capability can never ever match China. Pakistan's military and nuclear capability would seem to be of little value. On the other hand, was India to chase the gap with China significantly, how much would Pakistan's nuclear forces help China? A nuclear Pakistan would of course divide India's forces, but not very substantially given that India does not need a large force to deter Pakistan, whatever Pakistan may possess. If Pakistan's nuclear capability is not in a position to divide or affect India's nuclear capability to any extent, then surely Pakistan would be of little help to China. One can assume, in terms of the general balance of power Pakistan's nuclear capabilities would have little impact.[213]

The nuclear analysts feel that by promoting Pakistan's nuclear capability, China would be at loss. *First,* by promoting Pakistan's nuclear programme, China would be instigating Indian to further strengthen their nuclear capability. While it was conceivable that India could live with a nuclear China, it is hard to imagine that it could live with a nuclear Pakistan. *Second,* China's strategic location in Asia is complex enough without a nuclear India and nuclear Pakistan on its southern periphery. China has more neighbours than any other country in the international system. While they are nowhere near Beijing's nuclear power, but they are fairly formidable to local powers and could pose a serious threat if they choose to adopt the nuclear weapons programme. India of course, has always posed a potential nuclear threat to China. Why should Beijing add a nuclear power to those that already are or could be ringed around China? No doubt, the Sino-Pak Axis is at present on strong footings, but that could well change in the future because in the game of nations, there are no permanent friends "only permanent interests." There is unfortunately precisely little, if any hard evidence on the nature of Chinese thinking on its nuclear relationship with Pakistan. Officially China has strongly denied any role in Pakistan's nuclear programme. Scholarly analysis of Pakistan's nuclear progress hardly touch Beijing motivations beyond suggestions that China seeks a balance in South Asia.[214]

An Indian nuclear analyst Bajpai firmly believed that "the Pakistan China nuclear alliance has been detrimental to India's security by raising the possibility of a two-front nuclear confrontation and by allowing Islamabad to achieve strategic parity with India. The only way out for India would have been to strike a deal with Pakistan. Agreements on final disposition of Kashmir and other bilateral disputes as well as on the conventional force levels could well have eliminated Pakistan's incentive to approach China for nuclear weapons technology. With Pakistan out of the nuclear game, China could hardly have forced nuclear weapons technology on Islamabad. Giving up nuclear weapons jointly with Pakistan even now may lead to dramatic break through with both Islamabad and Beijing. India's security would thereby be greatly enhanced, not harmed.[215]

After the nuclear tests by India and Pakistan, "the collaboration in lethal technologies and the Chinese support on the core issues which are affecting Indo Pak ties might have been diluted but it is by no means evident that the Chinese stand during the Kargil conflict is one that will reflect the nature of China's engagement with Pakistan in the years to come." Pakistan is still considered to be of paramount importance for the Chinese in achieving its strategic goals. Pakistan's significance may stem from its inherent potential to play a role of considerable importance in China's troubled North West. The Chinese leadership feels that China's close relationship with Pakistan would help in seeking the support of the Muslim World, and front-line Muslim states in the battle against separatists tendencies to Xingjian province (a Muslim dominated area), but also make available an uninterrupted flow of funds from China's conventional arms merchandising, once these two core criteria's for continuing engagement and friendship with Pakistan have been met, China may still consider Pakistan a reliable strategically of yore, and this may be fundamentally well disposed towards it.[216]

Recent indications of a qualitative shift in Chinese attitude towards its close friend Pakistan, might be limited to only one area, i.e. of Pakistan going overtly nuclear than anything else. At a time when China is in the need of international support for its rapid economic development programmes, the leadership in Beijing could very well barter support for Pakistani nuclear ambitions in Southern Asia for the larger goal of being considered a responsible international player. Pakistan has counted on China's support in maximizing its power capabilities down the years, China, on the other hand, may have little to gain from a consistently strong and long-term strategic association with Pakistan.[217]

China's most important strategic preference for the future of South Asia appears to be its own desire to play safe in the South Asian security tangle. The Chinese leadership had realized the dangers of stitching to the balancing game in South Asia. It can pull China deeper into the region's myriad problems. Already, world opinion feels that it was China which has encouraged the arms race in South Asia by secretly helping Pakistan for the missiles and nuclear development programmes. The Chinese elites now are worried to clear the suspicion because such an image in the years to come will do it good in terms of the roles and responsibilities expected of a potential great power. As China seeks to enhance strategic cooperation with the US, and leave the pull of the Southern Asian deadweight behind, we might very well see a new institutionally oriented China constantly learning and adopting so as to adjust to the emerging realities of world politics.[218]

The US failed in fact miserably in convincing China regarding the help it has provided and is still giving for Pakistan's missiles and nuclear weapons development programmes. It seems, the US doesn't feel threatened in any way in achieving its objectives in South Asia, with the growing Sino-Pakistan politico-military relationship. Considering the way successive US administrations had tuned a blind eye to repeated transgression of the MTCR and even of the NPT. It was clear that the US felt itself helpless in enforcing its non-proliferation agenda on Pakistan and China. Far from punishing China for such blunt violations of its treaty obligations, the US has been an active salesman of military equipment to China.[219]

As after the 9/11, Pakistan once again became the frontline state for the US due to the critical situation which is still fluid in Afghanistan and Iraq. During the 1980s when Pakistan enjoyed the same position, the US Administration conveniently looked the other way when Islamabad acquired its nuclear capability clandestinely. Even after that the US only behaved like a paper tiger and did nothing substantial to dissuade China from giving nuclear and missile technology to Pakistan. The history has taken a full circle. The Chinese have joined hands with the US openly in the struggle against curbing and checking terrorism of any form. Therefore, "the chances are that Pakistan will continue to get required supplies for its nuclear and missile manufacturing facilities without any hindrance."[220]

But since 1995, China's support to Pakistan in the field of nuclear and missile technology has become a constant irritant in Sino-US relations. When it was reported that China had transferred 500 magnetic rings to Pakistan's unsafe guarded nuclear facilities, the US administration got worried. The US tried using economic sanctions against the Chinese, but after few months of imposition, it lifted by announcing that it had won a specific Chinese promise not to sell such nuclear equipment to any country. Despite the US desire to punish China on the technology transfer issues, it could not do so because it would have harmed the US more than China, in economic terms.[221]

During his visit to the US in November 1997, Chinese Premier withstood American pressure and stated that China would not compromise on its commitment to Pakistan regarding transfer of nuclear technology for peaceful purposes. He made it clear to his counterpart that Beijing had contractual obligations with Pakistan involving the setting up of power plants and it could not renege on the Chinese sincerity firmness and reiteration of support for Pakistan in the face of US pressure was another reminder of the strength and depth of Sino-Pak relations.[222]

India conducted the five nuclear tests on 11-13 May 1998. Earlier in an interview broadcast on the Indian television on 3 May 1998, Indian Defence Minister, George Fernandis argued that Chinese defence strategy was working to encircle India "China has provided Pakistan with both missiles as well as nuclear know-how and China has its nuclear weapons stockpiled in Tibet right along our borders." On the Eastern frontier, George maintained that China had trained and equipped the Myanmar Army whose strength had increased from 170,000 to 4,50,000. The Defence Minister concluded that China must be perceived as a threat by "any person who is concerned with India's security."[223]

The reaction of China to Indian tests was low key. However on 13 May when text of letters of Prime Minister Atal Bihari Vajpayee to President Clinton and other leaders was released. Beijing attitude went a change and its criticism of India's additional tests was much stronger. The second series of tests led China to make four important points one that Indian action reflected "an outrageous contempt for the common will of the international community" in favour of the CTBT. *Second,* India was using the "China threat" as an excuse for the development of its own nuclear weapons. *Third,* India was seeking hegemony in South Asia. *Fourth,* "If international community should adopt a common position by strongly demanding that India immediately stop its nuclear development programme.[224]

Indian nuclear policy has been marked by restraint and openness. It has not violated any international agreements either in 1974. The restraint exercised for 24 years after having demonstrated its capability in 1974, is in itself a unique example. Restraint, however, has to arise from strength. It cannot be based upon indecision or doubt. Restraint is valid only when doubts are removed. The series of tests taken by India led to the removal of doubts. The action involved was balanced as it was the minimum requirement, and component of national security. The government decision was, therefore to be seen as part of the tradition of restraint that has characterized India's policy.[225]

After the tests Indian Government categorically stated that it would observe a voluntary moratorium and refrain from conducting nuclear tests explosions and also indicated its willingness to move towards a dejure formalization of this declaration. According to Indian sources, the basic obligation of the CTBT was, thus met "to refrain from undertaking nuclear test explosions." The 'voluntary declaration was for the consumption of international community to know the seriousness of India's faith in the non-proliferation of nuclear weapons. It was also stated that India might take more decisions in this regard after assuring and analyzing the security needs of the country.[226]

The Indian Government had also indicated its willingness to participate in negotiations in the conference on disarmament in Geneva on a Fissile Material Cutoff Treaty. The main objective of this treaty was to prohibit future production of Fissile Materials for use in nuclear weapons or nuclear explosive devices. India's approach to these negotiations was to ensure that this treaty emerges as a universal and non-discriminatory treaty, backed by effective verification mechanism.[227]

China strongly condemned the Indian action to introduce nuclear weapons in South Asia which had destabilized the strategic balance in South Asia. The official Chinese media said, "India's explosions had sabotaged the fragile trust build up with Beijing over the past decade and raised the chances of nuclear war in South Asia.[228]

Not surprisingly, the Indian nuclear tests had created public outrage in Pakistan. In the first few weeks followed India's tests, Pakistani news papers were understandably obsessed with nuclear issue. The national dailies published well over 100 articles on this issue, written by noted defence and political analysts, scientists and academics. Dozens of editorial and numerous statements by a cross section of society were also splashed across the daily papers. Most of them urged Pakistan to go nuclear.

It also came as no surprise when an overwhelming number of politicians urged Pakistan to test its own device in order to rectify the "strategic balance" in the sub-continent. For Pakistan, the nuclear question quickly became a matter of pride and honour. From the comparatively liberal Prime Minister Benazir Bhutto to Qazi Hussain Ahmed, leader of the hardliner Jamaat-i-Islami, a variety of political leaders were urging the governmental to cross the nuclear threshold.[229]

While the tirade of public opinion was clearly in favour of Pakistan going nuclear, a small section of opinion makers boldly challenged the majority view, urging the government to desist from a tit-for-tat response. Instead of embarking on a dangerous nuclear arms race in the region, they believed that Pakistan ought to make the best of the situation. While India was weighed down by international sanctions, the US and other Western powers would reward Pakistan generously if it showed restraint. Indeed, the argument for restraint was compelling. Such a course of actions would guarantee Pakistan a steady flow of foreign aid investment and perhaps would have led to rescheduling if not waiving of foreign debt. There was also a destine possibility that Pakistan would be supplied more sophisticated conventional weapons including of course, the famous F-16 fighter aircraft, it had paid for but not received. In the eyes of the West, at least, Pakistan would also have scored a moral victory, emerging as the responsible one in South Asia and perhaps further isolating India in the international community. It was incentives such as these which the US President Clinton later described as the "priceless opportunity which Pakistan had missed by deciding to go nuclear."

For the Pakistani establishment, however this was clearly a difficult decision. On the one hand was the prospect of becoming the global community, favoured power in South Asia. On the other hand, were questions of strategic balance and national pride?[230]

By going ahead with the tests, Pakistan would have to face international sanctions that could well deal a moral blow to the economy. The other opinion was to cap the nuclear threshold at least for the time being. Nawaz Sharif must have realized that such a course of action would be nothing short of political suicide. Not only would be the risk involving the wrath of the army, he would also be forced to face the decisive taunts of his political opponents.[231]

So all things considered, Sharif was clearly strapped for choice. As noted Pakistani defence analyst felt "explode the bomb, and be prepared to eat the grass or decide against it, and eat humble pie." As it turned out, the government opted for grass, without having the slightest idea of what it actually tastes like.

Faced with two equally undesirable options, the Pakistan establishment initially seemed unable to make up its mind. It was a tricky situation, government officials maintained and that was what they had repeated to foreign officials when they descended on Islamabad, calling on it to show restraint. Nawaz Sharif had echoed this position when he spoke to the US President and the British Prime Minister. But this period of studied silence, it appeared that the Government was not locked in debate over the issue or mired in silence in diplomatic manoeuvering. It was clear that despite the public show of indecisiveness, the government and the armed forces had decided to be reactivating the Pakistan's nuclear weapons programme almost immediately after the Indian blasts. It was decided at the highest level while the Prime Minister considered all the options, preparation for nuclear testing would begin without further delay.

As the debate on Pakistan's future course of action intensified outside the country, Foreign Minister, Gohar Ayub openly declared the government's intentions to restore strategic balance in South Asia. When he was asked whether or not Pakistan would conduct a nuclear test, his stock reply was that "the decision will be about when not if." He clearly spoke for the hawks within the Pakistani establishment and, as it turned out, they had the last say.

Meanwhile, the Prime Minister's own position was uncertain. He talked about a befitting reply to India's increasingly aggressive posture, but also appeared to be considering other option. Indeed at one stage his pronouncements were being interpreted to mean that Pakistan had finally decided not to detonate a nuclear device any time in the near future. It was said that perhaps an international pressure, especially from the US, had worked or that the package offered by Washington was tempting. Some analysts described the government's response as conditional claiming that Pakistan had been promised that it would not be asked to sign the CTBT if it openly stated that it would not test any nuclear device. During this period of intense speculation, divisions within the establishment also appeared. Although sources in the government said the "security doctrine" presented by the army and the intelligence agencies left the government with little choice in the matter.

On 28 May 1998 Pakistan became the world's seventh nuclear weapons states, finally admitting openly what had been shrouded in ambiguity for the past fifteen years. Besides, the threats dangers of a nuclear South Asia, there were real possibilities to be considered. Hard line Hindu nationalist party hanging on by the skin of its teeth to a razor thin majority in the Lok Sabha, largely in order to consolidate its position, it had adopted a confrontationist stance with respect to its neighbours. The Bharitiya Janata Party also had a track record of acting on its promises whether vowed to demolish the Babri Masjid or to turn India into a nuclear weapon state. The above assumptions were in the minds of the Pakistani scholars and common men. Similarly, in Pakistan the situation was not reassuring either. It had a history of unstable and ambiguous political situation and its decision-making procedures are highly erratic. A fanatical ruler in Islamabad or in New Delhi might easily trigger a holocaust, and a single irresponsible decision in either capital could spell nuclear disaster.[232]

Since the Indian tests, the internal debate on the future directions of Pakistan's nuclear policy was clearly divided into three factions—the nuclear hawks, the nuclear doves and those who wished to see a continuation of the long standing policy of nuclear ambiguity that is relating nuclear weapons capability without opting for overt weaponization.

As far as the nuclear hawks were concerned, it included all the major Islamist parties, some secular political parties opposed to the Muslim League government as well as some key figures of the ruling political party especially Foreign Minister Gohar Ayub Khan, who after submitting his resignation, was given a new lease of life by the nuclear crisis. This camp was also composed of ultranationalist journalists and academicians, a number of retired civil and military bureaucrats, some members of the business community and the odd political economists. In their collective opinion, Pakistan had no choice but to test a nuclear device, and, moreover, they felt, it should declare itself a nuclear weapon state, rejecting all the incentives proposed by the external actors, attempting to pressurise or to persuade Pakistan from adopting an overt nuclear course. In their view, any other policy choice would jeopardize national security and undermine national sovereignty by emboldening India. The Kashmir cause would suffer, and Pakistan would become hostage to the whims of external benefactors, especially the US, which had always failed to come to Pakistan's rescue in times of need.

The nuclear doves, of which surprisingly several surfaced in the wake of the Indian tests, included a number of regional parties and their student groups such as Sindhi Awami Tehrik, the Sind Democratic Party, as well as its student wing, the Baloch Students' Organization. Asghar Khan's Tehrik-e-Istiqlal and the Pakistani National Party were also strongly opposed to the nuclear tests. Other nuclear doves included influential opinion makers in the print media, human rights groups and activists, most economists, some members of the business community and the odd retired civil or military bureaucrats.[233]

For the nuclear doves, the Indian nuclear weapons programme was a grave threat to South Asian security and also undermined the international non-proliferation regime. However, they believed a Pakistani retaliatory test would not only threaten Pakistan's national security by triggering a regional nuclear arms race but could also devastate Pakistan's politically and economically, as a result of harsh economic sanctions. The nuclear doves also argued that Pakistan's national security was dependent on economic development and democratic functioning and not on a simple minded reliance on weapons, conventional or nuclear. Hence, they called for a dialogue on easing tensions with India accompanied by an internal redefinition of national security.[234]

The third group in the nuclear debate supporters of Pakistan's long standing policy of nuclear ambiguity unlike the nuclear doves, who favoured denunciations of nuclear weapons, wanted retention of nuclear weapons capability on the grounds that an untested nuclear capability, which they also equated with national sovereignty and independence would be a sufficient deterrence against India. Ever since the creation of Pakistan's nuclear weapons programme, supporters of ambiguity have dominated the public debate since their stand had been in consonance with the directions of official policy. After the May 1998 Indian nuclear tests there were defections to the camp of nuclear hawks since many supporters of the then official policy of ambiguity believed that a more overt nuclear weapons policy was then required. However, there were also some interesting defections of nuclear hawks to the cause of ambiguity on the assumption that the threat of international sanctions required restraint on Pakistan's part. Hence, in their view, a demonstration of nuclear weapon capability would undermine Pakistan interests. These defections include a number of academicians, opinion-makers, and a particularly high profile hawks like former Army Chief, Mirza Aslam Beg. They appeared to be on the verge of defection. Other more consistent supporters of ambiguity included former policy-makers such as ex-Chairman, Pakistan Atomic Energy Commission, Munir Ahmed Khan. Political parties such as Awam National Party and influential factions of the PPP, though PPP leader Benazir Bhutto motivated by political expediency had adopted a hawkish posture. The Muslim League Government could also have been included within the field of nuclear ambiguity. In his statement on the eve of the Pakistan nuclear tests, Prime Minister did not support a policy of overt weaponization. He appeared hesitant to opt for a nuclear test, conscious of the threats of international military and economic sanctions. Sharif support for ambiguity, however, eroded as nuclear hawks gained ascendancy in the nuclear decision-making process and his political survival was at stake.[235]

This internal elite discourse on the pros and cons of nuclear testing did not influence the ultimate decision to test, since the closed circle of Pakistani decision-makers, with its traditional aversion to dissenting views was unfamiliar with democratic bargaining process. In the aftermath of the Pakistani nuclear tests and the imposition of sanctions by the

US, a rallying around the flag response had resulted in supporters of three schools of nuclear opinion initially joining hands. Even the doyen of the political doves, Asghar Khan had reluctantly expressed his support in the cause of national solidarity for the government decision to demonstrate its nuclear capability.[236]

Pakistani leaders seemed to view nuclear weapons both as deterrent to conventional weapons and war, even war fought for limited aims, as an option forwarding off defeat, even if the existence of state was not at stake. If statements made by Pakistani leaders and military experts were not intentionally misleading, they suggested that Pakistan requires tactical nuclear weapons and to use them first, under very demanding circumstances of course. Pakistani planners and decision-makers were also aware that the very existence of India's nuclear weapons was very risky, so they could be expected to see the need for an offsetting arsenal of long range missiles as well.[237]

Pakistan, after conducting the tests had offered to enter into a dialogue with India to ensure "Mutual Restraint" in the wake of nuclear tests by both sides but said should address all outstanding issues, including the thorny Kashmir problem. The Pakistani Foreign Secretary Shamshad Ahmed also stressed the need for[238] equitable measures or nuclear stabilization in the region. No doubt, the tests by India and Pakistan "signal the beginning of a nuclear arms race in the Indian sub-continent. The issue no longer is of creating a strategic symmetry but of doing one better than your adversary in developing weapons of mass destruction. The Pakistani tests came at a time when the national consensus an the nuclear tests was finally coming to end. The unquestioning enthusiasm, which seemed all set to engulf India in the immediate aftermath of the nuclear tests, appeared to be tapering of."

As the debate over the Pakistan tests in Parliament showed that Indian opposition leaders across the political spectrum had realized the ruinous consequences of a nuclear arms race. Former Prime Minister I.K. Gujral, lambasted the BJP government's claim of being prompted by security considerations *vis-à-vis* China. He stated categorically that when he demitted the office there was no such threat. The Congress urged it to reiterate a commitment to disarmament, nuclear non-proliferation and the elimination of all nuclear weapons, on its part, the left warned government against weaponisation and deployment.[239]

The jingoistic behaviour of Vajpayee advisers and cabinet colleagues in the aftermath of the tests had put India in immensely greater peril. It made credible Pakistan's claim that it tested its nuclear weapons because of direct threat from BJP Ministers, and because India was on the point of launching the attack on its nuclear installations.[240] Pakistan Foreign Secretary even notified to the Clinton Administration and the UN Secretary General Koffi Anan that it expected attacks by Indian and Israeli fighter jets on Pakistan nuclear installations. Pakistan's information was based on reports collected by its external spy agency, ISI. Islamabad's fears were assuaged by firm assurances from the State Department that there were no Israeli aircraft based in India. Unconvinced, Gohar Ayub and Ambassador Kamal embarked on a media campaign in Washington with allegations of Israel and Indian war planes equipped with long range refueling gear poised to attack."[241]

The US officials had offered many theories why such a scenario might have been conjured up by Pakistan. But essentially the argument was that it might have been "cooked up" to justify the tests. One intelligence officer was however quoted a saying that there were also fears that Islamabad might use the pretext of unspecified external aggression to launch one of their Gauri missiles against an Indian target with an untested nuclear warhead. One US official had warned that any "miscalculation" could have triggered off a conflict. One another reason why there had been such press accounts about Pakistani fears about Indo-Israeli alliance was due to the fact that there have been several half-baked theories floating in the Arab press that Israel might have assisted India's nuclear programme and helped accelerate its course towards nuclear testing. There was a talk of secretive conclaves between India's nuclear scientists and Chief of Israeli Nuclear Energy Programme. But following the Pakistani tests, news dispatched from the Middle-East had started talking about the pride of many Arabs in the "Islamic bomb" as detonated by Pakistan.[242]

The New York Times reported that it required Pakistan "more than three decades, a global network of theft and espionage, and uncounted millions for Pakistan one of the world's poorest countries to explode the bomb. But it could not have happened without the smuggled Chinese technology and contradictory shifts in American policy." The report further said that China a "staunch ally of Pakistan provided blue-prints for the bomb, as well as highly enriched uranium, titanium, and key components for a nuclear weapons production complex."

The report also catalogued the US assistance to Pakistan which proved essential to its nuclear programme (especially uranium and tritium), provided extensive to Islamabad's nuclear scientists between the fifties to the late seventies, and turned a blind eye to the nuclear weapons programme in the 1980s because Pakistan was providing the crucial link for the CIA's efforts to smuggle billions of dollars worth weapons to Afghan guerrillas attempting to drive out Soviet invaders. When that cover action ended "it left Pakistan feeling defenceless.[243]

A secret State Department report based on evidence gathered by the CIA stated that there was "Unambiguous evidence that Pakistan had a secret blueprint for a bomb." That blueprint was made in China. Belatedly the US officials had approached Pakistani officials at the highest levels. The news reports quoted Milt Bearder, a former CIA officer based in Pakistani between 1986 and 1989 said that "we went to them and said, "Here is what your bomb looks like, even showed them the model I believe."[244]

No doubt, it was the political and moral support of the Chinese leadership that had helped Pakistani to reach a decision for conducting nuclear tests. In a briefing on 20 May to newsmen on his arrival from Beijing where he had gone for consolations with the Chinese leadership, Foreign Secretary said, "There is a complete identity of views between Pakistan and China on the gravity of the situation which has resulted from India's reckless actions agreed that Indian nuclear explosions were a threat to Pakistan's security.

He further said, that China has promised not to retaliate with economic sanctions against Pakistan exploding a nuclear device and the Chinese leadership reaffirmed that the "all weather friendship between the two countries was above any political expediencies." He also said that China would not impose economic sanctions against Islamabad should it conduct a nuclear test. The US media reported that Beijing had made no public promises to provide a "nuclear umbrella" to Pakistan against any potential threat from India. Television commentaries and *New York Times* maintained that although China was sympathetic to long-term ally Pakistan, it was unlikely to make Pakistan such an offer of nuclear protection and "will probably" quietly oppose any Pakistan test.[245]

In a report from Beijing *The Times* quoting Chinese sources said that China would not encourage Pakistan to conduct its own nuclear tests and it was not a country that provided nuclear umbrella to other countries.

Although China had publicly refrained from joining chorus urging Islamabad not to respond to India's nuclear tests, it had strongly condemned the Indian tests. However, the Pakistan tests came at a time when Beijing was trying to evolve a "new and delicate" rule for itself. It came at a time when it had been compelled to single its friendship with Pakistan alongside the demands of "important nations like the US and India with which China has been seeking to improve ties." Quoting a China expert *The Times* reported that "China's challenge is to reassure Pakistan that they will not stand by it without inflaming relations with India or the US." And despite the irritants of Chinese assistance to Pakistan in missile technology, the former placed a great value on their developing relationship with India. Citing the views of Shong Hui Peng, a Professor at Beijing University, the paper said that "China has now adjusted its policies in South Asia so that it now places importance on relations with India and Pakistan. I think that's very important regional security."[246]

The report also said some Chinese experts were surprised to hear comments emanating from New Delhi that Chinese threat had necessitated the Indian threat and it had used it as an "excuse" for conducting them. An unnamed former Chinese official was quoted as saying, "Since the world has come out for disarmament, it is no longer acceptable to say we are testing because we are a great power to be a part of the nuclear club. It is much better to say that there is this big nuclear power on our borders so we have to."[247]

On the other hand, Indian security analysts and defence experts felt that the tests were long overdue and they were entirely in tune with the strategic security environment prevailing in the Indian neighbourhood. The choice was between inaction while being slowly squeezed by smiling faces with deceptive hands or acting on the direction that a country's national interests are permanent whereas friends need not be so. China had been pursuing a major defence modernization and she launched missiles programme that included nuclear tipped land, air along with long range aircraft. China was keen to resolve its border dispute with Russia but was slow in resolving the same with India. With monotonous regularity, it was publishing false maps of the Sino-Indian border while sending foot patrols on incursion mission into Indian territory. More deviously, Beijing had since long been arming Pakistan with both conventional weapons (aircraft, tanks, etc.) as also with both missile and nuclear technology. While issuing public denials and pledging itself to improving relations with India.[248]

Chinese modernization of missile technology included fuel technology, improved accuracy and mobility, Multiple Independently Targetable Re-entry Vehicles (MIRV), improved reaction time, hardened silos, and a more sophisticated satellite navigation technology China was engaged in developing the XXJ Stealth fighter and was helping Pakistan develop the Super F-7 fighter.

Similarly, Pakistan's major technology thrust had been on maintaining nuclear warheads for delivery through ballistic missiles supplied by China (M-11s) and North Korea (Nodong-11). Pakistan had been building a missile factory at Fateh Ganj located at a distance of 50 km from Islamabad. The US had chosen to go soft wink at the Sino-Pakistan nuclear and missile cooperation despite regular pronouncements by the US government officials that this was still continuing."[249] It was speculated that the US would like to counter India's tests by ensuring regional balance by asking "all the government in the region to enhance regional stability."[250]

Pakistan and CTBT

Pakistan had called for a ban on underground nuclear tests when the "Partial Test Ban Treaty" was being negotiated and again when it was being signed.[251] Also during the negotiations for the NPT, Pakistan proposed the Comprehensive Test Ban (CTBT) and fissile material cutoff to have a more balanced responsibility between the nuclear weapon states and the non-nuclear weapons states.[252] From 1984 to 1986, Pakistan supported all the resolutions concerning the CTBT in the UN General Assembly.[253]

Pakistan had not been a major player in the CTBT negotiations but it drove importance from the fact that nuclear proliferation must be maintained and checked. Pakistan's basic concern relating CTBT have been that the treaty should not put it at disadvantage *vis-à-vis* India. Pakistan being the country with the smaller nuclear capability, found it difficult to accept any transparency in its nuclear programme as a result of the signing of the CTBT. Pakistan's support to the CTBT was to be subject to the gains in return.

Officially Pakistan had said that it was ready to sign the CTBT provided India did it too. There was also a non-official minority within Pakistan which was in favour of unilaterally signing of the CTBT for getting economic or moral objectives fulfilled. They argued that CTBT is not dangerous to Pakistan's security. They said, the treaty had a clause "national interest option" which said that any state which had signed the treaty could withdraw if it felt that "extra ordinary events related to the subject matter of the treaty had jeopardized its supreme interests."[254]

Nawaz Sharif had committed at the UN General Assembly that Pakistan would sign the CTBT before September 1999. He said that Pakistan had always opposed to both vertical and horizontal nuclear proliferation but was also concerned about some loop-holes in the treaty. It had some worries on the verification and onsite inspection causes of the treaty. Pakistan like India was working for a consensus to develop before it was in a position to take a decision on the question of signing the CTBT.[255]

To sign or not to sign has always been a major controversy in Pakistan. In Pakistan, there has always been suspicion regarding the establishment setting out on critical issues. The supporters of the CTBT range from pure moralists, who support non-proliferation at all costs, to those who view this treaty as harmless. They argue that by signing the CTBT after having tested, Pakistan may have something to gain, and nothing to lose. They quote clauses and develop their arguments logically, but there remains suspect in the eyes of the detractors. Both sides continue to seek the hidden agendas on the other, which merely, "The government's desire to evolve a consensus is understandable, though this effort should have preceded any statement, rather than follow it."

There are different perceptions about the CTBT in Pakistan. All religious parties are opposed to the signing of the CTBT and are always in contact with each other to formulate a joint line of action if the government signed the CTBT, and this played in the hands of the enemies who are out to deprive the only Islamic state of its nuclear capability.

Maulana Noorani, the President of the JUP said that Islamabad should not follow New Delhi on this issue as India, Japan, Israel and the US were joining hands against Pakistan and China. Noorani appealed to the military leadership to beware of the enemies intrigues against Pakistan who wanted to create gulf between the people and their beloved armed forces. In his opinion, the military government should reject all pressures about the CTBT like its pre-decision had done to carry out nuclear tests in May 1998. He said had Pakistan not acquired nuclear capability, India would have attacked long ago to make it a part of what it called united India,[256] the logic of the situation is overwhelmingly in favour of signing, but when has Pakistan ever followed logic? At its very creation, logic said it would collapse in six months—but it is still here. Logic said that Pakistan should merely accept Indian hegemony—but it is still definitely upright. Logic said a poor country like Pakistan would be unable to withstand sanctions against nuclearisation but it matched India test for nuclear test. Too much, both direct cost and indirect development foregone, has been invested in Pakistan's nuclear programme for it to be given up, and under the circumstances, signing the CTBT would appear the first step to accepting defeat on this issue.[257]

A retired army officer Lt. Gen. Javed Nasir felt that, if the signing of the CTBT was that innocent and innocuous, why has the US Senate not ratified it? It was strange that a country which has not ratified the CTBT itself is blowing hot and cold on others to sign it.

"They are all honey and sugar and sparkly smiles when they talk to the Indians but when they talk to us, they frown with all sorts of threats and coercions.... loans, temptations and the newly found bait of legitimacy to the present military regime. In any event, why is Pakistan so scared of the sanctions... is sanctions instil a quality of sacrifice? Nations are always built on the laurels of their sacrifices. The sanctions against us when compared to what the Iranian underwent ... when these were imposed on Iran, they brought down its imports from $80 billion to just $18 billions, are not huge. Pakistan should sign CTBT if the following conditions are met:

- "The signing should remain linked to signing it by India.
- Coercive and discriminatory attitude of the West/ US/G-8 towards Pakistan *vis-à-vis* India must change.
- Acceptance of Pakistan as a nuclear weapon state.
- Compelling India to remove the most dangerous nuclear-flash-point, i.e. Kashmir by starting a dialogue with Pakistan immediately and giving a time frame for the settlement of the Kashmir issue.
- Declaration by NATO that Pakistan will not be made a target of its initiative on weapon of mass destruction.
- Saving and rescheduling loans.
- The inspection/monitoring team will remain confined to a specific area and will remain under

command of the host country and will move out of it only with specific permission of the government.

- Finally, the CTBT must give time table for destruction of all nuclear weapons in the world, otherwise it will remain an incomplete treaty."[258]

Hamid Alvi, a noted political observer, was strongly in favour of Pakistan joining the CTBT regime. He felt that the opponents of the CTBT, particularly the right wing type did not seem to have closely studied the text of the CTBT, nor they seem to realize that Pakistan participated in preparation of the text and approved it prior to its opening up for state parties' signature in 1996. Further, the opponents seemed to be confusing CTBT with NPT when they argued that Pakistan's acceptance of the former would weaken its defenses. Whether such arguments were forwarded deliberately or because of ignorance was hard to understand. However, a glance over the treaty text might help in dispelling the mist which over the period had gathered around the subject.

Article I of the CTBT lays down basic obligations of the states which sign the CTBT. It reads, "Each state party undertakes not to carry out any nuclear weapon tests explosions, or any other nuclear explosions and to prohibit and prevent any such nuclear explosions of any place under jurisdiction or control." It must be noted that the obligations of signatory to CTBT is confined not to testing. Inspection of nuclear facilities or rollback is not involved. Basically, the treaty does not intend to weapon the defence line of a state which NPT definitely does.

Article II of the CTBT is longest in context and fundamental to its organizational structure. In contrast to the organization of UN, the treaty structure is free from discriminations and gives no veto power.

Unlike the UN Security Council, no member in Executive of CTBT has the dominant power. In matters of procedure, it shall take decision by a majority of all its members and on matters of substance, by a two third majority of elite members. Its firmest function shall be to implement the treaty which in turn involves monitoring of nuclear explosion anywhere in the world, and proposed action against such activity. A technical secretariat and vast network of monitoring system shall help the Council to discharge its functions. Articles III, IV and V list measures which could be taken to ensure compliance with treaty.

From the point of view of Pakistan fears and apprehensions, the Article IX provides the necessary security checks and balances. Thus, Pakistan if at any point of time feels threatened by nuclear related developments in the region, nothing could stop it from withdrawing from CTBT and conducts its own nuclear tests. It must be mentioned that besides political gains, the only objective to conduct a test is to check on the working of a technology. At this juncture, Pakistan seemed to have lot to gain and nothing significant to lose by signing the CTBT. Entry into CTBT would be a boon for Pakistan economy as it would be getting liberal economic aid and other facilities. As regards matching Pakistan's nuclear clout with India, the latter is sure to come under tremendous pressure once Pakistan inks the CTBT. In any event, Pakistan should not let Delhi decide Pakistan's policy in this regard. Making CTBT conditional to its signing by India, as some political parties demand, is a sure way to pass the initiative and accompanying gains to Pakistan's adversary.[259]

Nuclear Proliferation: Some Observations

The preamble of the Draft Report of National Security Advisory Board on Indian Nuclear Doctrine, 17 August 1999 clearly stated that "The Use of nuclear weapons in particular as well as other weapons of mass destruction constitutes the gravest threat to humanity and to peace and stability in the international system. Unlike the other two categories of weapons of mass destruction, biological or chemical weapons which have been outlawed by international treaties, nuclear weapons remain instruments for national and collective security, the possession of which on a selective basis has been sought to be legtimized through permanent extension of the NPT in May 1998. Nuclear weapons states have asserted that they will continue to rely on nuclear weapons with some of them adopting policies to use them even in a non-nuclear context. These developments amount to virtual abandonment of nuclear disarmament. This is a serious setback to the international community to abolish weapons of mass destruction... However, the very existence of offensive doctrine pertaining to the first use of nuclear weapons and the insistence of some nuclear weapons states on the legitimacy of their use, even against non-nuclear weapons countries constitute a threat to peace, stability and sovereignty of states."[260] The Indian nuclear doctrine which envisages, according to Pakistan, in the guise of credible minimum nuclear deterrence is an exercise for a massive expansion of strategic as well as conventional forces. With a large loud air and sea based strike force of bombers and missiles, capable of reaching every nook and corner of Pakistan, India would pose a threat far more serious in future than at present. Pakistan has always blamed India for the proliferation of nuclear weapons in the region and jeopardizing the military balance, posing a serious threat to it.

There is a widespread feeling in the minds of Pakistani political, military, religious and bureaucratic circles that major powers have failed miserably to prevail on India to abandon its ambitious plans. Their capacity and the desire to promote nuclear restraint in South Asia has ebbed. They do not have effective leverage or lack the will to use it for fear of detriment to their economic and political interests in India. Aga Shah, Zulfikar Khan and Abdul Sattar discussed the various issues related with seeking nuclear peace in the region.[261] Their source of anxiety and concerns were related with the following discussions: (1) "What is needed to focus on objective analysis and assessment of the implications of India's plan for Pakistan's defence and security? How long will India take to realize the projected force goals? (2) To what extent might our minimal deterrent capability become vulnerable to a surprise attack by Indian missiles and strike aircrafts? (3) India might consider its pre-emptive strike and interception capability, enhanced by the anti-ballistic missile system. New Delhi is planning to acquire of to make it immune from Pakistan attack? (4) What are the concrete steps Pakistan should take to ensure the survival, ability and credibility of its deterrence force?"[262]

They all strongly believed that "restorations of the credibility of Pakistan's deterrence capability was a very important issue. There was a need to ensure the continued efficacy of Pakistan's deterrence force." The Pakistan's leadership had realized the importance of nuclear deterrence from the past experiences and that was the reason they "instructively assimilated the deterrence rationale and embarked on a programme to acquire the nuclear weapon options." Even though nuclear weapons were not assembled, the recessed capability was credible enough to induce restrains against escalations. The Kargil crisis of 1999 had tested and illustrated the deterrence assumption.[263]

It is a well known fact that Pakistan does not have a "No First Use Policy." A top ranking military officer General Khalid Kidwai, while interacting with the members of the London Network Centro Volta, which prepared a concise Report on "Nuclear Safety, Nuclear Stability and Nuclear Strategy in Pakistan" said that Pakistani nuclear weapons would be used only "if the very existence of Pakistan as a state was at stake." He further elaborated that "Nuclear weapons are aimed solely at India. In case that deterrence fails, they will be used if (a) India attacks Pakistan and conquers a large part of its territory (space threshold), (b) India destroys a large part either of its land or air forces (military threshold), (c) India proceeds to the economic strengthening of Pakistan (economic strengthening) included an blockade of Pakistan and the stopping of the waters of the Indus river, (d) India pushes Pakistan into political destabilization or creates a large internal subversion in Pakistan (domestic destabilization)."[264]

That was not an official version of Pakistan government as it has not articulated or perhaps even defined the contingencies in which Pakistan might use nuclear weapons. The assumption has always been that if the enemy launches a general war and undertakes a piercing attack, threatening to occupy large territory or communication junction, the weapons of last resort "would have to be invoked. That possibility cannot be ignored and acts as a deterrent."

It seemed the combination of a diversity and broadness of the motivations that might justify the use of the nuclear weapons, on one side, and the use of the nuclear threat to enforce a rational decision-making, i.e. not too aggressive behaviour by the opponents, on the other. It is also clear that the nuclear weapons are perceived in Pakistan as an instrument to counter veil a manifest conventional inferiority *vis-à-vis* the Indian military force. Presumably, Pakistan feels or will feel compelled to enlarge and diversify its nuclear arsenal so to increase the nuclear options and make the threat of nuclear retaliation more credible. If this diversification will move Pakistan away from the doomsday machine vision, it will also increase the likelihood of the use of nuclear weapons in a situation of crisis. Thus, the Indian sub-continent might follow on a reduced scale (but not necessarily on a reduced risk) the pattern of the US-USSR nuclear race during the cold war. The alternatives might come from dialogue between India and Pakistan on the one side and from some kinds of international constraints and pressure on the two nuclear programmes in the sub-continent, on the other side.[265]

Since late 1980, political and military changes have transformed East-West relations. The collapse of the Soviet Union after the introduction of widespread reforms popularly known as "Glasnost and Perestroika, communist collapse in the Eastern Europe, and the German unification, have altered the world map completely."[266]

The security environment in the Middle East and Gulf, South Asia and South East Asia and other regions referred as "Third World" stands in sharp contrast. Here political, economic, ethnic and military conflicts have surfaced quite later. Many regional rivals are fielding sophisticated conventional weapons, including ballistic missiles, and acquiring capabilities to manufacture the same. Biological and nuclear weapons proliferation is underway, and it is felt that biological weapons proliferation would gain momentum in the years to come.[267]

Why should we worry about the spread of nuclear weapons? The answer is by no means obvious. After all, we have lived with nuclear deterrence for more than half a century now. The two super powers maintained a long peace throughout the cold war, despite deep political hostilities, numerous crisis situations emerged and followed by a prolonged armed race.[268]

A prominent group of scholars have pointed out to the apparent contradiction between a peaceful nuclear past and a fearful nuclear future and argued that the further spread of nuclear weapons will be a stabilizing factor in international relations. A number of prominent political scientists have also jumped into the pro-proliferation band wagon. Bruce Bueno de Mosqueto and William Riker advocate the selective spread of nuclear weapons into areas when non-nuclear states face nuclear armed adversaries. Since the choice of bilateral conflict becoming nuclear... decreases to zero when all nations are nuclear and a superb deterrent and argues that the world would have been more safe if Germany, Ukraine and Japan become nuclear powers in the post-cold war era. Other scholars reach similar conclusions for different countries. Stephen Van Evera advocates German's acquisition of a nuclear weapon arsenal to deter Russia. Barry Posen recommends that Ukraine should keep nuclear weapons as a deterrent against future Russian military interventions; Peter Lavoy predicts that nuclear weapons would prevent future war between India and Pakistan. Both Martin Van and Shiu Feldman maintain that nuclear proliferation in Middle-East would help in reducing tension between Arabs and Israel. This "proliferation optimist" position is considered to be the product of rational deterrence theory. The possession of nuclear weapons by two powers can reduce the likelihood of war precisely because it makes the cost of war so great.[269]

There is of course *status quo* doctrine also which intends to keep someone else from actually doing what they may be contemplating doing. But it had not worked with any consistency in the pre-nuclear era, indeed the study of deterrence failures prior to 1945 gave rise, during the latter years of the cold war, to repeated warnings that deterrence might be less robust than it appeared to be. It is difficult to determine, even today, just how revisionist each of the great powers was with respect to the cold war *status quo* partly because the documents are still insufficiently available for the Soviet and the Chinese sides, but partly also because even when documents do exist, they do not always fully reflect the intentions of those who produce them. And then, there is the additional difficulty that the statements themselves may not always know what they intend.[270]

The Pakistani nuclear analysts argue that deterrence was the sole aim, and a small arsenal was considered adequate. Consistently with that purpose, Pakistan was satisfied with nuclear capability. For years after years achieving that capability, it realized on recessed deterrence, refraining from test restraints. At no time did Pakistan contemplate use of nuclear weapons for war fighting or seek to develop capability for a pre-emptive attack. Believing that its minimal capability was then sufficient for deterrence, it even discontinued further production of fissile uranium in 1989. They also advocate the up-gradation of the deterrence force in proportion to the heightened threat of pre-emption and interception. But minimum deterrence has been and should continue to be the guarding principle of Pakistan's nuclear pursuit. Of course, the minimum cannot be described in static numbers. In the absence of an agreement on mutual restraints, the size of Pakistan's arsenal and its deployment pattern have to be adjusted to ward off the dangers of pre-emptive strike and interception. Only then can deterrence remain efficacious.[271]

Implicit in nuclear deterrence is the assumption that nuclear weapons are intended to prevent wars, and not only for fighting wars. The contingencies in which nuclear weapons may have to be used have not been articulated and may even be difficult to define. It is obvious however that a weapon of last resort is by definition not a weapon to be used for conquest or expansion. Pakistan can therefore declare that it will never resort to the threat or use of nuclear weapons, or for that matter conventional force, for aggression. A unilateral non-aggression proclamation automatically rules out the first use of nuclear or conventional weapons.[272]

So far Pakistan has not declared any nuclear doctrine except that its strategy remained premised on basic security considerations—to construct a credible nuclear deterrence, therefore, the calculus of Pakistan's nuclear threshold has been deliberately shrouded in vagueness with a view to sustain a viable deterrent *vis-à-vis* India's much larger conventional and strategic forces. On 30 May 2002, Pakistan Ambassador to the UN, Munir Akram defended Islamabad's right to "rely on means to deter India's aggression." He further reiterated that Pakistan possessed the means and we will not neutralize it by any doctrine of "No First Use." If India reserves the right to use conventional forces, how can Pakistan, a weaker power be expected to rule out all means of deterrence. Adding that India had an advantage over Pakistan in the conventional forces, Munir Ahmed declared that "We have not said we will use nuclear weapons. We possess nuclear weapons, so does India."[273]

The deep-rooted rivalry between India and Pakistan is characterized by a high degree of hatred and mistrust. Besides both countries presently do not possess the level of mutual assured destruction potentials, which the US and the former Soviet Union possessed during the cold war that had finally maintained the critical deterrent from the 1940s down to the 1990s. Michael Krepon writes, "The US and the Soviet Union managed to avoid nuclear and conventional war force during the cold war, while Jockeyeing for advantage in myriad ways, including proxy wars and a succession of crisis that becomes surrogates for direct conflict... The stability instability paradox was embedded in the enormity of the stakes involved in crossing the nuclear threshold. As positioned by western deterrence theorists, offsetting nuclear capabilities and secure, second strike capabilities would induce special caution, providing the basis of war prevention and escalation control offsetting nuclear deterrents channelled the super powers competitions into "safer" pursuits, the object of which would be to impose penalties on an adversary without inducting direct conflict."[274]

At the present juncture, India and Pakistan are primarily aiming their nuclear deterrence as based on counter-value instead of counter-force targets. The subsequent advancement of their nuclear and defence related technologies, which of course includes the second strike capabilities, both countries would then be able to attack the counterforce targets as well. Therefore, even in the foreseeable future, superiority in the nuclear weapons would not be of great consequence. Therefore, India and Pakistan should not formulate strategies that subject their security, or even their survival, hostage to the luck factor, which could possibly spiral out of control in crisis.[275]

The entire concept of security of South Asia is based on principles of "security", "fear" and "hegemony." Both India and Pakistan have entangled themselves in a perpetual cobweb of "offensive" and "defensive" types of solutions respectively. As a result, India has sought to prevent the emergence of "peer" competitor on the sub-continent, Pakistan to challenge its supremacy. This "peer" competition between India and Pakistan took a turning point in 1974 when India conducted its first nuclear test, which then started a new period of nuclear arms race in South Asia.[276]

The Pakistan Foreign Minister Abdul Sattar, while delivering a speech at the Institute of Strategic Studies on 25 November 1999 said that, "Minimum nuclear deterrence will remain the guiding principle of our nuclear strategy." In order to ensure the survivability and creditability of the deterrent, Pakistan will have to maintain presence and upgrade its capability. In the absence of alternatives, acquisition of the nuclear option was conceived as a means of deterrence against aggression and prevention of war. Safeguarding the peace and security of the country was the sole objective and Pakistan entertained no ambition to a great power status or regional domination.[277]

Shamshad Ahmed, then Foreign Secretary of Pakistan, categorically said that India developed its nuclear option as a matter of choice and policy consistent with its long held vision as a regional hegemony and a major global power. In contrast, Pakistan exercised nuclear optional in response to the compulsion of its security environment. He further said, "The nuclearization of South Asia is neither of our choice, but it is now a reality that cannot be wished away. The international community should fully comprehend the near and long-term strategic implications of India's proposed nuclear doctrine, asserting that New Delhi sought to establish in the next two decades its total military hegemony in South Asia and beyond... India's nuclear ambitions aimed at creating a nuclear trial employing upto 400 nuclear warheads on land, sea and in air at a cost estimated by independent experts as anywhere between 20 billions and hundreds of billions of dollar India intends to destroy Pakistan's economy but Pakistan can and will find ways and means to maintain credible nuclear deterrence against India without the need to match it—bomb for bomb, missile for missile."[278]

He called upon the international community to check the Indian nuclear designs in time, as India's nuclear doctrine would give a deadly blow to all international efforts at halting fissile material production, apart from undermining other major nuclear disarmament and non-proliferation objectives. He also feared that unless the international community responded in a coherent and determined way to this doctrine in order to arrest India's dangerous plans for nuclear and conventional arms satisfaction. India should assure its neighbours and the world on 10 points on nuclear doctrine.[279]

- "Both India and Pakistan would not conduct nuclear tests until the CTBT comes into force.
- They will not operationalize or deploy nuclear weapons.
- India will not build hundreds of nuclear warheads as indicated in its doctrine.
- No further production or possession of large stock of fissile materials.
- India will not seek to create a sea-based and sub-marine-based nuclear armed forces.
- It will not acquire, develop or deploy anti-ballistic missiles which could boost nuclear arms race in this region.
- It will refrain from any military related actions in space.
- It should put a restraint on its plans for acquisition and development of advanced aircraft and nuclear sub-marines.
- It will seriously address and resolve the outstanding problems with Pakistan, particularly the Kashmir issue.
- It will enter into negotiations with Pakistan on an "elaborate strategic restraint regime for South Asia."[280]

When nations with deep grievances acquire nuclear weapons, tensions increase and their crisis becomes more wrecking. It is therefore, not surprising that India and Pakistan are traversing a very dangerous passage marked by periods of intense confrontation. Offsetting nuclear capabilities on the sub-continent have made crisis avoidance and conflict resolution more imperative, but also more difficult to achieve.

One reason why crisis has become more prevalent under the nuclear shadow is that some in Pakistan have sought to use unconventional warfare, backed by nuclear weapons to leverage a more favourable outcome of the Kashmir dispute. Decades of Pakistani diplomacy, two conventional wars, and unconventional means have failed to wrest territorial gains from New Delhi. Pakistan's failed Kashmir policies have instead worsened social, economic and political conditions at home, while penalizing those living across the Kashmir divide.[281]

Nuclear Threat Reduction: A Need for South Asia

Zawar Haider Abidi feels that "security and stability in South Asia pivot on relations between India and Pakistan... The growth of Indian conventional capabilities has resulted in an asymmetry in the regional conventional military balance... Reduction of the military threat will diminish the chances of escalation up to and across the nuclear threshold, avoiding an outcome with devastating consequences for not only the region but also the entire international community."[282]

Krepon has suggested ten key commandments to reduce the risk of nuclear escalation:

- Do not change the territorial *status quo* in sensitive areas by use of force.
- Avoid nuclear brinkmanship.
- Avoid dangerous military preaches.
- Put in place special reassurance measures for ballistic missiles and other nuclear forces.
- Implement properly treaty obligations, risk reduction, and CBM's.
- Agree on verification arrangements, including intrusive monitoring.

- Establish reliable lines of communication between political leaders and between military leaders.
- Establish redundant and reliable command and control arrangements as well as intelligence-gathering capabilities to know that the other side is up to, especially in a crisis.
- Keep working hard on these arrangements. Improve them and do not take anything for granted.
- Hope for plan dumb luck or divine intervention.[283]

Nuclear stabilization presumes adequate backup from conventional forces. Conventional balances are not easy to calculate, because advantages in some categories might be offset by others. Moreover, it is easier to defend than to advance, particularly in the rugged terrain much of the Kashmir divide. In South Asia, the conventional military balance is shifting steadily in India's favour from 1995-99, South Asians military expenditure grew more than for any regions of the world with India's growth rate three times that of Pakistan.[284] This disparity which could enable the Indian military to employ new tactics in future conflicts with Pakistan, has grown even more appreciatively. As the Indian armed forces begin to absorb the necessity for combined arms operations, Pakistan's armed forces remained plagued by a "lack of coordination and joint planning.[285] Critical defiance in Pakistan and growing capabilities in India could increase nuclear risks, unless new peace-making initiatives are forthcoming.

New Delhi's procurements of advanced combat aircraft, deep surveillance capabilities, and supersonic cruise missiles are sources of concern in Pakistan. These capabilities appear well suited to support new conventional and limited war fighting options. Growing Indian air superiority has ramifications for escalation control and for the stability of a nuclear deterrence on the sub-continent in at least two major respects. *First,* the attrition of the Pakistani Air Force in air-to-air combat in a limited war scenario could constitute a "redline" that cannot be predicted with assurance. *Second,*

Pakistani military planners would view Indian air force power as the quickest and most accurate means for deep strikes against nuclear, as well as conventional target.[286]

Pakistan has two options in addressing the issue of the military imbalance in the region. The first is to enter into an arms race and use all available avenues to increase its conventional military capabilities. This approach, however, is undesirable, as it will lead to an unending arms race. The second option is to employ diplomacy to build confidence between the two states and to take concrete steps to demonstrate non-hostile intent. One model for doing so is Conventional Forces in Europe Treaty (CFET) negotiated to reduce threatening conventional capabilities at the end of the Cold War.[287] India and Pakistan must move towards such an agreement to downplay the threat of conventional and thus nuclear warfare in the region. The following section lays out three stages for achieving this goal.

Stage I

This stage would be short-term. The five steps advocated need not be connected with resolving the Kashmir dispute.

Agreement to Stop Firing at the Line of Control (LOC)

The exchange of small arms and heavy caliber fire has become routine along the LOC. This exchange of fire has caused more damage to the civil population than to military personnel against whom the fire is directed. Most of the residents of these areas have become internally displaced refugees and have not received any help from the UN refugee relief programmes. President Musharaff had then shown his willingness to accept a ceasefire.[288] If an agreement was to be concluded, it would not take long to implement, simply requiring an order from both sides' army headquarters. As far as monitoring the LOC is concerned, the United National Military Observer Group (UNMOG) is already present in Kashmir and could impartially monitor the ceasefire.

Agreement to Demilitarize the Siachen Glacier Area and Revert to its Pre-1984 Status

Two Indian divisions and one Pakistani division have been deployed in this area, the highest battle ground in the world, for the past twenty years, confronting not only each other but also facing extremely inhospitable weather conditions. Both sides have suffered significant losses in terms of men, material, money, and equipment. An understanding was reportedly reached in the late to withdraw these divisions; however, for reasons unknown to the public, the agreement was not finalized. The demilitarization of this area is critical as it will not only end an undeclared limited war between India and Pakistan but also reduce the economic burden both countries have incurred in holding their positions. Officials of both countries' Military and Foreign Service Office can once against finalize the details of such an agreement.

Military Maneouvers

In order to reduce the threat of conventional offensive strikes against each other, India and Pakistan must clarify the vague language utilized in existing CBM's. Specifically, in the Agreement between India and Pakistan on the Advanced Notice of Military Exercises, signed on April 6, 1991, a provision such as "Both sides may not conduct exercises of Land Forces at Divisional level and above within five kilometers (Km) of the areas specified at Paragraphs (1)a, (1) and (2)" provides considerable flexibility to both sides in interpreting the agreement and concentrating sufficiently large forces near the international border. The term "may not" should be replaced with "should not." The force level should be reduced to no more than a brigade within 25 kilometers of the international border and no more than a division within 50 kilometers of the international border. Thus, the language of the agreements could be improved by being more specific, and the obligations undertaken by both sides might be expanded.

Joint Consultative Group (JCG)

For the purpose of mutual consultation and inquiries,

there exists a hotline between the two Director-Generals Military Operations; however, in the light of post-1998 tensions, the establishment of a JCG would be more beneficial in facilitating close communication between the two sides.

Organization

The JCG might be headed by an officer of the rank of at least Brigadier from each side. A staff of five officers could assist him: one from each of three services, one from the Ministry of Defence, and a secretary of the group from each side.

Mandate

The JCGs could meet at least twice a year, preferably after every six months. In addition, meetings could also be convened upon the request of either side. These meetings would provide a forum to resolve misunderstandings related to current arrangements, exchange information about activities that potentially violate the spirit of agreements reached, or address general issues of concern. Such meetings could be hosted alternatively by India and Pakistan.

Monitoring and Inspection Regime

To lend credibility to the arrangements, India and Pakistan agree upon a monitoring regime be established. The regime's mandate might include:

Attendance of Military Maneouvers

Military maneouvers planned by either side of a large scale, or maneouvers that appear to be larger than notified could be witnessed by the representatives of the other state, perhaps the member of the JCG, and also by independent and neutral observers from mutually friendly countries at least once a year.

Patrolling of the Line of Control

India has voiced concerns about infiltration in Jammu and Kashmir across the LOC. Both the Indian and Pakistan armies have in place a system of patrolling the LOC on the respective sides. To address this issue to the satisfaction of both India and the international community, Pakistan has suggested a system of multilateral monitoring, which has received favourable international comments and such a system could be established with little difficulty by expanding UNMOG's presence in the area.

Use of International Technical Means

In the absence of national technical means in India and Pakistan to monitor each other's compliance with agreed arrangements, third parties in possession of such technology could potentially collaborate with India and Pakistan.

Cooperative Aerial Monitoring

A great deal has already been written on cooperative aerial monitoring that could be applied subsequently as the level of trust between the two neighbours increases.[289]

Stage II

A long-term planning that can be linked with the resolution of the Kashmir dispute.

Agreement Not to Deploy Additional Forces in the Disputed Area

Such an agreement could help reduce the threat of conventional offensive strikes that seek to alter the *status quo* in the disputed area. Force reductions could also be contemplated after the demilitarization of the Siachen area.

Military Technologies

The technological ascendancy of India's armed forces is a major concern of Pakistan. Regional stability would be greatly enhanced if both India and Pakistan could agree to regulate the induction of advanced military technologies into their forces. If no agreement is possible, then such technologies should at least be inducted in a non-threatening manner.

Agreement for Re-Deployment of Offensive Forces

India and Pakistan could redeploy their strike formations further away from international borders.

Agreement for Low Military Zones or No Military Zones

Both countries could agree to declare certain areas as low or no military zones, keeping in view the strategic and operational sensitiveness. These zones could be mutually or internationally monitored, as discussed above.

Stage III

This stage would be linked with the mutually satisfactory resolution of the Kashmir dispute.

During the third stage, India and Pakistan would seek an agreement on the proportionate reduction of conventional forces. Such an agreement could perhaps evolve into a no war pact, bolstered by enhanced mutual economic interests.

The leaders of India and Pakistan face a similar challenge to transition from recurring crisis to nuclear safety. This passage can only be traversed safely with sustained collaboration. If so deterrence optimists will be proven right. After all India and Pakistan have experienced severe crisis, but national leaders have avoided a conventional war that could result in a crossing of the nuclear threshold. National leaders are well aware of the adverse economic consequences of severe crisis. They understand the potential consequences of war and the spectre of unintended escalation.

Perhaps, now at long last, Pakistan and India are at the beginning of nuclear risk reduction. Deterrence pessimists are correct in warning that nuclear risk reduction measures are not in place. Much can go badly wrong on the sub-continent unless Pakistan's national security establishments reassess its Kashmir problem and unless New Delhi engages substantively on Islamabad's consensus and with dissident Kashmir. The way out of this morass is widely appreciated but rarely acted upon. This exit strategy point to placing a much higher priority on the well-being of Kashmir's – something both governments profess to hold clear, but rarely act upon. If the governments of Pakistan and India were to follow this fundamental guidelines, firing would cease permanently along the LOC, the crossing of Jehadis and human rights abuses would virtually cease, divided families would be free to meet, and trade and development projects would be encouraged across the Kashmir divide. At the same time, if New Delhi and Islamabad take concrete actions to change course, those opposed to the reconciliation will attempt to blow up process. The best chance of defusing nuclear danger and controlled escalation lies in political engagement.[290]

Apart from the indispensable political will required by India and Pakistan to move this peace process forward, the international community has a critical role to play in bringing, peace to the region. It is incumbent on the international community and friends of South Asia to become more actively involved in nuclear risk reduction in the region so that its inhabitants, almost one-fourth of the world's population, can enjoy the benefits of the abundant resources in their nations. Thus, far these resources either remain untapped or have been squandered due to the India-Pakistan conflict. If third parties can not broker a peace, they can at least facilitate it by acting as neutral umpires to guarantee that the two side abide by the rules they draw for themselves.[291]

The fact that the military structural imbalance in South Asia exists and there is a possibility that it will widen further. There are strong reasons for finding ways to assure the systematic safety, security and stability of strategic and nuclear command and control arrangements. Cooperation in this area has been delicate, almost taboo, for legal and political reasons, and the US or western actions would have to be carefully formulated and implemented to avoid treaty impediments. The NPT restrictions forbid parties from assisting states to acquire or take control over nuclear weapons. This would prohibit direct assistance to new nuclear weapons states with nuclear command and control. The NPT obligations tend in the way of offering technical improvements or mechanism for nuclear weapons, even to improve their safety against accidents or safeguards against their unauthorized use, because it is difficult to differentiate these features from ones that would also enhance the host's capability to deploy and use nuclear weapons. These restrictions would not necessarily stand in the way, however, if expert consultations focused on good practices and earlier lessons learned that could be applied to organizational, training, and safety procedures. Nuclear security consultation could provide an avenue for objective discussions on historical incidents, close calls, and things that could go wrong in foreseeable contexts, stimulating Indian and Pakistani examinations and scrutiny in their approaches.[292]

Cooperative threat reduction measures that might take hold in bilateral discussions between India and Pakistan should be encouraged. These could provide direct buffers against certain command and control shortcomings, and generate commitments on both sides to develop effective accident prone, risk reduction and crisis management tools and procedures.[293]

The US, Russia, China, Iran, Saudi Arabia and Israel each have major stakes in South Asia, whether in energy resources, financial capability, or arms control options and could affect nuclear stability in the region. Gaining improved means of early warning could contribute to crisis prevention and nuclear stability but this can depend in practice on whether the early warning is available to both sides, and on whether the instruments that serve early warning purposes and employed instead as offensive force multipliers, to guide missiles or aircrafts to newly found targets. Missile defence is intrinsically appealing if it can buy time for crisis decision-making and bilateral communication, or for leadership and asset survivability, thus restraining the impulse to respond at the nuclear level. If, however, missile defence deployment is perceived to erode one side's deterrence credibility in favour of the other, or to multiply offensive options, it would have destabilizing effects.[294]

Notes and References

1. Tariq Ali, *Pakistani's Military Rule or People's Power*, (New York, 1970).
2. *Ibid.*
3. *Ibid.*
4. See, http://countrystudies.us/Pakistan/15.htm
5. *Pakistan: A Political History* in The Encyclopedia of Asian History, see www.arches.uga.edu/sga/readings/Pakistan_%20pol_his.htm
6. *Ibid.*
7. *Ibid.*

8. Stephen, P. Cohen, *The Idea of Pakistan* (New Delhi, 2005).
9. Sohail Mohammed, *Islamic Fundamentalism* in *Pakistan, Egypt and Iran* (Lahore, 1955), pp. 254-63.
10. Ayesha Siddiqa Agha, "Can Pakistan Turn Around, see, www.asian_affairs.com/terriorism/siddiqa_agha. The conclusion was drawn from the several interviews with militant group in Pakistan.
11. *Ibid.*
12. *Ibid.*
13. *Ibid.*
14. *Ibid.*
15. *Ibid.*
16. *Pakistan Times,* 14 October, 1999.
17. "Pakistan at the Crossroad: Crisis of Democracy & Trial of Military Leadership", see www.Jamaat.org/isharat/1999/ish1199.htm
18. *Ibid.*
19. *Ibid.*
20. *Ibid.*
21. Edward Shills, "The Military in the Political Development of the New States", In John J. Johnson (ed.), *The Role of Military in Under-Developed Countries* (Princeton, 1962,), p. 33.
22. Robert E. Lone, *Political Life: How People Get Involved in Politics?* (Glenco, 1959), p. 75.
23. Bruce M. Russett and Elizabeth C. Hanson, Interest and Ideology: *The Foreign Policy Beliefs of American Businessmen* (San Francisco, 1975), pp. 59-99.
24. Robert L. Wendzel, *International Relations: A Policy-maker Focus* (New York, 1977), pp. 253-56.
25. *Ibid.*
26. S.E. Finer, *The Man on the Horseback: The Role of the Military in Politics* (London, 1962), pp. 3-54.
27. Samuel P. Huntington, *The Common Defence: Strategic Programme in National Politics,* (New York, 1961).
28. S.E. Finner, n. 26.
29. Morris Janowitz, *The Military in the Development of Two Nations: Essay in Comparative Analysis* (Chicago, 1964).
30. Fred R. Von Der Mehden, *Politics of Developing Nations* (Englewood Cliffs, 1964).
31. A.R. Luckham, "A Comparative Typology of Civil-Military Relations", *Government and Opposition,* Vol. VI, No. 1, Winter 1971.
32. Sang Seck Park, "Political System in Black Africa", *Journal of African Studies,* Vol. IV, No. 3, Fall 1977.
33. P.J. Vantikiontis, "The Military in Politics: A Review", *Journal of Conflict Resolution,* Vol. IX, No. 1, 1963.
34. Moshe Lissak, *Military Role in Modernization: Civil-Military Reforms In Thailand and Burma,* (Bevery Hills, 1976).
35. Claude E. Welch, Jr. and Arthur K. Smith, *Military Role and Rule: Perspectives on Civil-Military Relations* (Massachusetts, 1974).

36. J. Stephen, *Soldiers and Politics in South Asia: Civil-Military Relations: A Comparative Perspective* (Cambridge, 1976).
37. For more details see, Veena Kukreja, Military Intervention in Politics, (New Delhi, 1985), pp. 16-43.
38. Lawrence Radway, "Militarism" in David L Shells, (ed.) *International Encyclopedia of Social Sciences,* Vol. X, pp. 301-02.
39. Kenneth Fidei, "Militarism and Developments: An Introduction," in Kenneth Fide (ed.), *Militarism in Developing Countries* (New Brunswick, 1975), p. 1.
40. Stephen P. Cohen, *The Pakistan Army* (New Delhi, 1984), pp. 133-34.
41. Lawrence Ziring, "Pakistan", in George E. Slurry (ed.) *World Encyclopedia of Political Systems,* Vol. II, (Harla, 1983), pp. 783-84.
42. For a detailed account of Indo-Pak war of 1971 see, S.S. Bindra, *Indo-Pak Relations :Tashkant to Simla Agreement,* (New Delhi, 1981).
43. Robert Laporte Jr. Power and Privilege, Influence and Decision-making in Pakistan (New Delhi, 1975), pp. 114-15.
44. *Ibid.,*pp. 115-16.
45. Veena Kukreja, n. 37, p. 104.
46. *Ibid.,* p. 106.
47. L.F. Rushbrook Williams, *The State of Pakistan,* (London, 1966), p. 39.
48. Herbert Feldman, Omanibus, (New Delhi, 2001), pp. 46-47.
49. Khalid Mohammed Arif, "The Role of Military in Politics: Pakistan 1947-97", Hafeez Malik, *Pakistan: Founders Aspirations and Todays Realities,* (Oxford, 2001), pp. 90-91.
50. *Ibid.,* pp. 91-92.
51. Political Parties in Pakistani, See www.hrcpelectoralwafch.org/partyprofiles.com
52. *Ibid.*
53. Hasan Askri Rizvi, *Military and Politics in Pakistan* (Lahore, 1976), p. 286
54. Robert Lapore Jr., n. 43, pp. 43-44.
55. Lawrence Ziring, "Pakistan: A Political Perspective", *Asian Survey,* Vol. XV, No. 7, July 1975, p. 630.
56. Satish Kumar, *The New Pakistan* (New Delhi, 1978), pp. 326-27.
57. Jasjit Singh, "The Army in the Power Structure of Pakistan", *Strategic Analysis,* Vol. XVIII, No. 7, October 1995, p. 878.
58. Veena Kukreja, n. 37, p. 125.
59. Benazir Bhutto, "*Pakistan: The Gathering Storm,* (New Delhi, 1983), p. 12
60. *The Patriot* (ed.), "The Pak Coup 6 July 1977. Also see *Hindustan Times,* (ed.), "Setback in Pakistan", 6 July 1977, *The Tribune,* (ed.), "They Had it Coming", 7 July 1977.
61. Bilal Hashmi, "Dragon Seed Military in the State" in Hasan Gardezi and Jamil Rashid (Ed.), *Pakistan: The Roots of Dictatorship* (London, 1985), p. 164.
62. Kt. General Eric A. Vas (Retd.), "Pakistan Security Future<", in

Stephen P. Cohen (ed.), *The Security of South Asia: American and Asian Perspective* (New Delhi, 1987), p. 89.

63. Veena Kukreja, "Military Politics in Pakistan, 10 Years of Zia's Rule", *Strategic Analysis*, Vol. XII, No. 5, August 1988, p. 470.
64. *Ibid.*, p. 451.
65. Abha Dixit, "Between Scyllo and Charybdis: The Legacies of Zia-ul-Haq", *Strategic Analysis*, Vol. XIII, No. 1, April 1989, p. 32.
66. *News Week*, 16 December 1989 as cited in Veena Kukreja, "Restoration of Democracy in Pakistan", *Strategic Analysis*, Vol. XII, No. 11, February 1990, p. 1196.
67. Abha Dixit, "Pakistan: After a year of Benazir Rule", *Strategic Analysis*, Vol. XIII, No. 2, May 1990, p. 200.
68. Mohammed Waseem, "Pakistan's Lingering Crisis of Dyarchy", *Strategic Digest*, Vol. XIII, No. 2, December 1992, p. 1602.
69. Kalim Bahadur, "Pakistan Back to Square One", *Hindustan Times*, 17 October 1993.
70. Veena Kukreja, "Pakistan's 1993 Elections: Back to Square One", *Strategic Analysis*, Vol. XVI, No. 10, January 1994, p. 1364.
71. Hari Jai Singh "Pakistan Today", *The Tribune*, 6 March 1997.
72. *Ibid.*, Also see, B.M. Bhatia, "Pakistan's Ailing Economy," *Hindustan Times*, 20 February, 1997.
73. K. Natwar Singh, "Choices and Challenges," *Main Stream*, Vol. XXXV, No. 12, 1 March 1997, p. 10.
74. Kuldip Nayyar, 'Pakistan' After the Polls", *Hindustan Times*, 21 February, 1997.
75. Khalid Mohammed Asif, "The Role of the Militancy in Politics: Pakistan 1994-97, in Hafeez Malik (ed.), *Pakistan: Founders Aspirations and Today's Realities* (Oxford, 2001), p. 101.
76. *Ibid.*
77. *Ibid.*
78. *Ibid.*, pp 102-03.
79. *Ibid.*, p. 103.
80. *Ibid.*
81. S.M. Zafar, "Constitutional Developments in Pakistan, 1997-99," in Craig Boxter and Charles H. Kennedy (ed.), *Pakistan 2000* (Oxford, 2001), pp. 27-29.
82. *Ibid.*, p. 28
83. *Ibid.*, pp. 28-29.
84. Stephen P. Chohen, n. 8, pp. 154-55.
85. *Ibid.*, pp. 155-56.
86. *Ibid.*, pp. 158-59.
87. *Ibid.*, pp. 159-60.
88. Khalid Mohammad Asif, n. 75, pp. 4-118.
89. Robert Laporte Jr., n .43. pp. 4-8.
90. Lewis Dunn and William Ooverhall, "Next Phase in Nuclear Proliferation Research", William Overhall (ed.), *Asia's Nuclear Future* (Colorado, 1977), p. 7.

91. Praful Bidwai and Achin Vanyak, *South Asia on a Short Fuse: Nuclear Politics and the Future of Global Disarmament* (New Delhi), p. 1.
92. *Ibid.*, pp. 1-2.
93. *Ibid.*, p. 2.
94. *Ibid.*
95. K.J. Holisti, *International Politics: A Framwork for Analysis* (New Delhi, 1978), p. 310.
96. *Ibid.*, pp. 310-11.
97. *Ibid.*
98. Edmind A. Walsh, "Changing the How's of Foreign Policy", *ISD Reports*, George Town University, Vol. IV, no. 2, January 1996, p. 5.
99. Alva Myrdal, *Game of Disarmaments: How the US and Russia Run the Arms Race* (New York, 1976), p. 293.
100. Albert Wholestetler *et. al.*, *Swords from Ploughshares* (Chicago, 1979), p. 5.
101. Itty Abraham, *Making of the Indian Atomic Bomb* (Delhi, 1998) p. 10.
102. Ravi Shastri, "Nuclear Issues and Securities of States", *Strategic Analysis*, Vol. XII, No. 1, February 1989, p. 1268.
103. Shaukat Hussain, "Environmental Issues and Security in South Asia", *Adelphi Papers, 262* (London, 1991), p. 41.
104. *Ibid.*, p. 42.
105. Parvez Iqbal Cheema, "Implications of Arms Buildup. in South Asia", *Regional Studies*, Vol. XX, No. 182, Summer 1995-96, p. 19.
106. P.S. Jayaram, *India's National Security and Foreign Policy*, (New Delhi, 1987), pp. 1-50.
107. P.V. Rao, *Indian Defence Policy and Organisation Since Independence* (New Delhi, 1977), pp. 6-7.
108. Introduction in M.G. Weinbaim and Chetan Kumar (eds.), South Asia Approaches the Millennium: Re-examining National Security (Bouldercalo, 1994), p. VIII.
109. K. Subramanyam, *Our National Security*, (New Delhi, 1972), pp. 1-4.
110. S.N. Das, *National Security in Perspective* (New Delhi, 1987), pp. 1-25.
111. V.P. Malik, "India's Economic Development An Essential of National Security", *The Tribune*, 13 September 2002.
112. S.N. Das, n. 110, pp. 1-25.
113. D.K. Palit and PKS Namboodri, *Pakistan's Islamic Bomb* (New Delhi, 1979), p. 10.
114. George Perkovich, *India's Nuclear Bomb: The Impact on Global Proliferation* (Berkeley, 1999), pp. 14-21.
115. See, Summit Ganguly, "India's Nuclear Weapons Programme", *International Security*, Vol. XXIII, Spring 1999, p. 157.
116. www:globalsecurity.org/wind/library/report/crs/90-116.
117. *Ibid.*
118. *Ibid.*
119. *Weapons of Mass Destruction (WMD)* CRS Issue Brief 93-243: South Asia: US interests and Policy Issues, See www.globalsecurity.org/wind/report/crs/93-243.

120. *Ibid.*, pp. 6-7.
121. *Ibid.*, p. 8.
122. *Ibid.*, pp. 8-9.
123. *Ibid.*
124. For more information, see US Library of Congress, Congressional Research Service: US Non-Proliferation and Foreign Policy Consideration, No. 1B90149, Washington, 1992.
125. Brahma Chellaney, "US Plans Separate Talks on India-Pakistan Nukes", *Washington Times*, 12 October 1992.
126. *The Dawn* (ed), "Nuclear Non-proliferation", 5 July 1968.
127. Z.A. Bhutto, *The Myth of Independence* (London, 1969), p. 183.
128. *Ibid.*
129. Robert C. Hardgrave, Jr., *India Under Pressure Prospects for Political Stability* (London, 1984), p. 155.
130. Pradyot Pradhan, "Nuclear Pakistan: India's Response", *India Quarterly*, Vol. XLIII, No. 1, January-March 1987, p. 7.
131. Parvez Iqbal Cheema, "Pakistan's Security Dilemma-1", *The Muslim*, 22 May 1982.
132. As Cited in T.C. Bose, "Nuclear Proliferation: A Case Study of Pakistan" in Surendra Chopra (ed.), *Perspectives on Pakistan's Foreign Policy* (Amritsar, 1983) p. 394.
133. For the text of the Press Conference, see *Foreign Affairs: Pakistan* (Islamabad, Ministry of Foreign Affairs, Vol. 1994), p. 5.
134. *Ibid.*
135. Shrin Tahir Kheli, *The United States and Pakistan: The Evolution of an Influence Relationship*. (New York, 1984), p. 89.
136. For details see B.M. Kaushik and P.N. Mehrotra, *Pakistan's Nuclear Bomb* (New Delhi, 1980), P.B. Sinha and R.R. Subramanyam, *Nuclear Pakistan: Atomic Threat of South Asia* (New Delhi, 1980), A. Ali, *Pakistan's Nuclear Dilemma* (New Delhi, 1984), S. Swissman and H. Krosney *The Islamic Bomb* (Times Books, 1981), B. Sen Gupta, *Nuclear Weapons* (New Delhi, 1981), John Kaniyalil, *Pakistan's Bomb Strategic Analysis*, Vol XII, No. 2 May 1987
137. *Times of India*, 5 November 1986.
138. *The Tribune* 1 March 1987.
139. *The Muslim*, 2 March 1987.
140. *Times of India*, 25 March 1987.
141. Warren Donnelly, "Pakistan and Nuclear Weapons", *Strategic Digest*, Vol. XVII, No. 5, May 1987, p. 893.
142. *Ibid.*
143. *Ibid.*, p. 894.
144. *Ibid.*
145. For the full text of the speech see, *Strategic Digest*, Vol. XVII, No. 5 May 1987, pp. 881-88.
146. Robert L. Hardgrovet n. 129, p. 159.
147. Leonard S. Binder, *Nuclear Proliferation Today* (Cambridge, 1984), pp. 71-106.

148. Official Records of the General Assembly, 29th Session, Agenda Item No. 107, Document No. A/9706.
149. *The United Nations and Disarmament, 1970-75* (New York, UN Publication, 1976), p. 104.
150. *Ibid.*, p. 105.
151. *Foreign Affairs Records*, New Delhi, Vol. XXI, No. 12, December 1975, p. 330.
152. John W. Garver, *Protected Contest: Sino-Indian Rivalry in the Twentieth Century* (New Delhi, 2001), p. 354.
153. Ashley J. Tellis, *India's Emerging Nuclear Posture* (New Delhi, 2001), p. 120.
154. Praful Bidwai, "Foreign Policy in Mess", *Times of India*, 27 November, 1991.
155. Ashley J. Tellis, n. 153, pp. 120-21. Also see, Praful Bidwai, "India and NPT Review, Grasping the Disarmament Nettle", *Times of India*, 22 October 1995, P.R. Chari, *India-Pakistan Nuclear Stand : The Role of the US* (New Delhi, 1993).
156. www.pas.org/nucl/guide/pakistan/india.html
157. *Ibid.*
158. *Ibid.*
159. *Ibid.*
160. *Ibid.*
161. Gaurav Kampani, "Seven Years after the Nuclear Tests Appraising South Asia's Nuclear Realities", www.nH.org/e_research_649html.
162. *Ibid.*
163. *Ibid.*
164. *Ibid.*
165. *Ibid.*
166. *Ibid.*
167. *Ibid.*
168. *Ibid.*
169. Ashley J. Tellis, "US Strategy: Assisting Pakistan's Transformation", Vol. XXVIII, No. 1, *Washington Quarterly*, Winter 2004-05, p. 108.
170. *Ibid.*
171. *Ibid.*
172. *Ibid.*, pp. 98-99.
173. *Ibid.*, p. 99.
174. See, http://ipriph.org/jounral/winter 2001/the politics, 8 htm.
175. *Indio Abroad*, 9 November 2001.
176. See, www.jid.janes.com, 1 November 2001.
177. "Fear Prompts US to Beef up Nuclear Terror Detections", *Washington Post*, 3 March 2002.
178. Samina Ahmed and David Cartwright (ed.), *Pakistan and the Bomb* (Oxford, 2000) p. 33.
179. *The Dawn*, 13 July 1978.

180. Rajesh Kumar Mishra, "Nuclear Pakistan: Implications for National and International Security", Paper No. 429, *South Asia Analysis Group*, 20 March 2002.
181. CRS Issue Brief 93-243, South Asia: *US Interests and Policy Issues* by Richard P. Cronin and Barbara L. Le Poer, 12 February 1993. See, www.globalsecurity.org/wind/library/report/crs/93-243f.html.
182. Abdul Sattar, Reducing Nuclear Dangers in South Asia, *The Proliferation Review*, Vol. II, No. 2, Winter 1995, pp. 50-51.
183. Mohammed Ramjan Ali, "US and South Asia in the New Millennium", *Regional Studies*, Vol. XXII, No. 3, Summer 2004, p. 9.
184. See CRS Report RL 32115, Missile Proliferation and the Strategic Balance in South Asia and KRS Report RL 31900, Weapons of Mass Destruction: Trade Between North Korea and Pakistan.
185. See CRS Report RL 31559, Proliferation Control Regimes; CRS Report RS 20995, India and Pakistan Current US Economic Sanctions, and CRS Report RL 31589, Nuclear Threat Reduction Measures for India and Pakistan.
186. The Agricultural Export Relief Act of 1998 (PL 105-194) allowed US wheat sales to Pakistan after July 1998. The India-Pakistan Relief Act of 1998 (in PL 105-207) authorized one year sanctions Waiver exercised by President Clinton in November 1998. The Department of Defence and Appropriations Act 2000 (PL 106-179) gave the President permanent authority after October 1999 to waive nuclear-test-related sanctions applied against Pakistan and India on 27 October 1999, President Clinton Waived economic sanctions on India (Pakistan remained under sanctions as a result of the October 1999 Coup). The Foreign Operations Export Financing and Related Appropriations Agencies Act, 2001 (PL 106-429); (section 97) provided an exception under what Pakistan could be provided US foreign assistance funding for basic education programmes. (see also CRS Report RS 20995, India and Pakistan: Current US Sanctions).
187. CRS Issue Brief for Congress Pakistan US Relations, 8 October 2004 (Washington, Library of Congress, 2004) See, Waheb Siddiqui, "Sino-Pakistan Nuclear Accord", *Pakistan Horizons*, Vol. XXXIX, No. 4, Fourth Quarter, 1986, p. 53.
188. Rajiv Naryan, "Sino-Pakistan Missile Cooperation", *Peace Initiatives*, Vol. V, Nos. 3 and 4, May-December 1999, p. 76. Also see, Cameron Binkley, "Pakistan's Ballistic Missile Development: The Sword of Islam?" Van William C. Potter and Harlan W. Jencks (ed.), *The International Missile Bazar*, The New Suppliers Network (Boulder, 1994), pp. 76-80.
189. P.R. Chari *Indo-Pak Nuclear Standoff* (New Delhi, 1995), p. 72.
190. Kapil Kak, "Pakistan's Ballistic Missile: Sword Arm of a New Influential?" *Asian Strategic Review* (Delhi, IDSA, 1997-98), p. 296.
191. Praful Bidwai and Achin Vanyak, n. 91, p. 216.
192. Kapil Kak, n. 190, p. 290.
193. *Washington Post*, 6 April 1991.
194. *Ibid.*, 22 February 1992.

195. *Ibid.*, 26 December 1993.
196. Jon B. Walfsthal, "US-China Reach New Ackerson: MTCR, Fissile Cutoff Issues", *Arms Control Today*, Vol. XXII, No. 9, November 1994, p. 28.
197. R. Jeffrey Smith, "China Linked to Pakistani Missile Plan", *Washington Post*, 25 August 1996, Douglas Walter, "The Secret Missile Deal," *The Time*, 30 June 1997.
198. http://cns.miis.ed/research/india/China/mpahposs.html
199. Nyan Chanda and Susan L. Lawrence, "US-China Relations: Fund Deadline", *Far Eastern Economic Review*, Internal Edition, 18 May 2000
200. *New York Times*, 2 July 2000.
201. *Ibid.*, 6 July 2000.
202. Rajiv Nayar, n. 188, p. 81.
203. John W. Garver, *Protracted Contest: Sino-India Rivalry in the Twentieth Century* (New Delhi, 2001) p. 327.
204. *Ibid.*
205. Zulfikar Ali Bhutto, *If I am Assassinated* (New York, 1979), pp. 221, 107, 137-138 and 168-69 as cited in *Ibid.*, pp. 327-28.
206. *Ibid.*
207. Karan R. Sawhny, "The Sino-Pakistan Nuclear Atomic Prospect and Retrospect," *Peace Initiative*, Vol. V, No. 324, May-December 1999, p. 28
208. M.V. Rappai, "Indian-China Relations and Nuclear Real politic." *Strategic Analysis*, Vol. XXIII, No. 1, April 1999, p. 16.
209. *Ibid.*, Also see, P.K. Ghosh, India-Pakistan Nuclear Parity: Is it Feasible or Necessary? *Strategic Analysis*, Vol. XXV, No. 4, July 2001, pp. 519-32.
210. Anil Josephe Chandy, "India, China and Pakistan", in Kanti Bajpai and Amitabh Mattoo (ed.). *The Peacock and the Dragon: India-China Relations in the 21st century* (New Delhi, 2000), p. 323.
211. Philips Saunders *et al.*, "How and why China proliferates missiles to Pakistan", The Rediff Special, http//www.rediffcom/news/2000/org.
212. *Ibid.*
213. Kanti Bajpai, "Strategic Threats and Nuclear Weapons: India, China and Pakistan", in M.V. Raman and C. Ram Manohar Readdy, *Prisoners of the Nuclear Dream* (New Delhi, 2003), pp. 40-41.
214. *Ibid.*, pp. 42-43.
215. *Ibid.*, pp. 51-52.
216. Anil Joseph Chandy, n. 210, pp. 328-29.
217. *Ibid.*, p. 331.
218. *Ibid.*, pp. 332-33.
219. Shri Parkash, "Sino-Pakistani Relations Comparing Changes over Three Decades", *Peace Initiative*, Vol. V, No. 3 & 4, May-December 1999, p. 128.

220. M.V. Rappai, "China's Nuclear Arsenal and Missile Defence," *Strategic Analysis*, Vol. XXVI, No. 1, Jan-March 2002, p. 78.
221. Fazal-ur-Rahman, "Pakistan's Relations with China", *Peace Initiative*, Vol. V, Nos. 3-4, May-December 1999, p. 183.
222. *Ibid.*, pp. 183-84.
223. Maqbool Ahmad Bhatty, "China's Emerging Role in the World", in *Ibid.*, pp. 163-64.
224. *Ibid.*
225. "Evaluation of India's Nuclear Policy" Papers laid on the table of the Lok Sabha, 7 May 1998. See, *Strategic Digest*, Vol. XXVIII, No. 7 July 1998, pp. 1079-1984.
226. *Ibid.*
227. *Ibid.*
228. *Hindustan Times*, 14 May 1998.
229. Zaffar Abbas, "The Nuclear Debate in Pakistan", *The Hearld*, June 1998.
230. *Ibid.*
231. *Ibid.*
232. *Ibid.*
233. Samna Ahmed, "The Nuclear Debate", *Newsline*, June 1998.
234. *Ibid.*
235. *Ibid.*
236. *Ibid.*
237. Eric Arnett, "Test of Endurance", *Newsline*, June 1998.
238. *Hindustan Times*, 1 June 1998.
239. *Ibid.*
240. Prem Shanker Jha, "Adverse Fallout", *Hindustan Times*, 4 June 1998.
241. *Times of India*, 2 June 1998.
242. *Ibid.*
243. *Ibid.*
244. *Ibid.*
245. *Ibid.*, 22 May 1998.
246. *Ibid.*
247. *Ibid.*
248. *Ibid.*, 18 May 1998.
249. *Ibid.*
250. *Ibid.*, 22 May 1998.
251. Zeba Moshaver, *Nuclear Weapons Proliferation in the Indian Sub-Continent* (London, 1991), pp. 58-62.
252. *US Arms Control and Disarmament Agency Documentation on Disarmament*. (Washington DC, US Government Printing Office, 1960), p. 319.
253. S. Fetter, *Towards a Comprehensive Test Ban* (Ballinger, 1988), p. 179.
254. *The Dawn*, 11 August 1996. Also see, D. Albright, "India-Pakistan Nuclear Arms Race", *Defence Journal*, Vol. XX, Nos. 3-4, 1994, pp. 25-31.

255. Kamal Matinuddin, "The CTBT Controversy: Need for a Consensual Approach", Moonis Ahmar, (ed.), *The CTBT Debate in Pakistan,* (Delhi, 2001), p. 123.
256. *The Dawn,* 18 January 2000.
257. *The Nation,* 21 January 2000.
258. *Ibid.,* 25 January 2000.
259. *Pakistan Observes,* 21 January 2000.
260. Available at http://www.meadev.gov.in/govt/indiaucld.htm accessed on 17 August 1999.
261. Securing Nuclear Peace, *The New International,* 5 October 1999.
262. *Ibid.*
263. *Ibid.*
264. Available at http://www.mi.infn.it/londer
265. *Ibid.*
266. Lewis A. Dunn, "Contouring Nuclear Proliferation", *Adolphi Paper,* 263 (Oxford, 1991), p. 3.
267. *Ibid.*
268. Scott D. Sagan, "More Will be Worse", in Scott D. Sagan and Keneth N. Waltz (eds.), *The Spread of Nuclear Weapon: A Debate* (New York, 1995), p. 247.
269. *Ibid.,* pp. 48-49.
270. John Lewis Gaddis, "Nuclear Weapons and Cold War History" in Olav Njolastad (ed.), Nuclear Rivalry and International Order (London) 1996) p. 44.
271. Seeing Nuclear Peace, n. 261.
272. *Ibid.*
273. Pakistan Firm as First-Strike Nuclear Policy. See, http://headlines.sify.com/915news.htm., 5 May 2005.
274. Michael Krepon, "The Stability-Instability Paradox, Misperception and Escalation Controlling South Asia, In Michael Krepon *et. al.* (ed.) Escalation Control and Nuclear Option in South Asia (Washington, 2004), p. 1
275. Zulfqar Khan, India-Pakistan Nuclear Rivalry: Perceptions, Misperceptions and Mutual Deterrence", *IPRI Paper,* 9 (Islamabad, January 2005), pp. 22-25.
276. *Ibid.,* p. 39.
277. *The Dawn,* 26 November 1999.
278. *Ibid.,* 7 September 1999.
279. *Ibid.*
280. *Ibid.*
281. Michael Krepon, n. 274, "Introduction."
282. Zawar Haider Abide, "Threat Reduction in South Asia", The Hungry L. Slimson Center, Feb 2004.
283. Michael Krepon, Nuclear Risk Reduction: Is Cold War Experience Applicable in South Asia?" in Michael Krepon and Chris Gagne, (ed.), *The Stability-Instability Paradox* (Washington, 2004), 00.1-14.

284. India's defence expenditure rose on average of 2.9 percent in 1999, India spent $11.3 billion on military expenditures, Pakistan spent $3.5 billion (US Department State, Bureau of Verification and Compliance), *World Military Expenditure and Arms Transfer*, 1999-2000 (Washington DC, Library of Congress, 2002), pp. 2-3.
285. Parvez Iqbal Cheema, The Armed Forces of Pakistan (Karachi, 2003), p. 184.
286. Michael Krepon, n. 274, p. 10.
287. The text of the Conventional Forces on Europe Treaty is available online at http://www.fas.org/nuh/control/efe/text
288. *Times of India*, 12 August 2003.
289. See John H. Hawes and Teresita Schaffer, "Nuclear Risk Reduction and Cooperative Aerial Observation," in Michael Krepon and Chris Gagne (ed.) *Nuclear Reduction in South Asia* (New Delhi, 2003).
290. Michael Krepon, n. 274, p. 24.
291. Zawar Haider Abidi, n. 282.
292. Rodney W. Jones, "Nuclear Stability and Escalation Control in South Asia: Structural Factors in Michael Krepon *et. al.*, n. 274, p. 55.
293. *Ibid.*, p. 56.
294. *Ibid.*

Index